Sherman's
Woodticks

Sherman's Woodticks

The Adventures, Ordeals, and Travels of the Eighth
Minnesota Volunteer Infantry During the Civil War

Paul Hodnefield

NORTH STAR PRESS OF ST. CLOUD INC.

WWW.NORTHSTARPRESS.COM

First Edition
Printed in the United States of America.

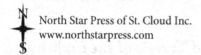 North Star Press of St. Cloud Inc.
www.northstarpress.com

ISBN: 978-1-68201-137-9

Library of Congress CIP data available upon request.

Book cover design and text layout and design by Liz Dwyer of North Star Press.
Text set in Minion Pro and Gryphius MVB.

Cover painting: *The 8th Minn. Infantry (Mounted) in the Battle of Ta-Ha-Kouty* by Carl Boeckmann (1910). Used with permission from the Minnesota Historical Society. The original painting was prominently displayed in the Minnesota Capitol building for decades. In 2016, the Minnesota Historical Society's Executive Council decided to remove the painting, along with one other, because they were "painful reminders of our shared history" and the events depicted took place in North Dakota, not Minnesota.

The author is available for presentations and promotions related to the subject matter of this book and welcomes comments. You can reach Paul Hodnefield at: author@8thminn.com

Acknowledgements

This book could not have been written without the accounts of the soldiers who participated in the adventures of Company E and the entire Eighth Minnesota Volunteer Infantry Regiment. I am especially grateful to the soldiers' families who donated primary materials to various historical societies, including diaries, reminiscences, and letters, thus ensuring that such important part of our history could be preserved for future generations.

I offer a big thank you to my extended circle of friends, too numerous to mention, who encouraged me and shared suggestions throughout the course of this project. I especially want to thank Joel Friedman, Steve Olmanson, Mark Campbell, and his wife Leila, who provided extremely helpful comments on my early drafts of the book.

Several historical societies deserve credit for the assistance they provided during my research for this book. I especially want to thank the Minnesota Historical Society for allowing me to use several photographs and for their valuable research assistance. Thanks also to the Wright County Historical Society, the Holdingford Area Historical Society, and the State Historical Society of North Dakota, all of which were very helpful while I worked on this project.

I also want to thank my brother-in-law, Jeremy Dando, for his assistance with photography.

Finally, I want to extend a special thank you to my wife Patty for her encouragement and unfailing support of my efforts on this book.

Contents

Introduction

The Civil War ended well over 150 years ago and for many it may seem like ancient history. Yet we are not so far removed from that conflict as many people realize. There are still people alive as of this writing who are old enough to have living memory of the last surviving veterans of that era. In fact, the U.S. government was still paying at least one survivor's pension for the child of a Civil War veteran in the year 2020, and the last widow of a veteran from that conflict died on December 16, 2020.

Perhaps most striking of all is that the same issues that bitterly divided the nation in the mid-nineteenth century are much the same as those facing the United States today. Both race and states' rights continue to be divisive. Even as the finishing touches were made to this work, riots, destruction, and looting took place around the country, sparked by the death of an unarmed black man while being arrested by Minneapolis police. Protestors have attacked and destroyed what they call symbols of oppression, including monuments commemorating historic figures from the Civil War, Confederate and Union alike.

Looking back, the riots and vandalism we experience today would not have surprised those who lived in the United States during the Civil War era. In the three decades leading up to the great conflict, riots were common, including mob attacks on abolitionists and street violence between free blacks and recent immigrants who were competing for the same low-paying jobs.

Despite the unsettled times, people carried on then as they do today. They worked to support themselves and make a better life for their children. At the time, both those born in the United States and recent immigrants recognized the opportunity that the country offered. Many of them believed that there was something special about the country that made it worth preserving. These men put their plans on hold and volunteered to defend their country during the Civil War.

Well over 1,500 volunteer infantry regiments served the Union cause during the Civil War. Each had its own story to tell. Minnesota alone provided eleven volunteer infantry regiments to the cause. Much has been written about some of the more famous regiments from the state. Numerous books and other works, for example, cover the heroic charge of the First Minnesota at the Battle of Gettysburg. Likewise, Minnesota regiments played a key role in the Battle of Nashville in late 1864.

Until now, however, relatively little has been written about the Eighth Minnesota Volunteer Infantry Regiment. There are snippets of information about the regiment mentioned in various historical works on other topics. The only full account of the regiment from enlistment to the end of the war was a brief history written by William H. Houlton of Company E for a publication commissioned by the State of Minnesota to document the state's participation – *Minnesota in the Civil and Indian Wars*. This publication, however, was written in large measure to cast the state and its soldiers in the most favorable light for posterity. It largely omits incidents and criticism of that would reflect poorly on those involved.

The history of the Eighth Minnesota is both unique and fascinating. It deserves to be told in far more detail than has previously been published. During the last year of the Civil War, the Eighth Minnesota traveled more miles and served under more extreme conditions than any other unit in the Union Army. Across the Dakota plains to the Yellowstone River and then on to North Carolina, the soldiers endured dehydration, hunger, and exhausting marches, often while exposed to scorching heat or bitter cold. Along the way, the regiment fought against formidable adversaries such as Sitting Bull and General Nathan Bedford Forrest but came away victorious each time.

Nevertheless, the extended story of the Eighth Minnesota is difficult to tell, which may explain why it has not yet been attempted. There are a couple of reasons that make it a formidable task. For one, there is no "one" history of the regiment. The Sioux Uprising, which coincided with the enlistment drives from which the Eighth Minnesota was formed, resulted in the army making a hasty deployment of the new recruits to defend the Minnesota frontier. As a result, the ten companies that comprised the regiment were isolated for nearly two years defending a string of forts along a line that stretched almost 200 miles from near present-day Fargo, North Dakota south to central Minnesota. During that time, it was rare for even four of the ten companies of the Eighth Minnesota to be in the same location at the same time.

With the regiment's companies being scattered across the state, one could say that each had its own unique history. In addition, the companies themselves often further divided into squads which were stationed at remote locations within a company's assigned territory. As a result, even soldiers from the same company might have entirely different experiences.

The other challenge to drafting a history of the Eighth Minnesota is that it cannot be effectively communicated through statistics, which tend to be the focus of many regimental histories. The quantifiable facts, such as dates of service, battles fought, casualties and decorations, cannot do justice to what the soldiers experienced during their service. While statistical facts are relevant, more is needed to fully convey what the soldiers went through during the regiment's time in service.

Sherman's Woodticks deals with the foregoing challenges by telling the history of the regiment through the recollections, impressions and personal experiences of the men who were there. The book focuses on Company E, which consisted mostly of volunteers from Wright County, Minnesota. It records their experiences and impressions—humorous, mundane, and terrifying alike—from their enlistment in 1862 through to their discharge almost three years later.

The soldiers who served in Company E were drawn from Minnesota's first settlers, who flowed into the state from the mid-1850s to the early 1860s looking for opportunity. Most of them came to farm, for rich, arable land was cheap and plentiful. The new territory also needed mills, stores, and transportation, which brought mechanics, merchants, and tradesmen to the new settlements as well.

Among those who came to Minnesota during that time were the men who would become the Eighth Minnesota Volunteer Infantry Regiment. Most of them arrived with their families while they were still in their early teens or even younger. They endured brutal winters, hot summers, insect plagues, and other trials. Yet they persevered. By 1862, the men who would join the Eighth Regiment were tough, independent frontiersmen who were perhaps a little rough around the edges.

Nevertheless, most of them were good, moral men. They largely consisted of Protestants with New England roots. Nearly all believed in God, most regularly attended worships services with their families, and they cared about each other. They had a strong sense of right and wrong. These men were also patriotic citizens who were willing to give up three years in the prime of their lives to serve their country.

These men volunteered for the army of their own free will and wanted to become the best soldiers possible. This they accomplished. However, they never forgot that they were citizens first. They had little patience of army bureaucracy and actively rebelled against any perceived injustice. Above all, they wanted to have all the fun out of soldiering that they possibly could, and to a great extent, they did.

When the Eighth Minnesota arrived in Washington D.C. in early 1865 on its way to join Sherman's army in North Carolina, the local provost guard garrison called the Minnesota soldiers "Sherman's Woodticks." It was not intended as a compliment. The provost guard, in their clean, crisp, fancy new uniforms, considered themselves of higher class than the motley band of Minnesota soldiers.

The Eighth Minnesota had been constantly on the move or on the front line for nine months before it reached Washington D.C. The men looked rough, and their uniforms were dirty, faded, and tattered. Despite their appearance, they were by then tough veteran soldiers and proud of it. The Minnesota soldiers held the provost guard in contempt. Besides, they admired General Sherman. As a result, they took the intended slur of "Sherman's Woodticks" and wore it a badge of honor.

The inspiration for this book began routinely enough through genealogical research into my family's history in Minnesota. As I traced my family tree, two men stood out: George Cambell and Charlie Gibbs. They both married into the same family after the Civil War and I was curious about their backgrounds. Their stories fascinated me, especially as I found more materials about their Civil War service in Company E of the Eighth Minnesota Volunteer Infantry Regiment.

As I dug deeper, more materials from these ordinary soldiers began to shed light on their day-to-day activities. They also shared their thoughts about the conflict, their leaders and service in the army. It was the stories of army life from the individual soldiers' point of view that most grabbed my attention, and I decided to tell the story of the regiment through that lens.

For anyone looking for regimental history told from a strategic point of view, this is not the story for you. While this book does offer brief descriptions of higher-level strategy and command decisions, it does so only to provide context for the story of the soldiers who made up the Eighth Minnesota Volunteers. This is the story of the soldiers, what privates, corporals, and sergeants experienced during the war.

This story is told primarily through the eyes of Company E of the Eighth Minnesota. Company E was raised at Monticello, Minnesota in August 1862. Several members of Company E left behind diaries or reminiscences of their time in the service, which form the basis for this book.

Company E's recollections are supplemented with sources from other companies within the regiment, primarily from Company F. Other accounts from soldiers who were present with other units are included as well to provide additional detail. In many cases multiple accounts described the same event but, with significant differences. Wherever possible, I have tried to reconcile different accounts to describe a more accurate version of the events.

One challenge in writing this book was how to address the Sioux Uprising, the Indian attacks of 1863, and the Northwest Indian Expedition in 1864. Most of the primary sources from the era were written from the white perspective and often dehumanized the Indians, a propaganda strategy which is as old as warfare itself. Sadly, the practice continues around the world to the present day as a way to justify actions that would otherwise be unthinkable.

The soldiers of the Eighth Regiment reflected the attitude of the time towards the Sioux, and recorded the events in the language of the day. Many referred to the Indians as "savages," "heathens" and other dehumanizing terms that are patently offensive to the modern ear. I have tried to avoid the gratuitous use of offensive terms, such as "savage" and "squaw," by only using them in direct quotes from the soldiers' materials.

The reality of how the soldiers viewed the Indians was more nuanced than accounts from the time might suggest. Not all the Minnesota soldiers thought of the Indians as less than human. There were some who sympathized with their plight. Other soldiers found their hatred tempered after witnessing the bravery of the Indians as they defended their families in Dakota Territory. Many of them returned from the Dakota plains with a newfound respect for their adversary.

Likewise, not all the Sioux Indians in Minnesota hated the whites. A significant number of them opposed the 1862 uprising and refused to take part in it. Some even risked their own lives to help hundreds of white settlers escape.

In writing this book, I wanted to cover the story from the soldiers' perspective but, in the process, not gloss over the injustices done to Native Americans. To this end, I have tried to present a balanced description of the Sioux and the events leading up to their Uprising. I confess that I may have fallen short in this goal.

To tell the soldiers' story, I had to place their experiences in context. To do so, it was necessary to provide background on the events that led to the 1862 uprising, including the nature and role of warfare in Sioux culture. This book describes the terror of the Uprising, including what the whites considered barbaric atrocities, to provide perspective of the impressions these happenings had on the soldiers. However, I also wanted to be clear that the whites were just as guilty of atrocities during the Sioux War, if not more so. Therefore, the book includes several incidents that do not reflect well on the soldiers.

Critics might claim that the book doesn't fully explain the injustices done to the Native Americans or provide enough Indian perspectives. I agree. While I sympathize with the injustices committed against the Indians both before and after the Sioux Uprising in 1862, this book is about the Eighth Minnesota and its soldiers. It was never intended to be about the Sioux Indians or Native Americans in general. Others can and have done a far better job of presenting that aspect of history than this author could hope to achieve.

I encourage anyone interested in learning more from the Native American perspective on history and government policy to seek out additional resources. There are a multitude of books available on these subjects. Ironically, one of the more influential books in this area was *Custer Died for Your Sins: An Indian Manifesto* by Vine Deloria, Jr. Deloria was the great-grandson of General Alfred Sully and his Yankton Sioux wife. It was General Sully who commanded the 1864 Northwestern Indian Expedition against the Sioux in which the Eighth Minnesota participated.

A note on usage. I decided to use the older term "Sioux" rather than the more currently accepted word "Dakota" to describe the native people of that tribe. I also use the term "Chippewa" in some cases to describe the Ojibway people. The use of these terms is done not to cause offense but because these were the labels used by the soldiers in their contemporary accounts and are often included in quotations taken from primary sources.

Prologue

December 7, 1864

Hugging the cold mud of a picked Tennessee cotton field, the boys of Company E, Eighth Minnesota Volunteer Infantry Regiment knew they were in grave trouble. They were advancing on a gentle downhill slope across the field when their captain ordered them to halt, lie down, and hold their fire. While puzzled by the order, the soldiers promptly obeyed, even though they were now fully exposed and within range of the Confederate rifles and cannon to their front.

It did not take long for the Confederates to take advantage of the situation. The rebels, under the command of General Nathan Bedford Forrest, poured rifle and cannon fire down upon Company E with terrible effect. Within minutes, a third of the company, including their captain, lay dead or wounded on the field.

Quickly realizing their predicament, Company E, and the rest of the Eighth Minnesota, did not wait for orders. They took the initiative and began to return fire. It started as a shot here and there but soon grew to general fire across the line. Still, the soldiers remained trapped in the open. They must have been terrified as bullets smacked into the damp soil all around them, even more so when they heard the sickening crack as a bullet struck flesh and bone. Every instinct told these solders to turn and flee for safety. Yet, none turned his back to the rebels.

As they lay on that killing ground amid the cacophony of battle, few of the Minnesotans would have taken time to reflect on the long series of events that had brought them to the old cotton field. Their primary focus was on nothing more than survival. Yet, their journey from the warm August day when the company formed in 1862 to the battlefield of December 7, 1864 and beyond makes a remarkable story, and it deserves to be told.

The Nation Calls

August 12 to 17, 1862

When the Civil War began early on April 12, 1861 at Fort Sumter in the harbor at Charleston, South Carolina, the opposing sides both expected a quick and relatively painless resolution to the conflict. From the Union perspective, it was thought "that a show of force would suffice to bring the rebels to terms."[1]

Immediately following the surrender of Fort Sumter, President Abraham Lincoln issued a call for 75,000 volunteers to serve for three months unless sooner discharged. Coincidentally, Minnesota Governor Alexander Ramsey was in Washington D.C. at the same time. First thing the next morning, Ramsey paid a call on the Secretary of War Simon Cameron and offered to tender 1000 troops to the Union cause, and thus, Minnesota was the first state to offer a regiment in response to Lincoln's call for troops.

Before the end of April 1861, the First Minnesota Volunteer Infantry Regiment had formed at Fort Snelling.[2] Among the initial volunteers in the First Regiment was a man who would later command the Eighth Minnesota Volunteer Infantry Regiment, Minor T. Thomas from Stillwater.

When the president called for another 42,000 volunteers the following month, Minnesota again responded by forming the Second Minnesota Volunteer Infantry Regiment. In fact, Minnesota went on to furnish more than its proportionate share of troops during the first year of the war. Despite the small number of people in the state—Minnesota ranked thirty-first out of thirty-three states in population size during the 1860 Census—Minnesota produced enough volunteers during the first

---

1   The Board of Commissioners, *Minnesota in the Civil and Indian Wars: 1861-1865*, vol. 1, St. Paul, MN, Pioneer Press Company, 1891, 2.

2   The recruits for the First Minnesota initially signed up for three months' service. In May, 1861, however, the secretary of war wired the governor and suggested that the regiment instead muster in for three-year period. Governor Ramsey obliged and the men who were unwilling to enlist for the longer term were mustered out. *Minnesota in the Civil and Indian Wars: 1861-1865, vol. 1, 4.*

year of the war to furnish the Union Army with five infantry regiments, two battalions of cavalry and two batteries of light artillery.[3]

By the summer of 1862 there was no longer any illusion that the war would end quickly. The Union and Confederate armies had repeatedly clashed during the previous year. The engagements were bloody and generally not decisive. The Confederates were more than holding their own on the battlefield. It was becoming increasingly clear to the authorities that more manpower would be needed for the Union to defeat the Confederate forces.

On July 2, 1862, President Lincoln issued another call for volunteers. This time it was for 300,000 men to serve for three years or until the end of the war. The War Department issued a quota to each state based on population. Minnesota's quota was for one regiment of 1000 men.

Lincoln had to issue another call for 300,000 more troops only a month later. To ensure that the states provided the full requirement of 600,000 troops, the War Department threatened to implement a draft. If the quotas could not be met by the recruitment of volunteers, then conscription would follow.

Minnesota again responded to the call. Governor Ramsey issued recruitment quotas by county, and the county governments then began their enlistment efforts in earnest. By mid-August 1862, recruitment meetings were scheduled to take place throughout the state.

Wright County Recruiting

Wright County is located on the west side of the upper Mississippi River in central Minnesota. In 1862, Monticello was the largest town in Wright County and served as the county seat.[4] Monticello's location on the bank of the Mississippi approximately forty-five miles from Minneapolis provided excellent access to transportation by road and water. Therefore, it was the natural meeting place for potential recruits from the area.

In response to earlier calls for troops, Wright County had only furnished about twenty men for the Minnesota regiments.[5] The Wright County quota for the July 2 call was for only twenty-two more recruits.[6] Now, following Lincoln's August 4, 1862

---

3   The state's contribution to the war effort by mid-1862 was approximately 6000 men. At full strength, a regiment consisted of 1000 soldiers.

4   The county seat was moved about 15 miles south to the town of Buffalo in 1868.

5   N.H. Winchell, et al., *History of the Upper Mississippi Valley*, Minneapolis, MN, Minnesota Historical Company, 1881, 489.

6   *The North-Western Weekly Union* (Monticello, Minn.), Aug. 2, 1862.

call for another 300,000 volunteers, making 600,000 total, Wright County would have to produce significantly many more men for the war effort.

Wright County men had not rushed to volunteer following Lincoln's call of July 2. It was not from a lack of patriotism or interest. Most of the military-aged men who lived in and around Wright County were farmers. Their wheat crop wouldn't be ready until the first part of August, and if they enlisted before then, there would not be enough labor to bring in the harvest. Money was also a factor. It was common for county governments to offer bounties as an incentive to those who volunteered for army service.[7] Wright County had offered a small bounty early in the war but had not increased the amount as some other counties had done to fill their quotas.

With the added burden of the August 4 call for troops, the Wright County government realized that a greater effort was needed to fill its quota of volunteers. The county had a vested interest in doing so, as if the county could not find enough volunteers, then the remaining quota would have to be filled by a draft. The citizens of Wright County did not like the idea of a draft.[8]

To find enough volunteers, the county leaders decided to organize a War Meeting of local military-age men in Monticello. The meeting was to begin on August 12, 1862. It was more of a multi-day recruiting drive. The meeting would include bands playing patriotic music and feature prominent speakers from throughout the county. The whole affair was intended to be a focused appeal to the attendees' patriotism. The War Meeting would go on until the county reached the minimum number of volunteers to form a company, which might take several days.

As they planned for the War Meeting, Wright County officials grew concerned that the county's enlistment bounty was insufficient. Nearby counties were paying better. There was a risk that prospective recruits would simply go to a nearby county and enlist there for the higher bounty.[9] If that happened and the county fell short of its quota, there would be no choice but to implement a highly unpopular draft.

To sweeten the pot for prospective volunteers, the Wright County government approved an enlistment bounty of $25, a significant sum at the time. Coupled with the federal bounty of $100 for a three-year enlistment, it was a powerful financial incentive to the prospective recruits. To put the bounties in perspective, farmland in Wright County was selling for just over $4 an acre. A farmer in Minnesota at the time could expect to earn under $200 a year, assuming there was no drought, grasshopper plague or other natural disaster. Together, the federal and state bounties would provide the frugal soldier with a nice nest egg when he returned from the war.

7 A bounty was a form of enlistment bonus.

8 *The North-Western Weekly Union*, Aug. 9, 1862.

9 Ibid.

Despite the generous bounty, county officials were by no means certain that the War Meeting could raise the required number of volunteers. That meant the county had to also prepare for the unpleasant prospect of a draft. Consequently, the township assessors in Wright County quietly began to compile lists of able-bodied men just in case the War Meeting failed to attract enough volunteers.

Another motivating factor for the county to fill its quota was the matter of pride. Some of the citizens believed that Wright County wasn't getting enough recognition for its role in the war effort. Many of the early volunteers from the county had signed up individually or in small groups of two or three. With numbers so small, these volunteers found themselves assigned to fill out companies from other parts of Minnesota. Those few Wright County volunteers were now scattered among all the existing Minnesota regiments.

The company was the basic unit of the Union Army, both for recruiting purposes and in the organization of a regiment. On paper, a volunteer infantry company consisted of one hundred enlisted men and officers. However, very few companies ever reached full strength. For recruiting purposes, it wasn't necessary to have the full complement of one hundred men to form a company. If somewhere between fifty and seventy men enlisted together, that would be enough to ensure they could be organized together as a company.

There was a growing sentiment among local officials and residents of the Monticello area that they should raise a company that Wright County could call its own. As a volunteer unit, the men could choose officers from among their own ranks and perhaps even be able to pick a name for the unit that would make their region proud, such as "The Wright County Volunteers."[10]

It was not unusual for freshly recruited units to adopt a name that identified their geographic origin and perhaps their role, "The Sibley Guards," for example. In some cases, the unit might take the name of a ferocious mascot, such as "The Le Sueur Tigers," much as modern sports teams do today. However, the name would not matter all that much in the long run. Once the new unit was mustered into a regiment as a company it would become known by the company letter. The group of men recruited from Dakota County during the War Meetings that began on August 12, for example, initially named themselves "The Dakota Rifles." When they were mustered in to the Eighth Minnesota, the unit was thereafter known simply as "Company F."[11]

---

10 *The North-Western Weekly Union*, Aug. 2, 1862.

11 There's no evidence that the Wright County recruits ever formally adopted a nickname prior to the time they became Company E. However, they are referred to in this work as the "Wright County Volunteers" up to the point when the unit was mustered in as Company E.

On August 9, 1862, local newspaper headlines announced the "WAR Meeting" to commence at 10 a.m. on Tuesday, August 12 at Academy Hall in Monticello. The newspaper encouraged all citizens to turn out for the meeting as "We want a full expression of the people."[12]

Word of the War Meeting quickly spread throughout Wright County and bordering townships in Stearns, Benton, and Sherburne counties. The military-age men in the area knew that it was only a matter of time before they would need to enlist. Most of them had sat out the first calls for volunteers waiting to see whether, as many had predicted, it would be a short conflict. Now, with the war not going well for the Union, they began to realize that the time had come to join the army. They now had to face the hard decision of whether to leave their families behind and go to war or stay behind and risk being drafted.

One motivating factor for the prospective recruits was that by volunteering, they would serve in the same company as their friends and neighbors. If the quotas were not filled and a draft became necessary, those conscripted would have little control over where and with whom they served. George Cambell, a carpenter and mechanic from Clearwater, recalled that the men of the area thought it better to enlist together "so that we might not be strangers among strangers when we went South."[13] Moreover, draftees did not receive the significant enlistment bounties paid to volunteers.

Edson Washburn, a 20-year-old farmer who lived with his parents and siblings in a small log house near Monticello, was one of those who struggled with the question of whether to enlist. His sense of duty told him to "go!"[14] On the other hand, he was concerned about whether he had the courage and stamina to "endure a soldier's life."[15]

In the end, Edson's patriotism got the better of him. He finally made up his mind one day while working in the fields. His mother, on hearing his decision, put her hand on his head, gave him her blessing, and told him "go, my boy and fight manfully for God and your country."[16] With that inspiration, Edson and his older brother Elbridge set out together for the War Meeting on August 12.

12 The North-Western Weekly Union, Aug. 9, 1862. The Academy Building was the public school. It was located in downtown Monticello between Pine and Walnut Streets, south of where they intersect with 3rd Avenue. The site was used for various public schools for many years. Today, a bank building and parking lot occupy the property

13 George T. Cambell, Personal Reminiscences of the Civil War, George T. Cambell family papers, 1857-circa 1890, Minnesota Historical Society.

14 Edson Washburn, Autobiography of Edson Dean Washburn, Washburn Family Papers, 3, Wright County Historical Society.

15 Ibid.

16 Ibid.

Another young farmer from Monticello, twenty-three-year-old William Houl-
ton, had wanted to enlist since the start of the war. In fact, the captain of Company
D, First Minnesota Volunteer Infantry Regiment, who had some acquaintance with
William prior to the war, wrote a letter urging Houlton to enlist in his unit.[17]

Enlisting in 1861, however, would have created problems for his family. His
father, Samuel Houlton, was seventy-two years old and could not handle the farm
alone. Moreover, the elder Houlton was unwilling to give his blessing to William's
enlistment. As a result, William Houlton didn't enlist during that first year of the war.

Now a year had passed, and the Union remained in peril. It was apparent to
all that the war could be much longer and require more men to step up and do their
duty. When Lincoln made the call for additional troops on August 4, 1862, Houlton's
father relented.

As the date of the War Meeting approached, there was great excitement
throughout Wright County. Local farmers were working night and day to finish their
harvest before the meeting so their affairs would be in order should they decide to
enlist.[18] William Houlton was one of them. He was up all night cutting and binding
wheat to finish the harvest.[19] Then he then went off to the War Meeting.

As the meeting finally commenced on August 12, 1862, young men began to
arrive at Monticello. There, the attendees were entertained with patriotic speeches
by local dignitaries, music, and refreshments. The festivities were designed to build
up a patriotic fervor among the attendees so the young men would feel compelled
to enlist.

Although no detailed description of the War Meeting at Monticello is known
to exist, War Meetings around the country generally followed substantially the same
program. One soldier from a Massachusetts regiment described the format of such
meetings he had attended:

> *Musicians and orators blew themselves red in the face with their*
> *windy efforts. Choirs improvised for the occasion, sang "Red,*
> *White, and Blue " and "Rallied 'Round the Flag " till too hoarse*
> *for further endeavor. The old veteran soldier of 1812 was trotted*
> *out, and worked for all he was worth, and an occasional Mexican*

---

17 Captain H.R. Putnam to William Houlton, Sept. 30, 1861, William H. Houlton and Family Papers.
Minnesota Historical Society.

18 *The North-Western Weekly Union,* Aug. 9, 1862.

19 William Houlton, untitled autobiography manuscript, William H. Houlton and Family Papers.
MNHS. The manuscript consists of a family history and autobiography. Houlton wrote it in 1910 when he
was 70 years old (hereinafter cited as "Houlton, *Autobiography*").

War veteran would air his nonchalance at grim-visaged war. At proper intervals the enlistment roll would be presented for signatures. There was generally one old fellow present who upon slight provocation would yell like a hyena, and declare his readiness to shoulder his musket and go, if he wasn't so old, while his staid and half-fearful consort would pull violently at his coat-tails to repress his unseasonable effervescence ere it assumed more dangerous proportions. Then there was a patriotic maiden lady who kept a flag or a handkerchief waving with only the rarest and briefest of intervals, who "would go in a minute if she was a man."[20]

It was not particularly difficult to drum up a sufficient level of patriotism to drive enlistment in Wright County. Many of the men who attended the War Meeting were born in New England, and a good number of those had grandfathers or great-grandfathers that served in the Revolutionary War.[21] They understood that it was their duty to preserve the Union that their forebears had fought so hard to create.

By the second day, the War Meeting had secured the requisite number of volunteers to meet the county's quota and more than enough to form a company. On Thursday, August 14th, the new volunteers began their journey to Fort Snelling, where they would be examined, equipped, and mustered into the army. They set off on foot, following a rough road along the Mississippi River. They spent the first night of their travels sleeping under the stars; the next day, they obtained some boats and floated down the Mississippi to Minneapolis.

The volunteers reached Minneapolis at about dusk on Saturday, August 16. There, the tired and hungry men dragged the boats out of the water only to discover no arrangements had been made for their reception. Although word had been sent ahead well in advance of the group's arrival, there was no food or accommodations awaiting them.

It was too late for the men to continue on to Fort Snelling. Darkness was rapidly falling. In the days before artificial light, traveling unknown paths in the inky blackness of night could be hazardous and the fort was still a good seven miles away. Without accommodations and the prospect for further travel that night out of the question, the exhausted recruits slept wherever they could. Some spent the night on the floor of a stable and others in vacant rooms nearby.[22] The next morning, the men set out on foot for the final seven-mile hike to the fort.

20 John D. Billings, *Hardtack and Coffee: or The Unwritten Story of Army Life*, George M. Smith & Co., Boston, 1887, 38.

21 George Cambell's grandfather, for example, was a veteran of the Revolution.

22 *The North-Western Weekly Union*, Aug. 23, 1862.

A Profile of the Wright County Volunteers

Just who were the men from Wright County that enlisted at Monticello? Most were of New England Yankee origin. Many had roots in Maine, New Hampshire, and Vermont. Several members of the Wright County company came from other Northern states, including Ohio, Michigan, and Illinois. They had all emigrated to Minnesota Territory after the region had opened for settlement.

A few of the men were immigrants from other countries. Thomas Tollington, Samuel Murry, and John Ponsford, for example, were all born in England. Michael Murphy and Michael Batterbury were from Ireland. Lewis Goyette and Joe Vadner had been born in French-speaking Quebec, Canada. The Monticello company also included recruits from Germany and other parts of Canada.

In fact, it does not appear that any of the Wright County men, or perhaps anyone else who later served in the Eighth Minnesota were actually born in Minnesota. They all came to the newly opened frontier with their families, many as children or young adults, seeking cheap land or other opportunities.

Those who came from New England Yankee stock tended to bring their Protestant work ethic along with them to Minnesota. And that dedication to work was sorely needed on the frontier. Earning a living in the unsettled upper Midwest required extensive labor. These men were accustomed to hard work.

Most of those who enlisted at Monticello were farmers, but a variety of other occupations were represented as well. The new recruits included tradesmen, such as carpenters, mechanics, and at least one blacksmith. There were professionals, including a surveyor, a clerk, and two attorneys. Other occupations represented in the company were lumbermen, a wheelwright, and two schoolteachers.

The men were generally healthy and strong. The average height of the Wright County men was 5'9", which was about the same as the average Civil War soldier. Obesity didn't seem to be a problem among the recruits. Nearly all the men were of slender build, the result of daily hard work on the farm or elsewhere. There was, however, one notable exception.

At 5'8" and well over 200 pounds, William Lane stood out from the rest. His rotund figure is easy to spot in photographs taken of the company. It is unlikely that he could have performed well in battle due to his weight. Fortunately, he enlisted as one of the two company musicians, a role that generally did not require a high level of fitness.

The new recruits were by nature frontiersmen and ruggedly self-sufficient. Yet, they did not fit the stereotype of the hard-drinking, coarse ruffians, as the inhabitants of frontier towns are often portrayed in Hollywood movies. Many were deeply religious. They all found their way to Minnesota hoping for a better life. Their goal was to settle with their families, establish communities, and build solid Christian lives.

Nevertheless, these were strong and tough men, especially the farmers, though they often didn't realize it. They had a deep, quiet strength built by the daily struggle with the hardships of farming on the frontier. The settlers that arrived in Minnesota starting in 1853 had to endure brutally cold winters and hot humid summers. The mosquitos and other biting bugs were a constant nuisance. The farmers faced a multitude of risks every year, including drought, hailstorms, prairie fires, and grasshopper plagues, all of which could quickly wipe out their crops.

Grasshoppers were especially destructive and posed a great threat to the new settlers. The species responsible for this plague was sometimes called the "Rocky Mountain Locust."[23] These grasshoppers traveled in thick clouds covering hundreds of square miles. These massive swarms could contain trillions of individual bugs. The grasshopper clouds were often so thick that they would darken the sky and might take days to pass by overhead.

Minnesota suffered from grasshopper plagues in both 1856 and 1857. The clouds of grasshoppers ate everything in their way, including grass, leaves and the settlers' crops. Nothing growing seemed to escape the destruction of these hungry pests. They often consumed entire fields, eating every plant down to the soil.

It seemed as though nothing could stop the grasshoppers. Farmers tried smoke, noise, and even fire to scare the bugs away, but without effect. Even attempts by settlers to protect their vegetable gardens by covering them with blankets proved futile. The grasshoppers simply ate their way through the blankets.[24] The most recent settlers were usually the hardest hit because they had no surplus from prior years to fall back on.[25]

When considering the harsh living conditions and the wide variety of threats facing their crops it is a wonder that many settlers didn't pack up and seek a more hospitable climate. Some of the earliest arrivals did just that but the hardiest stayed to tough it out.

Those that remained persevered through the harsh conditions. Eventually, they were able to make a good home and earn a good living. Needless to say, these early Minnesota settlers were made of formidable stock and would make good soldiers.

---

23 Surprisingly, considering the vast numbers that existed in the mid-nineteenth century, this species is now believed to be extinct. The extinction appears to have occurred suddenly, perhaps due to agricultural practices in the breeding grounds on the western plains The last confirmed sighting of a Rocky Mountain locust was in 1902.

24 William Bell Mitchell, *History of Stearns County, Minnesota*, Vol. II, Chicago, IL, H.C. Cooper, Jr., & Co., 1915, 1410.

25 Ibid.

One example of a gentle man with deep inner strength built of hardship as a settler was Edson Washburn. His father had set out for Kansas in 1855 to stake a claim on cheap land and then build a farm for the family. While on the way, he learned about the political situation in Kansas and became concerned. Tensions arising from differences over the extension of slavery to the territory resulted in an ongoing bloody fight between the opposing factions. Washburn's father changed course and instead took a land claim in Wright County, Minnesota Territory. There, he intended to plant crops, build a home, and then send for his family to join him.

In September 1856, when Edson Washburn was just fourteen years old, he arrived along with the rest of his family at the new Minnesota farmstead. It consisted of little more than a small shanty with a roof made of bark. The permanent family home was not yet finished.

Edson was impressed with the rolling open country. He was quickly disgusted, however, by the quality of the water. It happened to be the same year that one of the grasshopper plagues struck the area. Many of the bugs flew into waterholes and died. Washburn recalled that the water they fetched would be full of the wings, legs, and heads of decaying grasshoppers. They boiled the water before drinking it, but a disgusting smell and taste remained. For the rest of that fall, Edson chose to walk two and a half miles to the Mississippi River for water rather than drink the nearby bug-infested liquid.

To make matters worse, the family's belongings were delayed in transit and did not arrive for several months. As a result, the entire Washburn family, consisting of mother, father and eight children, spent their first long, cold Minnesota winter in an unfurnished home with barely the clothes on their backs.

Whatever concerns Edson had about whether he had the courage and stamina to be a soldier, his life as a settler in Minnesota demonstrated an ability to endure despite hardship. He was also deeply religious, patient, and tolerant of others. His faith and endurance would serve him well in the harsh conditions that he would encounter in army service.

William Houlton was another recruit who had endured adversity in the harsh Minnesota conditions. He arrived in Monticello during 1856 at the age of sixteen, along with his widowed sixty-seven-year-old father. At the time, the area was still very much a frontier. Most of the land in the area was still pristine. There were only poor roads and no bridges, so the travel was difficult. [26]

Houlton and his father took a squatter's claim and began to farm outside Monticello. The second year, they were hit by the grasshopper plague, which destroyed all their crops. Their livestock also died off. They lost their last cow that year and all but

26 Houlton, *Autobiography*, 11,

their last horse. For the Houltons, it became a struggle to find enough food to sustain life.[27] Starvation was a very real possibility.

To survive, William's father had to mortgage the farm. The burden of that mortgage weighed heavily on young Houlton during his late childhood.[28] By the time the war came, Houlton was already well-accustomed to living with hardship, deprivation, and uncertainty. He didn't let it bother him. William later wrote that he had been doing a man's work since the age of fifteen and had led a strenuous life of privation and sacrifice.[29]

Washburn and Houlton were far from alone. Many of the Wright County volunteers were more than tough enough to endure even the harshest conditions that army life might throw at them. Moreover, they knew they could count on each other.

Relationships

Despite their varied careers and origins, the men who enlisted together at Monticello were far from strangers. Every one of them either knew or had a mutual friend with every other member of the company. This was not unusual in volunteer companies as those units tended to be raised in a particular geographic area. This group of recruits, however, might have been a bit different. They seemed to have closer bonds among themselves than did companies raised in other parts of the country.

As pioneers in Minnesota Territory, their families had learned to rely on each other to survive and build new communities. Together, they all had endured harsh winters, hot summers, grasshopper plagues, and all the other hardships that go with settling wild country. Their families looked out for each other. In some cases, the older members of the company had helped raise the younger members from childhood. Moreover, there were many close family ties within the newly formed company. The Wright County volunteers would include nine sets of brothers. There were other family relationships as well. Homer Markham and Randolph Holding, both of whom resided in Clearwater, were first cousins. Others were related by marriage.

The close relationships did have a downside for the young men leaving the constraints of home for the first time. If any misbehaved while off on their grand adventure, they could expect that their family, friends, and sweethearts would learn of it soon enough.

---

27 Ibid., 12.

28 Ibid., 13. Houlton was forced to take on outside work to support his father, earning $12 a month as a farm laborer and later worked in a store for $15 a month.

29 Ibid., 21.

Politics

The citizens of Wright County and surrounding areas tended to be both religious and conservative. Having been settled mostly by New England Yankees who sympathized with the Abolitionist cause and preferred to eliminate slavery, the county residents overwhelmingly favored President Lincoln and the Republican Party. In the 1860 presidential election, the county voted for Abraham Lincoln over the Democrat nominee, Stephen Douglas, by a three-to-one margin. The political views of the recruits would have generally reflected those of the Wright County area.

The Democrat Party was not particularly popular in Wright County in 1862. The *North-Western Weekly Union* newspaper, which was published in Monticello, seemed particularly hostile to Democrats. The newspaper could not risk offending its readership so the views it expressed likely reflected the overall politics of the city. In one short article, the newspaper stated:

> From all we can learn by observation and otherwise, the "Democratic" party of this day amounts to just this - that they are the Secessionists of the North. You will always find one of these so-called Democrats to be in favor of everything conservative, and in favor of nothing that really tends to hurt the rebels. You will always hear them indirectly praising the superiority of the South over the North; and always opposed to any measure that is calculated to terminate the war with defeat to the rebels; and generally calling the rebels "our erring brothers.[30]

The newspaper included other smaller snippets from time to time to remind readers of the publisher's opinions. One example, slipped in between stories, equated the Democrats with the treasonous Confederates: "The Rebels call Lincoln a 'usurper.' So do Democratic platforms, leaders and newspapers."[31]

Other newspapers that covered the area had similar sentiments and were not afraid to take controversial political positions. A Saint Cloud newspaper provides one example. The paper was published by Jane Gray Swisshelm, who was an ardent Abolitionist.

Swisshelm was an early pioneer of women in journalism.[32] She began her career by publishing a newspaper in Pennsylvania during 1848, *The Pittsburgh Visiter* [sic].

---

30 *The North-Western Weekly Union*, Oct. 25, 1862.

31 *The North-Western Weekly Union*, Nov. 15, 1862.

32 For a more detailed biography of Jane Gray Swisshelm, see Mitchell, *History of Stearns County, Minnesota*, Vol. I, 62.

The paper was a vehicle for her to express views on many social issues of the day, including Abolition and equal rights for women.

In 1857, Swisshelm moved to Saint Cloud, Minnesota and began publishing a new newspaper, *The Minnesota Advertiser*. Her anti-slavery articles in that paper enraged some powerful people in the town. On the night of March 24, 1858, an angry mob of vigilantes broke into the newspaper's office, destroyed the printing press, and threw it into the nearby Mississippi River.

The destruction of the printing press didn't put Swisshelm out of business for long. Sympathetic locals, even some who disagreed with her Abolitionist stance, pitched in and purchased a brand-new printing press for her. She soon resumed publication. Not long afterwards, she took over ownership of *The Saint Cloud Visiter* and later changed its name to *The Saint Cloud Democrat*.

The Saint Cloud papers also circulated in nearby Wright County. Swisshelm's anti-slavery position would have been well-known to the young men from the area who showed up to enlist at Monticello. The majority of them probably sympathized with her sentiments.

Motivations

Most of the men that signed up for the army at Monticello on that warm August day in 1862 did not record their reasons for enlisting. There can be little doubt that many of the men from the Wright County area enlisted primarily out of a sense of duty to their country.

These men were patriots at heart. They had grown up hearing tales of the Minutemen, Concord Bridge and Yorktown. Many of the enlistees had grandfathers or great-grandfathers who served in the Continental Army during the Revolutionary War.[33] As a result, many felt they had an investment in this country that was well worth defending. But it wasn't just duty and patriotism that led the men to enlist. The promise of bounties and steady pay would have helped sway those who were still undecided. That would have been especially true for the farmers.

After barely getting by trying to eke out a living in the harsh Minnesota farming conditions, the financial benefits of the army had to be enticing. Regular pay, a clothing allowance, and generous bounties, would have made even the meager pay of a private look good to the men.

---

33 There were numerous members of Company E with Revolutionary connections. To take but two examples - George Cambell's paternal grandfather had served in the Continental Army until he was discharged for disability after nearly dying from disease and William Houlton's great-grandfather, Amos Putnam, was among the first to enlist in the weeks following the battle at Lexington and Concord in the spring of 1775.

Surprisingly, slavery, the most divisive issue of the day, did not appear to be a significant motivator for the men who enlisted at Monticello. While most would have agreed that the institution of slavery was wrong, they were not necessarily so passionate about abolition that they were willing to fight a war over it.

There were, however, a few exceptions. George Cambell was one man who enlisted specifically for the purpose of fighting to end slavery. He was a carpenter and mechanic who had settled in Lynden Township outside Clearwater. His story is worthy of exploring in more detail.

The Abolitionist Family of George T. Cambell

Twenty-six-year-old George Cambell could honestly say that he was born into the Abolitionist or anti-slavery movement. In the 1830s, his parents, David and Sylvia Cambell, ran a boarding house in Boston. They were involved in various social reforms of the day, including the temperance movement, pacifism, and opposition to the institution of slavery.

The Cambells soon became involved in anti-slavery activities led by their neighbor, a young firebrand newspaper publisher named William Lloyd Garrison.

Garrison published the anti-slavery newspaper *The Liberator* from an office on Washington Street, just around the corner from the Cambells' boarding house at 33 Brattle Street in Boston.[34]

Garrison passionately believed that the institution of slavery was evil. It was by his fearless advocacy for Abolition in *The Liberator* that he became a national leader of those who sought to abolish slavery.

As the Cambells grew more involved in abolitionist activities they became acquainted not only with Garrison, but with many other famous Abolitionists of the

PRIVATE GEORGE THOMPSON CAMBELL TRYING TO LOOK FIERCE IN HIS NEW UNIFORM.

34 The location of the house was across Congress Avenue from Faneuil Hall on the site of the current Boston City Hall Plaza.

time. These included Angelina and Sarah Grimké, the poet John Greenleaf Whittier, and Arthur Tappan.

The abolition of slavery was a controversial and divisive issue in those days, even in reform-minded Boston. Passions ran high on both sides of the issue. The abolitionists in the mid-1830s, however, were in the minority. When they held meetings or publicly expressed their views on the issue, the risk of violence at the hands of pro-slavery ruffians was always present.

On the afternoon of Wednesday, October 21, 1835, George Thompson, a noted British abolitionist and temperance advocate, was scheduled to address The Female Anti-Slavery Society in Boston. During the day, an angry mob of between two and three thousand pro-slavery agitators gathered outside of William Lloyd Garrison's offices, hoping to find Thompson there. When informed that Thompson was not present, the mob turned its anger on Garrison.

Garrison, trapped inside his office by the mob, tried to escape out a back window into a carpenter's shop. There he hid under a pile of wood shavings hoping that the crowd would get tired and disburse. He was wrong. The mob eventually found his hiding spot, and he was, as one witness described, "dragged out onto State Street with the avowed purpose of applying a coat of tar and feathers."[35]

Only an effort by the mayor and a small band of friends saved Garrison from the cruel and painful application of hot tar to his body. The mayor managed to drag Garrison away from the mob and into City Hall. Soon after, Garrison was moved to the Leveret Street Jail, where he was locked up for his own protection. The mob never did locate George Thompson.

David and Sylvia Cambell could not have missed the commotion going on just outside their door. They had to be afraid of what the mob might do if they caught Thompson and Garrison, both of whom the Cambells held in high esteem. The couple were probably also concerned for their own safety, especially since they were expecting a baby any day. Fortunately, all of them escaped any real harm. Just one week later, on October 28, 1835, the Cambell's baby entered the world in the family's boarding house and was christened George Thompson Cambell.

George grew up surrounded by famous abolitionists and their children, first in Boston and then later at Oberlin College in Ohio. The Cambells moved to Oberlin in 1840 not because they were abolitionists, although the college was certainly a hotbed of activity for the Abolitionist cause, but rather for their experience with another popular reform movement of the time: Grahamism.

---

35 Bradley Newcomb Cumings Journal, Oct. 21, 1835. Massachusetts Historical Society at http://www. masshist.org/database/viewer.php?item_id=2445&img_step=1&pid=3&mode=dual#page1 accessed July 19, 2019.

Grahamism was a healthy eating reform movement based on the teachings of the Reverend Sylvester Graham. The Reverend Graham promoted a strict vegetarian diet consisting entirely of bland vegetables, coarsely ground whole wheat flour and water. This diet, devoid of stimulants and spices that might inflame the passions, was purported to combat drunkenness and other forms of intemperance.[36] Today, one remnant of the Graham's dietary reform movement remains on grocery store shelves, the Graham cracker.[37]

As a leader in all types of social reforms, Oberlin College decided to implement the Graham Diet for its students and staff. For this, the college needed a steward experienced with this strict regimen. "Steward" was the title of the person responsible for providing room and board for the students.

David Cambell was the ideal candidate for Oberlin's new steward. David and Sylvia Cambell were staunch advocates of the Graham diet and had promoted their operation in Boston as a "Graham Boarding House." From 1837 to 1839, David also published *The Graham Journal of Health and Wellness*, a weekly newsletter, for the express purpose of promoting the benefits of the diet.[38] The Oberlin board of trustees were familiar with the Cambells' Grahamism experience through various abolitionist connections.

In late 1839, the board of trustees decided to offer David Cambell the position of steward and he eagerly accepted. The Cambells sold their Boston boarding house and set out for Oberlin with their three sons, Moses, James, and George. They arrived at Oberlin in the spring of 1840.

The Cambells quickly imposed a strict Graham diet on both the college faculty and students. It wasn't long, however, before the complaints began. The bland diet failed to satisfy the students and quickly fell out of favor. Students and faculty alike complained of constant hunger and boring meals.[39] Resentment over the strict diet eventually boiled over into open revolt following the dismissal of a popular instructor after he was caught smuggling a pepper shaker into the dinner hall.

36 The social reforms of the 1830s were often interrelated. Grahamism was aimed at promoting temperance or abstention from alcohol.

37 The modern Graham cracker, however, bears little resemblance to its 1830s predecessor. Today's Graham cracker is much sweeter and made with lighter flour.

38 Cambell often used related stories of how the diet benefitted his own family, including one tale where the Reverend Graham himself saved the life of infant George Cambell by prescribing molasses instead of mother's milk. David Cambell, *The Graham Journal of Health and Longevity*, Case of George Thompson Cambell, Boston, Mass. 1839, 348.

39 As proof that history repeats itself, the widely-reported complaints expressed by many high school students in 2014 over the content of school lunches designed to comply with the new federal standards promoted by First Lady Michelle Obama mirrored the complaints made by Oberlin students forced to follow the Grahamite diet more than 170 years earlier.

In 1841, Oberlin College discontinued the Graham Diet experiment and ended its employment of the Cambells. Despite the setback, the Cambell family remained on friendly terms with the Oberlin community and stayed in town for several more years.

During that time, the Cambells continued to develop relationships with other prominent abolitionists. One of those was Owen Brown, a trustee of Oberlin College. It was Brown's son John who would push his own more violent form of abolitionist movement. His raid on Harper's Ferry in 1859, intended to capture arms for a slave revolt, arguably set the nation on a path that would inevitably lead to civil war.

There is evidence that John Brown visited Oberlin during the time the Cambells were there. In such a small community it is likely that the Brown and Cambell children would have become acquainted. Those days may have led to a long-term friendship between John Brown's son Owen and George Cambell's older brothers.[40]

The Cambell family moved again in 1845, this time to New Lebanon Springs, New York. David and Sylvia had been summoned by two doctors from New York City to manage the affairs of a new water-cure establishment. The "water-cure" was quite popular at the time. It treated nearly every known malady of the time through bathing in both hot and cold water spas, a healthy Graham-type diet, and light exercise in the fresh air.

George grew to adulthood working at the water-cure establishment with his parents and older brothers. It was there that he learned carpentry, mechanics, and the hospitality trade.

In 1850, his two older brothers, Moses and James, enraged at the adoption of the Fugitive Slave Act,[41] returned to Oberlin in Ohio. Using Oberlin as a base, the two brothers worked as conductors on the Underground Railroad[42] until 1853. George, who was too young for such risky work, stayed behind in New York and continued to help his parents.

---

40 The younger Owen Brown, grandson of Owen Brown the trustee, was a survivor of the 1859 raid on Harper's Ferry. Moses and James Cambell were certainly acquainted with Owen. They were all ardent abolitionists with ties to Oberlin. Later on, both James and Owen were early settlers in Pasadena, California. An 1884 travel diary of Joseph Whittemore, George Cambell's brother-in-law, describes being introduced to Owen Brown by James Cambell.

41 The Fugitive Slave Act of 1850 required Northern officials to assist in the recapture and return of fugitive slaves. Citizens who assisted fugitive slaves faced stiff fines and criminal penalties. In effect, the anti-slavery Northern states were compelled to assist in the enforcement of slavery in the South. This increased opposition to slavery and led to active resistance.

42 The Underground Railroad was a series of escape routes from the slave states north to Canada. Along the way were safe houses where the fugitive slaves could find food and shelter. Many of these routes to freedom ran through Ohio. Conductors on the Underground Railroad, such as Moses and James Cambell, would guide the fugitives from safe house to safe house during the night, keeping them out of sight along the way.

After James and Moses Cambell returned from Ohio, they decided to explore opportunities in a quieter location far from the growing political turmoil of the east. George, who was by then eighteen years old, joined them. At the time, there was cheap land available on the western frontier and it made sense to try and get some of it.

In the mid-nineteenth century, the U.S. did not have a lot of money in the treasury, but it did have a lot of land. In lieu of paying pensions to veterans of America's early wars, the Revolution and War of 1812, the government gave them land warrants. The warrants allowed the bearer to claim 160 acres in any area open to settlement.

Most of those old veterans, all of whom were at least in their sixties and seventies, had no intention of picking up and moving west. Those veterans were simply too old and wise to relish the prospect of back-breaking work and hardship on the frontier.

The better option for most of the veterans was to sell the land warrants to younger men who were more enthusiastic and in better shape for the rigors of frontier life. The buyers could often get the warrants for less than ten percent of what they would pay to purchase land in the settled East.

The Cambell brothers were among those who took advantage of the opportunity to pick up cheap land on the frontier. They tapped their savings and purchased land warrants from local veterans of the War of 1812.

In early 1853, the Cambell brothers set out for Minnesota Territory, which had recently been opened for settlement. James and Moses took claims along the north bank of the Clearwater River, which runs into the Mississippi River about fifteen miles above Monticello. Although the Clearwater River was just thirty to fifty feet wide, it provided a strong steady flow which could be used to power mills.

Multiple mills eventually sprang up along the Clearwater River in the 1850s. Life would have been even more difficult for the early settlers without access to mills. The water-powered mills were essential to grind flour, cut lumber, and make all the other products necessary for settlers to scrape out a living in the wilderness. James Cambell built one such mill outside the village of Clearwater, next to his brother Moses' 160-acre land claim.

George, however, must have decided he wasn't ready to move so far from his parents and returned to New York. There he continued to work as a carpenter and mechanic for the next five years.

George Cambell returned to Clearwater in 1860 after the death of his mother. For the next two years he worked as a carpenter building houses and commercial buildings in and around Clearwater. He also worked as a mechanic in the local mills.

In May 1862, Moses Cambell's brother-in-law, Charles Whittemore, arrived in Clearwater by riverboat, along with his wife Betsy Jane, five daughters, and two sons. The Cambells and the Whittemores knew each other from New Hampshire, where a young David Cambell had worked in mills near the Whittemore's hometown of Dublin. They met again when twenty-year-old Charles Whittemore moved to Boston and apprenticed as a spruce beer brewer just a couple doors down from David Cambell's Boarding house on Brattle Street.

Years later, in 1845, Moses Cambell married Charles Whittemore's youngest sister, Paulina. After the Whittemores fell on hard times following the Panic of 1857, Charles decided to go back to his farming roots. By then, Moses and Paulina Cambell had settled in Minnesota. However, Moses was spending most of his time working as a mechanic in the mills and was not actively farming. Therefore, Moses and Paulina sold their 160-acre land claim to Charles Whittemore, who then moved his family west.

George was no doubt happy to have these family friends move to town. However, it was the prospect of being near eighteen-year-old Martha Whittemore that had George particularly thrilled. Martha was intelligent, well-educated, and attractive. George Cambell was smitten. He began visiting the Whittemores at every opportunity and soon began courting Martha.

Just when the budding romance between George and Martha was taking off, the war intervened. After only three months of courting, news arrived of the War Meeting in Monticello. George was no doubt reluctant to leave, but his romance with Martha would have to wait.

George Cambell knew that he had to enlist and continue the family's Abolitionist tradition. If it meant he had to fight to end the institution of slavery, he would. And he did.

Other Anti-Slavery Monticello Recruits

George Cambell was certainly one of the few who could say he enlisted expressly to fight slavery. Charles "Charlie" Gibbs may have been another. His family were all Republicans and strong supporters of the Union cause.

Charlie Gibbs was born in Maine. His father Seth moved the family to Minnesota during the 1850s and established a sash-and-door mill in Clearwater. As a leader in the new community, Seth Gibbs became involved in politics. He was elected as a Republican in 1860 to represent the area in the state senate. [43]

---

43 Gibbs only served one term as there was some question whether he actually lived in the senate district he was elected to represent. It appears he resided on the south side of the Clearwater River, but his district was on the north side.

Seth Gibbs supported the party's anti-slavery platform, and it is reasonable to assume that Charlie Gibbs shared his father's political views. If so, he was likely moti-

vated at least in part, to enlist so he could fight against the institution.

The slavery issue may have also served as a motivation for William Houlton to join the Wright County Volunteers. As a nineteen-year-old in 1858, Houlton drafted a long paper condemning slavery and setting forth various detailed arguments against expansion of the institution into the territories, including Kansas. He drew a contrast between platforms of the two major political parties:

CHARLES "CHARLIE" GIBBS IN AN UNDATED PHOTO.

But we must now decide between [the Democrats] position, which is allow Slavery to exist in the territories until they form state governments and then if the majority of the people approve it they may abolish it, and that of the Republicans, which is allow no more Slave States or territories under any consideration.[44]

In response to the question some might ask as to why oppose its extension, Houlton went on to explain: "Because it is a political and social curse to the country where it exists. That it is a political evil can easily be proved."[45] Houlton ended the piece by framing the issue in religious terms and suggesting the importance of opposing the institution:

To stop the progress of Slavery would be taking one step toward that promised time when War and contention, oppression and tyranny shall be known no more, but peace and good will to men shall reign on earth. God speed the day![46]

---

44 William Houlton, *untitled manuscript*, April 9, 1858, Houlton Papers. From the format of the writing it may have been a speech delivered at school or some other civic function.

45 Ibid.

46 Ibid.

Minnesota in 1862

Welcome to the Army!

"What have we gotten ourselves into?" – Cpl. William Houlton

August 17 to 23, 1862

The Wright County volunteers arrived at Fort Snelling expecting to be sworn in and immediately begin their training. They were eager to receive their uniforms, arms, and equipment. What awaited them at the fort, however, would turn out to be quite different from anything they had imagined.

Fort Snelling

Construction of Fort Snelling began in 1819 at a strategic position high on the bluffs overlooking the confluence of the Minnesota and Mississippi Rivers. Originally designated Fort St. Anthony, it was later renamed Fort Snelling after Colonel Josiah Snelling, who designed and oversaw construction of the fort in the early 1820s.[47]

The fort had been decommissioned in 1857 and then sold at a cut rate price to Franklin Steele, a friend of President Buchannan. When the Civil War began, Steele leased it back to the federal government at a healthy profit. During the war it was used primarily to train and equip Minnesota's volunteer regiments. In fact, the very first volunteer regiment formed after President Lincoln's call, the First Minnesota Volunteer Infantry, trained at Fort Snelling before setting out for the south.

---

47 General Winfield Scott recommended the fort be named after Snelling. https://www.cem.va.gov/cems/nchp/ftsnelling.asp, accessed September 2, 2021.

Fort Snelling also played a background role in one of the major dramas that put the nation on a course to civil war. In 1836, Dr. John Emerson, an army officer from Missouri, was assigned to Fort Snelling as post surgeon. He brought with him two slaves, Dred Scott and his wife Harriet. The fort was in what was at the time still part of Wisconsin Territory. Slavery was prohibited in Wisconsin Territory under the Missouri Compromise of 1820.

Dr. Emerson served at Fort Snelling for only a year before he was reassigned to a post near St. Louis. However, he left Dred and Harriet Scott behind and leased their services out to another officer. In 1838, Dr. Emerson was yet again reassigned to a post in Louisiana. He sent for the Scotts, and they returned to join him. It was on a steamship during this trip, while still in free territory on the Mississippi River, that the Scott's first child was born.

Later, the Scotts returned to St. Louis with Mrs. Emerson. For the next several years, Mrs. Emerson continued to rent out Dred and Harriet Scott. In 1846, Dred Scott attempted to buy his freedom from Mrs. Emerson, but she refused. Being denied after earning the money to buy his way out of slavery, Scott filed a lawsuit in Missouri state court seeking his family's freedom based on their time living in free territory.

The Missouri state courts ruled against the Scotts. The Scotts then appealed to federal courts. Eventually, the case went all the way to the United States Supreme Court.

FORT SNELLING IN AUGUST 1862.

The infamous 1857 decision in *Dred Scott v. Sandford* ruled that the Scotts were not entitled to their freedom. As slaves, they were not citizens and could not bring their action in federal court. Therefore, the state court decisions stood. This ruling enraged Abolitionists and helped solidify Northern opposition to the continued existence of slavery.

Reaching the Fort

If the new Wright County recruits expected to find an efficient and orderly military operation when they arrived at Fort Snelling, they were sorely disappointed. Monticello had not been the only county seat to host a War Meeting between August 12 and 14; there were several other such meetings held across Minnesota on those dates. Volunteers who enlisted during War Meetings at Anoka, Hennepin, and several other counties all began to arrive at the fort around the same time. Over the span of just a few days, hundreds of men poured into Fort Snelling.

The army was in the process of forming a total of five new Minnesota regiments. The volunteers arriving from the various counties were not yet formally organized as companies or assigned to regiments. That would come later. First, the army had to find the men a place to stay and arrange for meals. Then the recruits would go through physicals, be issued uniforms and equipment, and complete the other induction formalities. Only once that process was complete would the unit "muster in" to a numbered regiment and be assigned a company letter.

The large number of arriving volunteers quickly overwhelmed the fort's capacity to process the recruits. In some cases, the men would wait for days before being called up to complete the induction process.

The most immediate concern of the Wright County men when they arrived at Fort Snelling late in the morning of August 17, however, was food. The men had little to eat since leaving Monticello. Not having much else to do, they began looking around for a meal.

As the Wright County volunteers passed one of the soldiers' quarters, a cook stepped out and shouted for "Company C" to come in for their meal. The men had not yet been mustered in or assigned a company letter. Therefore, they quickly decided that "C" would do as well as any. The hungry recruits rushed into the quarters and helped themselves to the meal. When the real Company C later showed up to find their meal gone, "you never saw such a crowd of long-faced boys."[48]

This incident was perhaps the first expression of a certain attitude possessed by the Wright County volunteers and probably many other soldiers during the war. The volunteers considered themselves citizens first. They all expected that army life would involve

48 Cambell, *Personal Reminiscences,* 110.

hardship but they were glad to endure it to serve their country in its time of need. Nevertheless, they expected the army to treat them fairly and properly, even if that meant they had to take the initiative and bend the rules to achieve that result. As their later escapades would show, the men sometimes contorted the rules beyond all recognition.

That first meal the Wright County volunteers received at the fort provided them with a rude awakening to army life. The meal consisted of sour bread, bean soup, and "a dirty liquid called 'coffee.'"[49] George Cambell recalled that someone in the mess hall had mistakenly used a bucket of "acid vinegar" when they brewed the coffee.[50] The result was an almost unpalatable meal washed down with equally disgusting coffee. Sadly, it was far from the worst coffee they would receive during their time in the service. This first impression of army life led many of the volunteers to question their decision to enlist.

The men grew concerned that this fare or worse would be their lot for the next three years.[51] Recalling their first army meal at a reunion years later, William Houlton said that soldiers never tasted food so bad outside of a rebel prison camp.[52]

It was also at Fort Snelling where many of the men had their first encounter with an adversary they would constantly battle throughout their service. The cramped conditions and constant flow of troops through Fort Selling provided an ideal environment for a dreaded enemy – vermin. Within a short time after arrival, the recruits found themselves suffering nasty bites from lice and bedbugs. The ferocity of this foe took many of the men by surprise.

The bites from both types of bugs caused intense itching and were constantly annoying, making for an unforgettably miserable experience. Andrew Bertram later described their first encounter with the pests at Fort Snelling in a tongue in cheek poem about Wright County Volunteers' Civil War experience:

> 'twas there for our dear country
> that our first blood was shed
> not on the post of duty
> but in our humble bed.[53]

---

49 William Houlton, handwritten draft of a speech, William H. Houlton and Family Papers, MNHS (hereinafter cited as "Houlton, *Speech*"). The speech appears intended for delivery at the Company E reunion in Monticello on Dec. 7, 1878.

50 Cambell, *Personal Reminiscences*, 2.

51 Ibid.

52 Houlton, *Speech*, MNHS.

53 Andrew H. Bertram, *Reminiscences & Incidents of Co. "E" 8ᵗʰ Minn. Vol. Inf., being A Sketch of The Droll Side of Army Camp Life In Field and Garrison from actual facts, by one who was present*, December 7, 1878, Dakota Conflict of 1862 Manuscripts Collections. Minnesota Historical Society.

Lice were especially a nuisance for soldiers throughout the Civil War. The crowded conditions for the soldiers in barracks and tents made ideal conditions for lice to spread from man to man. Once infested, a man might find dozens of lice on his body with many more hidden in his clothes.

The little pests would lay their eggs in the seams of the soldier's uniforms and underclothing. Upon discovery of a louse, the afflicted soldier might find an isolated spot outside of the camp to do what the men called "knitting," which consisted of scraping the eggs out of the seams of his garments. This process, however, was frequently ineffective.

The bites and constant itching sometimes led men to take extreme measures. One soldier described how a distressed victim might deal with the problem:

> He would hang the suit on a bush, strip off every piece of the old, and set fire to the same, and then don the new suit of blue. So far well; but he was a lucky man if he did not share his new clothes with other hungry [lice] inside of a week.[54]

A soldier would have to foot the bill for a new uniform out of his meager pay. It was therefore unlikely that he would destroy an otherwise perfectly good set of clothes except out of desperation.

The only truly effective method for getting rid of lice was to boil the infested clothing, in salt water if possible. Large laundry kettles were available to the soldiers for this purpose while in camp. It was a different story, however, when the troops were in the field. Desperate soldiers would be driven to boil their clothes in cooking kettles to rid themselves of the lice.

The food, cramped conditions, and vermin led several of the Wright County volunteers to reconsider the prospect of spending the next three years in the army. The army enlistment process allowed volunteers to back out up until they took the oath and were mustered in. After a day or so, some of the original enlistees, perhaps less than ten, resigned and promptly went home.

Processing

During the first few of days at Fort Snelling, the volunteers went through the induction process. The fort surgeon, Dr. Poll, examined each man and, if found in acceptable condition, certified him as fit for duty. The physical examination was not particularly difficult to pass. Generally, if the volunteer appeared reasonably fit and

54 Billings, *Hardtack and Coffee*, 81-82.

was over 5'3" he would be in good enough physical shape as far as the army was concerned.[55] Even the height requirements were not written in stone.

Records show that at least two Wright County volunteers were shorter than the minimum height, Michael Batterburg and nineteen-year-old George Kriedler. At 5' 2½", Batterburg's height may have simply been rounded up to the nearest inch so he could meet the minimum requirement.

Rounding, however, wouldn't help George Kriedler, who stood only 5' 1". Fortunately, Kriedler had other leverage. He enlisted along with his two older brothers, Daniel and Samuel. If George had been rejected, it was possible that both of his brothers would decide to pack up and leave with him. After all, the men were still free to go until they were formally mustered in. The recruiting officer may simply have decided to allow George to join despite his height rather than risk losing all three brothers.

Despite the lax physical standards, several of the original group of Wright County volunteers failed the physical exam and were sent home. Among those found unfit was George Gray, the publisher of the Monticello newspaper. Soon afterwards, he wrote that "our ardor was somewhat damped by being rejected by the examining surgeon."[56]

The large influx of volunteers for the five newly formed Minnesota regiments didn't just overwhelm the induction process, it quickly drained the quartermaster's office of supplies. When their turn came, the quartermaster did not have enough uniforms and equipment to outfit the Wright County volunteers. It didn't make sense to have the men sit around for days until more supplies arrived by steamboat, so they were sent home on ten days' furlough.

The men were not altogether disappointed. The unexpected leave would give them a chance to help finish the wheat harvest at home. When the leave was over, they would finally get their gear, undergo their training, and then set off to whip the rebels. Before they went on leave, however, the Wright County Volunteers had to elect their officers.

A company had three commissioned officers, five sergeants and eight corporals. The men who had enlisted at Monticello didn't consider officers as being any better than the rest of those who served as privates. In fact, all the men had initially enlisted as privates. Those who they elected as officers were simply viewed as having different duties, not as having any special privilege or higher station.

---

55 Later in the war, the minimum height was reduced to 5'.

56 *The North-Western Weekly Union*, Aug. 23, 1862. It does not appear that George Gray was any relation to Jane Gray Swisshelm.

Reflecting their egalitarian views, the Wright County men agreed that anyone elected an officer must turn over the amount of their pay in excess of $13.00 each month, the amount of a private's pay, to the first sergeant. The first sergeant would then divide the pooled assets equally among all the men in the company.[57] Thus, the company's captain would receive no more than any private, except perhaps for the clothing allowance. All the candidates in the officer election had to pledge to abide by this condition.

On Sunday, August 23, with Willie Houlton serving as secretary to record the events, the Wright County volunteers sat down to elect their company officers. The men unanimously elected Edward Hartley the company's captain.

Hartley was a prominent attorney in Monticello. Born in 1836, Hartley earned a law degree and practiced for a short time in his hometown of Portland, Maine. He left Portland in 1857 to seek his fortune in Minnesota Territory.

In 1858 he settled in Monticello and quickly became involved in civic affairs. Between 1858 and 1862, Hartley held various positions in Monticello and Wright County government, including postmaster, county attorney, court commissioner and judge of probate. At 5'6", Hartley was not physically imposing but he was well-known and well-respected throughout Wright County.

Another prominent citizen of Monticello, Micah Croswell, received the company's unanimous vote for first lieutenant. Croswell was a New Yorker who settled in Monticello. He and his brother operated a general store in town.

The second lieutenant position went to twenty-eight-year-old Harvey S. Brookins. Brookins was born in Shoreham, Vermont. He journeyed to Minnesota in 1856 along with his brother George. He quickly found work as a surveyor in Silver Creek, not far from Monticello. In late 1861, Harvey Brookins was elected as Wright County Sheriff. He succeeded to the duties of the office almost immediately because the prior sheriff was in a hurry to leave town.[58] He wasn't sheriff for long. Brookins resigned that position after less than a year in office to enlist as part of the Wright County volunteers.

The men next elected their non-commissioned officers. Thomas Tollington from Clearwater was chosen as first sergeant. Tollington was twenty-nine years old and a recent immigrant. He was born in England and a cabinet maker by trade. Prior to enlisting he had operated a door-and-sash mill in Clearwater.

---

57 Cambell, *Personal Reminiscences*, 8; William H. Houlton, *Record of the Proceedings of the Company at the Election of Officers, Aug. 23, 1862*, Houlton Papers. Houlton served as clerk to record the proceedings.

58 Harvey Brookins to Thurman Brookins, Monticello, Oct. 27, 1861, George W. Brookins and family letters, 1861-1865, Minnesota Historical Society. The previous sheriff was William Smith Brookins, who appears to be a distant cousin of Harvey Brookins. It is unclear why William Smith Brookins was in such a hurry to vacate his position.

The other sergeants elected that day were Albert Barker and John Parvin from Monticello, James Bradley from Minneapolis, and Edward Woodworth from Clearwater. The men also selected eight corporals:

Asel E. Hulett, Silver Creek.
Charles E. Post, Monticello.
William H. Lord, Monticello.
Henry W. Fuller, Orono.
Charles L. Smith, Monticello.
Emerson T. Woodward, Richfield.
William H. Houlton, Monticello.
George W. Carpenter, Silver Creek.

Following the election, the men set off for home on their furlough. As they left Fort Snelling that morning, none could have known of the historic events taking place along the Minnesota frontier not far from Monticello that would change the course of their service far more than any of them could have imagined.

The Sioux Uprising

All the men who volunteered at Monticello in mid-August, 1862 did so with the intent and expectation that they would be quickly trained and then sent south to fight the rebels. They could not imagine, however, the momentous event that would take place just days after they departed Wright County – what became known as the Sioux Uprising. In an instant, the U.S. found itself at war on a second front against a new foe.

Although the Sioux Uprising lasted for barely six weeks, it had a lasting impact and drew precious resources away from the war effort against the Confederates. It also changed everything for the Eighth Minnesota.

Minnesota in 1862

The name "Minnesota" derives from the Dakota language and is variously translated to mean the land of sky-tinted or sky-blue waters, a reference to the thousands of lakes and other waterways that stretch across the state.

The dominant waterway within the state is the Mississippi River. It begins as a mere trickle at Lake Itasca, about 180 miles northwest of Minneapolis. The river loops around to the north and east before running down the center of the state. It then passes through Minneapolis to Fort Snelling, where it is joined by the other major waterway in the state, the Minnesota River. From there, the Mississippi proceeds east past St. Paul a few miles until it merges with the St. Croix and flows south, forming the border with Wisconsin.

In August 1862, Minnesota was still the northwestern frontier of the United States. It had gained statehood only four years earlier in 1858. There were not yet any railroads in the state, so the Mississippi and Minnesota rivers provided the fastest and most efficient transportation routes. Steamboats were the primary means of transportation for settlers and traders prior to the Civil War.

Minnesota Territory was formed in 1849. By that time, French voyageurs and English fur traders had been active in the area for almost 200 years. There were a few settlements near Fort Snelling, including St. Anthony, later to be part of Minneapolis, and Pig's Eye, now known as St. Paul. Trade routes mostly ran along the rivers and waterways. However, the Red River oxcart trail provided overland transportation north to the British settlement at Fort Garry in Canada.[59]

A significant portion of Minnesota territory was covered by a hardwood forest. The "Big Woods" as the area would be called, consisted of nearly four thousand square miles of sugar maples, oak, elm, basswood, and other deciduous trees. The Big Woods extended north from Mankato, which formed the southwestern corner, in a swath about 40 miles wide running as far north as Stearns County near present day St. Cloud.

Large stands of old growth pine forest, which ran north to the arctic, formed the northeastern boundary of the Big Woods. From the western edge of the woods, a vast prairie spanned more than 700 miles to the foothills of the Rocky Mountains.

The variety of trees and other vegetation within the Big Woods provided sufficient food and shelter to sustain a large and diverse population of wildlife. Deer, bear, elk, and ruffed grouse were all abundant within the Big Woods. As a result, Indian bands throughout central and southern Minnesota depended on the Big Woods for much of the food they needed to survive in the harsh climate.

Native Americans

Until the mid-seventeenth century, most of what became the State of Minnesota was inhabited by the Sioux Indians.[60] French voyageurs and early missionaries found various Sioux tribes throughout the area, from the shores of Lake Superior in the north to the Big Woods, plains, and Minnesota River valley in the southwest part of the region.

The Sioux were many different bands that shared the same language family. They roamed a territory running from western Wisconsin and stretching west for several hundred miles across the plains. The eastern bands were known as the "Santee" and occupied most of what is now Minnesota. The "Yankton" and Western Sioux

---

59 The settlement at Fort Garry was incorporated in 1873 and was renamed the City of Winnipeg.

60 This book uses the term "Sioux" as it was the term used by the soldiers and primary sources of the time to describe the people of the Dakota Nation.

or "Teton" bands covered parts of southwestern Minnesota, the Dakotas, and west into Montana.

At about the same time the first French voyageurs arrived, the Chippewa or Ojibwe, an eastern Algonquin tribe, began encroaching on lands occupied by the Sioux. The Chippewa had migrated west through Canada and then traveled down the north shore of Lake Superior into Minnesota's northern pine forests. As they moved south, the Chippewa began to encounter the Sioux. The two tribes clashed over resources. The result was an ongoing bloody war for territory between the two peoples.

By the late eighteenth century, the Chippewa had driven the Sioux out of northern Minnesota, pushing them to the south and west. They had conquered the lands near Lake Superior and around Mille Lacs Lake in central Minnesota. The Chippewa drove the Sioux into the Big Woods and beyond. No Sioux villages remained east of the Mississippi River, which formed a rough boundary between the two warring Indian nations.

The two tribes continued to fight during the early days of settlement. Painted warriors could be seen on the streets of St. Paul with scalps of their dead enemies on their belts. In 1853, the Sioux and Chippewa engaged in a small battle at Third and Jackson Streets in downtown St. Paul.[61] That fight killed one Indian, wounded several others, and sent the white residents diving for cover.

Attempts by the U.S. government to prevent the Sioux from engaging in warfare against the Chippewa only bred bitterness against the whites.[62] Warfare was simply too important in Sioux culture. It was primarily through warfare that young Sioux men could prove their bravery.

Demonstrations of bravery were very important to the Sioux. Young men knew they could not advance in the tribal hierarchy unless they had proven their bravery in battle. Returning from a war party with enemy scalps and horses would increase the warrior's status within the tribe.

Perhaps the most highly regarded act of courage by plains Indians, including the Sioux, was "counting coup."[63] This entailed getting so close to an enemy in battle that the warrior could touch him with a stick and get away without injury to himself or his opponent. A Sioux warrior would often carry his own decorated "coup stick" for this purpose.

While counting coup was important when the opportunity arose, warfare between the Indian tribes bloody and brutal. Neither the Sioux nor Chippewa hes-

61 Willoughby M. Babcock, "Sioux versus Chippewa," *Minnesota History Magazine*, 41-45, March, 1925.

62 Ibid., 45.

63 "Coup" comes from the French language and is pronounced "coo."

itated to kill women and children of the other tribe when the opportunity arose. Men who fell into Sioux hands were nearly always killed, often through slow torture. Women and children might be taken hostage but were often killed as well. Age and sex did not matter. It was understood and accepted by the Sioux and Chippewa alike that war involved killing the full range of their enemies, from babies to the elderly of both sexes.

Indians also sometimes mutilated the bodies of those they killed in battle. In the culture of many Indian tribes, including the Sioux, it was believed that those killed in battle went into the afterlife in the same form in which they died. Mutilation of a vanquished foe's body would also mutilate the dead man's spirit.[64] The warrior might cut off the limbs or head of a fallen enemy or poke out the dead man's eyes. To the victor, it made sense to further cripple the deceased opponent in this world just in case they might have to fight again in the next.

To the white settlers, the Indian customs of warfare must have seemed horrific, and it may have been somewhat unnerving to be living in proximity to the warring tribes. Nevertheless, the settlers tended to believe that they were in little danger. An article about the ongoing war between the Sioux and Chippewa in the St. Cloud newspaper summed up that attitude:

> Generally, the white settlers had no fear of them, for they knew that the murder of a white by them, would be apt to result in the speedy extermination of the tribe; and they attempt no greater injury than stealing provisions.[65]

Many of the settlers, however, were not aware of the growing frustration and anger among the Sioux arising from treaties made with the U.S. Government during the 1850s. It was mistrust from the treaty negotiations and resentment caused by the U.S. government's failure to fulfill its obligations that finally boiled over into the Sioux War.

Treaty of Traverse des Sioux

Shortly after the formation of Minnesota Territory, the U.S. government began negotiations with the various Indian tribes to open land for white settlement. The

---

64 It has been widely reported that the body of George Armstrong Custer was mutilated after he fell at the Battle of Little Big Horn. The Indian women stabbed sewing awls through the ears deep into Custer's head so that he could listen better in the afterlife.

65 *St. Cloud Democrat*, Nov. 3, 1859.

first such treaty was negotiated with the Sioux in 1851 at the small trading village of Traverse des Sioux.

Traverse des Sioux was located along the west bank of the Minnesota River, about sixty miles southwest of Fort Snelling and just north of St. Peter. The settlement was located at the point where a well-used trade route crossed or forded the Minnesota River. Hence, the French term "Traverse" (to cross or ford) of the Sioux.

It was at Traverse des Sioux in the summer of 1851 that the Sioux Indians and U.S. government negotiated a treaty to open more of Minnesota territory to white settlement. The treaty required the Sioux to cede approximately 24 million acres of land to the U.S. government. The ceded territory stretched from the Mississippi River in southeast Minnesota, north to the Chippewa lands, and west into what is now South Dakota.

In exchange for the land, the government agreed to pay the Sioux what amounted to about seven-and-a-half cents per acre. In addition, the government set aside a reservation for the Sioux. The new Sioux reservation was seventy miles long and twenty miles wide along the Minnesota River. It started just east of New Ulm and ran northwest covering about ten miles on each side of the river.

At the conclusion of the negotiations, the parties sat down to sign two copies of the Treaty of Traverse des Sioux. As they were doing so, traders gave the Indian negotiators a third document to sign that the Indians had not previously seen. The traders often sold goods to the Indians on credit and drafted the additional document to ensure they received payment.

The trader's document was never read aloud or translated into the Dakota language, so the Indians never knew what they were signing. The document authorized the government to deduct from the treaty payments the unpaid claims of traders. When the Indians realized what had occurred, it created great lingering mistrust and resentment.

Payments under the treaty were to be a sore spot for the Sioux for the next several years. The government did not pay over the amount due under the treaty in a lump sum. First, as provided in the traders' document, the government deducted from the payment the unpaid claims of traders. Then, a portion of the treaty money was used to move the Indians onto the reservation and teach them to be farmers.

The remaining portion of the treaty money would be paid out as an annuity. The annual annuity payments were to be paid in gold each July after deducting any debts the traders claimed were owed them.

Two agencies were established on the reservation to administer the treaty. The Lower Sioux Agency was located on the east end of the reservation, approximately twenty-five miles upriver from the town of New Ulm. The Upper Sioux Agency was located farther west on the reservation near the Yellow Medicine River, about six miles downstream from the present location of Granite Falls, Minnesota.

An Indian agent for each agency was appointed by the federal government. The Indian agent served as the liaison between the Indians and the government. In that capacity, the agent was also responsible for managing the government plans for the reservation.

Each agency was set up much like a very small town. They included the administrative office of the agency, shops for carpenters and blacksmiths, and the stores and warehouses of the traders.

To help maintain the peace between Sioux and nearby settlers, the government decided to build a fort not far from the Lower Sioux Agency. Construction began in 1853 on what would become Fort Ridgely. The location was on the north side of the Minnesota River about midway between the Lower Sioux Agency and New Ulm. One of the first commanders of Fort Ridgely was a young West Point graduate named Alfred Sully.[66]

For much of the year, the Indians would roam their former territory hunting game. Then, just before the annuity payments were due in early July, they would congregate at the agency. There they would wait for the payment, which was inevitably late. Without money and unable to leave for hunting until after the treaty payment, many of the Indians had to rely on the traders.

> *"During this time they had to depend upon what they could find in the vicinity and what credit they could get at the stores for means of subsistence. The scanty supply was the cause of great suffering and a constant source of complaint..."*[67]

The Indians were largely dependent on the traders for food and goods while they awaited their payments. These supplies were usually purchased on credit. Then, when the treaty payments were made, the traders would be waiting with their books showing how much each Indian owed and collect it on the spot.

The traders' books were the only evidence of the debt owed and the Indians had no receipts or written evidence of their own to dispute the traders' claims. No doubt some of the traders took advantage of the situation to cheat the Indians with

---

66 Sully would later command the Northwest Indian Expedition of 1864, in which the Eighth Minnesota would play a key role.

67 Jared Waldo Daniels, Jared Daniels Reminiscences, Ch. 4, Indian Outbreak 1862, 22, Minnesota Historical Society.

inflated amounts due.[68] To make matters worse, the Indians did not have access to the courts as a remedy for inflated claims. This arrangement only fueled the Indians' growing anger at the white traders.

The Indians were also aware that many of the white settlers and traders viewed them as somehow inferior. "Many of the whites always seemed to say by their manner when they saw an Indian, 'I am much better than you,' and the Indians did not like this."[69] That was somewhat ironic as Chief Big Eagle noted "the Dakotas did not believe there were better men in the world than they."[70]

By 1857, as Minnesota Territory moved closer to statehood, there were concerns in Washington, D.C and in Minnesota

BIG EAGLE.

about allowing the Sioux to remain in the territory at all. The government again entered into treaty negotiations with the Sioux, this time for the purpose of reducing the size of the reservation.

Several Sioux chiefs, including Little Crow, Big Eagle, and others, traveled to Washington for the negotiations. The result was a new treaty that eliminated that portion of the reservation north and east of the Minnesota River. In exchange, the Indians were to receive a cash payment and were promised an increase in the annuities.

The new treaty was highly unpopular with the Sioux. Any change to a long-standing way of life will always meet some resistance. In the case of the Sioux, however, the magnitude of the change was immense. For many generations, the Sioux

68 Big Eagle. "A Sioux Story of the War," *Saint Paul Pioneer Press*, July 1, 1894.

69 Ibid.

70 Ibid.

roamed about a vast territory whenever and wherever they pleased. By ceding the land north of the Minnesota River, the Sioux lost access to the best hunting grounds. Moreover, the Sioux never saw the bulk of the cash payment promised by the 1858 treaty. The funds were mostly used to pay off the Indians' debts to the traders.

Nevertheless, some of the reservation residents did give up their traditional way of life and became farmers. The government supplied them with seeds, implements and other necessities. A growing divide developed between these "Farmer Indians," as they came to be called, and those who stuck to their traditional ways or "Blanket Indians."

The government looked after the Farmer Indians by building them houses and providing supplies. "The 'farmers' were favored by the government in every way" recalled Chief Big Eagle.[71] This made the Blanket Indians jealous and perhaps envious. They referred to the farmer Indians as "cut-hairs," which was intended as a slur to those Indians who abandoned wearing their hair in the Indian style and instead took to cutting it in the manner of the whites.

Indian-Settler Interactions

Many early settlers, including those in Wright County, had plenty of contact with the Sioux, despite the treaties that moved them on to the reservation along the Minnesota River. Groups of Indians frequently traveled north from the reservation to the Big Woods on hunting and trapping expeditions. "They roamed over the country at will hunting deer," recalled one settler[72]. Along the way, it was not unusual for the Indians to stop at settlers' houses and ask for something to eat or drink.[73] The Indian parties often camped near the lakes in Wright County and the surrounding area, including those around Lake Minni Belle in Meeker County, about forty miles west of Monticello.[74]

As recently as the winter of 1861-1862, a large group of 300 Sioux camped for a time near Silver Creek, about midway between Monticello and Clearwater. The Indians were hunting for deer and other game in and around the Big Woods. One settler described the Indians' method of hunting deer:

71 Ibid.

72 Rachel A. Maservey Linn, *Account of building a block house at Maine Prairie, Minn. during the uprising, 1932*, Dakota Conflict of 1862 Manuscripts Collections. MNHS.

73 Peter P. Quist, *Mrs. Pernilla Ofelt's account of the Sioux uprising*, 1862, Dakota Conflict of 1862 Manuscripts Collections. MNHS.

74 Irene Persons, *Notes of interview with Elizabeth Whitcomb*, June 11, 1937, Dakota Conflict of 1862 Manuscripts Collections. MNHS, 2.

There were lots of deer in the timber so the Indians would form a
great circle of perhaps two miles and then close in and finally get a
lot of them in the circle and then shoot them all.[75]

George Cambell recalled that these hunting parties "had been known to kill sometimes one-hundred deer in a day."[76] On the whole, most of the white settlers who encountered the Indian hunting parties thought them peaceful.

Nevertheless, the nearby presence of the Sioux, coupled with stories of the brutal acts committed by both sides in battles with the Chippewa, seemed to leave many settlers with a constant sense of anxiety about the Indians. While the settlers generally believed they were safe from attack, they never really trusted the Indians despite their outwardly peaceful demeanor. On occasion, events took place that seemed to reinforce the settlers' worst fears.

The most significant incident on the minds of Minnesota settlers was the Spirit Lake Massacre in 1857. At the end of an unusually harsh winter, even by Upper-Midwest standards, a small band of Indians led by a Santee Sioux chief named Inkpaduta were camped in northwest Iowa. Inkpaduta had not participated in the 1851 treaty of Traverse des Sioux, which ceded much of the Sioux Minnesota lands to the U.S. Government.[77]

For months, the Indians and settlers in the area had been quarreling over various disputes and perceived slights. The growing anger of the Indians finally came to a head after a settler killed Inkpaduta's brother and family. Inkpaduta led a small party of warriors to take revenge. They killed approximately three dozen settlers near Spirit Lake in northwest Iowa before fleeing north through Minnesota and into Dakota Territory. There, they were taken in by local tribes.

Between the Spirit Lake massacre of 1857 and the summer of 1862 there had not been any significant Indian trouble in Minnesota. Nevertheless, many settlers remained on edge, especially when a large number of Indians camped nearby. The settlers, it was claimed, knew the friendship of the Indians "did not emanate from the heart, and that in their inmost souls they hated the whites."[78]

---

75 Dick E. Blanchard reminiscence, July 5, 1933., Dakota Conflict of 1862 Manuscripts Collections. MNHS, 4-5.

76 Cambell, *Personal Reminiscences*, 7.

77 William E. Lass, "Inkpaduta (Scarlet Point)" *The Biographical Dictionary of Iowa.* University of Iowa Press Digital Edition, 2009, http://uipress.lib.uiowa.edu/bdi/DetailsPage.aspx?id=193, accessed Sept. 8, 2019.

78 E.H. Atwood, *Early History of Maine Prairie, Fair Haven, Lynden, Eden Lake, and Paynesville*, St. Cloud, 46.

Indian scares at the time were frequent.[79] "Settlers would come racing through the country with their livestock and other possessions only to return to their farms in a brief time."[80] One example of such a scare occurred in the vicinity of Maine Prairie.

On July 8, 1860, a rumor reached the citizens of Maine Prairie that claimed twenty thousand Sioux warriors were attacking from the west, killing and torturing the settlers as they went and burning their buildings.

> A panic seized the citizens. All the women and children were hast-
> ily started for St. Cloud, accompanied by some of the older men.
> In their fright they took only those things that were handiest and
> would be most needed, and poured into St. Cloud. Some traveled
> with horse teams, some with oxen, and some on foot.[81]

A number of men remained behind to defend the area against the invasion. They fortified a house, collected arms and ammunition, and then began drills in preparation for the coming fight.

A terrified rider soon arrived in St. Cloud to report that the Indians had risen up at the treaty payment over on the Minnesota River. The bearer of this news, a census marshal, reported that the Indians had murdered the agents and interpreters at the agency, and were then crossing the country, murdering, burning, and pilfering. According to the local newspaper, "This courier had seen them, and estimated their numbers at thousands, had seen them burn two houses and murder the inhabitants."[82]

When the terrified refugees reached St. Cloud, rumors began circulating that the last of those who fled Maine Prairie had seen the flames of the burning buildings and could hear the shrieks of the tortured victims.[83] A unit of militia was promptly dispatched from St. Cloud to relieve the embattled men who stayed behind at Maine Prairie.

Of course, there was no Indian attack. It was simply a false alarm. There were no Indians anywhere near the area, much less the thousands claimed in the rumor. By the next day, the hysteria had died down and the refugees returned to their homes.

The white settlers continued to believe that the Sioux would never dare rise up and go to war against them. Nevertheless, the Maine Prairie incident demonstrated

---

79 Irene Persons, *Notes of interview with Elizabeth Whitcomb, June 11, 1937*, Dakota Conflict of 1862 Manuscripts Collections. Minnesota Historical Society, 2.

80 Ibid.

81 Atwood, *Early History of Maine Prairie*, 8-9.

82 *St. Cloud Democrat, July 12, 1860*. These rumors in 1860 would bear an unsettling resemblance to what actually occurred two years later.

83 Ibid.

that the settlers never really felt entirely safe when the Indians were around. If anything, the false alarm at Maine Prairie showed that the settlers would flee in a panic if an uprising were ever to occur.

Tension Builds

The combination of a poor crop, plus the effect of insects and birds resulted in a poor harvest on the Sioux reservation in 1861. There simply wasn't enough food raised to feed all the inhabitants of the reservation. The Farmer Indians were able to get by because they could earn some money cutting wood or doing other work. However, it was not as easy for the Blanket Indians. It became necessary for the Indian Agent to buy flour and other essentials to feed the Indians from December 1861 until the beginning of April 1862.

Many of the Indians on the reservation had to purchase supplies on credit from the traders who had set up shop there and, in the process, ran up large bills. As spring turned into summer, the traders began to cut off credit to the Indians. Without access to the traders' supplies and being largely cut off from their hunting grounds, many Indians were forced to beg for food to avoid starvation.

The Indians' anger and resentment at the situation increased when July came and went without the annual annuity payment. Rumors circulated among the Indians that the payment would not be made that year due to the Civil War. Many of the Sioux had long regretted the treaties made by their chiefs and seethed in anger over the conduct of the white traders. It was time, some thought, to act.

More militant factions of the Indians began to argue that the time had come for war with the whites. To the Indians, the timing for war may have seemed right. They might encounter minimal opposition. Thanks to the Civil War, many white men had gone south to fight against the Confederates. Moreover, many men from the reservation were about to leave for the army. They had enlisted in a company of volunteers from the area that called themselves the "Renville Rangers."

Many of the men who enlisted in the Renville Rangers were of mixed parentage, one Sioux parent and one white parent. They were referred to by the derogatory term "half-breeds." Both the Sioux and whites tended to look down on them. When the Sioux learned that the army was recruiting from among the half-breeds, it only reinforced their belief that the whites were weak and vulnerable. "The Indians now thought the whites must be pretty hard up for men to fight the South, or they would not come so far out on the frontier and take half-breeds or anything else to help them."[84]

---

84 Ibid.

LITTLE CROW

By June 1862, the Indians living along the Minnesota River quietly began whispering among themselves of possibly going to war against the whites. With so many white men gone to fight the Confederates, some of the Indians argued that they could push the settlers out and retake their land. Moreover, they believed their mortal enemies, the Ojibway and Winnebago, would not stand idly by in the event of war. If fighting began, the Sioux hoped and expected that these tribes would instead join them as allies.

While there was strong sentiment in favor of war, several respected chiefs, including Little Crow and Big Eagle, argued instead to keep the peace. Chief Big Eagle later recalled:

I had been to Washington and knew the power of the whites and that they would finally conquer us. We might succeed for a time, but we would be overpowered and defeated at last. I said all this and many more things to my people...[85]

Another factor weighing in favor of peace was that the annuity payment was expected to arrive soon. Although much of it would go first to the despised traders, the payment would relieve some of the hardships. In the end, the peace faction prevailed, at least for the short term.

To help calm the tensions on the reservation, a delegation of Indians traveled to Fort Ridgely, where they met with the commander, Captain Marsh. They asked Captain Marsh not to send soldiers to the annuity payment. Captain Marsh replied that he would have to send soldiers, but he would not allow them to be used to collect

---

85 Ibid.

debts owed to the traders.[86] This seemed to satisfy the Indians and they returned to their villages in triumph.

When the traders learned that the Indians had gone to Captain Marsh they became outraged. Andrew Myrick, who ran a trade house owned by his brother, was particularly angry. He cut off credit to the Indians and refused to sell them any goods. Myrick purportedly told the Indians:

> ...you will be sorry. After a while you will come to me and beg for meat and flour to keep you and your wives and children from starving and I will not let you have a thing. You and your wives and children may starve, or eat grass, or your own filth.[87]

Other traders followed Myrick's lead and no longer allowed the Indians to buy goods on credit. This placed the Indians on the reservation in a desperate situation. The Blanket Indians had exhausted their credit and could no longer buy food or other essential supplies. All they could do was wait for the annuity payment. Needless to say, the traders only stoked the Indians' anger through their actions.

The annuity payment, however, did not arrive when promised. The Indians waited throughout July without any word of when they could expect their payments, and anger grew with each passing day. The Sioux chiefs believed the situation might lead to some sort of trouble, but few expected outright war. "Little Crow and other chiefs did not think so," recalled Big Eagle, "but others were getting ready for it."[88]

As July gave way to August, the tensions began to reach a peak. With no annuity payment and their credit cut off, many of the Indians had run out of provisions and were beginning to starve. Many had already been forced to eat their own dogs.[89] It was reported that six children died of starvation in the first part of August.[90] Some of the starving Indian women were forced to trade sexual favors for food or credit.[91] The situation was becoming desperate.

Settlers in the area around the Lower Sioux Agency began to notice a subtle change in the demeanor of Indians they encountered. Some Indians even hinted

---

86 Ibid., 286.

87 Ibid., 286.

88 Big Eagle. "A Sioux Story of the War," *Saint Paul Pioneer Press*, July 1, 1894.

89 Franklyn Curtiss-Wedge, *History of Renville County Minnesota*, Vol. I., Chicago, H.C. Cooper, Jr. & Co., 1916, 132.

90 L.A. Fritsche, M.D., Editor, *A History of Brown County Minnesota: Its People, Industries and Institutions*, Vol. 1, Indianapolis, B.F. Bowen & Company, Inc., 1916, 151.

91 Ibid.

that trouble was coming. Many of the settlers dismissed these concerns as nothing but unfounded rumors. The failure to take the hints seriously was a decision many settlers would come to regret.

The Spark – Hen's Eggs at Acton

Sunday, August 17 1862, began as a warm sunny day in the central part of the state. On this beautiful day, tragic events were set to take place that would cause the Indians' smoldering anger and resentment to explode into a conflagration that would quickly take hundreds of lives throughout the western half of Minnesota.

It began near Acton in Meeker County, which is about forty-five miles west-southwest of Monticello. The area was near the edge of the Big Woods along a trading route that ran to Pembina in Dakota Territory far to the north. The Big Woods was a popular hunting destination for Indians from the reservation along the Minnesota River forty miles to the south.

A few days before, on August 12, a small hunting party of twenty Sioux Indians set out from the Lower Agency to the Big Woods.[92] They were starving along with the rest of their people and hoped to find some game for themselves and their families. As they neared the Big Woods, the hunting party split up into smaller groups.

On the morning of August 17, one group of four Indians from the hunting party were traveling across property near the Big Woods owned by a settler named Robinson Jones. One of their number came across a nest of hen's eggs along a fence line on the property. According to various accounts, their names were Sungigidan, which translates to English as "Brown Wing," Ka-om-de-i-ye-ye-dan or "Breaking Up," Kagi-wi-cak-te or "Killing Ghost," and Pa-zo-i-yo-pa or "Runs Against Something Crawling."[93] All of the Indians were young men under thirty years of age.

As one of the hungry Indians picked up the eggs, another member of the party cautioned him "Don't take them, for they belong to a white man, and we may get in trouble."[94] The first Indian responded by calling his colleague a coward. This was a supreme insult in the Sioux culture and prompted the offended man to respond that he was not a coward and would go up to the house and shoot the owner to prove it. The other Indians all agreed to go along and prove their bravery as well.

The Indians were already acquainted with the property owner, Robinson Jones. Jones both farmed and maintained a public house, which doubled as a trading post. From his establishment, Jones sold goods to other settlers and traded with the Indi-

92 Curtiss-Wedge, *History of Renville County Minnesota*, 146.

93 Big Eagle. "A Sioux Story of the War," *Saint Paul Pioneer Press*, July 1, 1894.

94 Ibid.

ans for furs. The Jones house also served as the post office for Acton. Robinson Jones and his wife Ann lived on the property with two children recently adopted from relatives, fourteen-year-old Clara Wilson and her eighteen-month-old baby brother. When they arrived at the door, the Indians did not shoot Jones as they had discussed. Instead, they asked Jones for whiskey. Jones, who knew all four Indians, refused and a heated argument developed. Jones quickly grew alarmed at the Indians' conduct, which was unusually menacing and threatening.[95] Growing concerned over the hostile demeanor and rising anger of the Indians, Jones left young Clara and her baby brother at the house and set out for a neighbors' farm, that of his son-in-law Howard Baker and his wife Emily.[96]

The Bakers had settled on their farm in 1856 with their two children and Howard's mother Anna. Shortly thereafter, Robinson Jones had married Anna. Anna Jones was already at the Baker home that morning, having arrived earlier to pay them a Sunday visit. Also at the Baker farm that day were Viranus Webster and his wife Betsey, newly arrived pioneers. The Websters were living in a covered wagon, which they had parked in the Bakers' yard while they searched for land on which to settle.

Robinson Jones reached the Baker farm just before 11 a.m. The four Indians arrived a few minutes later, having followed Jones to the Bakers'. It appeared that the Indians had calmed down from their earlier confrontation with Jones. Two of the Indians spoke some English and Jones spoke the Dakota language reasonably well. They conversed in the house for a few minutes.

According to some accounts, Jones was trying to sell Baker's gun to one of the Indians. The Indian asked for Jones to shoot the gun before he would buy it. The group then went outside for a little target shooting to test the weapon.

Jones and two of the Indians fired their guns at the target. One of the other Indians claimed his gun wasn't working and asked to borrow Webster's gun. After everyone had taken a turn shooting, the Indians reloaded their guns. Robinson and Webster did not, leaving them conveniently unarmed.[97]

What happened next was described by Emily Baker at the coroner's inquest held the next day:

> *About 11 o'clock A. M., four Indians came into our house; stayed*
> *about fifteen minutes; got up and looked out; had the men take*
> *down their guns and shoot them off at a mark; then bantered for*

95 Hubbard and Holcombe, *Minnesota in Three Centuries*, 305.

96 William Watts Folwell, *A History of Minnesota*, Vol. II, Saint Paul, MN, Minnesota Historical Society, 1924, 416.

97 Fritsche, *A History of Brown County Minnesota*, 157.

a gun trade with Jones. About 12 o'clock two more Indians came and got some water.[98] Our guns were not reloaded; but the Indians reloaded theirs in the dooryard after they had fired at the mark. I went back into the house, for at the time I did not suspect anything, but supposed the Indians were going away.

The next thing I knew I heard the report of a gun and saw Mr. Webster fall; he stood and fell near the door of the house. Another Indian came to the door and aimed his gun at my husband and fired, but did not kill him; he then shot the other barrel of the gun at him, and then he fell dead. My mother-in-law, Mrs. Jones, came to the door and another Indian shot her; she turned to run and fell into the buttery; they shot at her twice as she fell. I tried to get out of the window, but fell down cellar. I saw Mrs. Webster pulling the body of her husband into the house; while I was in the cellar I heard firing out of doors, and the Indians immediately left the house, and then all went away.[99]

By the time the Indians departed, Robinson Jones, his wife Ann, Howard Baker and Viranus Webster all lay dead or dying. Betsey Webster, Emily Baker and the two Baker children were not harmed.

The killing at Acton, however, was not over. As the Indians fled from the Baker farm, they again passed the Jones house. Standing in the door of the house was Clara Wilson. Unaware of the massacre that had just taken place, she was casually watching the Indians as they passed by on the road.

It is believed that one of the Indians, seeing Wilson in the doorway, fired his gun from horseback. The bullet pierced Clara Wilson's heart and she died instantly. The Indians apparently did not stop for there was no evidence they entered the home. Robinson Jones' stock of whiskey was later found untouched and Clara's baby brother was discovered sleeping in a back bedroom.

The Fire Spreads

After fleeing from the murders at Acton, the Sioux hunting party set out as fast as they could back to their village along the Minnesota River. They stole fresh horses

---

98 Other accounts indicate the two Indians who stopped for water left after receiving their drink and were not present at the murders. Curtiss-Wedge, *History of Renville County Minnesota*, 145.

99 Hubbard and Holcombe, *Minnesota in Three Centuries*, 305-306.

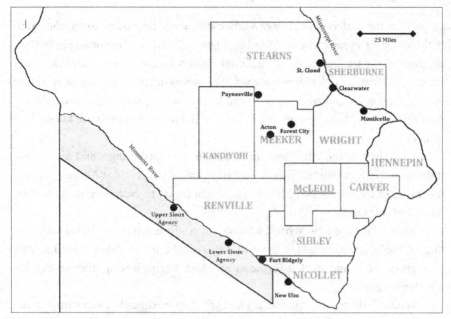

MAP OF CENTRAL MINNESOTA SHOWING LOCATIONS OF EVENTS AT THE BEGINNING OF THE SIOUX WAR.

from a farm not far from the Robinsons and covered the forty-mile distance back to their village in a few hours. They arrived near dusk.

Upon reaching the village, the hunting party jumped from their exhausted horses and called out: "Get your guns! There is war with the whites, and we have begun it!"[100] This caused great excitement throughout the small village. Messages were sent to chiefs of the other villages to meet at the house of Little Crow, one of the more respected chiefs.

Throughout the night, debate raged at Little Crow's home over whether to go to war. It was not a decision taken lightly. Many of the chiefs, including Little Crow, urged caution and restraint, knowing that the chances of success were slim. Nevertheless, before the night was over, Little Crow was swayed to declare war on the whites. It would start early in the morning.

The rest of the night was spent in preparation for the coming conflict. The warriors readied their arms and painted their bodies for battle. There were chants of "Kill the whites and kill all of these cut-hairs who will not join us."[101]

---

100   Ibid., 311.

101   Big Eagle. "A Sioux Story of the War," *Saint Paul Pioneer Press*, July 1, 1894.

Assault on the Lower Agency

It was the traders at the Lower Agency who would be the first to feel the wrath of the Sioux. At about 7 a.m. on Monday, August 18 1862, a group of armed Indians approached the trading house at the Lower Agency run by Andrew Myrick. James Lynd, a clerk at Myrick's store watched the Indians intently as they were acting strange. One of the Indians rode up to Lynd, drew his gun and said, "Now I will kill the dog that would not give me credit."[102] The Indian then shot Lynd, killing him instantly.

With the first shot, the Sioux unleashed all the pent-up anger and resentment they had towards the whites. Their hatred was especially directed at Andrew Myrick, the owner of the warehouse. Myrick was caught trying to escape from the trading house and was killed.

After killing Andrew Myrick, who was especially hated by the Indians for cutting off credit and then telling them to eat grass, the Indians shot several arrows through his body and stuck a scythe in his chest. Before leaving, they stuffed his mouth with grass.

Within a short time, the Indians had killed approximately twenty men at the Lower Agency. The killing spree only let up when the Indians became distracted by all the goods stored in the warehouses. They began looting the stores and then set fire to the buildings.

After the attack on the Lower Agency, a large number of warriors set out along the road running from the Lower Agency to New Ulm, about twenty-five miles to the southeast. As they went, the Indians killed any settlers that they came across. In Milford Township alone the Sioux killed fifty-two settlers that day, a substantial portion of the township's population.

The settlers tended to make easy targets for the Sioux. They were not prepared, nor could they believe what was happening. As recorded in one history of the area:

> There was no resistance worthy of the name. Very few settlers had firearms or were accustomed to them. There were many Germans that had never fired a gun in all of their lives. Then, too, the Indian attacks were wholly unexpected. The savages approached their victims in a most friendly and pleasant manner and slew them without warning.[103]

---

102 Hubbard and Holcombe, *Minnesota in Three Centuries*, 313.

103 Curtiss-Wedge, *History of Renville County Minnesota*, 149.

The attacks on settlers continued throughout August 18 on both sides of the Minnesota River. Those who escaped from the early ambushes quickly spread the alarm as they fled. Settlers in the area could see the smoke of burning farms and sometimes hear gunfire. For most, that was all it took to realize that they were in grave danger. Many of the settlers quickly set out for what they thought would be safety in New Ulm.

The population of New Ulm quickly swelled from about 650 to nearly double that number as refugees from the nearby countryside poured into the town. As it turned out, New Ulm would not be quite so safe as the refugees hoped.

On Tuesday, August 19, a small group of Indians attacked New Ulm. They managed to kill six residents and wounded several more. Already alerted to the danger, the citizens and refugees in the town quickly drove off the attackers. It is unknown whether the Indians suffered any casualties in this skirmish.

The next day, Wednesday, August 20, approximately 400 warriors attacked Fort Ridgely but were repulsed after a five-hour battle. Two days later, a much larger number of Indians attacked the fort. The vastly outnumbered soldiers managed to hold out, thanks in large part because they had a cannon. The Indians did not attempt another direct attack after Friday, August 22. However, the warriors kept the fort under siege for the next several days.

On the morning of August 23, the Indians again turned their attention to New Ulm. This time they attacked with a force of approximately 600 warriors under the command of Little Crow. By then, there were about 2500 citizens and refugees crammed into the small town. Most of the refugees were women and children.

The Indians surrounded the town and then began the attack. The outnumbered defenders, who consisted of about 300 armed citizens and soldiers, put up a stubborn defense. There was heavy fighting all around New Ulm throughout August 23. By the end of the day the defenders had suffered ten killed and many wounded. Nearly eighty percent of the town was destroyed in the process.

Over the next few days, hundreds of warriors spread out from the reservation across the Minnesota frontier. They killed settlers and burned farms from near the Iowa border all the way north to almost present-day Fargo, North Dakota. Hundreds of settlers and soldiers would die in the first several days of the Uprising.[104]

The Uprising might have been avoided if the treaty payment had reached the reservation before the killings at Acton. Tragically, the payment left St. Paul for Fort Ridgely under escort on the morning of August 17, 1862. By the time the payment reached the fort, it was too late. The Uprising had already been underway for several hours.

---

104 Estimates of the total number of settlers killed during the 1862 uprising run between 450 and 800 settlers. Indian casualties from the fighting were far less, although the Sioux ultimately paid a terrible price in lives over the next several years.

Panic Along the Frontier

The Wright County Volunteers were happy to be going home and, it seems, blissfully unaware of the events that were taking place across the western part of the state. It had been just over a week since they left Monticello for Fort Snelling. Many of the men had never been away from their families for so long and were beginning to feel a little homesick at the fort. Now on the road home, the men were in good spirits. They would soon see their families and be able to share their experience with the induction process.

The route home to Monticello would take the men through Minneapolis and then north along the Mississippi River to Anoka. From there, they would travel by road along the east side of the river past Elk River. At Big Lake, they would cross the river to Monticello, while the men from Silver Creek, Clearwater, and adjoining Lynden Township would continue several more miles north to their homes.

The furloughed men set out on Saturday, August 23 1863, after electing their company officers. The first day they traveled about three miles north of Minneapolis. A farmer let the whole crew sleep in his barn that night. The volunteers got up early Sunday morning and started out for their sixty-mile walk home.

If the men had heard any reports about the Sioux uprising while still at Fort Snelling, the news was probably dismissed as false rumors.[105] There had been many false alarms since Inkpaduta and his band had conducted the massacre at Spirit Lake five years earlier.

It wasn't until leaving the farmer's barn on Sunday, August 24, however, that they first realized the seriousness of the Sioux Uprising. By then, Indian attacks along the Minnesota frontier had been underway for almost a week.

As the merry band of newly minted soldiers set out on the road to Anoka that morning, they began to encounter refugees fleeing from the Indians. Soon, wagon after wagon of terrified settlers passed them heading south to safety in Minneapolis. "We met scores of panic-stricken families fleeing from the Indians who are currently reported to be in the woods just beyond" recalled William Houlton.[106]

Many of the Wright County men didn't take the exaggerated panic of the refugees seriously at first but something seemed different than with previous scares. William Houlton later wrote:

---

105 None of the surviving diaries or later reminiscences of men in the Eighth Regiment suggest the men were aware of Uprising until they encountered refugees while traveling home on furlough.

106 Houlton, *Speech.*

To us the whole thing was so ludicrous we felt like laughing, as we were sure there were no Indians there, but there was no mistaking the real terror which had signed upon the faces of the people so that no reasoning availed in the excitement was kept up by arrivals of people who imagined they had fled for their lives and that all beyond them had been killed.[107]

George Cambell, seeing the stream of refugees clogging the road, made a similar observation:

Everybody we met, to take their word for it, had a very narrow escape from death by the Indians; and the stories so increased by the telling that it seemed, at one time, that there would be nobody left outside the cities of St. Paul and Minneapolis.[108]

Men from other companies who returned home on furlough had the same experience. Thomas Hodgson from Company F of the Eighth Minnesota recalled the panic that awaited when he returned to his home in Dakota County on furlough:

No tornado ever swept over a country with more dreadful and blinding terror. No continent-shaking earthquake ever froze the heart of man with more fear than did this strange report of an Indian massacre.[109]

As more terrified refugees came down the road, the Wright County men grew increasingly anxious for the safety of their own families. Their fears were reinforced when they arrived at Anoka and found it filled with people that had poured in from the surrounding countryside. A stockade was being erected by the residents, and guards were placed around the town.

The Wright County volunteers discovered the same activities going on in other towns they passed. They finally arrived at Monticello to find the townspeople erecting a stockade around the academy building, the very spot where they had all enlisted less than two weeks earlier.

---

107 Ibid.

108 Cambell, *Personal Reminiscences*, 3.

109 Thomas Hodgson, "Recollections of the Sioux War No. 2," *Dakota County Tribune*, Sept. 26, 1889, Farmington and Lakeville, Minnesota.

The men were no doubt relieved to learn that their families were safe and that no Indian attacks had taken place in the immediate vicinity. The closest killings at that point had been those during the initial massacre at Acton, about forty-five miles to the west. Nevertheless, the men from Clearwater and Lynden Township rushed past Monticello to their own homes in fear for their families.

When George Cambell arrived at Clearwater, he found the town full of refugees from Forest City and Kingston.[110] They had taken the shortest route to safety, the well-traveled Fairhaven Road, which ran north from Meeker County to Clearwater. At Clearwater, the refugees could cross the Mississippi River by ferry and reach Chippewa territory, which they thought would be safe.

The village of Clearwater was a hub of activity as the townsfolk prepared for the expected Indian attack. A few were attempting to conduct militia drills so they could be organized for the defense. On the west side of the village, volunteers were digging a well and building a stockade around the First Congregational Church. The church sat on a low bluff and offered a good defensive position from which to protect the town.[111]

George Cambell immediately went out on the Fairhaven Road about three miles to visit the Whittemore family and especially to see his girlfriend Martha. Martha's father, Charles, had just built a nice new house for the family at their farm along the Fairhaven Road.

All of the refugees coming from Meeker County had to pass the Whittemore house on their way to Clearwater. Many stopped their wagons at the farm to water their animals and to share news. When George arrived, he had to navigate through quite a cluster of wagon teams that had stopped at the Whittemores' house.

In quieter days, George always enjoyed visiting the Whittemores' place and passing time in conversation with Charles. Satisfied that Martha was safe, he sought out Charles, who he found to be wholly defiant. Cambell later told his children "He had no idea of leaving on account of the Indians."[112]

Other men in Company E were also worried about their wives and girlfriends. Upon returning to Monticello, Edson Washburn checked in on both his family and that of his girlfriend, Amelia Wells. Edson appeared to be deeply in love with Amelia. The two corresponded frequently throughout the war and Edson stopped by to call

110 Cambell, *Personal Reminiscences*, 4.

111 The First Congregational Church building still stands in Clearwater at the intersection of Bluff and Elm streets. The wooden structure is no longer used as a house of worship and is now under private ownership.

112 Cambell, *Personal Reminiscences*, 4.

on Amelia whenever he could get a break from his duties. Edson was almost certainly relieved to find Amelia safe and sound.

Instant Soldiers
September 3 to 30, 1862

Return to Fort Snelling

The Wright County volunteers returned to Fort Snelling from their furlough in early September to complete the outfitting process and be mustered into a regiment. They remained apprehensive for their families. William Houlton later reminisced:

> *I have often thought that many of the soldiers' wives who were left alone with the care of their homes and helpless little ones suffered more in those few days of war and suspense than their husbands did in their three years' service.*[113]

For peace of mind, some of the soldiers sent their families either to Minneapolis or back East to safety. Joseph Perkins, for example, sent his wife and two daughters to live with relatives in Illinois until he returned from the war.[114]

Despite their concerns, the men were eager to become real soldiers. They didn't even wait to be mustered in at Fort Snelling before they began to study the Army Manual of Arms and learn basic drills. As it turned out, however, the Sioux war caused a change in plans. The men found themselves called upon to serve as soldiers immediately upon their return to Fort Snelling, without real training, uniforms, or equipment. The Wright County volunteers were needed elsewhere and would have to wait a while longer before they could join a regiment.

The panic in many towns along the Upper Mississippi River had not let up since the beginning of the Uprising. Thousands of settlers fled to the east as news of the attacks spread throughout Minnesota. They abandoned farms, livestock, and their

---

113   Houlton, *Speech.*

114   Perkins family file, Wright County Historical Society.

possessions. Without added protection, there was a significant risk that more settlers would leave. This concerned both state and federal government officials because if the countryside remained depopulated it could impact the production of wheat and other products that were essential to the war effort.

As it turned out, the fears of the settlers were well-founded. Isolated settlers were set upon and killed across western Minnesota. Between September 2 and September 4, up to 300 Sioux warriors attacked small settlements in Meeker and McLeod counties. Fortunately, casualties were light in those engagements. Settlers had erected stockades at Forest City and Hutchinson. These were heavily defended when the Indians attacked. Realizing the risks of attacking strong fortifications, the Indians directed most of their efforts at plundering and burning nearby buildings.

To prevent further flight from central and western Minnesota, the government turned to the army in the hope it could provide security for the area. However, there was one problem. The army was already spread too thin and didn't have the resources to recall trained troops from the South.

The government's solution was to make use of the untrained and mostly unequipped companies raised during the August War Meetings. These units would be armed as best they could and then posted in towns and forts along the frontier. There, they would guard against Indian attacks. The presence of soldiers, even if they were little more than untrained militia, would give the settlers a greater degree of security and, it was hoped, prevent more of from abandoning the towns and farms in the area.

Guarding Monticello

As luck would have it, shortly after their return to Fort Snelling the Wright County volunteers were assigned to provide protection for their hometown of Monticello. They were thrilled. At the very least it would give the new recruits the opportunity to show off as the guardians of their friends and family.

It probably didn't matter to the soldiers that they were ill-equipped to defend the town if the Indians attacked in force. An effective defense against the highly mobile Indians required both horses and reliable weapons. The Wright County volunteers had neither.

Weapons and uniforms were still in short supply at Fort Snelling when the men were equipped for their duty at Monticello. A few managed to obtain a uniform shirt or jacket. Most of the men had to wear their own civilian clothes for this assignment.

For arms, the quartermaster could only scrape together twelve old Belgian muskets for the eighty men who would be deployed as part of the new company.[115] Those obsolete muskets, however, were too few and too inaccurate to be of much defensive value if the towns were attacked.

Muskets are shoulder-fired long guns. Unlike modern firearms, which use brass cartridges that contain a primer, powder and bullet, the muskets had to be loaded through the muzzle. Loading was a multi-step process that merits more explanation.

In the first step of the loading process, the soldier tore open a rolled paper cartridge that contained the gunpowder and bullet. Then, the soldier poured the powder down the barrel. Next the bullet was inserted into the barrel along the paper cartridge wrapper to hold it in place. The soldier then pushed the bullet and wrapper down to the bottom of the barrel using a metal ramrod. Finally, the soldier pulled the hammer back to a half cock position and placed a percussion cap on a hollow post called a nipple. At this point, the musket is fully loaded. To fire it, the soldier first pulled the hammer back all the way until it clicked into place. This was called full cock. When at full cock, the musket was ready to fire with a pull of the trigger.

When the soldier pulled the trigger, it released the hammer. A spring snapped the hammer down onto the nipple where it struck the percussion cap. The hammer strike ignited a pressure-sensitive chemical called mercury fulminate contained within the percussion cap. This sent a small jet of flame through the hollow nipple, down a channel and into the breach at the rear end of the barrel.

The flame ignited the powder packed at the breach that had previously been loaded through the muzzle. The gasses resulting from the burning powder created a high-pressure explosion that propelled the bullet down the barrel in the direction of the target.

A musket barrel is smooth on the inside. It could fire a large round ball of lead measuring up to .75" or it could be loaded with smaller pellets called buckshot and used like a shotgun. Muskets were generally inaccurate at more than a few yards. When fired, the ball, which was often slightly smaller than the bore diameter, would travel down the barrel, bouncing as it went. As it exited, the bullet's path was unpredictable. Consequently, it was difficult for muskets to hit their point of aim at anything but short range.

To compensate for the lack of accuracy, the standard military drill for musketry called for units to stand close together and mass their fire, effectively creating a giant shotgun. That way at least some of the soldiers on the receiving end might be hit. Even then it was questionable. The Belgian muskets were so inaccurate that one soldier from Company F of the Eighth Minnesota claimed that they should have been stamped with the disclaimer "Warranted not to hit except by accident."[116]

115 Houlton, *Speech.*

116 Hodgson, "Recollections of the Sioux War No. 4," *Dakota County Tribune*, Oct. 17, 1889.

The Belgian muskets issued to the Wright County volunteers were notorious for their heavy recoil and the pain they inflicted upon the soldier that fired it. It was a matter of simple physics. The same energy expended by the powder charge to send the large heavy bullet out of the barrel also caused the gun to "kick" and drive the buttstock deep into the shooter's shoulder.

Had the Indians attacked Monticello in force, it would have been a vicious fight. The Indians had weapons roughly equal to those of the solders. Some of the Sioux were armed with trade muskets or shotguns, and only a few had rifles. Many of the Indians, however, were still armed with nothing more than the bow and arrow.

However, those armed with bows and arrows had one advantage over soldiers equipped with muskets. In a warrior's skilled hands, the bow was quiet and deadly accurate at short range. Moreover, a warrior could shoot several arrows within the same time it took a solder to load and fire the musket once.

The soldiers drilled regularly until loading and firing their weapons became so familiar that they could do it without thinking. That was critical because a soldier's efficiency in the loading process diminished in the adrenaline-charged chaos of battle. Without extensive training a soldier could lose track of where he was in the loading process and render his weapon useless.[117] Nevertheless, even a well-trained soldier could fire no more than two or three shots in a minute.

After receiving their orders, the volunteers again set out for Monticello during the second week of September 1862. This time they returned as a military unit. The first order of business was to set up camp, which the townsfolk watched with interest.

When the initial setup was complete, the soldiers discovered with delight that the ladies of Monticello had prepared a hearty supper in anticipation of their arrival. The residents set out tables for the men, which were weighed down with piles of rich food.[118]

Before they could indulge in the feast, however, an incident occurred that soured the soldiers' attitude towards certain officers. Captain Hartley stood up and, apparently without any cause, admonished the soldiers not to make hogs of themselves.[119] This humiliated the men in front of their families and friends.

Despite the anticipatory rebuke by Hartley, the Wright County company enjoyed a wonderful supper that evening. After living on army rations for the pre-

117 It has been widely reported that a large number of rifles recovered from the battlefield at Gettysburg were found with multiple unfired cartridges rammed down the barrel. The soldiers involved were probably so disoriented by the noise and intensity of the battle that they didn't realize they skipped steps of the loading process and didn't notice that the rifle failed to fire when they pulled the trigger.

118 Bertram, *Reminiscences*, December 7, 1878, MNHS.

119 Houlton, *Speech*.

vious couple of weeks, which might charitably be described as edible, it appears the men disregarded Hartley and enjoyed their fare with relish.[120]

After supper Captain Hartley further humiliated the men by placing armed guards around the camp with orders to allow no one to pass without permission. The soldiers were only allowed to communicate with their families with a guard and Belgian musket between them.[121] This was even more degrading than the admonishment at supper. Thus, were planted the seeds of resentment towards Captain Hartley and, to a lesser degree, Lieutenant Croswell. That resentment would continue to build over the next several months.

The soldiers' presence went a long way toward calming the citizens' fears of Indian attack. The soldiers were glad to be there, but they quickly realized neither they nor the town were in any real danger while they remained at Monticello. The residents were safe and secure under the soldiers' protection. The same could not be said for livestock in and around town.

One thing all the soldiers seemed to have in common was an insatiable appetite. The food furnished by the army was edible and generally met the nutritional needs of the soldiers. Yet, it never seemed to be enough. Shortly after the somewhat disorganized company of volunteers arrived in town, the citizens of Monticello became concerned about the mysterious disappearance of livestock. At first it was just a couple of chickens. As time went on, a few turkeys, hogs and sheep went missing. The culprits, of course, were soldiers who snuck out of camp "to draw their rations" while the farmers were asleep.[122] If the citizens of Monticello ever caught on, they didn't let it be known. Even so, they must have been relieved when the company was finally ordered back to Fort Snelling after only a month.

During their short time in Monticello, the company began drilling in earnest. Each day they had six hours of marching and drill. Not all the boys took quickly to the drills. Keeping in step while at the same time obeying marching commands did not come naturally to some of the new soldiers. They all tried hard, however, because nobody wanted to be assigned to what became known as the "awkward squad."

The awkward squad was composed of those who simply did not take to drill. They had to drill twice as long as the rest of the company. As the drill schedule for the rest of the company was already six hours a day, "those in the awkward squad found they had no picnic."[123]

---

120 Bertram, *Reminiscences*, December 7, 1878, MNHS.

121 Houlton, *Speech*.

122 Bertram, *Reminiscences*, December 7, 1878, MNHS.

123 Cambell, *Personal Reminiscences*, 6.

Sioux Defeated

As the Wright County volunteers were guarding Monticello, the Sioux army had pulled back to the west along the Minnesota River. Since the Uprising began at Acton on August 17 the Indians had killed over 600 settlers. In addition, the Sioux had taken about 260 hostages, nearly all of them women and children.

In early September, Little Crow realized that despite the Indians' early successes, the whites were too numerous and strong to be defeated. The Indians had failed in attacks on small settlements like Forest City and Hutchinson, not to mention the defeat at the larger town of New Ulm. Little Crow himself had been wounded during the unsuccessful attacks on Fort Ridgely. Realizing the futility of further hostilities, Little Crow opened negotiations with the commander of the army troops, Henry Sibley.

Henry Hastings Sibley[124] was a long-time resident of Minnesota, even before it became a territory. He was born in Detroit in 1811. His father, a prominent attor-

ney, wanted Henry to become a lawyer as well. As a result, the elder Sibley made sure his son was well educated.

By the time Henry was eighteen years old, he was sure that he did not want to follow in his father's footsteps. He decided to leave home and seek his own fortune. Sibley worked for a time as a clerk in a store at Sault Ste. Marie and then obtained a position in John Jacob Astor's American Fur Company.

In 1834, at the age of twenty-three, Sibley was made a partner in the fur company and placed in charge of affairs in the far Northwest. It was this opportunity that brought him to what was then Wisconsin Territory, but is now Minnesota.

Sibley established his headquarters at Mendota, the spot where the

HENRY HASTINGS SIBLEY, FORMER GOVERNOR AND COMMANDER OF THE DISTRICT OF MINNESOTA.

---

124   Much of Sibley's biography described on these pages is drawn from his obituary in *The Saint Paul Daily Globe*, February 19, 1891.

Minnesota River flows into the Mississippi and directly across the river from Fort Snelling. Aside from the fort, there was little else in the area at the time. The little hamlet of Mendota consisted of nothing more than a few mud huts. Sibley soon built a stone house, the first in Minnesota.[125]

Sibley learned some of the Dakota (Sioux) language and became acquainted with the ways of the tribe through his trading post operation. In fact, he took a Sioux bride, Red Blanket Woman, in 1839. The couple had a daughter in 1841. Red Blanket Woman died a couple of years later.

In 1848, Sibley entered politics. He served in Congress as a territorial delegate from Wisconsin. During that time, he was instrumental in the push to establish Minnesota as a territory. That occurred in 1849. Sibley continued to serve in Congress, now as the territorial delegate from Minnesota, until 1853.

After years of work to establish Minnesota as a territory, it was only natural for Sibley to continue the push to make Minnesota a state. He served in the territorial legislature for a time and later became president of the state constitutional convention in 1857.

Perhaps not surprisingly, Sibley was elected to serve as the first governor of the State of Minnesota. He took office shortly after Minnesota gained statehood on May 11 1858. He continued to serve as governor until 1860.

At the beginning of the Sioux Uprising, the governor, Alexander Ramsey, turned to Henry Sibley for leadership. The governor appointed Sibley as colonel of the state militia and gave him command of an expedition to quell the uprising.

In his trade with the Sioux at Mendota, Sibley met many of the Sioux leaders, including a young Little Crow. Now, twenty years later, he found himself in negotiations with his old acquaintance.

Corresponding by written messages, Little Crow offered to return the hostages if Sibley would grant amnesty to the Indians who participated in the uprising. Sibley refused. He demanded total surrender. Before long, the negotiations broke down. The war would have to continue.

On September 23, more than a month after the Uprising began, Sibley's troops engaged a large number of Sioux warriors commanded by Little Crow in what would be called The Battle of Wood Lake. This fight turned into a decisive defeat for the Sioux. Little Crow and about 300 warriors were forced to retreat west into Dakota Territory.

---

125 The Sibley House still stands and is a historic site. *See*, http://www.sibley-friends.org/sibleyhouse. htm, accessed June 4, 2020.

Following the Battle of Wood Lake, the remaining Sioux in Minnesota surrendered. The hostages were freed at a spot not far from the Upper Sioux Agency that would be called Camp Release.

It didn't take long before news of the victory at Wood Lake reached the overall commander of forces in the region, General John Pope. General Pope had recently taken command of the newly formed Department of the Northwest. The Department was formed on September 6, 1862 to oversee the forces engaged in the Sioux War.

Pope graduated from West Point in 1842 and had seen service in the Mexican War. He had shown promise as a leader during the early days of the Civil War. Within a short time, he rose to the rank of major general and took command of the Union Army of Virginia.

Pope's career suddenly came crashing down at the Second Battle of Bull Run. On August 30, 1862, Pope's command was caught by surprise when Confederates under General James Longstreet counterattacked. The Union troops suffered a significant defeat and had to withdraw.

Pope was blamed for the disaster. Rather than run Pope out of the army, his superiors decided to just transfer him out of the way. On September 6, 1862, Secretary of War Edwin Stanton ordered General Pope to take command of the new Department of the Northwest, and directed him to proceed immediately to the Department's headquarters at St. Paul, Minnesota.[126]

General Pope was almost certainly humiliated at being removed from main theater of operations against the Confederates in the East. Nevertheless, he did his duty and reported to St. Paul as ordered. There, he took command of the new front that had opened against the Sioux on the Minnesota frontier.

After receiving news of the Battle of Wood Lake, Pope wanted Sibley's forces to pursue Little Crow and his remaining band into Dakota Territory. However, from Sibley's point of view such a pursuit would have been almost impossible. The supply lines had already been stretched too thin. The soldiers were terribly short on food an ammunition. Consequently, Sibley wrote to General Pope: "It is unnecessary to make a further advance at present; indeed, it would be folly to attempt it without more supplies of provisions than are at present to be looked for."[127]

Sibley's performance against the Sioux did not go unrecognized by General Pope or army commanders back in the East. On October 7, 1862, while still

126   Stanton to Pope, Sept. 6, 1862, *Official Records*, series 1, vol. 13, 617.

127   Sibley to Pope, Oct. 3, 1862, U.S. War Department, *The War of the Rebellion: A Compilation of the Official Records of the Union and Confederate Armies*, 128 parts in 70 vols. And atlas. Washington D.C., Government Printing Office, 1880-1901, series 1, vol. 13, 708 (hereinafter "*Official Records*").

GENERAL JOHN POPE, COMMANDER OF THE DEPART-
MENT OF THE NORTHWEST

at Camp Release, Sibley received word from General Pope that President Lincoln had appointed him to brigadier general.[128]

On October 10, 1862, General Pope wrote to Henry Halleck, General-in-Chief of all the Union Armies, to report that the Sioux War was at an end.[129] There was still the question of what to do with the Sioux that were captured or surrendered. Many were sent to Fort Snelling, where they would be detained through the winter. At the same time, hundreds of Indians who participated in the uprising were tried before military tribunals. More than 300 of them were convicted of rape or murder and sentenced to death.

General Pope was still concerned about the Yankton Sioux tribe in eastern Dakota Territory. Although the Yanktons had not been involved in the Uprising, Pope considered them too close for comfort. On October 10, Pope sent orders to Sibley directing him to conduct an expedition against the Yanktons. Sibley responded that he would do so but pointed out that the expedition would not be successful without sufficient forage for the horses. Nevertheless, Sibley vowed that the proposed expedition would "be pushed ahead forage or no forage."[130]

With winter rapidly approaching, General Pope must have realized the futility of sending an expedition into Dakota Territory without adequate supplies of food, warm clothing, and forage for the animals. Sibley never left on the planned expedition that fall. Instead, he was focused on the aftermath of the uprising.

The idea of such an expedition was not forgotten, however. There were still fears about the Indians in Dakota Territory. As 1862 drew to a close, General Sibley wrote to General-in-Chief Halleck pleading that no other troops could be sent south

---

128   Ibid., 717.

129   Ibid., 724.

130   Ibid., 741.

from the District of Minnesota because "The Indians of the plains are gathering for a general onslaught as soon as weather permits."[131]

In early November 1862, approximately 1600 of the Sioux still at Camp Release were moved to imprisonment on Pike Island, which sits in the middle of the Minnesota River just below Fort Snelling. The Indians spent a brutal winter confined to the island where almost 400 of their number died of disease.

After reviewing transcripts of the trials for the 303 Indians who had been condemned to death by the military tribunals, President Lincoln commuted most of the sentences. On December 26, 1862, the remaining thirty-eight condemned Sioux were hanged at Mankato, Minnesota. It was the largest mass hanging in U.S. history.

The following spring, the Sioux confined on Pike Island were removed from Minnesota by riverboat. They were taken down the Mississippi River to St. Louis and then back up the Missouri River, where they were banished to a reservation in Dakota Territory.

Mustering in at Fort Snelling

Shortly after the Battle of Wood Lake, Monticello was deemed safe enough that it was no longer necessary to keep a garrison of soldiers at the town. The Wright County volunteers were ordered back to Fort Snelling. There, they could finally ditch their civilian clothes, be fully equipped as soldiers, and mustered into a regiment, where they would finally start their real training.

After arriving at Fort Snelling on October 1, the Wright County volunteers went into camp near a place within the fort boundaries known as Coldwater Spring.[132] The natural spring sits on the bluffs high above the Mississippi River about a mile west-northwest of the fort. During the Civil War, Coldwater Spring was the primary source of drinking water for both troops and animals passing through Fort Snelling.

On October 2, 1862, the men entered into the service of the U.S. Army. They were officially mustered when they took the oath:

> I, _____, do solemnly swear that I will bear true allegiance to
> the United States of America, and that I will serve them honestly
> and faithfully against all their enemies and opposers whatsoever,
> and observe and obey the orders of the President of the United
> States, and the orders of the officers appointed over me according

---

131 Sibley to Halleck, Dec. 27, 1862, *Official Records*, series 1, vol. 22, part 1, 880.

132 The area surrounding the spring is now under the control of the National Park Service, which is restoring the landscape surrounding the spring to its former mix of oak savannah and prairie. https://www.nps.gov/miss/planyourvisit/coldwater.htm, accessed July 14, 2019.

to the rules and articles for the Government of the armies of the United States.[133]

Until that point, a volunteer who enlisted at Monticello would have been free to change his mind and return home. After taking the oath, however, the volunteer was committed to serving his full three-year enlistment. There was no backing out from then on.

The Wright County volunteers were assigned to the newly-formed Eighth Minnesota Volunteer Infantry Regiment. For the rest of their service, the volunteers would be known simply as "Company E."

Organization of the Eighth Minnesota Volunteer Infantry Regiment.

The Eighth Minnesota followed the same structure as other volunteer regiments formed during the Civil War. It was composed of ten companies, numbered A through K. Regiments did not have a Company J, perhaps because the "J" and "I" too closely resembled each other. In addition to the ten companies, the regiment included several field and staff officers.

A regiment was under the command of a full colonel, who was assisted by a lieutenant colonel and a major. The lieutenant colonel would assume command of the regiment if the colonel became incapacitated or unavailable. The major would serve as the third in command.

In the field, the regiment was often divided into two battalions of up to five companies, one commanded by the lieutenant colonel and the other by the major. The regimental commanders were supported by other regimental officers, including a surgeon, quartermaster, chaplain, and various other staffers.

The principal commanders of volunteer regiments were appointed by the state's governor. Minnesota Governor Alexander Ramsey gave command of the new Eighth Minnesota to Colonel Minor T. Thomas, age thirty-two.

Thomas was a civil engineer by trade. He arrived in Minnesota during 1854 hoping that the climate would help ward off bouts of malaria, which he had contracted in his native Indiana. He liked the area so well that he returned home to Indiana and convinced several family members to move to the territory. While he was back in Indiana, Minor Thomas married Carrie Bolton.

With his new bride and extended family in tow, Thomas returned to Minnesota in 1855. The family made their home near Stillwater. His father, "Judge Thomas," soon built and operated a mill.

---

133 Billings, *Hardtack and Coffee*, 44.

From 1857 to 1860, Minor
Thomas worked as a surveyor in and
around Washington County. He also
served for a time as county sheriff.
In 1860, he became the Washington
County Surveyor and held that post
until he enlisted in the army.

In 1859, Minor Thomas joined
the local Masonic Lodge. He became
a Master Mason at St. John's Masonic
Lodge #1, the first Lodge formally
chartered by the Grand Lodge of
Minnesota.[134]

In response to Lincoln's call
for troops following the fall of Fort
Sumter in April 1861, Minor Thomas
enlisted as a private in the Stillwater
Guards. This unit became part of the
First Minnesota Volunteer Infantry
Regiment.[135] He quickly rose to the
rank of lieutenant in Company B.

COLONEL MINOR T. THOMAS, COMMANDER OF THE
EIGHTH MINNESOTA VOLUNTEER INFANTRY REGIMENT.

Just three months after its formation, on July 21 1861, the First Minnesota participated in its first serious engagement with the enemy – the Battle of Bull Run. The
First Minnesota fought well and gained a solid reputation because it did not break
and run like so many other Union regiments involved in the battle. In doing so,
however, the Minnesota troops suffered heavy casualties. Among the wounded was
Lieutenant Minor Thomas.

Thomas recovered quickly from his wounds. Two months later, Thomas was
promoted to lieutenant colonel of the Fourth Minnesota Infantry Regiment, which
was then being formed at Fort Snelling. After spending a year in the Fourth Minne-

---

134 The first three Lodges in Minnesota, which initially operated under authority of Grand Lodges in
Wisconsin, Illinois and Ohio, banded together in 1853 and formed the Grand Lodge of Minnesota. The
Grand Lodge then issued charters to each of its constituent Lodges. Lodges are generally numbered based
on the order in which the charter was issued, not necessarily the order in which they began operation. The
original Minnesota Lodges were St. Johns #1 at Stillwater, Cataract #2 at Minneapolis and St. Paul Lodge
#3. More information on the history of the Grand Lodge of Minnesota is available at the Minneapolis
Lodge #19 web site, http://mpls19.org/grand-lodge-minnesota/, accessed Aug. 6, 2020.

135 *The Saint Paul Daily Press,* Sept. 21, 1862. Regiments were numbered in the order in which they were
raised.

sota, Thomas was again promoted, this time to full colonel, and placed in command of the newly formed Eighth Minnesota.

Colonel Thomas was well respected by the troops, one of whom provided a description of the man:

> *In personal appearance the colonel was an ideal military officer. Tall, straight and self-possessed, with a heavy, black, full and flowing beard and a dignified demeanor, he was every inch an officer... He was one of those men whom it is easy to obey because he had the respect of his subordinates to a degree that few officers even attain.*[136]

LIEUTENANT COLONEL HENRY C. ROGERS, SECOND-IN-COMMAND OF THE EIGHTH MINNESOTA VOLUNTEER INFANTRY REGIMENT.

Governor Ramsey appointed twenty-eight-year-old Lieutenant Colonel Henry Rogers as second in command of the Eighth Minnesota. A native of Vermont, Rogers was a successful farmer and merchant from Mower County in southern Minnesota. He had engaged in politics and served for a time in the Minnesota legislature. He was described as short in stature and bearing a resemblance to General Ulysses S. Grant.[137] Rogers had a gentle manner and an unassuming demeanor, but he also had the respect of his troops.

As major of the Eighth Minnesota, Ramsey appointed Minneapolis businessman George A. Camp. Camp arrived at St. Anthony in Minnesota Territory during 1851. St. Anthony was a small but booming town on the Mississippi River, thanks to the wide waterfall at that spot. The dropping water from St. Anthony Falls provided a vast amount of power for a variety of mills erected along the riverbank. Camp took advantage of this great resource and entered the lumber business.

In addition to his business activities, Camp was involved in civic affairs. In 1857, he was appointed by the legislature to serve as surveyor of logs. Camp was also

---

136 Hodgson, "Recollections of the Sioux War No. 14," *Dakota County Tribune*, March 6, 1890.

137 Ibid.

an active Freemason. He was a founding member of Cataract Lodge #2[138]
and served as Master of the Lodge in
1860.

At thirty-three years of age,
Camp was already quite successful
when he resigned from the lumber
business in 1862 and raised a company
of volunteers for the war effort. The
company he raised became Company
A of the Ninth Minnesota Volunteer
Infantry. In accordance with the usual
custom, Camp was elected captain of
Company A because he recruited the
unit. He led the company during the
first months of the Sioux Uprising
before being promoted to major and
assigned to the Eighth Minnesota.

Camp presented quite a contrast
to both Thomas and Rogers. He took
no guff from anyone. One member

MAJOR GEORGE CAMP OF THE EIGHTH MINNESOTA, A
TOUGH AND OFTEN COARSE MINNEAPOLIS LUMBERMAN

of the regiment described Camp as a man who was big and strong, a bit uncouth,
and, at times, demonstrated a somewhat despotic manner.[139] His language and tem-
perament were probably developed from years of dealing with tough, no-nonsense
lumbermen. Yet, he could also be kind and charitable. Regardless, the troops greatly
respected him because, as later events would show, they knew Major Camp would
always look out for them.

The Eighth Minnesota was initially placed within the newly formed Army
Department of the Northwest, which included the forces in Wisconsin, Iowa, Min-
nesota, and the Territories of Nebraska and Dakota.[140] Colonel Thomas reported to
General Sibley. Sibley, in turn, was directly under the command of General Pope.

---

138 Cataract Lodge # 2 is named in honor of the waterfall at St. Anthony. "Cataract" is an obsolete
English word meaning a cascading waterfall. St. Anthony Falls was vitally important during the early days
of Minneapolis because the falling water powered the saw mills and flour mills for which the city became
known.

139 Hodgson, "Recollections of the Sioux War No. 14," *Dakota County Tribune*, March 6, 1890.

140 *See*, General Orders No. 128, Sept. 7, 1862, *Official Records*, series 1, vol. 13, 618.

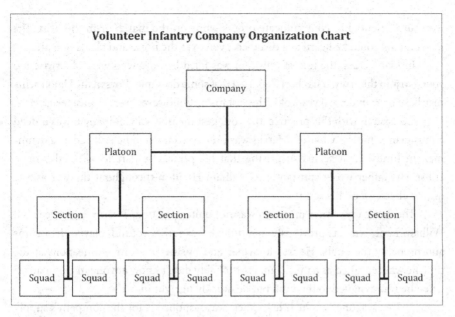

Volunteer Infantry Company Organization Chart

Organization of Company E

The authorized strength of an infantry company was 100 men. This number included three commissioned officers, five sergeants and eight corporals, all of whom would be elected by the men in the company. In addition, each company was allotted two musicians, and a wagoner. The remaining eighty-one men of a company were privates.

The company was divided into two platoons and each platoon was further divided into two sections. Each section was broken down into two squads, making a total of eight squads within the company.

The captain was the ranking commissioned officer at the company level. He had overall command of the company. The other two company officers were a first lieutenant and a second lieutenant. The lieutenants were each responsible for one of the platoons. The first lieutenant was next in line to command the company in the absence or incapacity of the captain.

In addition to the commissioned officers, each company would have five sergeants and eight corporals. The first sergeant was the ranking non-commissioned officer. He had responsibility for much of the record-keeping duties within the company. Each of the other four sergeants was assigned to a section, two per platoon. One corporal was assigned to lead each squad.

Each company was authorized to have two musicians. The musicians played the drum and either a fife or bugle. This was an important role within the company. The musicians used their instruments keep the cadence as the men drilled. They were also essential to communicate orders while on the march or in the field. The instruments could be heard at a distance, even over the noise and chaos of battle.

In many cases, the role of musician was filled by boys who were otherwise too young to join the army. It has been reported that some drummer boys in the Union army may have been under ten years old. The vast majority, however, were at least teenagers.

Consistent with this practice, the youngest member of Company E was indeed a musician. Charles "Charlie" Merrill was only sixteen when he enlisted as a drummer. In hindsight it seems surprising that his protective parents allowed him to enlist. His father wrote constantly to William Houlton throughout the war asking him to check up on his son.[141]

The company's other musician was not quite so young. Twenty-eight-year-old William Lane, who, as previously mentioned, was rather rotund, played the drums and probably the bugle. He was a farmer and businessman in Minneapolis at the time he was recruited as a musician. He probably didn't know anyone in Company E when he was assigned to the unit, but he quickly fit right in.

The wagoner, as the title implies, was responsible for the company's supply wagon. He not only drove the wagon, but also had to maintain it and care for the mule team that pulled it. The assignment of a soldier as wagoner was often temporary. The soldiers, at least in Company E, tended to rotate through that position and returned to their squads within the company after taking their turn.

Outfitting Company E

Once the company settled into camp, the quartermaster began to properly outfit the men as soldiers. Each man was issued a uniform consisting of sky-blue wool trousers with suspenders, a dark blue wool fatigue coat, a wool forage cap and brogan shoes. The soldiers also received heavy woolen overcoats with capes for use in cold weather.

Along with the uniform, each soldier was equipped with the gear he would need in the field. This included a heavy leather belt that was worn at the waist on the outside of the fatigue coat. On the belt, the soldier wore a bayonet scabbard and a cap box for his rifle. Each soldier was also issued a knapsack, which was a backpack painted to be waterproof, or at least water resistant. In the knapsack, the soldier carried his spare clothes and other personal items, as well as a wool blanket, a rub-

---

141 See, e.g., M.E. Merrill to William Houlton, March 19, 1865, Houlton Papers. MNHS. M.E. Merrill was Charlie Merrill's father. He wrote Houlton to express his anxiety over the health of his son.

berized blanket, and a shelter half. When camping, two soldiers would combine their shelter halves to form what the soldiers called a "dog tent."[142]

In addition to the knapsack, each soldier was issued a smaller haversack, which was worn over the shoulder. Soldiers used the haversack to carry food, eating utensils, tin cup, and various personal belongings.

Other equipment issued to the soldiers included a canteen and cartridge box. The canteen was made of tin with a cork stopper. It was covered in cloth and had a shoulder strap.

The cartridge box was made of leather and had a leather shoulder strap. The cartridge box contained forty rounds of ammunition for the soldier's rifle within a metal insert. The insert protected the highly explosive black powder cartridges from sparks that might fly from the rifle when it was fired. The cartridge box also contained a gun cleaning kit.

The men began to feel more like soldiers in their new uniforms with all the accompanying gear. They were especially impressed with all the shiny brass on the equipment they were issued. There were brass buttons on the uniforms, brass buckles on their belts and straps, and even brass insignia on their caps. The men got so caught up in showing off their new sparkling metal gear that George Cambell referred to it as the "Brass Age."[143]

Eager to show off, the men went to a photographer who set up near the fort. There, they each had their photos taken in all their shiny new gear. George Cambell recalled that they all did so "with as fierce an expression as we could summon up."[144]

The photos were tintypes, a common method of photography in the 1860s where the image was created on a small metal sheet. The cameras in use at the time generally didn't have shutters. Instead, the photographer would remove the lens cap from the camera to expose the negative.

The subject of the photo would have to remain totally still for several minutes, depending on the amount of light, while the cap was off the lens. Any movement during that time would cause the photo to become blurred. To help the subjects, the photographer often used stands to help the men hold their pose without moving. These stands can sometimes be seen in old tintypes.

The soldiers commonly placed the metal sheets with their photos in a small folding frame behind glass for protection. Then, they proudly sent the photos back home to their friends and family.

The men also finally received their weapons. Each man was issued an old Austrian rifle. These were a big improvement over the Belgian muskets. The rifles were

142   The name evolved over time and today this style of small tent is commonly known as the "pup tent."

143   Cambell, *Personal Reminiscences*, 5.

144   Ibid.

loaded in the same manner as muskets through the muzzle. However, the inside of a rifle's barrel has grooves that twist slightly between the breech and muzzle. When fired, the grooves cause the bullet to spiral. That makes the bullet more stable in flight. The result is much greater range and accuracy.

Like the Belgian muskets they replaced, the Austrian rifles were heavy and kicked the shooter's shoulder like a mule. Nevertheless, the soldiers were thrilled to receive them. Each man in the company finally had his own gun. At last, they truly felt like soldiers.

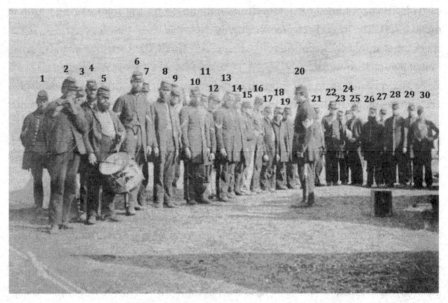

A PORTION OF COMPANY E, EIGHTH MINNESOTA VOLUNTEER INFANTRY REGIMENT. THE PHOTO WAS PROBABLY TAKEN AT FORT SNELLING IN OCTOBER, 1862. THE ORIGINAL INCLUDED MOST OF THE SOL-DIER'S NAMES AND IDENTIFIED THEM AS FOLLOWS:

1. ALBERT BARKER	11. GEORGE CARPENTER	21. CRAMER SWARTOUT
2. AMIDE PHILBROOK	12. LEWIS CHAFFIN	22. JOHN BOYD
3. UNIDENTIFIED	13. CPL. HENRY FULLER	23. JAMES AMBLER
4. JOHN PARVIN	14. WILLIAM HOULTON	24. ELBRIDGE? WASHBURN
5. WILLIAM LANE	15. JOSEPH DUPRAY	25. NICHOLAS FLYNN
6. CPL. WILLIAM LORD	16. ALONZO BRYANT	26. HENRY BRAUGHTON
7. SAMUEL WILDER	17. UNIDENTIFIED	27. EDWARD WOODWORTH
8. MARTIN LORD	18. BAZLEY	28. CHARLES VORSE
9. DANIEL DESMOND	19. HENRY CRAWFORD	29. CHARLES SMITH
10. CPL. CHARLES POST	20. SGT. THOMAS TOLLINGTON	30. JOHN PONSFORD

Training at Fort Ripley

November 4, 1862 to April 30, 1863

The newly designated Company E didn't get to spend too much time at Fort Snelling. Within days of being outfitted, the company was ordered north to Fort Ripley, where the Eighth Minnesota would be temporarily headquartered. Initially, all the field and staff officers were stationed at the fort, along with several of the regiment's companies.[145] The companies assigned to Fort Ripley would spend the winter of 1862 to 1863 performing guard duty and drill.

One unusual aspect of the Eighth Minnesota's service was that the ten companies of the regiment were scattered across central Minnesota for almost two years after the regiment was formed. Security concerns following the Sioux Uprising required the new regiment to be split between Fort Ripley, Fort Abercrombie in Dakota Territory and a string of smaller forts and outposts running through central Minnesota. It wasn't until the spring of 1864 that the regiment would come together for the first time.

Fort Ripley was established in 1849 on the west bank of the Mississippi River, about 110 miles north-northwest of Fort Snelling. It was situated about seven miles south of Crow Wing, a small trading town that had sprung up along the river.

The fort was located within the heavily wooded country of northern Minnesota. The climate there was harsh. During the winter, temperatures could easily drop to -40F.[146] The severe cold sometimes made it dangerous for the troops to be out-

---

145 *Minnesota in the Civil and Indian Wars: 1861-1865*, vol. 1, 386.

146 This is bitter cold whether measured in Fahrenheit or Celsius. It is the one point on the thermometer where the two scales read the same temperature.

side the barracks for any length of time, especially those unfortunate enough to be assigned guard duty.

Company E was among the last Eighth Minnesota units to leave Fort Snelling to join the other companies assigned to Fort Ripley. Company E set out on November 4, 1863. The company's gear would follow behind in a wagon pulled by a six-mule team. Sergeant Tollington led a detail of six soldiers who were assigned to handle the mules and get the wagon safely to Fort Ripley. Among those selected to drive the mules were Corporal William Houlton and Private George Cambell.

The Mule Train

During their short time at Fort Snelling, Company E had been assigned a well-trained team of mules to pull its wagon. Those beasts were relatively tame and easily managed. As the Company E detail was loading their wagon for the trip north to Fort Ripley, however, the quartermaster ordered them to turn their mules over to Company A. Company E would have to make do with a replacement team of mules, which the detail would have to select from the fort's corral.

Mules were the essential draft animals for the Union Army during the Civil War. Horses were bigger, faster, and easier to train. Nevertheless, horses had some significant limitations when it came to pulling army wagons. Horses were high maintenance animals and required constant tending. They needed a good supply of grain and grass for forage. In addition, horses were susceptible to injury when pulling freight over rough terrain.

In contrast, mules were more sure-footed. They could travel unharmed over much rougher ground than could horses. Mules could endure neglect and sustain hard usage that would kill a horse. Moreover, mules could go longer without food and survive on poor forage. The animals would eat just about anything. When food was scarce, mule drivers would sometimes even cut up branches for them to eat. In one case, a mule driver claimed that one of his mule team actually chewed and swallowed a good portion of his army overcoat without ill effect.[147]

Mules had their own drawbacks for some uses in the army. They had a well-earned reputation for stubbornness. Furthermore, mules were harder to train than horses, and tended to be easily frightened by rifle and cannon fire. As a result, there was a division of labor amongst the army animals. Horses were used for cavalry and drawing artillery because of their speed and ability to cope with the sounds of gunfire. Mules, on the other hand, were better suited for drawing the heavy wagons that carried ammunition, food, and other essential supplies to an army in the field.

---

147   Billings, *Hardtack and Coffee*, 282.

The standard supply wagon in the army was pulled by a team of six mules. When new mules were needed to form a team, the mule drivers would select two larger animals for the back pair of the team, slightly smaller animals for the middle pair, and even smaller mules to form the lead pair.

This arrangement made sense because the smaller mules in the front of the team would presumably be easier for the driver to control. With nowhere else to turn, the larger animals in the back would have no option but to follow the smaller mules in the lead.

When the army purchased mules from suppliers, the untrained animals were usually held in a corral to await selection. Catching the mules in a corral was no easy task. The untrained animals were frequently belligerent and tended not to go willingly. Experienced mule drivers had developed techniques to isolate a particular mule, bridle it against the fence, and then lead it out to be joined to the others in a team. The Company E men, however, knew none of this.

In fact, not one of the Company E men assigned to drive the wagon to Fort Ripley had any experience working with mules. Sergeant Tollington, a cabinet maker by trade, and George Cambell, a carpenter and mechanic, probably never had occasion to deal with mules before in their lives. The farmers in the Company E wagon detail, such as William Houlton, had used draft horses to pull a plow or mower through the fields but that was no preparation for trying to drive mules. Houlton later recalled that "we knew as much about handling mules as a mule does about a newspaper."[148]

The Company E detail arrived at the Fort Snelling mule corral as instructed by the quartermaster. There they found several hundred wild mules from which to choose their team. With no experienced help or guidance, the men simply got out their ropes and set to the task of capturing the reluctant animals.

The scene quickly degenerated into utter chaos with hundreds of loudly braying beasts stampeding about the corral to avoid their captors. William Houlton described their approach to the task:

> We would select an honest-looking mule and make a dive for him and sometimes we caught the mule and sometimes our mule caught us. Sometimes we came out top of the heap but more often we didn't.[149]

---

148 Houlton, *Speech.*

149 Ibid.

The process wasn't pretty. While the men managed to catch some of the more docile animals in the corral, others kicked and brayed so much after being roped that they almost had to be dragged over to the wagon. It was dangerous work as well. Mules had a well-deserved reputation as kickers. The sharp heels of an angry mule could do a lot of damage to even the toughest soldier.

The battle wasn't over once the Company E men captured a mule. The stubborn beasts violently resisted being harnessed to the wagon. They kicked out in every direction and tied their harnesses up in knots."[150]

It took quite some time before the mules were finally under control. "After several hours severe skirmishing we had a six-mule team and we were ready for a trial trip."[151] As it was nearing evening, the men decided to delay their departure until the following day. Due to the difficulties they had experienced during the previous several hours, the men decided to leave the mules harnessed to the wagon overnight so they would be ready to get an early start.[152]

The next morning the Company E detail was ready to set out for Fort Ripley. By then, the rest of Company E was at least a full day's march ahead of them. The stubborn animals, however, refused to cooperate with the departure plans. The mules simply would not budge. Hours later, and only after one man was assigned to coax each mule, did the beasts slowly decide one at a time to get moving.

The ride did not go as planned. No sooner did the mules begin moving forward than they bolted out of control. "They dragged us uphill and downhill over brush and logs till we had almost concluded our military careers were about to come to an ignominious end and our epitaph 'trampled to death by a jackass.'"[153]

The wild ride only ended when the mule team crashed into a sturdy rail fence, which resulted in a twisted tangled pile of men, animals, and harness straps. Fortunately, none of the men or animals were seriously hurt.

Sergeant Tollington ordered the men to tie the mules to the fence post while they held a meeting to determine what to do. Tempers were almost as out of control as were the mules. The first part of that meeting consisted of a strong and steady stream of profanity calling for the damnation of the mules, the quartermaster, and anything or anyone else responsible for their predicament.

In the nineteenth century, the use of profanity was generally not socially acceptable. In fact, the army strictly prohibited it, although such rules were all but

---

150 Cambell, *Personal Reminiscences*, 6.

151 Houlton, *Speech*. Houlton may have accidentally omitted the word "of" before "severe" from his handwritten speech but, more likely, it was the common usage of the period.

152 Cambell, *Personal Reminiscences*, 6.

153 Houlton, *Speech*.

impossible to enforce. In a report on the moral condition of the Eighth Minnesota to the adjutant general in Washington, Regimental Chaplain Lauren Armsby expressed far more concern about the soldiers' use of profanity than their drinking, gambling, or chasing women of questionable virtue.[154]

Those on the Company E wagon detail were not the first God-fearing men to be so frustrated in dealing with mules that they resorted to profanity. It seemed that these stubborn beasts tended to draw out the most profane language from their overseers. Mule drivers were almost admired for their prolific and creative use of cuss words. It was said that "the propulsive power of the mule-driver was increased many fold by the almost unlimited stock of profanity with which he greeted the sensitive ears of his muleship when the latter was stubborn."[155]

When the men on the wagon detail finally calmed down, they turned to the issue of how they would resolve the mess. The prevailing sentiment was "We didn't enlist to fight mules. Tell Company A break their own mules."[156] With that, the men tied those wild mules to the rail fence and returned to Fort Snelling.

Surreptitiously, the men retrieved their original mule team from Company A and quietly led them away. When they reached the Company E wagon, the men hitched up the new team and snuck off. Once the Company E detail was on the road, they set out to the north as fast as they could, expecting to be pursued by "a regiment of mule drivers commanded by a mad quartermaster."[157] If any such pursuit were ever attempted, the Company E wagon detail was never caught.

The debacle finally ended when Tollington and his tired band of Company E men arrived at Fort Ripley a few days later. As far as they knew, those wild mules that had caused them so much grief were still tied to the rail fence a short distance from Fort Snelling.

Off on the Wrong Foot

While Sergeant Tollington and his brave band of men were engaged in battle with the mules, the rest of the company proceeded north to Fort Ripley. The 110-mile march took them from Fort Snelling along the Mississippi River to St. Cloud. From there, the path continued along the river straight north to Fort Ripley. It took

154 Lauren Armsby, Report of the chaplain of the 8th Regt., Minnesota Vols., for the month of May, 1864, June 3, 1864, Dakota Conflict of 1862 Manuscripts Collections. Minnesota Historical Society.

155 Billings, *Hardtack and Coffee*, 285

156 Houlton, *Speech*.

157 Houlton, *Speech*.

several days to make the trip on foot. The company stopped for the night along the way at Anoka, Monticello, St. Cloud, and Little Falls.

Having received advance notice that Company E was just a short distance away, the regimental officers organized the other companies into an assembly to formally welcome the new arrivals. Company E, led by Captain Hartley, arrived at the fort to find the garrison awaiting them in crisp military formation. What followed would further erode the company's confidence in its elected officers, especially Captain Edward Hartley.

Colonel Minor Thomas, the regimental commander, and other senior officers were waiting at the at the gates to welcome Company E into the fort. As Company E arrived, Captain Hartley ordered them to halt, placed the company at attention, and as a sign of respect for the regimental officers, ordered the men to "Present Arms."

The Present Arms command was and remains in use as a type of salute given by armed soldiers (unarmed soldiers use the hand salute). It is given only from the position of attention. The solder presents arms by holding his rifle vertically, muzzle up, about 4 inches from the center of his body, with the bottom of the rifle facing the person receiving the salute. After the Present Arms salute, the soldiers are given the "Order Arms" command to return to attention.

Captain Harley might have been a little flustered and perhaps intimidated by commanding officer and the assembled ranks of soldiers watching Company E arrive. Instead of returning Company E to attention after giving the order to Present Arms, Hartley skipped a step and ordered the company to "Forward March." Following Hartley's order, Company E marched on into Fort Ripley holding their Austrian rifles at Present Arms. Company E looked ridiculous marching in that position, much to the amusement of the assembled troops.

Hartley's jumbled up commands no doubt raised the eyebrows of the regimental officers. It also embarrassed the members of Company E in front of the other companies. The men were proud to be in the army and wanted to be the best soldiers possible. It was a humiliation that the men would not forget. From then on, the men began to view Captain Hartley as more of an embarrassment to the company than a leader.

The Long Cold Winter

The first order of business upon Company E's arrival at Fort Ripley was finishing construction of the barracks. Prior to the Civil War, the fort had never held more than one hundred men at a time. Now it needed quarters to accommodate almost 1000, including companies from the Eighth Minnesota and various other units training at the fort.

Construction of additional barracks, each designed to hold an entire company of one hundred men, had been started by previous residents. Company E's first assignment upon arrival was to complete the work on the barracks. There was an urgency to get the job done. It was already November, and the snow was beginning to fly. Moreover, some companies had to be quartered elsewhere until the barracks were completed. Company F, for example, was occupying an unfinished hotel in nearby Little Falls until there was room for them at the fort.

Much work still had to be done and it took Company E nearly until Christmas to finish the barracks. George Cambell described their new abode:

> *They [the quarters] consisted of a building about 100 feet long with an L in about the middle for a kitchen and dining room. Around the walls of the main building bunks were built, three high, and the officers had rooms finished out under the roof at each end for their accommodation.*[158]

Once the new barracks were ready, Company F moved to Fort Ripley from their temporary quarters in Little Falls. There were now four companies of the Eighth Minnesota stationed together, the largest single gathering of the regiment since its formation.

The Treaty Payment

Before Company E could begin drilling at Fort Ripley, they had one further assignment. After the Sioux Uprising, the U.S. government was taking no chances when it came to making annuity payments to the Chippewa. Company E was ordered north to oversee the payments at the Chippewa Agency.

The Chippewa Agency was located about twelve miles north of Fort Ripley, near the present-day town of Pillager. Ojibway (Chippewa) Indians were camped outside the agency to await their payments. Both Company A and Company E were sent to the agency to maintain order. A few soldiers from these companies were assigned to guard the paymaster's table as the money was paid out.

The payment process was much the same as at the Sioux agencies. The Indians were brought into the room with the paymaster one at a time when their name was called. There, the Indian would sign the payroll ledger and take his money.[159]

---

158 Cambell, *Personal Reminiscences,* 8-9.

159 Cambell, *Personal Reminiscences,* 7.

As each Indian left the room, he was accosted by sutlers[160] and Indian traders who intended to collect the Indian's debts. Some of the soldiers were disgusted by the dishonesty of the traders "…who often forcibly collected of the Indians the moneys due them."[161]

Some of the soldiers seemed to sympathize with the plight of the Indians after this experience. After seeing how the Chippewa were treated by the agents and traders, it seemed clear to George Doud of Company F where blame for the Sioux Uprising should lie. He wrote:

> *The agents and traders are guilty, and for every drop of blood of innocent women & children shed on the western frontier in the autumn of 1862, God will hold them responsible at the great day when all things shall receive a [righteous] judgment.*[162]

The behavior witnessed at the treaty payments would also color the soldiers' perception of the traders they would later encounter. The soldiers came to despise the traders who sought to take advantage of them and the army through price gouging and sale of inferior goods.

Duties at Fort Ripley

The treaty payment duty completed, Company E returned to Fort Ripley and settled in for the winter. Most of the soldiers spent their days learning the drills and standing guard duty. Weather permitting, the soldiers would spend the morning in drill as a company and in the afternoon drill with one or more other companies in battalion tactics.

As they drilled, the men became more proficient in the essentials of soldiering. They learned formations and tactics, commands and how to efficiently load their weapons. They also had to rotate through more monotonous duties, such a police (cleanup) and guard.

One important duty for which there was no dedicated position within the company was that of cook. The men were generally left to figure out how best to cook for

---

160 A sutler was a merchant that generally sold wares from a wagon or tent. They often set up near army camps or anywhere else that people congregated so they could have high customer traffic.

161 Cambell, *Personal Reminiscences*, 7.

162 George W. Doud, *George W. Doud Diaries*, Minnesota Historical Society, September 13, 1862-October 15, 1864, 110. Although the typed transcript of Doud's diary is mostly chronological, it contains a lot of commentary without clear dates. Consequently, cites to his diary in this book are by date, if known, or by page number.

themselves. Surprisingly, few of the troops knew much about how to cook food. The women in their households generally took care of all the food preparation.

Many companies solved that problem by having one of their own take on the role of cook. For Company E, that responsibility largely fell on Private Edson Washburn. He didn't enjoy cooking very much but at least he was paid extra for it. The other soldiers in the company chipped in a few cents each out of their own pockets to pay him to cook their meals. This amounted to an extra $6.00 a month on top of his monthly $13.00 from the army.

The army rations were not exactly mouthwatering. The army supplied soldiers with the very basics – coffee, flour, vegetables, and meat. Vegetables were especially important for the men at Fort Ripley. These were essential to ward off scurvy during the long winter. The army provided them as compressed cakes of desiccated mixed vegetables. The cakes had to be rehydrated before they were fit to eat, and it was not a particularly appetizing dish.

The army provided meat rations in the form of bacon, salt pork, and sometimes beef. The army cattle, however, were generally of poor quality. To supplement these rations, the soldiers went out hunting near the fort whenever they had free time. The woods around Fort Ripley had plenty of deer, elk, and bear. Bear meat was especially prized by the soldiers because it had more fat than other wild game, which made it tastier. The men could also catch fish in the Mississippi River just a short distance from the edge of the fort.

Foods that the soldiers often took for granted in civilian life, such as butter and cheese, were not commonly provided as part of the rations at Fort Ripley. Fortunately, while the army rations were not exactly appetizing, they were at least plentiful. So much so that the soldiers would take some of their rations up to Crow Wing and sell them. They would use the proceeds to buy luxuries like butter and cheese.[163]

The army rations, supplemented by wild game and whatever else they could buy in Crow Wing, allowed the men of Company E to eat like kings during their time at Fort Ripley. Meals were a bright spot in the otherwise dark, dull, and cold winter.

Boredom

The newly-constructed quarters at Fort Ripley were relatively comfortable, which was fortunate as the men would spend a lot of time indoors due to the rigors of the winter of 1862 to 1863. The winter nights are long in northern Minnesota. Near the winter solstice, it was light for less than nine hours during the day. Drill could only take place during daylight, so the soldiers had a lot of evening free time.

---

163 Cambell, *Personal Reminiscences*, 9.

All the men had their own methods of passing the time when not on duty. There were personal chores that a soldier might attend to, such as mending his clothing. Uniforms, socks, and other clothing were expensive and not easy to replace. The men quickly learned how to mend their own uniforms to save money.

Many spent their evenings writing letters, which all the soldiers seemed to enjoy. Those who did not know how to read and write would often seek help from their more literate comrades. Other leisure pursuits included reading books, engaging in hobby crafts, or playing games. Euchre and cribbage were popular card games with the soldiers while in quarters. The men also enjoyed checkers, backgammon, and dominos.

One pastime the men all seemed to enjoy was dancing. They would hold frequent dances in their quarters at Fort Ripley. Samuel Kriedler played the fiddle well and provided the music for these impromptu events. The only problem was that they didn't have any women at Fort Ripley with whom they could dance. The men solved this dilemma by designating the smaller soldiers to take the place of women for dancing purposes.

These routine distractions, however, did little to overcome the boredom of army life in an isolated camp. Despite the relative comfort of heated quarters, Fort Ripley was still a frontier fort. There were no restaurants or entertainment options in the immediate vicinity. The closest distractions were several miles away at Crow Wing. That left the men with little to do on cold winter days besides drill, guard, and police duty.

As the daily routine at the fort quickly became monotonous, the men of Company E began to make their own fun. They seemed to put a great deal of time and effort into one of their greatest amusements, playing practical jokes on each other.

Hijinks

Practical jokes were serious business at Fort Ripley. Something could happen any day at any hour. George Cambell was often on the receiving end. One evening, for example, the men came in from drill especially eager for dinner because they heard that there was to be a delivery of butter and cheese for their rations. Sure enough, one of those who had returned from the supply trip loudly noted as they sat down to dinner that "Ah, our cheese has come!" The man reached out and cut off a piece and set it beside his plate.

As the cheese platter was passed around, a couple other soldiers carefully cut off small pieces and set them besides their tin plates without saying a word. George

Cambell cut off his own piece and took a bite. He immediately realized from the foul taste that the joke was on him. The "cheese" was in fact a large cake of soap.[164]

There were two soldiers in Company E who were constantly fomenting various pranks, William Eberman from Clearwater, and Andrew Bertram from Monticello. George Cambell claimed these two "could not exist without perpetrating half a dozen practical jokes each day."[165] Bertram himself described the effort and planning that went into their practical jokes:

> *that winter we'll remember*
> *twill never leave our mind*
> *of the many jokes we used to play*
> *we use to go it blind*
> *we use to study daytimes*
> *and do it with all our might*
> *to try and hatch some devilry*
> *to perpetrate each night*[166]

The pranks were not really intended to be mean but could raise the ire of exhausted and short-tempered soldiers. One night, the men stationed at Fort Ripley gathered for a big dance. Sam Kriedler and his fiddle were to provide the music. As Kriedler first drew his bow across the strings, no sound came out. Someone had greased the catgut bow. With no friction across the strings, the fiddle was useless. The men, who had eagerly anticipated an evening of dancing, were mad as hornets. According to Andrew Bertram they would have willingly hung the culprit, but nobody ever figured out who it was.[167]

The jokers sometimes got into a tit-for-tat trying to outdo each other with their pranks. On the frigid New Year's Eve in the last hours of 1862, Bertram and Eberman set out to even the score with a few of their comrades who had apparently played a joke on them.

The two rigged a tub of water in the rafters over the bunks of their targets and tied a string to the handle. Sometime before the clock struck twelve to ring in 1863, the perpetrators pulled the string. The tub emptied its cold contents onto the bunks of the sleeping men. The irate victims, suddenly roused from their dreams of the new

---

164 Cambell, *Personal Reminiscences*, 10.

165 Ibid., 110.

166 Bertram, *Reminiscences*, December 7, 1878, MNHS.

167 Bertram, *Reminiscences*, December 7, 1878, MNHS. It was probably Bertram himself who had made the mischief.

year, sprang up from their wet bunks with fire in their eyes. They no doubt intended to cause great physical harm to the culprits. However, the soggy soldiers never found out who did it. George Cambell, in perhaps an understatement, later wrote "they stirred up quite a commotion in camp."

The Company E enlisted men also amused themselves with arbitrary unwritten rules for which an offender would be gleefully punished. One such rule was that the soldier had to have his clothes and gear carefully and securely stowed away by lights out at 9 p.m.

Once the lights went out, the men would try to grab anything loose and throw it across the room in the dark. Those who failed to stow their clothing or boots where they couldn't be reached might have to go out for roll call the next morning barefoot or partially clothed. There was little time between the sound of the bugle and roll call. The men couldn't waste it looking for missing apparel because anyone late to roll call would get extra duty.[168]

Another absurd rule was that no man should be allowed to wear his overcoat in the quarters. One dark evening, a couple of privates standing by the door saw a man about to enter the barracks in a common overcoat with no distinctive markings. The men quickly sounded the alarm and the company positioned themselves to deal with the approaching man, who apparently had no intention of observing the overcoat rule.

As the unknown man entered the door, two privates stationed at the entrance instantly threw a cape over his head and wrapped him up. Several soldiers then dragged the unfortunate rule-breaker around the quarters hooting and hollering, at least until the men realized they had captured Captain Hartley. The enforcers quickly dropped the captain and scattered.

By the time Hartley disentangled himself from the cape and scrambled up off the floor, he saw nothing but "the most busy and industrious men he ever saw, writing or reading or engaged in some other useful occupation and everything still and orderly."[169] Despite Captain Hartley's subsequent raving and demands to learn the identities of the guilty parties, nobody knew anything about it.[170]

Military Discipline

Captain Hartley's tormentors were lucky that they were never identified. The punishment for such a breach of military discipline could be harsh and demeaning.

---

168   Cambell, *Personal Reminiscences*, 9-10.

169   Cambell, *Personal Reminiscences*, 12.

170   Ibid.

Not that the men in Company E escaped discipline entirely. There were a few who ran afoul of the rules, whether intentionally or inadvertently.

There were many ways in which a soldier could get himself in trouble. According to one Civil War veteran, the most common offences punished by the army "were drunkenness, absence from camp without leave, insubordination, disrespect to superior officers, absence from roll-call without leave, turbulence after taps, sitting while on guard, gambling, and leaving the beat without relief."[171]

A wide range of punishments could be imposed on soldiers who violated the rules. For mild offenses, the penalty might be extra duty, such as digging latrines, or "sinks" as they were known during the Civil War. In some cases, the punishment was intended to humiliate the soldier in front of his comrades. A private named Fearing from Company F learned this the hard way. After being arrested for some infraction, he was made to dress up as a woman and march around the parade ground under guard. The rest of the garrison looked on this spectacle while the regimental band played the Rogues March.[172]

Most of the discipline was handled informally at the company or regimental level. Some of the most serious matters would be addressed by court martial. As would be expected, the more serious offenses would result in more severe punishments.

In one example, "Little Jo," probably Joseph Vadner, was caught drunk on guard duty and thrown into the guardhouse. Three days later, he was court-martialed and sentenced to ten days' hard labor with ball and chain.[173] In another case, Frank Colby, who had just arrived at Fort Ripley after transferring from Company G to Company E, was arrested for stealing money from Randolph Holding.[174] Colby was put in the guard house. He was ordered to stand trial at Fort Snelling two months later.

Randolph Holding, Charlie Merrill, and an officer had to attend the proceedings at Fort Snelling. Merrill was to serve as a witness at the court martial. There is no record of the outcome, but Colby was afterwards transferred to Company F, where he remained assigned for the rest of the war.

---

171 Billings, *Hardtack and Coffee*, 144.

172 Washburn, *Diaries*, March 6, 1863. MNSH. The Rogue's March had long been used in the British and later U.S. military to taunt the person subject to discipline.

173 Washburn, *Diaries*, March 14, 17 and 19, 1863. MNHS. The "Little Jo" mentioned in Washburn's diary was probably Joseph Vadner, who at 5' 3" tall was one of the shortest members of Company E and seems to have often found himself in trouble.

174 Washburn, *Diaries*, March 22, 1863. MNHS.

Replacement Officers

In early March 1863, Company E had finally had enough of Captain Hartley and, to a lesser extent First Lieutenant Micah Croswell. The men in the company were all volunteers and wanted to be the best soldiers possible. They were of the view, however, that their top officers were holding them back, especially Captain Hartley.

Bad feelings had been simmering ever since Captain Hartley prevented the men from mingling with their family and friends after they arrived at Monticello. It just got worse over time. Hartley's botched commands in front of the regimental officers during Company E's arrival at Fort Ripley had further humiliated the men.

Hartley didn't get much better as the company drilled throughout the winter of 1862 to 1863. "We all remember the humiliations we felt at what we regarded as the inferiority of our captain to those of other companies" William Houlton recalled during

Co. E Captain Harvey S. Brookins

a reunion speech many years later.[175]

Finally, the company could take it no longer. On Monday, February 23, 1865, the soldiers of Company E voted to have Hartley resign and replace him with Harvey Brookins. The men knew this action was a breach of military discipline and could lead to serious consequences. They decided to vote their convictions anyway. "The mass of the Company had reached the conclusion that the Company would never amount to anything with Hartley for Capt."[176]

The vote proved a stinging rebuke to Captain Hartley. He submitted his resignation a few days later. Colonel Thomas accepted Hartley's resignation with an

---

175   Houlton, *Speech.*

176   Ibid.

effective date of March 17, 1863. Hartley left the company for good shortly thereafter. Few were sad to see him go, and some had lingering resentments. William Houlton later wrote "however smart or useful he was as a lawyer he was utterly unfit for Capt. of the Company."[177]

After seeing what became of Hartley and being passed over for captain in favor of his subordinate, Harvey Brookins, Micah Croswell decided to leave as well. Croswell, however, did not resign. Instead, he sought promotion. He obtained a captain's commission in the Commissary of Subsistence, which was responsible for acquisition and provision of food for the army. He served with the Commissary of Subsistence for the rest of the war.

Colonel Thomas and the other regimental officers must have recognized that Company E's original officers were struggling. Perhaps for that reason, there is no record of any disciplinary action taken against the men of Company E for standing up against their officers.

With Croswell gone and Brookins promoted to captain, Company E no longer had any lieutenants. That situation was remedied on April 13, 1863, the same day that Croswell departed for his new assignment. The company elected Sergeant Thomas Tollington as its new first lieutenant.

The second lieutenant vacancy was not filled until June 6, when the company held a vote. There were two candidates competing for the honor, Corporal Charles Post and Sergeant James Bradley. Post won a narrow victory. He finished with thirty-eight votes to Bradley's thirty-two.

Freemasonry and Eighth Minnesota Leadership

The replacement officers that Company E chose were all men that the soldiers could trust and respect. They all had one other thing in common. They were Freemasons, or at least would be very soon. Harvey Brookins joined the Lodge in Monticello along with his brother, a soldier in the Third Minnesota Infantry, while both were home on furlough for ten days over Christmas in 1862. Thomas Tollington was not yet a Mason when he was elected as first lieutenant, but he joined the fraternity a few weeks later. Second Lieutenant Charles Post would also become a member of the Monticello Lodge.

It seems odd that all three of the company officers would be Freemasons, especially when members of the fraternity made up only a tiny percentage of the adult male population in Minnesota. Yet, Company E was not an anomaly in the Eighth Minnesota. There were several other companies where all the officers were Freemasons.

---

177 Ibid.

At the regimental level, nearly all the Eighth Minnesota officers were Freemasons. Colonel Thomas and Major Camp were both members of Masonic Lodges before the war. Lieutenant Colonel Rogers joined North Star Lodge No. 23 during 1863 while the regiment was headquartered in St. Cloud.

In all, just over seventy percent of the Eighth Minnesota officers had joined the Freemasons by the end of 1864. At the time, estimates suggest that Freemasons made up only between four and eight percent of adult male population in the United States. The estimates for Minnesota were even smaller, perhaps barely over two percent.[178]

Conspiracy theorists might believe that having so many Freemasons in the regimental leadership was the result of Freemasons promoting their brethren to positions of authority based on Masonic affiliation alone. However, this theory doesn't hold up.

Company officers in volunteer units were elected by the enlisted soldiers. Although Freemasons were often over-represented in the volunteer ranks compared to the adult male population, they were still a small minority. A man could not be elected as an officer without support from the majority of the company that were not Freemasons.

Nor did the regimental officers obtain their positions by virtue of their status as Freemasons. The field officers of a state volunteer regiment were generally appointed by the governor. Minnesota Governor Alexander Ramsey was not a Freemason.

It appears that the Eighth Minnesota's officer corps, from the regiment down to the company, earned their positions not because they were Freemasons but because they had leadership qualities that were over-represented among Freemasons, such as a strong moral compass, fairness, and a commitment to the welfare of the men they commanded.

The leadership example set by the Freemason officers inspired others in the regiment to join the fraternity. Several did so during the war. Lewis Paxson from Company G, for example, joined North Star Lodge No. 23 while he was stationed in St. Cloud during part of 1863. Lieutenant Colonel Rogers, himself a newly admitted Mason, was in attendance when Paxson became a Master Mason on November 5, 1863.[179]

Many of the regiment's enlisted men joined the fraternity during the war as well. Several did so during a brief, unofficial furlough in October of 1864. That was

178 Michael A. Halleran, *The Better Angels of Our Nature: Freemasonry in the American Civil War*, Tuscaloosa, AL, The University of Alabama Press, 2010, 49-53.

179 Lewis C. Paxson, *Diary of Lewis C. Paxson: Stockton, N.J. 1862-1865*, Bismarck, ND, (Reprinted from Vol. 2, Collections State Historical Society of North Dakota, Bismarck, N.D.) 1908, Nov. 5, 1863. Paxson often served as clerk and would later be promoted in 1865, first to regimental first sergeant and then to first lieutenant so he could serve as regimental adjutant.

certainly the case for Company E. Before the end of the war, at least twenty percent of the men from Wright County had joined the Masonic fraternity.[180] Nearly all of them joined the Lodges in Monticello and Clearwater.

FORT RIPLEY DURING THE CIVIL WAR.
THE PHOTO IS LOOKING TO THE NORTHWEST ACROSS THE MISSISSIPPI RIVER.

Spring Arrives

As the calendar moved from March to April and the weather warmed, the pace of life at Fort Ripley began to pick up. The men spent more time on the shooting range, a portion of the training they enjoyed very much. Some, like William McPherson and Edson Washburn turned out to be good shots. Washburn proudly recorded in his diary that he was the best shot a couple of days.[181]

Drill continued and became more intense. In addition to basic company commands, the soldiers were now learning how to skirmish against other troops. The men also ran through bayonet exercises, which Edson Washburn claimed were

---

180 Membership records of the Grand Lodge A.F. & A.M. of Minnesota.

181 Washburn, *Diaries*, March 30 and 31, 1863.

tough on the arms.[182] In fact, the men had been drilled into such shape that they felt lazy if drill was cancelled for the day.[183]

When not on duty, the men began spending more time in outdoor pursuits. A relatively new game quickly became popular with the men – baseball. They played it almost every day that the weather permitted.

The spring also brought with it new delicacies for the soldiers to eat. Some had tapped maple trees in March and boiled the sap down into syrup. Others traded for syrup with producers in Crow Wing.

A few of the men occupied their free time with less wholesome activities, such as drinking, gambling, or womanizing. Those pursuits could all be found in abundance at Crow Wing but there was one establishment nearby. A man named John Camels maintained a small saloon only a mile from the fort. At Crow Wing and Camels' place a soldier could find some forbidden whiskey, gambling, or perhaps female company. A number of Indian women stayed at both those places. A few possibly worked as prostitutes or were otherwise sleeping with soldiers.[184]

The majority of the soldiers that visited these places for the whiskey were well-behaved and respectful towards the women. The soldiers especially loved dancing with any female company. The Indian women, good dancers themselves, seemed to enjoy dancing as much as the soldiers.

It was perhaps inevitable that with a large gathering of drunken soldiers competing for the attention of a smaller number of women some conflict would result. George Doud of Company F recalled one such dance:

> The soldiers of Company H 8 Minn, and boys of the 3 Minn Battery had a dance at John Camels. The ladies consisted of squaws about 12 to 14 in number. They had not danced long before some of the boys got tight. Then they had a general knock down over the squaws. In the morning, their faces looked rather full and fat. Their faces did not look very fresh like the rosy cheeked boy, but was black and blue and their eyes were nearly closed.[185]

---

182   Ibid., April 24, 1863.

183   Ibid., April 4, 1863.

184   Private George Doud of Company F recorded a fight between one soldier and his Indian girlfriend, with "several married men hanging out under the covers very close." Doud, *Diaries*, 107.

185   Ibid., 107. The term "squaw" is now considered derogatory and is only used in this book in direct quotes from primary sources.

The Indian women were just as likely to fight over the soldiers. George Doud observed that these battles were not quite as dangerous as when the soldiers fought each other because they consisted mostly of hair pulling and tearing at each other's clothes. "Some had nearly all their garments torn off them and was in rather a destitute condition."[186]

A few soldiers, however, were violently abusive towards the women, especially when one refused a man's sexual advances. The barbaric actions of these men would shock and appall their comrades. George Doud described the first time he witnessed such an act, which took place at Little Falls in December 1862:

> Some hard cases was with some Indian women and gave them so much to drink they became drunk and senseless; the men who was with them was drunk too. They beat and pounded one of the women so bad that she died in three or four days afterwards. What for? Because she would not submit herself to their vile passions; and the penalty for her was death, which was no more or less than murder in cold blood. No notice was taken of it at all because she was an Indian woman.[187]

On another occasion, Doud witnessed a soldier from Company H say something insulting to an Indian woman, which prompted her to attack him with an axe. The soldier easily fended off the blow, knocked her senseless and then began kicking her over and over again in the face with his heavy boots. Doud, shocked at the attack, stepped in and made the soldier back away.[188]

Company H seemed to have more than its share of undisciplined and even brutish soldiers. George Doud recorded another man from Company H who got drunk and whipped his Indian girlfriend, "one whom he had had for his bed companion for some time."[189]

Some of the Indian women did not hesitate to fight back when insulted or attacked. They were at a disadvantage against the bigger, stronger soldiers so they often used weapons. The axe attack Doud described above is one such example. More often, the Indian women would use knives or clubs as weapons.

---

186 Ibid., 108.
187 Ibid., 105.
188 Ibid., 106.
189 Ibid., 107.

Some members of Company E also chased after the Indian women at Camels' and Crow Wing. In a few cases, the soldiers may have done something to provoke those women to anger.

On April 26, 1863, Herman Erath went up to Crow Wing. He came back with his hand cut. [190] Although the cause was not recorded, one could infer that it had something to do with one of the women.

The following day, Joe Vadner set out on a trip to Crow Wing and failed to return. Fearing that something had happened to Vadner, Sergeant Woodworth and Corporal William Houlton went out to retrieve him. Vadner might been in some sort of drunken dispute with one of the Indian women. It was not recorded whether Vadner was visiting one of the Indian prostitutes or otherwise attempted to mistreat one of them. Whatever the case, the sergeant and corporal brought Vadner back to the fort with "his face cut by a squaw." [191]

New Orders

As April came to a close, Company E learned of its next assignment. The previous November, General Sibley had been given overall command of the newly formed District of Minnesota of the Department of the Northwest. [192] General Pope would remain in command of the department from his headquarters in Milwaukee.

By that time, much of the panic and hysteria caused by the Sioux Uprising had subsided along the Minnesota frontier. Nevertheless, many of the settlers that fled the previous autumn were reluctant to return. And there was reason for concern.

As warmer weather returned to Minnesota, a few small Indian raiding parties returned to their old territory. While they mostly focused on stealing horses, the Indian raids generated news that would have made wary settlers reluctant to return to the area. As a result, the central Minnesota countryside remained largely deserted.

To give the settlers confidence that it was safe to return to their farms and small towns, the Eighth Minnesota was ordered to deploy its companies to a string of forts and towns running from Fort Abercrombie on the Red River to Fort Ripley and south to the Iowa border. There, the companies would patrol their assigned areas and, perhaps more importantly, serve as a conspicuous sign that the area was safe. The companies' activities were commanded from the new regimental headquarters at St. Cloud.

---

190   Washburn, *Diaries*, April 26, 1863.

191   Ibid., April 27, 1863.

192   *See*, General Orders No. 19, Nov. 23, 1862, *Official Records*, series 1, vol. 22, part 1, 788.

On April 28, 1863, Company E received it orders. The company would occupy a fort in the central Minnesota town of Paynesville. From there, Company E would be responsible for patrolling a sixty-mile stretch of country running from Sauk Centre in the northwest, south to Paynesville and then east to Fair Haven.

Paynesville had been attacked by the Indians the previous fall. The town had been largely abandoned when its citizens learned of the Sioux Uprising. When the Indians did arrive at the undefended town, they burned several buildings and looted the area. Once the Uprising had been suppressed following the Battle of Wood Lake, elements of the Second Minnesota Cavalry were stationed at Paynesville to guard the town. The settlers appreciated the military protection and were glad to have Company E take over that duty.

Before Company E departed for Paynesville there was one pleasant surprise for the men. They were to finally receive new rifles.

After drilling all winter armed with the old Austrian rifles, Company E would get an upgrade. On April 29, 1863, the troops were ordered to turn the old rifles over to the quartermaster. These were replaced with brand new Springfield rifles. The Springfield was the most modern rifle issued by the army during the Civil War. It was nearly as heavy as the Austrian rifles but had several advantages.

The Springfield rifle fired a .58 caliber bullet known as a "Minne ball." The Minne ball was not a "ball" at all. It was actually a cylinder-shaped projectile with a conical nose and hollow base. The bullet was made of soft lead, weighed more than an ounce and was over a half of an inch wide.

When fired, the hollow base of the Minne ball expanded under the pressure generated by burning powder. As the sides of the bullet pushed out, they sealed off the pressure and gripped the rifled grooves of the barrel. The result was that the bullet left the barrel at higher speed and with a steady spin. This, in turn, gave it greater accuracy and longer range than a round ball. Armed with a Springfield and Minne ball ammunition, soldiers could hit targets 200 yards away, or more. Skilled shooters could perhaps double that range.

After receiving the new rifles, Company E spent the next two days packing for their trip to Paynesville. Edson Washburn prepared rations for the march.[193] Many of the men sent unneeded possessions, including their heavy winter clothing, home to their families for storage. By the end of the day on April 30, Company E was ready to deploy.

---

193 Washburn, *Diaries*, April 30, 1863.

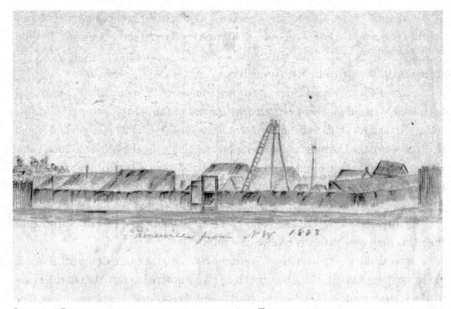

SKETCH OF PAYNESVILLE BY AN UNKNOWN PARTY IN 1863. THIS APPEARS TO BE A SKETCH OF THE FORT
RATHER THAN THE TOWN. NOTE THE STOCKADE CORNERS AND WATCHTOWER. THE ROUNDED WALLS
WERE MADE OF SOD CUT FROM THE PRAIRIE.

Patrol Duty

May 1 to September 30, 1863

The Paynesville Fort

Company E set out from Fort Ripley on the morning of May 1, 1863 for the march to their new post. They were joined by Company A, which would continue on from Paynesville to the towns of Kingston and Mannanah. With all their wagon teams and supplies in tow, the companies were only able to travel about eighteen miles per day.

It took five days of marching to reach Paynesville. When Company E arrived at about 4 p.m. on May 5 they were tired and footsore. To their disappointment, the men found the fort still occupied by Company A of the First Minnesota Regiment of Mounted Rangers, so the exhausted marchers had to set up camp outside the walls.

Like many frontier fortifications, the Paynesville fort was mostly made of sod. The townspeople hastily constructed the original defensive position when word of the Sioux Uprising first reached Paynesville about August 20, 1862.

The builders used a church, school building and two houses to serve as the four corners of the position. The buildings were connected by four-foot-thick sod walls. Over the course of a couple days, the walls were built up to five feet high. Sod was plentiful on the prairie and when properly constructed a sod fort provided good protection.

The fort quickly filled with refugees from the Sioux attacks to the west and south. For three days the men stood guard over the fort and sent scouts out to provide advance warning of the Indian attack they were sure would come.

Relief soon arrived in the form of a volunteer militia unit from nearby St. Cloud. The militia didn't stay, however. Instead, the relief force decided to escort a large number of the refugees out of the area to safety. The few defenders who remained behind then realized that their numbers were too few to successfully repel an attack on the fort. The Indians could quickly overwhelm such a small contingent so they decided to leave as well. Consequently, the Paynesville fort had to be abandoned. [194]

The refugees from Paynesville fled with such haste that they left behind their crops and livestock. A few days later it appeared that their fears had been for naught. No more reports came in of Indians in the Paynesville area.

On September 11, 1862, nine men returned to Paynesville hoping to retrieve some of their grain and livestock. The party first secured horse and wagon teams to haul the crops. Then they spent a couple of days threshing grain and gathering livestock. At night, they slept in the sod fort for security.

While the working party slept on the night of September 13, a raiding party of Indians entered the sod walls of the fort and set fire to the church. The light of the fire awoke the men. The Indians seemed unaware of their presence until a member of the working party, John Boylen, went to the door to see what was going on. One of the raiders saw Boylen by the light of the burning church and shot him. The wounded Boylen quickly dove under a wagon where he could not be seen by the attackers. From there he crawled back into the school.

The other men, who had been trying to stay out of the Indians' sight, grabbed their wounded comrade, escaped over the sod wall, and disappeared into the night. They eventually made it to an abandoned house three miles away where they attended to Boylen's wounds.[195]

The Indians stole about a dozen horses, several oxen and anything else they could find worth taking. Then they proceeded to burn the original fort buildings to the ground, along with much of the town.

Later in October, after the Sioux War had effectively ended at the Battle of Wood Lake, two companies of the Twenty-Fifth Wisconsin Infantry Regiment were assigned to Paynesville. The Wisconsin troops strengthened and expanded what remained of the fort. Feeling much safer with the presence of troops and the upgraded fort, settlers began to return. The Wisconsin troops occupied the fort until December, when mounted rangers occupied the post.[196]

The rebuilt fort could hold a full company. The quarters consisted of many small rooms, each measuring about ten feet by ten feet with accommodations for six soldiers.[197] The location of the fort was also convenient for the garrison. The north

---

194 Atwood, *Early History of Maine Prairie*, 77.

195 Ibid., 77-78.

196 Ibid.

197 Cambell, *Personal Reminiscences*, 13.

fork of the Crow River flowed just a quarter mile to the north of the fort and formed the northern boundary of the town. The trees along the riverbanks provided a haven for deer, bear, and other desirable game. The riverbanks also offered a reliable source of wood for fuel. About a mile and a half to the south was Lake Koronis, which teemed with fish and waterfowl.

By the time Company E arrived, there wasn't much to the village of Paynesville itself. Parts had been burned during the Indian attack the previous September. It consisted of little more than a few houses occupied by settlers and one hotel run by William Henry Blasdell. Blasdell, who came from Quebec and probably was a native French speaker, had lived in Joliet, Illinois for twenty years and served as the Will County Sheriff prior to his arrival at Paynesville.[198]

It was generous to call Blasdell's establishment a "hotel." It consisted of an eighteen foot by twenty-four foot log building with an adjoining twelve-foot-square shed.[199] The place was described by one soldier as a "whiskey shop" run by a French woman who tended the bar.[200] The French woman was no doubt William Blasdell's wife Harriet. The soldiers referred to the establishment as the "Frenchman's" on account of the owner's French-Canadian heritage. It quickly became the focus of Company E social activity.

It took two days for the mounted rangers to pack up and move out. On the same day, Company A of the Eighth Minnesota proceeded to its post at Mannanah. Only Company E was left to occupy the fort.

The soldiers were not happy with what they found when they moved in. Edson Washburn noted that the soldiers had to immediately commence cleaning up the "nasty mess" that the mounted rangers and their horses left behind.[201]

Cleanup was only the first task the men had to finish as they moved into their new quarters. Very quickly they began to reinforce the defenses of the fort. They formed work details to cut poles for a stockade and borrowed equipment from the local citizenry to plow sod so they could build up the walls.[202]

With anywhere from sixty to eighty men fit for duty at a given time, patrolling over the large area assigned to Company E presented some challenges. It would be hard to cover the entire territory from a central location in Paynesville. Therefore, the company was ordered to establish outposts across its patrol zone. These outposts

---

198   Atwood, *Early History of Maine Prairie,* 83.

199   Mitchell, *History of Stearns County, Minnesota,* Vol. II, 833.

200   Doud, *Diaries,* May 23, 1864.

201   Washburn, *Diaries,* May 7, 1863.

202   Ibid., May 19-29, 1863.

were located at Silver Creek, Fair Haven, and Green Lake. Patrols would also run from Paynesville to the towns of Richmond, Kingston and Mannanah, where other companies were stationed.

The outpost at the town of Fair Haven was roughly twenty-five miles east of Paynesville. At Fair Haven, Lieutenant Thomas Tollington rented an empty house to use as quarters. The Fair Haven detachment consisted of ten men who would guard the town and patrol the surrounding area. Along with Lieutenant Tollington, those assigned to the Fair Haven outpost included William Dallas, George Cambell, Franklin Clifford, Homer Markham, and Ellett Parcher.

Perhaps it was just a coincidence, but all these men were from Clearwater, which happened to be the closest town to Fair Haven. There were also a couple of men from the Monticello area stationed at Fair Haven, including Edson Washburn.

A similar situation was arranged at Silver Creek. A squad of Company E under the direction of Sergeant John Parvin rented a house near the shore of Silver Lake. The house was owned by one of their own, Private Joseph Locke. The town of Silver Creek was just a few miles east of Fair Haven. It also appears that those who were assigned to this location were all either from Silver Creek or nearby Monticello. In addition to Sergeant Parvin and Private Joseph Locke, the detachment included Andrew Bertram and Christopher Bailey, both of Monticello.

Company E also established an outpost on the shore of Green Lake near present day Spicer. A work detail of Company E was assigned to build a sod fort at Green Lake from scratch. As a result, the accommodations there were a little more primitive than at the other outposts.

While the men took turns on work details to improve the fort, the others began patrolling the area looking for Indians. After arriving in Paynesville, the company was issued approximately thirty-five horses for use in patrolling.[203] There were not enough for every man to be assigned a horse, but there were enough for training and small patrols.

Surprisingly, few of the soldiers had any experience as horsemen. Although most of Company E came from farming backgrounds, they didn't tend to ride their horses. They used them as draft animals for farm work. When these farmers took the reins, the horses were usually pulling a wagon, carriage, or plow. In fact, many farmers in the area didn't even own horses. They had to borrow or rent them.

Learning to ride became more of a priority as rumors began to swirl that the Eighth Minnesota would become a cavalry unit, or perhaps mounted infantry. In

---

203   Harvey S. Brookins to Thurmon Brookins, Fair Haven, Minnesota, Aug. 31, 1863, Brookins letters, MNHS. Capt. Brookins mentioned that he had 34 horses in his company for scouting purposes. as of August 31, 1863.

fact, Colonel Thomas had applied to have the regiment serve as mounted infantry or be transferred to cavalry service.[204]

Mounted infantry and cavalry units may have appeared similar but there were differences. Cavalry was used as highly mobile scouts, to harass an enemy's rear and to protect the army's flanks. In contrast, mounted infantry used the horses simply as a mode of transportation to quickly get troops into position for battle. Such units generally fought dismounted as conventional infantry. As the war went on, however, cavalry in the Union army was often used more like mounted infantry. By the end of the war, the two types of units became almost indistinguishable.

With horses at their disposal, the men practiced riding every chance they could. Their inexperience sometimes showed. George Cambell, for example, struggled to control the horse he was assigned. The animal had a habit of abruptly stopping whenever it chose, often at inopportune moments.

On one such occasion, the horse stopped so suddenly that Cambell was thrown forward over the animal's head. Poor George landed heavily right on his butt. He found himself sitting on his aching backside in the middle of the dusty road. When the laughing and jeers of his friends died down, George attempted to reclaim some of his dignity by explaining to these obviously ignorant fellows that "this is was the usual way a cavalier dismounted."[205]

Despite the patrols and work details, the men of Company E found plenty of time for recreation. Immediately after arrival, the soldiers began hunting and fishing to supplement their army rations. A hundred hungry young men could go through a lot of meat in a day and the livestock furnished by the army was not going to cut it.

While on patrol, the men would shoot any deer, elk, or bear that they might come across. If they were lucky, they would kill or capture some livestock abandoned by refugees the previous autumn. Hunting to supplement their rations became commonplace. Edson Washburn and John Ponsford, for example, participated in a patrol where they killed a deer and captured a hog.[206]

Almost immediately after they arrived at Paynesville the men discovered nearby Lake Koronis. They returned from the lake with geese and ducks to share with the company. Over the next few weeks, the men would make many trips to Lake Koronis for fish and game. On one such trip at the end of May some of the soldiers climbed up to an eagle's nest on one of the lake's islands and retrieved two of the young birds.[207]

---

204 Ibid.

205 Cambell, *Personal Reminiscences*, 15. "Cavalier" is an obsolete term for a cavalry soldier.

206 Washburn, *Diaries*, June 3, 1863; Ponsford *Diary*, June 3, 1863.

207 Washburn, *Diaries*, May 30, 1863.

It was a custom in the Eighth Minnesota for each infantry company to keep some sort of animal as mascot. Most of the companies had dogs for this purpose. Company E, however, seized the opportunity to have a bald eagle as its mascot. One of the young eagles survived its initial time in captivity. It was well fed and quickly grew into a formidable mascot.

The other companies' pet dogs didn't dare bother the eagle, which Company E kept chained up on the parade ground most of the time. The eagle also became attached to the men. They would let the majestic bird loose to hunt, after which it would return to the fort.

Remarkably, the eagle would leave the soldiers' supply of chickens unmolested. Instead, it would prey on the chickens of local farmers. Sadly, one of those farmers likely got tired of the predation on his chickens. Later that year, the young eagle failed to return from one of its hunting expeditions.[208]

Paynesville was not particularly far away from Monticello and Clearwater. Visitors from home could reach the soldiers with a full day's travel. It didn't take long after Company E arrived at their new post before a number of the ladies from these towns, the mothers, wives, sisters, and girlfriends of the soldiers, decided to pay them a visit. The ladies send word that they would attend church services with the soldiers on Sunday, May 25, 1863.

The men of Company E were excited to have the hometown visitors. George Cambell recalled that "a lot of us wanted to fix up extra fine" for the ladies.[209] Cambell and several others decided to get a fresh shave and sought out musician William Lane, known as the "little drummer" because of his enormous size, who acted as the company barber.

Lane explained that he too was in a hurry to get to the church that morning so he would have to expedite the shaving process. Lane ordered the men to lather up one side of their face and get in line. It was understood that Lane would work his way down the line, shaving one side of each man's face as he went. When he reached the end, the men would lather up the other side of their face and Lane would turn around and go back, shaving the other side. It was a personal grooming version of the assembly line process.

When Lane finished his first pass leaving only one side of each man's face shaved, he politely excused himself for a minute so he could step out and attend to some matter.[210] It didn't take long before the half-shaven men realized that they had been duped. Lane didn't return and could not be found anywhere. The soldiers, dis-

208 Cambell, *Personal Reminiscences*, 115.

209 Ibid., 113.

210 Ibid.

playing good humor, decided to go to the church anyway. George Cambell made the best of the situation and got a lot of fun out of it. "Some one would speak to me and I would turn the other side of my face to him and he would find he was talking to a stranger"[211] Cambell recalled years later.

Some of the married soldiers in Company E brought their wives and families to Paynesville. Charles Smith, Sam Kriedler, and Henry Braughton all arranged accommodations so they could live with their wives just outside the fort. In some cases, their temporary abodes had extra rooms, which the married soldiers would rent out to those who desired something better than sod-walled quarters

Indian Attacks Continue

The winter of 1862 to 1863 had been relatively quiet for Company E and most of the Eighth Minnesota. The sound defeat of the Sioux at the Battle of Wood Lake the previous September had forced the Indians to either surrender or flee west beyond Minnesota's borders. Little Crow and about 300 warriors fled the battlefield into Dakota Territory and spent the winter at Devil's Lake in present-day North Dakota.

Although the threat of large-scale Indian attacks had been all but eliminated, isolated raids continued. In the early spring of 1863, small bands of Sioux began filtering back into Minnesota. On April 15, 1863, a raiding party attacked along the south fork of the Watonwan River, about forty miles southwest of Mankato. Three settlers and a soldier from the Seventh Minnesota Infantry Regiment were killed in the skirmish.[212]

The Sioux made small scale attacks further north as well. In May, a band of Indians ambushed soldiers from Company D of the Eighth Minnesota in two separate attacks. A small detachment of Company D was stationed at Pomme De Terre under the command of Captain Samuel McLarty.[213] Their mission was to help protect the trail that ran between St. Cloud and Fort Abercrombie in Dakota Territory.

On May 2, two of the soldiers from Company D, Private H. Adams Hare and Corporal Zenas Blackman, went out hunting goose eggs. The soldiers often left the safety of the small fort at Pomme De Terre to hunt and fish to supplement their rations. The two soldiers were about a half mile from the fort when the Indians

---

211 Ibid. Cambell did not identify the date when the ladies visited in his reminiscence, which was written from memory 25 years after the Civil War. However, from Edson Washburn's diary it appears that this was the only date on which the event could have occurred.

212 *Minnesota in the Civil and Indian Wars: 1861-1865*, vol. 1, 353. The source is not certain whether the civilian casualties were 2 or 3 killed.

213 A small fort was established at Pomme De Terre in 1863. The location of Pomme De Terre is just south of Interstate 94 about midway between present day Alexandria and Fergus Falls.

attacked.[214] Both men were killed. Each was shot and then stabbed several times. The Indians took the soldier's weapons and disappeared.

Later that same day, Silas Foote, an employee of a company that supplied cattle to the army, was driving a small herd of livestock to Fort Abercrombie. He was accompanied by private Comfort B. Luddington, also of Company D, who served as escort. The men were near a crossing of the Otter Tail River approximately thirty miles northwest of Pomme De Terre when they were ambushed and killed by Indians.[215]

Reports of other attacks continued to alarm settlers along the frontier. Although they had elected to remain in Minnesota following the Sioux Uprising, these settlers were still terrified of the Indians. The state and federal government grew concerned that more settlers would abandon Minnesota at a time when the land needed to be productive to support the war effort in the east.

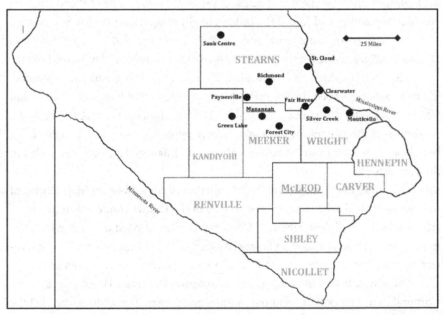

AREAS PATROLLED BY COMPANY E DURING THE SUMMER OF 1863. THE COMPANY WAS HEADQUARTERED AT PAYNESVILLE WITH OUTPOSTS AT GREEN LAKE, FAIR HAVEN, MANANNAH AND SILVER CREEK. THE REGIMENTAL HEADQUARTERS WERE IN ST. CLOUD.

---

214 *St. Cloud Democrat*, May 7, 1863.

215 Ibid.

1863 Sibley Expedition Against the Sioux

Even before the small-scale Indian attacks renewed in the spring of 1863, General Pope planned to launch the expedition against the Sioux in Dakota Territory that he had postponed the previous autumn. On February 17, 1863, Pope wrote General Sibley with plans for the expedition and an order to prepare his troops.[216] General Pope was deeply concerned at reports that Little Crow had organized a force of 7000 warriors near Devil's Lake in Dakota Territory and was planning to resume attacks in Minnesota or settlements near the Missouri River when the weather permitted.[217]

Pope's plan finally came together at the end of May. It was to be a two-pronged attack. General Sibley would lead a column of cavalry and infantry supported by a battery of artillery. Sibley would depart from near Fort Ridgely carrying three months of supplies and proceed directly towards Devil's Lake.

General Alfred Sully would lead the second column of the expedition, which would proceed up the Missouri River to a point southwest of Devil's Lake. From there, the column would go cross-country and meet up with Sibley's forces. Sully's column included 2000 cavalry and a battery of artillery.

The objective of the expedition was to force the Sioux in Dakota Territory to surrender. Pope was confident that the Indians wouldn't fight such an overwhelming force. "I do not doubt that a very large part of them will come on and deliver themselves up."[218] The rest were likely to flee north and take refuge in the British possessions (Canada).

After dealing with the Indians at Devil's Lake and near the James River, General Sully would lead his force southwest towards the Black Hills. Sully was to visit as many other Sioux tribes as he could find.[219]

The Minnesota troops under General Sibley set out from Camp Pope near the Upper Sioux Agency on June 16, 1863. The force was composed of the Sixth, Seventh, and Tenth Minnesota Infantry Regiments, along with the Third Minnesota Battery and the First Regiment of Minnesota Mounted Rangers. Company A of the Ninth Minnesota served as scouts.

---

216 Pope to Sibley, Feb. 17, 1862, *Official Records,* series 1, vol. 22, part 2, 115-116.

217 Pope to Kelton, Feb. 18, 1863, *Official Records,* series 1, vol. 2, part 2, 117-118.

218 Pope to Kelton, Feb. 18, 1862, *Official Records,* series 1, vol. 22, part 2, 304-305.

219 Ibid. It is not expressly stated what General Sully was planning to do on these "visits."

In all, Sibley's force consisted of almost 3,300 men.[220] The troops were supported by approximately 300 wagon teams loaded with ammunition, rations, and other supplies. The teamsters were civilians hired by the military for $25 per month plus rations.[221]

Among the troops that would accompany Sibley were several friends and relatives of soldiers in Company E. These included John Ponsford's younger brother James, who served in Company D of the First Minnesota Mounted Rangers, and George Tourtellotte, who had originally enlisted in Company E of the Eighth Minnesota but transferred to the Third Minnesota Battery effective May 1, 1863.

The soldiers of the Eighth Minnesota were certainly aware of Sibley's expedition. If they were disappointed not to be included, none of them made a record of it. As it turned out, they would have plenty to keep them busy guarding the frontier.

Death of Captain Cady – Company A

As Sibley's expedition was preparing for its mission at Fort Ridgely during the late spring, small Indian raids continued in central Minnesota, especially in Wright and Meeker counties. One Indian raiding party managed to slip undetected as far east as the Mississippi River in Wright County.

At Monticello, Mrs. Bertram[222] was up early on morning of June 7 when she looked outside and saw an Indian looking over her pig pen. On being spotted, the man ran for the river. Mrs. Bertram sounded the alarm. A hastily organized group of residents armed themselves and set out in pursuit. They quickly lost the trail north of town.[223]

Two days later, Indians quietly raided a farm at Silver Creek under cover of darkness. There, they stole a team of horses from a farmer named Ferguson.[224]

The following day, Wednesday, June 10, 1863, word of the Indians' horse theft at Silver Creek reached Forest City. At nearly the same time, Captain John Cady of Company A and three of his men, Privates George Secoy, Elias Pratt, and Edward

---

220   Arthur M. Daniels, *A Journal of Sibley's Indian Expedition During the Summer of 1863 and Record of the Troops Employed: By a Soldier in Company "H," 6th Regiment*, 51, Sherman & McNie Booksellers, Winona, Minn. 1864.

221   *Weekly Pioneer and Democrat* (St Paul, Minn.), June 5, 1863.

222   This appears to be Andrew H. Bertram's mother but it isn't clear from the various accounts.

223   Blanchard, *reminiscence*, July 5, 1933. MNHS.

224   Ibid.

Clinch, happened to be passing through the town. They were on their way back to their company's station in Richmond following a trip to St. Paul.[225]

Originally from Moravia, New York, John Cady had moved to Minnesota in the late 1850s seeking new opportunities. Like most of Company A, he was living nearby when Anoka County held its local war rally on August 14, 1862. Cady enlisted there along with the other local men. Cady was popular with the men in the company and it was no surprise that they elected him as their captain.

Upon learning of the incident at Silver Creek, Captain Cady, with his three soldiers and two civilian volunteers, set out after the Indian horse thieves. They quickly picked up the Indians' trail and followed it through the night for over twenty miles to near Kandiyohi Lake.

At about 8 a.m. on June 11, the soldiers spotted the stolen horses grazing along the edge of some nearby timber. Assuming the thieves were nearby, Cady took two men and began to sneak up on the horses. His intention was to take the Indians by surprise. Before the soldiers get close enough, however, the Indians spotted them. Within moments, the Indians mounted the horses and rode off down a thin stretch of dry land between the lake and swamp.

Cady and the two other soldiers followed the Indians. The rest of the force moved to cut off any escape route. Finding their path blocked, the Indians turned to fight their pursuers. A short exchange of gunfire followed between the Indians and the soldiers led by Cady. Cady fired at least three shots at the Indians and may have wounded one of their number.

One of the warriors was armed with a double barrel shotgun. As Cady was shooting, the Indian raised his weapon, took aim, and fired first one barrel and then the other at the captain. The second blast from the scatter gun struck Cady in the head and chest, killing him instantly.[226]

In the confusion that followed Cady's shooting, the Indians took refuge in a nearby thicket. Knowing that the Indians were armed with shotguns, which would be deadly in the close quarters fight that would ensue if they entered the thicket, the soldiers decided not to follow them. As a result, the Indians were able to escape.[227]

225 William E. Seelye, "Early Military Experiences in Dakota," *Collections of the State Historical Society of North Dakota*, vol. III, Bismarck, 1910. State Historical Society of North Dakota, 242.

226 *St. Cloud Democrat*, June 18, 1863; *St. Paul Pioneer and Democrat*, June 19, 1863.

227 Seelye, "Early Military Experiences in Dakota," 242.

The soldiers managed to recover the two stolen horses and decided to end the pursuit. Instead, they secured the body of their fallen captain to one of the horses and returned to Forest City.[228]

The pursuit of the Indians responsible for Cady's death did not stop when the Company A men returned. A detachment of Company E had been following on the trail of Indians in Wright County, perhaps in response to the sighting by Mrs. Bertram. They came close enough to exchange shots with them. However, they lost the trail in the dense woods.[229]

Those responsible for the death of Captain Cady may have been part of a small band of raiders that had returned to Minnesota, led by Little Crow himself. Due to Little Crow's failure to achieve victory the previous fall, he was deposed as chief while his band wintered near Devil's Lake in Dakota Territory.[230]

In early June, Little Crow and seven warriors, including two of his sons, infiltrated into Meeker County, within the territory patrolled by Company E.[231] The raiding party sought to steal horses and kill whites when the opportunity arose.

On Monday, June 29, 1863, the band of Indians were just west of the Wright County village of Howard Lake when they came across a wagon traveling down the road.[232] The wagon was occupied by six members of the Dustin family, Amos, his wife, their three children, and Amos's mother. The Indians attacked the settlers with arrows and tomahawks, killing Amos Dustin, his widowed mother, and Dustin's twelve-year-old son. Amos Dustin's wife was mortally wounded and left for dead.

It was two days before the massacre was discovered. A horrific scene awaited those who came across the wagon. The Indians had mutilated the bodies, which had been left out in the hot July sun. Amos was found with an arrow through his heart and his left hand cut off, apparently taken by the killers as a trophy. Dustin's mother was dead from arrow wounds. Her body was mangled and also missing the left hand. Amos's wife was still alive but died of her wounds shortly thereafter.[233]

---

228 Cady's body was taken to Clearwater and then to Anoka. From there, his former business partner arranged to have the body shipped back east to Cady's family in a metal casket. *St. Paul Pioneer and Democrat*, June 19, 1863.

229 *Minnesota in the Civil and Indian Wars: 1861-1865*, vol. 1, 387.

230 Justice Loren W. Collins, *The Expedition Against the Sioux Indians in 1863 Under Gen. Sibley*, St. Cloud, Journal-Press Print, 1895, 20.

231 Hubbard and Holcombe, *Minnesota in Three Centuries*, 408,

232 The site of the massacre is on Highway 12 a mile and a half west of Howard Lake. There is a pull off from the highway with a historical marker on the spot.

233 Story of the massacre was compiled from the *St. Cloud Democrat*, July 9, 1863; Folwell, *A History of Minnesota*, 283; and HL history; Dustin Massacre witness speaks, Howard Lake-Waverly Herald, October 2, 2000 (originally an uncited article from the early 1900s issue of the Howard Lake Herald), online at http://www.herald-journal.com/archives/1999/stories/dustin.html, last accessed on March 1, 2020.

On the same day that the terrified residents of Howard Lake discovered the bodies of the Dustin family, twenty-eight-year-old James McGannon, a resident of Champlin in Hennepin County, was ambushed nearby. He was traveling by road near Fair Haven when he encountered the small band of Indians and was killed. The killer, an Indian named Hinkpa, stripped McGannon's jacket from the body and later presented it to his father-in-law, Little Crow.[234]

Mid-Summer in Paynesville

Despite the nearby Indian attacks during May and June, having the Company E garrison in Paynesville gave the residents a sense of security as they worked in the fields and went about their business in town. To show their appreciation to the soldiers, the locals decided to throw a big Fourth of July party for the whole town, including the garrison. Preparations began days in advance as the local ladies baked cakes and pies for the occasion.

It might have seemed that there was little to celebrate on the Fourth of July, 1863. The war still seemed to be going badly for the Union. In early May, the Confederate Army of Northern Virginia under the command of General Robert E. Lee had routed the Union Army of the Potomac at the Battle of Chancellorsville in Virginia.

The Union defeat at Chancellorsville was all the more demoralizing because the Union troops outnumbered the Confederates by more than two to one. The Union commander, General Joseph Hooker, and his subordinates made numerous errors throughout the battle and were simply out-generaled.

As July 4 approached, the newspapers reported that General Lee had again invaded the North with the Army of Northern Virginia.[235] To the soldiers and civilians in Paynesville, it must have seemed like an unending stream of bad news coming from the east.

Farther to the west, the strategic Confederate stronghold at Vicksburg, Mississippi continued to hold out against the Union Army of the Tennessee under General Ulysses S. Grant. Vicksburg was strategically important because its fall would split the Confederacy in two and give the Union control of the entire Mississippi River.

Grant's forces had scored a number of small victories as they moved against Vicksburg, but the advance stalled on the outskirts of town. At the beginning of July 1863, the opposing forces at Vicksburg were at stalemate. The town was under siege by the Union troops, but the Confederates trapped in the encirclement continued to fight on.

---

234 Hubbard and Holcombe, *Minnesota in Three Centuries*, 408.

235 Lee had invaded Maryland the previous September and been defeated at the bloody Battle of Antietam.

The depressing news from the war did not stop the good citizens of Paynesville from their plans for a grand Independence Day celebration. On Friday, July 3, 1863, the residents and soldiers began preparing for the following day's festivities. Everyone pitched in to contribute food and refreshments for the big party.

Some of the soldiers picked wild gooseberries, which were then turned into various sweet edibles for the planned celebration.[236] Edson Washburn also helped. He joined Mrs. Hoover, one of the Paynesville neighbors in baking cakes for the celebration.[237]

Throughout the day on July 3 the soldiers' friends and family began to arrive in Paynesville from Clearwater, Monticello, and other locations in Wright County. There were many happy reunions, and all looked forward to the large picnic that would take place the following day.

Death of Little Crow

The soldiers and civilians in Paynesville didn't know it yet, but important developments in the Indian war took place on July 3 just thirty-five miles to the southeast near the town of Hutchinson. On that day, two local citizens, Nathan Lampson and his son Chauncy, took their rifles and went deer hunting about six miles north of Hutchinson.[238] As evening approached, the Lampsons spotted two Indians picking berries, perhaps fifty yards away.

Nathan Lampson raised his rifle and fired at one of the Indians, wounding the man just above the hip. Although taken by surprise, both Indians immediately fired back, slightly wounding Nathan.

Chauncey, who apparently had not been seen by the Indians, took aim and fired. His shot hit the previously wounded Indian. The bullet passed through the Indian's chest, and he fell. The other Indian fled. [239]

The Lampsons went back to Hutchinson, arriving late in the night. The following morning a detachment of soldiers was sent from Hutchinson to investigate the

---

236 Ponsford, *Diary*, July 1, 1863. On that day John Ponsford mentioned gathering "goose-berries for the fourth of July."

237 Washburn, *Diaries*, July 3, 1863.

238 July might seem a bit early for deer hunting in Minnesota. It was not unusual in the 1860s to hunt deer at any time of year. Hunting restrictions were few and there was no limit on the number of deer a hunter could take. Today, Minnesota strictly regulates deer hunting and, with some exceptions, limits the hunt to a three-week period in November each year.

239 Folwell, *A History of Minnesota*, 283-284.

Lampsons' reports. They found the Indian's body neatly laid out with new moccasins and a citizen's coat on or near it.[240]

The body was quickly identified as that of Little Crow. The Indian that fled was later identified as Little Crow's son, Wowinapa or The Appearing One. He was captured a month later near Devil's Lake in Dakota Territory, where he confirmed that it was his father that had been killed near Hutchinson.[241] According to Wowinapa, he had returned to his father after the Lampsons left and arranged the body with the moccasins and coat.

The soldiers returned to Hutchinson with Little Crow's body. There, events took a gruesome turn:

> The body of Little Crow was taken to Hutchinson and treated with great indignity. The head was cut off and almost literally skinned, the skin tanned, the bones of one forearm badly united after a bullet wound taken, the skull carried off and the rest of the carcass thrown into a pit of rotting beef entrails.[242]

Little Crow's scalp and arm bones were later donated to the Minnesota Historical Society, which put them on public display for decades. Thomas Hodgson of Company F described what he saw when he visited the capitol building many years later:

> At the foot of the staircase leading from the historical rooms in the basement to the first floor of the capitol, enclosed in a glass case or cupboard, may be seen the scalp of the once world-renowned Indian chief Little Crow, together with the bones of one of his arms.[243]

The relics remained at the Minnesota Historical Society until 1971, when they were returned to Little Crow's grandson, Jesse Wakeman, the son of Wowinapa. Wakeman buried them in South Dakota.

---

240   Ibid., 284. The coat was later determined to be the same one Hinkpa had taken from James McGannon's body and given to Little Crow two days earlier.

241   Ibid. Wowinapa would also be known as Thomas Wakeman.

242   Hubbard and Holcombe, *Minnesota in Three Centuries*, 409. Little Crow's skull, scalp and arm bones were later given to the Minnesota Historical Society, where they were put on public display.

243   Hodgson, "Recollections of the Sioux War," *Dakota County Tribune*, Sept. 19, 1889.

The Fourth of July

The Fourth of July dawned very warm and humid, which was not unusual in central Minnesota at that time of year. At 10 a.m., the soldiers of Company E left their sod fort and excitedly set out on the short walk to the picnic site along the Crow River, just a quarter mile away to the north. As they did so, the men noticed ominous dark clouds building to the west. Within minutes, a thunderstorm with heavy rain drenched the party goers.

The rain, however, passed quickly and failed to dampen anyone's spirits. The party was soon in full swing. More than 200 people were gathered at the picnic grounds. The soldiers spent the rest of the day enjoying the company of their families, friends, and the townsfolk.

For entertainment there were patriotic orations and plenty of food and drink. Later, a large number of soldiers from Company H dropped by and joined in the fun. William Houlton later recalled "It was one of the most enjoyable occasions I ever remember."[244]

As the soldiers, Paynesville residents, and their guests enjoyed the celebration, two far off events occurred, which, had the party goers known at the time, would have given them even greater reason to celebrate.

A thousand miles down the Mississippi River from Central Minnesota, the besieged Confederate defenders at Vicksburg finally surrendered to General Grant's Army of the Tennessee. The Union now controlled the entire length of the river, from its source in Minnesota all the way to New Orleans.

At the same time, a bloody battle was wrapping up in Pennsylvania. Beginning on July 1, 1863, the Army of the Potomac had clashed with Lee's Army of Northern Virginia in and around the small town of Gettysburg. After three days of heavy fighting, the Union had decisively defeated the Confederates. On July 4, General Robert E. Lee began withdrawing his troops to safety in Virginia.

The twin victories at Gettysburg and Vicksburg changed the course of the war and were indeed worthy of celebration. After that day, the Confederate Army would never again be able to seize the initiative. The Union would relentlessly pursue the Confederates from then until the end of the war. Nevertheless, it would still take almost two more years of bloody fighting to end the hostilities.

Company E and the rest of the Eighth Minnesota no doubt celebrated when word of Gettysburg and Vicksburg reached them several days later. The good news, however, would be tempered as the casualty lists came in.

---

244 Houlton, *Speech.*

Minnesota regiments were involved in the fighting at both Gettysburg and Vicksburg. At Gettysburg, the First Minnesota Volunteer Infantry Regiment earned a prominent place in in both Minnesota and Civil War history. That distinction, however, came at a terrible price.

On the afternoon of the second day of the Battle of Gettysburg, the Union's position was precarious as it held a thinly defended fishhook-shaped line running from just east of town, south about three miles and ending at two large hills, Little Round Top and Big Round Top. Several times that day rebel attacks had nearly broken through the line. All were repulsed but there were numerous points where the rebels nearly succeeded. Had the rebels broken through, the tide of the battle may have turned.

One of those close calls occurred near the center of the Union line. The spot was defended by the First Minnesota Volunteer Infantry Regiment. The First Minnesota was by then a combat-hardened regiment. It had seen plenty of fighting since the unit was formed more than two years earlier.

Through casualties and sickness, the regiment had been thinned to barely over 300 men. The ranks were further reduced because one company had been assigned to provost duty. On the afternoon of July 2, 1863, there were only 262 men of the First Minnesota under the command of Colonel William Colville available to hold their assigned position along Cemetery Ridge.

A deadly mistake by Union General Sickles placed the portion of the line held by the First Minnesota in grave danger. Sickles had been unhappy with the position that he was ordered to defend. The terrain was flat and offered little cover for his troops. He decided to move forward about a mile to a peach orchard, which offered a better defensive position.

The new position, however, was so far out in front of the Union lines that it left large gaps on either side of Sickles' position. The move left Sickles' troops isolated and exposed to the enemy.

The rebels took advantage of Sickles' mistake and attacked the troops in the peach orchard. For the next hour, some of the bloodiest fighting of the war took place while the Union troops fell back. In the process, they left the thinly held portion of the Union line held by the First Minnesota fully exposed to attack.

It did not take long for the Confederates to exploit the gaps left by Sickles. Nearly 4000 Alabama troops were ordered forward to attack the weak Union center. A breakthrough there could have changed the tide of the battle and perhaps the entire war.

As the Confederates neared the Union line, General Winfield Scott Hancock, commander of the troops in that section, quickly realized the danger. He sent for reinforcements, but those would take fifteen minutes or longer to arrive. Without bold action, even fifteen minutes would be too late. The entire Union Army was at risk of being cut in two.

Hancock, seeing no other option, rode up to Colonel Colville and asked, "What regiment is this?"[245] Colville responded that it was the First Minnesota. Hancock then commanded "Charge those lines!"[246]

None of the 262 First Minnesota men on the line that day had any illusions about what General Hancock's order meant. They knew that it would be nothing less than a suicide charge into the vastly superior number of Alabama troops advancing on them. Yet none waivered.

Coleville ordered the First Minnesota forward. They first advanced at the double-quick but the pace quickly grew into a full sprint. With their fixed bayonets leveled towards the enemy, the First Minnesota charged into the mass of Alabama troops.

The Minnesotans held their fire during the charge. The first line of rebels, unnerved by the Minnesota troops advancing with such momentum and desperation, broke and fell back. Then the First Minnesota opened fire, their rifle shots creating further chaos among the Alabamans.

The rebel advance stalled as a result of the surprise attack by the small Minnesota regiment. For the next several minutes a fierce battle raged as the Minnesota troops, outnumbered almost ten to one, fought on against the Alabama veterans.

The charge of the First Minnesota held up the rebels long enough for reinforcements to arrive. By the time the Alabama troops recovered from the charge of the First Minnesota, it was too late. The line was by then strong enough to repel the Confederate attack.

The efforts of the First Minnesota came at a great sacrifice. Of the 262 men who made the charge, only forty-seven returned to the line. In all, 215 members of the First Minnesota lay dead or wounded on the battlefield. It was the highest casualty rate of a Union Army unit in any engagement during the Civil War. The sacrifice, however, prevented the Confederates from breaking through the Union line and perhaps prevented a major defeat for the Union Army.

Those celebrating the Fourth of July at Paynesville knew nothing of what had transpired at Gettysburg. They would learn soon enough. The casualty figures for the First Minnesota would have been shocking to the men in Company E when the news did reach them. It must have been sobering to be reminded that their close-knit company would not be immune from the tragedy of war and might also suffer

---

245 *Minnesota in the Civil and Indian Wars: 1861-1865*, vol. 1, 35.

246 Ibid.

serious casualties when and if they made it into battle. Moreover, some of the men had family or friends who were in the First Minnesota.

The party eventually ended that night. The following day, Sunday, July 5, Company E, along with the many visitors who had participated in the previous day's celebration, attended morning church services. Then, everyone went home, and Company E returned to the boredom of its normal routine.

The Gordon Incident

The ongoing Indian threats, made real by the ambushes during the spring and early summer of 1863, continued to keep the settlers on edge. As a result, the citizens of Wright, Meeker and southern Stearns counties were grateful to have the Eighth Minnesota soldiers in the area. However, events in late July and early August of 1863 demonstrated that this warm feeling was not universally held.

On July 29, 1863, the squad stationed at Fair Haven set out on a routine patrol to the town of Clearwater. Nearly all the soldiers stationed at Fair Haven were from Clearwater, including the squad leader, Sergeant Ed Woodworth. It was a popular patrol destination for these men, and they looked for any excuse they could find to make the trip if enough horses were available.

Clearwater was only about twelve miles away, and the round trip could have easily been done in a day. Nevertheless, the men usually stayed in Clearwater for a day or two, just to make sure the town was safe. Apparently, that mostly involved spending time with friends and family.

The trip from Fair Haven to Clearwater took about four hours on horseback. The men passed the time with joking, singing and other activities. They were probably not too concerned about Indians as there hadn't been any seen in the immediate vicinity for weeks.

Upon arrival at Clearwater, they split up to pay their social visits. Edson Washburn and others called on Simon Stevens, one of the original town founders and brother of the founder of Minneapolis. From Stevens' house, they took in a nice view of the Mississippi River, which formed the eastern boundary of the town.

The men stayed in Clearwater that night. The following day, Edson Washburn, who, being from Monticello, didn't have any family or as many friends in the town, offered to help out some nearby residents as they stacked hay. Washburn and two other soldiers rode south about eight miles to Delhi Township,[247] which was by Clearwater Lake, and began to help several men with the haying work.

---

247 Delhi Township was renamed Corinna Township the following year.

Company E may have been the intended beneficiary of the hay gathered that day, which might explain why the soldiers volunteered to help. The horses used by Company E constantly needed hay. The army purchased it from local farmers. However, some of the farmers, like many who tried to make money off the government during the war, had a habit of cheating.

The standard practice was for the farmer to stack hay for sale to the army. The quartermaster would measure the stack and pay the farmer if it measured up to specifications. However, it was possible to fool the army and get paid the same for a much smaller amount.

One farmer tried to cheat by standing in one place and stacking a ring of hay as high as his head in a circle. Then he would get out on the edge and draw it in until he made it look like a good stack. In actuality, it was hollow and contained far less hay than the army would expect.

The men realized what was happening and notified the quartermaster. The quartermaster hid the rest of the day to avoid the farmer. The next morning when the farmer came back to have his haystack measured, he found it had collapsed into a flat mass. The quartermaster refused to even measure it and it is unlikely the farmer was ever paid for that aborted attempt at cheating.[248]

It is quite possible that the men of Company E were assigned to assist with stacking hay to make sure the army was not cheated by an unscrupulous farmer. Nevertheless, Washburn would have probably helped anyway. As farmers tend to do, he often assisted the neighbors with farm work, raising buildings, and other chores wherever he was stationed.

One of the farmers whom they helped stack hay on July 30 was Charles Gordon, who helped organize the township in 1860, along with Hanford Lennox Gordon. Charles and Hanford were half-brothers. They had settled on adjoining farms.

The day was hot and humid. When they finished stacking hay about supper time, Washburn and his comrades were no doubt tired and glad to enjoy a meal and trade stories with the other men in the working party. They probably bragged about how much fun they were having on patrols and entertained their new working friends with stories of their exploits.

The following day was again warm and muggy. Washburn and the rest helped stack hay for the farmers again in the morning. Then they returned to Clearwater.

The fog of time has largely erased any accounts of what happened when the Company E men assisted with the hay work. However, it appears that shortly thereafter Charles Gordon communicated something to Hanford L. Gordon, which left the latter Gordon upset and angry.

248 Cambell, *Personal Reminiscences*, 16-17.

Shortly after the patrol returned to Fair Haven, Col. Thomas received a terse letter from Hanford Gordon, which included the following passage:

> *I have seen a good deal of the soldier scouts now in the Big Woods, especially those of Co "E" 8th Regt. Col., their manner of scouting is a nuisance and a shame to themselves and their officers. They travel in large squads commanded by Sergeant, follow the roads strictly, sing and shout, fire at targets and in short do everything but try to find Indians. They are a nuisance to the section. They prowl over tearing down fences leaving open gates and bars so that the cattle destroy the crops and are more intent on securing the pigs, chickens and potatoes of the fugitive settlers than anything else. To my knowledge men of Co "E" 8th Regt have broken into five houses around Clearwater Lake (or Big Lake) eight miles south of this, helping themselves to everything they desired. The settlers actually fear them more than they fear the Sioux. I am not at all interested but tell you frankly what I have seen with my own eyes. I know Col what you are anxious to do and I speak thus frankly to you because I am acquainted with you and know that no one can be more disgusted with such soldiers than yourself. I know most often that it is difficult for you to get a true statement of these things. The officers and men of course will deny them but I tell you what I do know and what I can prove by a score of reliable men.*
>
>

Your Friend

HL Gordon[249]

Colonel Thomas could not ignore the letter. Hanford Lennox Gordon, the author, was a prominent attorney in Clearwater. Although only twenty-seven years old, Gordon was already a seasoned lawyer and had recently been appointed the Clearwater Postmaster. He was also a veteran, having volunteered to join the First Minnesota Infantry Regiment at the same time Minor Thomas joined in 1861. Gordon served as a private in Company D of the First Minnesota. It was during this stint in the army that Gordon likely became acquainted with the future Colonel Thomas, who then served as First Lieutenant in Company B.

Gordon's letter almost certainly refers to the Fair Haven squad of Company E. Some of the allegations in the letter were probably true. The men could be excused

---

249 Harvey S. Brookins to William Houlton, Aug. 14, 1863, Houlton Papers. Houlton served as Company E's clerk.

for breaking up the monotony of a patrol with some singing, target shooting and the exchange of good-natured banter, which onlookers might see as simply shouting. Edson Washburn recorded that the patrol was indeed shooting along the way, which had alarmed some of the nearby citizens.[250]

The most serious allegations in Gordon's letter, which would amount to burglary if substantiated, could have resulted in serious charges against the soldiers who participated in that patrol. However, the available information suggests that the charges made by Hanford Gordon were a combination of embellishments and second hand accounts.

The accused were all from the local area. Moreover, the squad included men who abhorred dishonesty and senseless destruction. Edson Washburn, for example, was deeply religious and proud that he kept his enlistment vow to never use intoxicating liquors or play cards.[251] Likewise, George Cambell later recalled that some men displayed dishonest behavior while the company was deployed in the East and South, which was a demoralizing influence, but that the dishonesty apparently ended with the war.[252]

With men such as Washburn and Cambell on patrol with the squad it is improbable that they and the other local boys would have tolerated burglary and vandalism, especially since the victims would have been their own friends and family.

There might be other motives behind Gordon's letter to Colonel Thomas. Perhaps he had an axe to grind with one or more members of the squad. It's also possible that he was simply jealous of the squad's freedom and relatively luxurious conditions of their assignment, especially considering that he himself had served with distinction.

Gordon's glorious moment came during the First Battle of Bull Run. It was during this battle that the First Minnesota established a strong reputation by being the last regiment to withdraw as the Confederates routed the Union Army, despite suffering heavy casualties. Among the wounded was then First Lieutenant Minor Thomas.

Gordon came through the battle unscathed, but not without a close call and a remarkable exploit. During the battle, Gordon was taken prisoner by the Rebels. However, he overpowered his guard, a sergeant of the Second Mississippi Rifles and returned to the Union lines with the sergeant, now Gordon's prisoner, in tow.[253]

---

250 Washburn, *Diaries*, July 29, 1863.

251 Washburn, *Autobiography*, 6. Wright County Historical Society.

252 Cambell, *Personal Reminiscences*, 74.

253 Mitchell, *History of Stearns County, Minnesota*, Vol. I, 538.

Despite his exploits at Bull Run, Gordon's Civil War service was short lived. He participated in several more skirmishes during 1861 and was slightly wounded. He was discharged for disability on December 1, 1861. The rigors of infantry life were apparently too great for his constitution.[254]

About the same time that he wrote the letter to Colonel Thomas, Gordon would have learned the fate of the First Minnesota at the Battle of Gettysburg earlier in July. During the First Minnesota's famous charge, nearly half of the men in Gordon's former company had been killed or wounded.

It may have grated on Gordon's conscience to learn of the deaths of so many former comrades while the men of Company E were having a grand old time running about in the relative comfort of the Minnesota countryside. Then again, it may have simply been his normal personality.

As an attorney, Gordon was described as a "fire-eater"[255] and earned the nickname of "Thunder Gordon."[256] He was known to be stubborn and inflexible. Perhaps he simply had a cranky disposition.[257]

One other possible explanation for Gordon's grudge with Company E was that he had tried to reenlist at the Monticello War Meeting in August 1862.[258] Based on his experience with the First Minnesota, Gordon may have hoped or even expected to be elected captain. However, it appears he was one of those rejected by the post surgeon, perhaps due to his prior disability.

Surprisingly, Gordon didn't mention any names in his letter to Colonel Minor. As the postmaster in Clearwater, he would have been personally acquainted with just about everyone in Company E, including most of the men in the Fair Haven squad.

---

254 Ibid.

255 Constance Oliver Skelton and John Malcolm Bulloch, *Gordons under Arms: A Biographical Muster Roll of Officers named Gordon in the Navies, and Armies of Britain, Europe, America and the Jacobite Uprisings*, Aberdeen, Aberdeen University, 1912, 484

256 Mitchell, *History of Stearns County, Minnesota*, Vol. I, 511.

257 Gordon appears to have had a significant ego, a difficult personality and the tendency to harbor grudges. He was married at least 3 times and divorced twice. A newspaper article published after his death claimed "He was an officer and organizer of the gallant First Minnesota regiment which made a magnificent charge at Round Top during the Civil War..." *Los Angeles Times*, November 13, 1920. However, he was discharged 18 months before the Battle of Gettysburg. Moreover, he was neither an organizer or an officer. He was also rather quirky when it came to his last wishes. It was reported that his instructions were that no professional funeral director be present at his services. He also dictated precise instructions for constructions of his casket and directed that nobody but his direct descendants be buried in the family plot, especially his son-in-law and two former wives. *Los Angeles Times*, November 19, 1920.

258 *The North-Western Weekly Union*, Aug. 23, 1862.

He certainly could have identified them to Colonel Thomas, but perhaps Charles Gordon chose not to when he related the events to Hanford.[259]

Colonel Thomas may have sensed that Gordon's allegations were only half-truths or secondhand reporting. Nevertheless, he had to at least see that the matter was investigated, and appropriate action taken. He delegated that task to Captain Brookins.

Captain Brookins was close to his men and certainly didn't want to get them in trouble with the regimental officers. At Brookins' direction, Sergeant Woodworth took his squad back out to Big Lake on August 10. There they found the men Washburn and the others had assisted with the hay work.

Those men provided the squad with written statements confirming that they had given the Company E men permission to enter their houses and get food. Word had probably reached H.L. Gordon that someone had seen the soldiers entering the empty houses. It is likely that Gordon assumed the soldiers were entering without permission, which prompted his complaint. Brookins forwarded the statements to Colonel Thomas, but it appears that nothing more came of the matter.[260]

The Lazy Days of Summer

By August, most of the men in Company E were having the time of their lives. William Houlton later recalled:

> Of our year at Paynesville I think every member of Company E must have many pleasant memories; with work and change enough to keep us occupied; with horses to go almost when and where we chose about the country; to a pleasant country with the people about us very grateful for friendly treatment; with game plenty and enough of the base of rations so that what [Pvt. Amiel] Philbrook said was sometimes literally true: that we had three kinds of pie for dinner - mince pie, pumpkin pie and hash; and our officers desirous after our work was well done that we should enjoy all else that we could.[261]

---

259 Curiously, Hanford Lennox Gordon remained close friends with Company E veteran Frank Parcher for the rest of his life. When Gordon died in Los Angeles on Armistice Day, Nov. 11, 1920, Parcher, who at the time lived in nearby Hollywood, was placed in charge of his funeral arrangements. *Los Angeles Times*, Nov. 19, 1920.

260 Brookins to Houlton, Aug. 14, 1863, Houlton Papers. Houlton was serving as company clerk. Brookins included the comment "I am afraid that Mr. H.L. Gordon may have a hard time in proving his statements." Also, Washburn made no further mention of the incident in his diaries.

261 Houlton, *Speech* at 6.

When their work was done, the men often left the fort to find entertainment. They largely had free reign with their spare time. A common destination for relaxation was the Frenchman's. In addition to selling whiskey, the establishment offered meals, company, and was just large enough to host the occasional dance. There may have been another factor drawing some of the soldiers towards the Frenchman's. Edson Washburn noted after his first visit to the Frenchman's "He has a very fine daughter."[262]

As it turned out, there were several attractive and eligible young women that drew the soldiers' attention. Lyman Reed and his wife Harriet lived with their children on a farm near the sod fort. Among the members of the family was the Reeds' twenty-two-year-old daughter, Francis.

Nancy Brown and her children, including twenty-two-year-old Alma, lived on a farm next door to the Reeds. Five men from Company E were especially enthusiastic about courting Francis Reed and Alma Brown. After roll call each evening, John Day, John Felch, and Levering Holgate, plus the brothers George and Daniel Kriedler, would go over the wall of the fort to visit the young ladies at the Browns and Reeds.[263]

William Houlton later recalled how the sod wall facing the Browns and Reeds "was worn down by the climbing in and out of members of the Company just to see that the ladies were safe, of course."[264] With so many suitors courting the limited number of local ladies the competition was fierce. Houlton was never sure whether they were going over the wall to kindly guard the ladies or were watching each other.[265]

Tragedy Strikes

It had been almost a year since the boys of Company E set forth from Monticello to enter army life. By July 1863, it had proven to be mostly an adventure with a lot of fun, good food and little hardship. It almost seemed that army life was too good to be true. That began to change quickly and tragically.

At the end of July, Corporal Charles Smith and his wife Erica both became seriously ill at Paynesville. The records do not show what illness they contracted, but typhoid fever was a likely culprit. The disease flourished in and around military camps during the Civil War.

---

262 Washburn, *Diaries*, May 16, 1863.

263 Houlton, *Speech*. Houlton identified the Kriedler brothers involved as "Kriedler two and Kriedler three." Samuel, the eldest Kriedler brother, was already married before enlisting so the two brothers mentioned by Houlton had to be Daniel and George.

264 Ibid.

265 Ibid.

Typhoid was a common and deadly disease. Unlike colds and flu, typhoid was not seasonal, as it was passed through contaminated food and water. As a result, the illness could strike any time of year. Large concentrations of men, such as those found in army camps, provided an ideal breeding ground for typhoid. The substandard hygiene and unsanitary conditions increased the likelihood that residents of the camps could be exposed. Similarly, typhus was endemic to army encampments, as rats were everywhere, and they spread disease-bearing fleas to the unsuspecting soldiers.

Both typhoid fever and typhus are caused by a bacterial infection. The symptoms were not for the squeamish. Victims might experience a high fever, which could often last for several days or even weeks, in addition to severe weakness, skin rash, stomach pains and other symptoms. After the fever had raged for a few days, the victim could become confused and delirious.

George Cambell may have been laid low by either typhoid or typhus at one point. He had been in the hospital for weeks with a fever during the previous winter at Fort Ripley. Reflecting on his time in the camp hospital, he wrote: "If one must have such things as fevers, camp was a better place than the field or on a march."[266]

If Cambell did in fact have one or the other of these miserable infections, he was lucky. Without antibiotics, there was not much doctors could do but let the disease run its course. The doctors could make the patient more comfortable, but death would visit more than half of those stricken with these diseases during the Civil War period.[267] Whatever the disease was that struck the Smiths at Paynesville, it was serious.

Erica Smith, like some of the other soldiers' wives, had joined her husband at Paynesville after Company E arrived. She and the other wives helped with the cooking and cleaning and became members of the Company E family.

Both Smiths suffered from their illness for a relatively long time, perhaps a couple of weeks. Then, Erica's condition rapidly deteriorated and she passed away on July 31, 1863.

News of Erica Smith's death spread rapidly through the ranks of Company E. John Ponsford learned of her demise while on the road back from an overnight patrol to Richmond, which was about eleven miles northeast of Paynesville.[268] Even though Edson Washburn was more than thirty miles away from Paynesville, he received the sad news on the same day when he returned to Clearwater after stacking hay for Gordon.[269]

266 Cambell, *Personal Reminiscences*, 12.

267 Mercy Street Article.

268 Ponsford, *Diary*, July 31, 1863.

269 Washburn, *Diaries*, July 31, 1863.

Immediately after her passing, Erica's body was sent to Monticello for burial. Charles remained deathly ill and was too weak to accompany his wife's remains home. Over the next several days Charles' friends sat by his side to console him and raise his spirits. John Ponsford and Frank Parcher visited him regularly when they were not on patrol. However, Charles' condition continued to worsen. On Sunday, August 9, Charles succumbed to his illness. As with his wife, Charles' body was transported back to his home at Monticello.

The deaths of Charles Smith and his wife cast a pall over Company E. The flag over the fort at Paynesville was lowered to half-staff in tribute. Many members of the company were excused from duty to attend the Smiths' funeral in Monticello. Life goes on, however. After the services, the men who attended spent time relaxing with a swim in the Mississippi. Soon after, they were back to their fun and games on patrol.

Later in August, John Ponsford would again have cause to grieve. He received a letter on August 28 with the news that his brother James had died of disease two weeks earlier in Dakota Territory. James was a private in Company D of the First Regiment of Minnesota Mounted Rangers, which was part of Sibley's Expedition.

James Ponsford and Andrew Moore, who died of wounds received in battle with the Sioux almost a month earlier, were buried outside Camp Arnold on August 15, 1863.[270] Camp Arnold was an overnight stop for Sibley's Expedition as it returned to Minnesota. The thought of his brother being buried in an isolated grave on the remote prairie must have been unsettling for John Ponsford.

Even the pranks and joking around eventually backfired in a horrible way. Combining the immature judgment of a young man with the deadly weapons of the army was a dangerous combination and led to yet another tragedy for Company E.

The Silver Creek squad of Company E included Christopher Baily and Andrew Bertram. Bailey and Bertram were close friends. They had known each other for several years, were the same age and had grown up together in Monticello. Therefore, it should come as no surprise that they managed to become part of the same squad.

Late in the afternoon of Tuesday, September 1, 1863, Bertram left the rented house where they were stationed and followed the path down to Silver Lake to get water. He quickly filled the bucket and started back to the house.

As he walked up the path, he heard what sounded like the growling and scratching sounds of a black bear moving through the brush a short distance away. Bertram rushed back and alerted the rest of the squad that a bear was just outside of the house. Five men grabbed their Springfield rifles and went out the door in pursuit.

---

270 The graves are now marked with headstones and are about three miles north of Oriska, North Dakota.

They were not afraid of bears. Rather, bear meat would make a welcome and delicious addition to their army rations.

Little did Bertram and the other squad members realize but the "bear" was actually one of their own. Christopher Bailey had earlier slipped into the woods to play a little prank on Bertram. It was he who was making the bear noises hoping to fool the squad into believing they had an easy hunt. It worked far too well. Bailey continued the charade as he moved around in the thick brush near the lake.

A black bear can move with surprising speed and the hunter has to be quick on the trigger. The hungry soldiers, looking forward to a fat bear steak, spread out around the dense brush where they believed the bear was hiding hoping to prevent its escape. As they started to move into position, a shot rang out.

It was Bertram. He had seen the dark mass of what he believed to be the bear and fired. Instantly there was as loud shriek as the large caliber bullet tore through Bailey's chest. He never had a chance. The wound was too extensive, and he died within minutes surrounded by the rest of his squad, who stood by helpless. There was nothing they could do for him.

This was a devastating shock to the squad. They were prepared for and could deal with the idea of death from disease or battle with the enemy. This, however, was something far different. An accidental death at the hands of a comrade and a longtime friend. If Baily's death was a shock to the squad, it certainly left Bertram devastated.

After the initial shock wore off, the squad sent a messenger to the nearby Company E post at Fair Haven. The rest of them took Bailey's body to Monticello. His family was understandably stricken with grief at the unexpected loss of their son and brother. They hastily arranged for a funeral, which was held the next day.

For Andrew Bertram, facing the family after killing their loved one, even accidentally, must have been terrifying. However, it does not appear that either the family or his fellow soldiers blamed him for Baily's tragic death.[271] Nevertheless, Bertram would forever bear the painful knowledge that he had killed one of his closest friends.

Sibley's Forces

There was great excitement among Company E in early September. General Sibley's forces were returning from their punitive expedition against the Sioux in Dakota Territory. They had made it as far north as Devil's Lake and then turned back to Minnesota by way of Fort Abercrombie.

---

271 Letter from Sgt. John Parvin reprinted in the *Mankato Weekly Union*, Sept. 11, 1863 at 2.

Contrary to General Pope's belief that the Sioux would either surrender or flee to the British possessions in Canada, the Indians chose to fight. Sibley's forces had participated in three battles against the Sioux during the summer. These took place at Big Mound, Dead Buffalo Lake and Stoney Lake. None were decisive nor did either side inflict any significant casualties on the other. Sibley's men, however, were able to destroy food, shelters and other supplies left behind as the Indians had fled their camps.

After chasing the Indians for more than two months, Sibley's supplies were running low, and his troops exhausted. Moreover, General Sully had failed to make the rendezvous as expected. With his troops tired and no sign of Sully, Sibley decided to return to Minnesota. On August 12, 1863, Sibley's forces set out for home.

General Sully's force had been delayed by low water on the Missouri River. Too late to participate in the battles with Sibley, Sully pursued some of the Indians that were still in the vicinity. This led to a large engagement at Whitestone Hill on September 3, 1863.

The Battle of Whitestone Hill resulted in much higher casualties for the Sioux than in the previous battles that summer. Up to 200 Indian men, women and children were killed or wounded. In contrast, Sully's forces suffered about twenty-two killed and thirty-eight wounded. Sully was also able to destroy all the supplies left behind in camp as the Indians fled.

There was one strategic blunder with the 1863 expedition against the Sioux. Few, if any of the Indians that were attacked had actually participated in the 1862 Uprising. Inkpaduta, who had led the Spirit Lake Massacre in 1857, was reportedly one of the Indian leaders involved in fighting against Sully and Sibley. While he was still a wanted man, Inkpaduta had nothing to do with the 1862 Uprising. The attacks against Sioux tribes that had not been at all responsible for the Minnesota Uprising did little more than turn them against the U.S. government. The resentment created by the expeditions would have repercussions the following year and far beyond that.

When the 1863 expeditions ended, the Sioux had been driven to the western side of the Missouri River. That was all Sibley and Sully were able to accomplish.

Some of Sibley's troops came back to Minnesota through Fort Abercrombie on their way to Fort Snelling. On September 4, Company E learned that the Tenth Minnesota Infantry Regiment had detached from Sibley's main force and was camped not far away. John Ponsford and a few others were able to get away that afternoon and pay a visit. There they listened to the returning soldiers' stories about the Dakota plains.

While they were visiting, the men traded for souvenirs. Among other things, the soldiers from the Tenth Minnesota brought back a number of buffalo horns. These must have seemed somewhat exotic to the men from Company E, and they managed to buy or barter for some of the horns.[272] The horns were especially prized by the men in Company E because they were perfect for making camp crafts, a popular pastime of the soldiers.

Two days later, eight men from Company E went out on a regular patrol to Richmond. Sibley's main force was camped near Richmond at the time. Upon reaching their objective, the Company E men dropped in to visit with the soldiers returning from Dakota Territory. They learned that Sibley's expedition was returning with Indian prisoners. Curious about their adversaries, the Company E men went to look at the prisoners. Among them was Wowinapa, Little Crow's son.

Wowinapa had initially fled when the Lampsons shot Little Crow in the field near Hutchinson. When the Lampsons left the scene, Wowinapa returned and tried to help his dying father. Little Crow, however, knew his fate. He told Wowinapa that he was dying and asked for water. He died shortly afterwards.

Wowinapa was devastated at the death of his father. He carefully laid out the body, placed a new pair of moccasins on Little Crow's feet and neatly folded the jacket that Hinkpa had given him a few days earlier after killing the previous owner. Wowinapa then took their guns and ammunition and started out alone for Devil's Lake in Dakota Territory.[273]

Almost a month later, a detachment from Sibley's expedition came across Wowinapa. He had nearly starved to death on the trip to Devil's Lake and was almost completely naked. The soldiers took Wowinapa into custody and brought him back to Minnesota.

Ambush Death of Sergeant Edwards

The risk of Indian attack had substantially diminished following the death of Little Crow. Only a few hostile Indians remained on the loose within Minnesota. Nevertheless, a chance encounter with some of these Indians would mean another casualty for the Eighth Minnesota.

On September 11, 1863, Captain Marcus Q. Butterfield, who had taken over Company A after Captain Cady was killed in a fight with Indians three months earlier, set out from Paynesville for Mannanah on horseback in the company of Sergeant William Edwards and a cavalryman who was tagging along.[274] They had spent the

272 Ponsford, Diary, Sept. 7, 1863.

273 Folwell, A History of Minnesota, 285.

274 Seelye, "Early Military Experiences in Dakota," 242. Seelye from Company A later wrote the third member of the party was a cavalryman, but did not further identify him. He may have been a member of the Second Minnesota Cavalry, which was also patrolling the area.

night with the Company E garrison in Paynesville as they returned to Mannanah from a visit to the Company A squad stationed at Kingston.

A squad from Company E was scheduled to make a regular patrol to Mannanah that day but it was cancelled because Butterfield would cover the same road. Butterfield, Edwards, and the cavalryman set out for Mannanah mid-morning.

They had not gone far, only about five miles from Paynesville, when they were suddenly ambushed by Indians firing from cover along the roadside. The Indians were so close when they fired that Butterfield always maintained he would never forget their faces.[275]

Edwards was shot from his horse and a bullet pierced Butterfield's uniform. The cavalryman fled immediately when the shooting started.[276] Under fire from the Indians, Butterfield was unable to retrieve Edwards and rode off to get help from Company E.[277]

Butterfield rode into the fort at Paynesville about noon and sounded the alarm. Lieutenant Thomas Tollington quickly assembled as many of the Company E soldiers as they could equip with horses. This amounted to seventeen men. The Company E squad then rushed to the scene of the shooting. "We went in pursuit as soon as we learned of it, but not soon enough to prevent them from scalping him [Edwards] beside mangling him in a horrid manner" recalled John Ponsford, one of the Company E squad.[278]

Lieutenant Tollington led his men on the trail of the Indians. The soldiers followed the Indians for many miles until they lost all sign of them. The Company E squad then turned around and returned to Paynesville with the body of Sergeant Edwards.

A Company E patrol set out from Paynesville the following day, but they found no further sign of the Indians. After returning to the sod fort, a few of the men solemnly loaded Sergeant Edwards' body into a wagon for the trip back to his home at Champlin, just across the Mississippi River from Anoka.

Edson Washburn and Frank Clifford were just entering Paynesville when they met the wagon that bore Edwards' body. The two were returning from St. Cloud with

275 Ibid., 243. Butterfield would later claim that the Indians involved were the wanted Sioux chiefs Little Six and Medicine Bottle, who had fled to Canada after the 1862 uprising. The two chiefs were drugged and smuggled out of Canada in early 1864 and taken to Fort Snelling for trial. Butterfield visited the fort and recognized them. Little Six and Medicine Bottle were hanged at Fort Snelling on November 11, 1864 after being convicted of atrocities committed during the opening days of the Sioux Uprising.

276 Ibid.

277 *St. Cloud Democrat*, Sept. 17, 1863. Reprint of report from Captain Butterfield to Col. M.T. Thomas dated Sept. 12, 1863.

278 Ponsford, *Diary*, Sept. 11, 1863 and memorandum.

a wagon full of grain for the company's horses. The sight of Edwards' body shocked Washburn. "We meet the corpse of Sgt. Edwards killed by the Indians 4 miles from Paynesville. He was terribly mutilated and scalped, blouse taken and pants leg also. Oh so sad."[279]

---

279 Washburn, *Diaries*, Sept. 12, 1863.

Paynesville Winter Quarters

October 1, 1863, to May 24, 1864

Company E Consolidates

By the beginning of October, the weather began turning cold and snow flurries served as a reminder that winter was not far off. The return of cold weather had one benefit, it would become more difficult for Indian raiders to move around without shelter or food. Thus, the risk of Indian attacks would rapidly diminish.

On October 1, 1863, the Company E squads stationed at Fair Haven and Silver Lake were ordered back to Paynesville for the winter. From Paynesville the company would continue to patrol the area, although not as frequently as during the summer.

One order of business that the company had to address was the reorganization of the non-commissioned officers. Sergeant John Parvin asked to be demoted to private. At forty-one years of age, Parvin may have realized that he was not physically up to the job. In any event, the company had to elect a replacement for him and for two corporals.

The election was held on Thursday, October 8. Timothy Desmond was elected sergeant. Desmond, the son of Irish immigrants, had been a lumberman in Maine before moving to Minnesota with his parents in 1856. At nearly six feet in height and strong from his lumbering days, Desmond made an imposing figure as sergeant.

The company also elected two new corporals. One was David Lansing Kingsbury. Kingsbury was originally from Michigan, where he was raised by his aunt. When his aunt's family moved to Minnesota in 1854, twelve-year-old David went with them. Now, at twenty years old, Kingsbury was educated, intelligent, and a natural leader. The other corporal elected that day was thirty-five-year-old James Ambler, a farmer from Buffalo in Wright County.

Company E continued to make patrols between Paynesville and nearby towns, including Richmond, Mannanah, Cold Spring, and Lake George. On October 9, 1863, during one of these routine patrols, the company nearly experienced another tragedy.

Milt Brown, a twenty-one-year-old private, was examining his pistol while riding back from a patrol to Richmond with his squad. As he did so, the pistol accidentally discharged, sending the bullet through Brown's head. The wound, however, was not fatal. In fact, Brown was not even in much pain.[280] He was lucky. It took two days for the doctor to arrive from St. Cloud after being summoned by the company. Despite the lack of prompt medical attention, he still survived. Moreover, it appears that Brown recovered completely. The army records show he was discharged with the rest of the company in 1865.

As Company E consolidated at Paynesville, they quickly became bored. At the outposts they were constantly on the move and often managed to arrange patrols so they could visit their homes. The soldiers also had an active social life with the locals. Edson Washburn was a favorite of the residents around Fair Haven. The local ladies often invited him to stop by for afternoon tea.

The outpost at Fair Haven was so close to Clearwater, Silver Lake, and Monticello that the soldiers would invite the young ladies of those towns to visit for the day. The soldiers enjoyed cooking for their friends. "After supper there might be a dance and we would see them home, all escort duty, of course" recalled George Cambell. George's girlfriend, Martha Whittemore, and a couple of her sisters were almost certainly among the visitors for these events.

All those activities ended when the company consolidated at Paynesville. Edson Washburn lamented "It's rather dull around here now. It's not like Fair Haven."[281] The soldiers noted the dullness of garrison duty. Washburn recorded that "Nothing worthy of note transpires. Nothing to dictate. The dull monotony of garrison life."[282]

---

280 Ponsford, *Diary*, Oct. 10, 1863.

281 Washburn, *Diaries*, Oct. 10, 1863.

282 Ibid., Oct. 12, 1863.

John Ponsford made a similar observation: "Well another dreary day has rolled into eternity and nothing will immortalize that it happened at Paynesville."[283]

The Daily Routine

Soldiering quickly fell into a regular routine at the Paynesville fort. It began every morning with roll call at 6 a.m. Days grow short in Minnesota during the autumn. By the winter solstice the sky would not begin to lighten until about 7:30 a.m and darkness fell again by 5 p.m. In 1863 there was no artificial outdoor lighting. It would have been so dark most mornings that the men would not have recognized someone standing a couple feet away.

Nevertheless, the soldiers had to turn out at roll call every morning. George Cambell described the routine:

> We all had to get out in the middle of the square formed by the quarters. It would have been amusing if there had been any light, to see the shape in which the men would turn out – wrapped in blankets or partly dressed – answer to their names and, when dismissed, go back to bed again.[284]

After getting a little more time in the bunk and grabbing a quick breakfast, the soldiers would form up at 9 a.m. for two hours of drill as a company. After lunch, it was common to have another drill as a battalion, where they would practice coordinating tactics in a larger group consisting of one or more other companies.

Another common part of the training was a dress parade. These assemblies took place intermittently, sometimes for several days in a row and sometimes only once a week. At the dress parade, all general orders were read, with charges, specifications, and findings of courts martial, etc.[285]

The winter of 1863 to 1864 was unusually cold, even by Minnesota standards. At times, the sub-zero temperatures created serious risk of frostbite for the soldiers, even in their heavy outdoor gear. As a result, drill was often limited to once per day. It sometimes got so cold that Company E was forced to conduct its training indoors. A nearby granary was large enough to accommodate the company for this purpose, but it was certainly not big enough to allow any maneuvering.

---

283 Ponsford, *Diary*, Oct. 13, 1863.

284 Cambell, *Personal Reminiscences*, 18.

285 Billings, *Hardtack and Coffee*, 188.

It takes a lot of wood to heat a drafty barracks in sub-zero weather. During the worst of the cold spell the soldiers spent the afternoons gathering firewood for their quarters rather than drill. The frigid temperatures, however, failed to numb their sense of humor.

One winter day, when the temperature had dropped to forty below zero, George Cambell was placed on "wood police." That duty made him responsible for gathering firewood for the Company E quarters that day. He would go out, cut the necessary wood, and bring it back to the barracks.

Every time he brought in a load of firewood, he found the men sitting around the stove, staying warm while quietly playing cards, mending clothes, or performing other menial tasks. With each trip, Cambell would refill the wood box and then go back out into the cold to gather another load. It was so cold that the wood box was nearly empty by the time he returned. Cambell noticed they were going through an unusual amount of wood but attributed it to the sub-zero temperatures.[286]

The next day was Charley Gibbs' turn on wood police. However, he had a much easier time of it than did Cambell. The previous day, Gibbs had been surreptitiously taking firewood from the wood box and hiding it in a small cellar beneath their quarters. Whenever Cambell went out for another load, Gibbs would clean out the wood box and stash the firewood in his hiding place. Much to Cambell's chagrin, Gibbs was able to fish enough wood out of the cellar during his turn on wood police to keep the barracks warm without having to go outside all day.[287]

Free Time

Just as they had the previous winter at Fort Ripley, the men all seemed to enjoy going out hunting. It gave them a chance to leave the fort, enjoy the countryside and sharpen their shooting skills all at the same time. Best yet, they continued to supplement their army rations with tasty venison, duck, and even an occasional elk.

There were still abandoned pigs and other types of livestock running wild. The men hunted them whenever they could. All things considered, the plentiful wild game and feral livestock allowed Company E to eat rather well during the long winter at Paynesville.

Perhaps out of boredom, to supplement their income, or both, some of the men began another pursuit in their spare time - fur trapping. The area around Paynesville

---

286 Cambell, *Personal Reminiscences*, 114.

287 Ibid. Cambell appears to have taken the joke in good stride. He and Gibbs would remain lifelong friends and eventually become brothers-in-law.

made an ideal habitat for many furbearing animals. It was nearing prime time of year when the animals' fur would be the thickest.

Many of the soldiers obtained traps, either purchasing them locally in Paynesville, or sending for traps from their families at home. The men initially had great success as trappers. Private Lewis Chaffin even managed to catch a mink. Edson Washburn, who was too busy cooking for the company to worry about outside pursuits, recorded that "Company E making a fortune at trapping."[288]

Crafts were also a common pastime in any army camp. Soldiers throughout the army often used their spare time to make various trinkets, often in commemoration of their unit or events during their time in the service. The soldiers would fashion their pieces of camp folk art out of whatever materials were available, including scrap metal, wood, bone, and antlers.

A particularly popular craft with the soldiers throughout the army was making rings. They would fashion the rings out of dried livestock horns, hooves, or bones. Sometimes large buttons would be used and worked into the rings.[289] The rings were often engraved with the soldier's name, regiment, and company.

Company E was soon engulfed in the ring-making fad sweeping the army. It began in September, shortly before the company concentrated at Paynesville. While visiting the Tenth Minnesota on September 7, members of Company E obtained buffalo horns from soldiers who had picked them up while in Dakota Territory on Sibley's Expedition.[290]

Soon, several soldiers from Company E began crafting rings out of the buffalo horns. Other soldiers saw the resulting rings and decided to try making their own. Soon, it seemed like all the Company E soldiers were engaged in making rings for themselves or that they could use to sell or to barter. Edson Washburn described the situation as "ring fever."[291]

Private Washburn got in on the fun along with everyone else. Between September 1863 and the end of April 1864, Washburn manufactured at least a dozen rings and probably many more.[292] Even as late as April 1864, Edson Washburn stated

288 Washburn, *Diaries*, Oct. 14, 1863.

289 Billings, *Hardtack & Coffee*, 67.

290 Ponsford, *Diary*, Sept. 7, 1863.

291 Washburn, *Diaries*, Oct. 17, 1863. Rings made from buffalo horns are still popular. A wide variety are available on Amazon, eBay and other electronic commerce sites.

292 Edson Washburn's diary recorded many of his ring-making activities during the seven-month period beginning in September 1863. However, he probably didn't record anywhere near all of the rings he crafted as it had become routine. He noted in his diary entry for April 11, 1864 that he made a ring "as usual," suggesting he was making them on a regular basis.

that "Rings are all the rage now."[293] The ring-making fad didn't die out until the soldiers received orders to join Sully's Expedition in May 1864.

However, dancing remained perhaps the most popular pastime for the soldiers of Company E. They had dances whenever they could round up a couple of violinists. Sam Kriedler frequently filled this role, but sometimes the men had to recruit musicians from other sources.

The only problem was that the soldiers rarely had any member of the opposite sex with whom to dance. As they had done the previous winter at Fort Ripley, the soldiers improvised. "The smallest and best-looking soldiers had to represent the ladies; and, to distinguish them from the others, had to take off their hats and were expected to be more polite."[294]

There were times, however, when dancing with other men just wasn't good enough. On January 22, 1864, Company E began to plan for a big dance and do it right. The next day, Sergeant Timothy Desmond was dispatched to round up some young ladies at Monticello and bring them back for the big event, which would be held on Tuesday, January 26. David Kingsbury accompanied Desmond to assist with his objective.

Lieutenant Tollington took Ellet Parcher and set out for Clearwater with a similar mission. Other soldiers were sent to visit Company B, which was stationed at Sauk Centre, to recruit more musicians for the upcoming dance.

Kingsbury returned from Monticello without any young ladies for the dance. Desmond stayed behind in Monticello to continue the recruiting effort. Tollington and Ellet Parcher didn't do much better at Clearwater. The only woman they managed to find who was willing to accompany them to the dance was Lieutenant Tollington's wife.

By the morning of the big dance, it appeared that the only women who would be in attendance were a few of the soldiers' wives. In a last-ditch effort, a recruiting party was sent to Mannanah.

Much to the relief of the company, Tim Desmond arrived from Monticello, bringing with him four patriotic ladies who were eager to dance with the soldiers. Shortly thereafter, the Mannanah party returned with five more young women.

Between the wives and visitors, Company E managed to put on quite a party. "They have a joyful old breakdown in the evening" recorded Edson Washburn.[295] The following day, the musicians from Company B returned to Sauk Centre and the girls

---

293 Washburn, *Diaries*, April 7, 1864.

294 Cambell, *Personal Reminiscences*, 17.

295 Washburn, *Diaries*, Jan. 26, 1864.

from Mannanah went back home. They left behind a lot of happy soldiers who were thrilled to have some real female dance partners.

Many of the Paynesville residents were happy to make room for the soldiers' out-of-town visitors so there were plenty of places for the young ladies from Monticello to lodge. As a result, several of them stayed at the fort for a few more days. The soldiers entertained them by sleighing, more dances and seeing a fortune teller at the Frenchman's. It wasn't until February 3 that the ladies returned to Monticello. Dan Desmond, Russell Wedgewood and Amiel Philbrook escorted them as far as Forest City.[296]

Several of the soldiers had not given up their attempts to court Francis Reed and Alma Brown. Many evenings throughout the winter, men snuck out over the wall to pay them a visit. Usually, they all met at the Reeds.

The Reed home seemed to be a central gathering spot for any time of day. John Ponsford noted that he spent a morning at the Reed house and "Played euchre most of the time."[297] In the evenings, the soldiers would play cards, engage in polite conversation with the families, and participate in other proper social activities until the older folks went to bed. After that, the young men and ladies could quietly sit together for a while longer and gaze into the fire.[298]

It appears that the men did not engage in any hanky-panky with the Brown and Reed daughters. They generally were on their best behavior. It is doubtful that any of the soldiers would be left alone with the young women. If the parents were not present, the other soldiers would be there to prevent any of their competing suitors from gaining an advantage.

People generally paid close attention to social norms of the time. Any pre-marital sexual activity was strongly discouraged. It still happened of course. Edson Washburn received a letter from home with local news and noted that "Mr. Snow has a son born four months from the time he was married. Fast young man."[299]

Often, other soldiers would tag along on visits to the Reeds just to break the monotony of winter in the fort. Edson Washburn recorded that life in the fort was "Dull dull dull, I wish I could see someone that would sharpen me up a little."[300]

Washburn sometimes joined gatherings at the Reeds as a diversion from the normal boredom. Washburn had no romantic interest in Francis or Alma, he already

296 Washburn, *Diaries*, Feb. 3, 1864.

297 Ponsford, *Diary*, Sept. 23, 1863.

298 Bertram, *Reminiscences*, Dec. 7, 1878, MNHS.

299 Washburn, *Diaries*, Jan. 1864.

300 Ibid., Jan. 9, 1864.

had his heart set on Amelia Wells, but he enjoyed a welcome opportunity to socialize outside the usual routine of camp life.

Alas, it all suddenly came to an end. One evening the soldiers went to Francis Reed's home as usual, only to receive an icy reception from her father. He told them not to come over anymore and sent them away. Later that night, the stunned and disappointed soldiers discovered that someone had told Lyman Reed that the soldiers had been seen drunk.[301]

With all the men confined to the fort in Paynesville during those long cold Minnesota winter nights, they had a little too much idle time on their hands. The usual suspects stayed busy with a steady stream of pranks and practical jokes. Some were harmless and others downright dangerous.

The barracks chimney was a tempting target of some pranks. All that was required was for the jokester to climb onto the roof and place a board over the top of the chimney. The smoke would quickly back up and fill the barracks, causing the men to dash outside for fresh air.

In a more dangerous version of the stunt, someone would climb up on the roof and drop a handful of rifle cartridges down the chimney. The gunpowder in the cartridges would explode the moment they hit the hot coals, instantly filling the barracks with thick gun smoke and perhaps sending a few bullets bouncing out of the stove.[302]

Departures from Company E

Nearly all of the men who enlisted as privates in August 1862 remained with Company E throughout the war. There were some exceptions. Two of the original officers, Edward Hartley and Micah Croswell resigned and left the company the previous winter after the men lost confidence in their abilities. Edward Hartley's brother John also left the company on January 1, 1863, but this departure was for a promotion. He was tapped to serve as the Eighth Minnesota's sergeant major for the rest of the war.

By the fall of 1863, only one other man, private George Tourtellotte, had transferred out of Company E. He left the company to join the newly formed Third Min-

301 Bertram, *Reminiscences*, Dec. 7, 1878, MNHS.

302 Cambell, *Personal Reminiscences*, 17. The gunpowder was not confined within the paper cartridges as it would be with modern brass shells. As a result, the powder in the cartridge would flash more than actually explode. The cooked off cartridges would still make a bang and send bullets bouncing around, but without enough force to do any real damage. Still, burning the gunpowder in use at the time of the Civil War would have generated huge amounts of smoke and created pandemonium in the barracks.

nesota Battery earlier in the year. Several other men from different Eighth Minnesota companies also transferred to the Third Minnesota Battery at about the same time.

As 1863 was drawing to a close, two other enlisted men decided to leave Company E for new opportunities in other units. Sergeant James Bradley and corporal Emerson Woodward both demonstrated leadership ability and probably felt under-employed as non-commissioned officers.

Prior to the war, Sergeant Bradley had been a lawyer. He originally settled at Monticello in 1857 but moved to Minneapolis a couple years later. He enlisted as a private to be with friends from his former abode. Bradley may have felt rejected in some way by Company E. In June, he was nominated for the position of second lieutenant along with Charles Post. Company E elected Post by a narrow margin of only three votes.[303]

Corporal Woodward was also well-educated. Until he enlisted, Woodward had been a schoolteacher living in Richfield,[304] which abutted Minneapolis. He was on good terms with the rest of the company but aspired to a rank higher than corporal.

In the fall of 1863, the army was in the process of forming several regiments of African-American troops. These were made up of free blacks and escaped slaves. The army wanted white officers to command regiments in the U.S. Colored Troops. The regular army officer corps generally looked down on service with the African-American regiments, leaving the army in need of officers for these units.

To find officers for the U.S. Colored Troops, the army began interviewing non-commissioned officers and even privates from volunteer units. Those selected would be quickly promoted to the appropriate rank.

Both Bradley and Woodward decided to seek commissions as officers in the U.S. Colored Troops. On October 27, 1863, the two were permitted to leave for St. Louis, Missouri, where they were interviewed for promotion. Bradley and Woodward did well in their examinations for they were both eventually promoted to captain.

Late in December 1863, newly-promoted Captain James F. Bradley took over as commander of Company F, 102nd Regiment, U.S. Colored Infantry. At the same time, Captain Emerson Woodard assumed command of Company E, 62nd Regiment, U.S. Colored Infantry.

---

303   Ponsford, *Diary*, June 6, 1863.

304   At the time of the Civil War, Richfield covered a much larger territory than it does today. It extended west from the Mississippi River about ten miles and north from Fort Snelling to what is now Lake Street in Minneapolis. It covered large portions of what later became Edina, Hopkins and St. Louis Park. Beginning in 1867, the City of Minneapolis began to annex portions of Richfield. The last annexation took place in 1927, and took the land between Highway 62 north to 54th Street. Today, the City of Richfield is barely one tenth of its former size.

Other Events

There are bad apples in every barrel and Company E was no exception. Some of the men committed acts that winter that resulted in court martial or some other form of military discipline. One of the worst occurred as the village of Paynesville was rebuilding some of the structures burned by the Indians in 1862.

On Friday, November 13, 1863, the citizens of Paynesville banded together and raised a new schoolhouse. The building was quickly finished. Within a month it was already being used for classes as well as for church services on Sundays. Edson Washburn attended religious services there on December 13.[305]

After a dance on the evening of December 17, one or more soldiers broke into the new schoolhouse and vandalized the place. The culprits tore up some books, stole others and stole some of the writing slates.[306] The stolen goods were found in Company E's quarters. The next day, Albert Erath was arrested for being drunk and disorderly.[307] In the course of the arrest it was determined that he had been responsible for the break-in at the schoolhouse. He was then charged for that the schoolhouse crime and thrown into the guardhouse to await trial by court martial.

The use of a court martial was not limited to crimes like burglary. Earlier in December, Joseph Fisher had refused to take his turn at guard duty, after which he was arrested. He remained confined in the guardhouse pending trial.

As the courts martial for Erath and Fisher were pending, the company almost experienced another tragedy. On Saturday, December 19, 1863, Captain Brookins, Lieutenant Post, and Private Hulett were scheduled to travel by sleigh to Richmond. There, they planned to buy books to replace those torn up in the schoolhouse incident. As they started to leave, the horses went out of control. In the ensuing chaos, Brookins was thrown from the sleigh and badly injured.

Brookins was carefully carried to his bed and the doctor summoned. The doctor arrived at midnight and attended to his injuries. Brookins eventually made a full recovery. However, it took a while. By early January 1864, the captain was moving about with a crutch. It took until a month after the accident, however, before Brookins was again able to venture out from Paynesville.

At about the same time Brookins was hurt, officers from other companies arrived for the pending courts martial. On December 21, Joseph Fisher was tried and convicted for refusing an order to stand guard. A week later, his sentence was read during the dress

---

305 Washburn, *Diaries*, Dec. 13, 1863.

306 Washburn, *Diaries*, Dec. 17, 1863. The slates were small chalkboards used as writing tablets by the pupils instead of paper.

307 Ponsford, *Diary*, Dec. 18, 1863.

parade, twenty days' hard labor cutting wood and a fine of $6.50.[308] The fine may seem small by modern standards, but it amounted to half a month's pay, a not insubstantial sum.

Albert Erath avoided trial by admitting his guilt in the schoolhouse break-in and was released from the guardhouse with an undisclosed penalty. He returned to duty and even received a coveted furlough for a short trip home at the end of January.

Furloughs were much sought after by the men in Company E. They did receive occasional visits from their friends and family, but it wasn't the same as being home. As the Christmas holiday approached, many of the young men grew homesick.

Furloughs were handed out to fifteen men at a time. The lucky recipients were allowed to go home for fifteen days. Married men were generally given a preference, but sometimes others got to go as well. On December 23, for example, Lieutenant Tollington, along with Charley Gibbs and Charley Vorse all received a furlough and the three set out together for their homes in Clearwater.[309] Of the three, only Tollington was married.

George Cambell didn't receive a furlough right away and was growing anxious. He finally went to the officer responsible and asked for one. The officer asked Cambell if he was married. Cambell recalled "I had to confess I was not, but wished to go home and make the necessary preparations."[310] He received his furlough. Presumably, he followed through with the engagement. Cambell and Martha Whittemore were married not long after he returned from the war.

Just before Christmas 1863, Company E received a nice gift from the ladies of Monticello. They had created a beautiful flag for the company.[311] Company E proudly displayed that flag throughout their service during the final year-and-a-half of the war. By the time Company E returned their homes in the summer of 1865, that flag had traveled several thousand miles.

As winter wore on, the men continued to drill, practice skirmishing tactics, and find fun ways to occupy their spare time. Riding was a popular activity. It was not only good practice in case the company was assigned to become mounted infantry, but also provided an opportunity to court the local young ladies.

Like sleighing, riding could be dangerous. John Louisiana took Gina Brown out for a ride late in February. As they were riding, Gina was thrown from her horse and dislocated her shoulder. [312]

---

308 Washburn, *Diaries*, Dec. 28, 1863. *See also*, Ponsford *Diary*, Dec. 28, 1863. It was Ponsford who recorded that the hard labor consisted of wood cutting.

309 Ponsford, *Diary*, Dec. 23, 1863,

310 Cambell, *Personal Reminiscences*, 18.

311 No photos of the Company E flag are known to exist.

312 Washburn, *Diaries*, Feb. 25, 1864.

While the soldiers mostly enjoyed their winter at Paynesville, preparations were underway for a new assignment. Various rumors had the Eighth Minnesota going south to fight the rebels or west to deal with the Sioux. Either way, the company had to be ready.

Over the previous year-and-a-half, the company had lost several men to resignation, transfer, or death. Some of the others who enlisted in 1862 were either too old or found to have ailments that limited their ability to endure the rigors of combat. Before going off to fight, Company E needed more men.

New Recruits

During February and March of 1864, the officers of Company E worked to increase the unit's strength in preparation for the expected deployment of the Eighth Minnesota. Captain Brookins made some recruiting trips to St. Cloud and other locations. His goal was to seek volunteers from among the ranks of veterans who were discharged when their term of enlistment expired.

Brookins managed to recruit seven veterans who had previously served in the First Regiment of Minnesota Mounted Rangers. The Mounted Rangers had been hastily formed in November and December of 1862 in response to the lessons learned about the limitations of infantry in an offensive war against the Indians:

> Infantry could only fight Indians when Indians chose to make the attack. When they chose to get out of the way there was no difficulty in doing so. Infantry could not patrol the long line of frontier, and were necessarily confined to the various stockades and garrisons.[313]

After the Battle of Wood Lake had at least temporarily secured the Minnesota frontier, the War Department authorized a regiment of mounted soldiers who would be armed with long-range rifles so they could engage against all types of Indian warfare.[314] Thus, the First Regiment of Minnesota Mounted Rangers was formed.

The Mounted Rangers included many men whose families had been killed during the early days of the Uprising in 1862. They had enlisted to serve for one year. During that time, the unit participated in Sibley's 1863 expedition against the Sioux in Dakota Territory. The men gained valuable experience on that expedition. Nevertheless, they were all mustered out by the end of 1863 when their term of enlistment was up.

313 *Minnesota in the Civil and Indian Wars: 1861-1865*, vol. 1, 519-520.

314 Ibid.

Some of the First Minnesota Mounted Ranger veterans were happy to re-enlist in Company E. These veteran volunteers received large bounties for signing up again because their experience was valuable to the army. The veteran volunteers from the Mounted Rangers were Henry P. Clark, Charles H. Keator, John Moore, John Morgan, Samuel Morgan, Samuel Murray, and Isaac Parks.

Company E also picked up ten other recruits. One of them was Joseph Reed from Paynesville, who enlisted in March 1864. Reed had met many of the men from Company E when they came calling on his sister at the family home in Paynesville. By the spring of 1864, Reed was old enough to enlist and he did so to serve among the men he already knew.

Two brothers of Company E soldiers also enlisted during March. Twenty-three-year-old William Ponsford, John Ponsford's older brother, and James Lyons, John Lyons' brother, arrived at Paynesville together on March 18, 1864. At just seventeen years old, James Lyons was the youngest member to serve in Company E.

The other recruits in the spring of 1864 included James Young, Edwin Persons, James Gates, William Stinchfield, and John Thompson, all from St. Cloud. In all, Company E gained fourteen new members in February and March of 1864. It is a good thing that several of them had military experience, for they did not have long to train before the regiment would start west to Dakota Territory.

Spring at Paynesville

Rumors had been circulating since the beginning of 1864 that the Eighth Minnesota would be sent west across the plains in pursuit of the Sioux. Sibley's expedition against the Sioux in 1863 had been far from decisive. In fact, the Eighth Minnesota suffered more casualties at the hands of the Indians while defending central Minnesota than did Sibley's expedition into Dakota Territory.

As the spring of 1864 approached, there was real concern among politicians and the military that the remaining Sioux would continue a guerrilla war along the Minnesota frontier. Furthermore, the Sioux in Dakota Territory that had not participated in the Uprising remained a perceived threat. Until the matter was resolved it would be difficult to convince settlers to return to Minnesota.

General Pope made the decision to finish what had been started the previous year. He ordered a new expedition against the Sioux in Dakota Territory. The goal was to drive the Sioux onto reservations and build a series of forts across the territory to maintain the peace.[315] This time, however, General Sibley would stay home. The 1864 effort would be solely under the command of General Alfred Sully.

---

315 *See,* Historical Society of North Dakota, Fort Rice State Historical Site, https://www.history.nd.gov/historicsites/rice/index.html, accessed June 13, 2020.

Despite the uncertainty as to their future movements, life carried on for Company E. They continued to drill, practice skirmishing, and conduct all the other monotonous chores of camp life. Riding horses was a welcome diversion. It not only gave the men more experience, but it was a chance to get out of camp for hunting or the occasional patrol.

Riding could be hazardous for both men and horses, especially in the unsettled weather of a Minnesota spring. Horses like those used by the military were not very hardy creatures. They could die easily from any number of causes. On March 31, for example, Tom Dill was out riding when the horse slipped and broke its leg. Dill had to shoot the animal to put it out of its misery. A month later, Dill's new horse died as well.[316]

It wasn't just the horses that paid the price. On May 13, Henry Crawford managed to fall off his horse. Like Gina Brown a few weeks earlier, he dislocated his arm. He recovered quickly from his injury and would later be able to serve with Company E during the excursion into Dakota Territory.[317]

At the end of April, orders finally arrived to confirm that the Eighth Minnesota would join "The Northwestern Indian Expedition," as the endeavor was formally known. However, it became known to history as "Sully's Expedition."[318]

On April 27, 1864, General Sibley wrote to Colonel Thomas and ordered him to consolidate the Eighth Minnesota at Sauk Centre.[319] The regiment would arrive piecemeal as each of their various garrisons from Fort Abercrombie to Princeton were relieved by other troops. The consolidation at Sauk Centre would be the first time the Eighth Minnesota had served as one unit since it was formed.

The entire regiment would participate in the new expedition. Only a small group of men would remain behind. Sibley ordered Thomas to leave a detachment of twenty-five to thirty men in garrison at Sauk Centre. Those men who were physically unfit for active duty in the field would be assigned to Fort Ripley.[320]

Before the trip to Sauk Centre, however, Company E arranged one last party with their family and friends. On Friday, May 6, several young ladies from Silver Creek and Monticello arrived at Paynesville. The soldiers' parents also arrived to send their children off to Dakota Territory.

---

316 Washburn, *Diaries*, March 31 and May 3, 1864.

317 Ibid., May 13, 1864.

318 David Lansing Kingsbury, "Sully's Expedition Against the Sioux In 1864," *Minnesota Historical Society Collections*, Volume Eight, St. Paul, 1898, 449.

319 Olin to Thomas, April 27, 1864, *Official Records*, series 1, vol. 34, part 3, 314-315.

320 Ibid.

The guests went home on May 10 and Company E went to work on the final preparations for their departure from Paynesville. Finally, on May 16, Company E left Paynesville and marched to Sauk Centre. There were already four other companies awaiting their arrival. Company E set up camp and waited for further orders.

The regiment received a delivery of ponies[321] the following day, along with all the equipment necessary to turn the Eighth Minnesota into mounted infantry. Company F also arrived at Sauk Centre with a herd of Canadian ponies they had procured at Fort Snelling. Over the next few days, the men were issued their horses, saddles, and other cavalry equipment.

Most of the men were pleased with the quality of the horses they received. Andrew Bertram, not so much. He later said to call them "horses" was an insult to horses. He described them as "Mere apologies of gristle, hide and bone."[322]

As the Eighth Minnesota was still gathering, the commanders began organizing the unit. The different companies were grouped together into battalions for maneuvering in the field.

On Saturday, May 21, the Eighth Minnesota set out for the trip to Fort Ridgely, where they would meet up with elements of the Third Minnesota Battery and the Second Minnesota Cavalry. These units, along with Brackett's Battalion of cavalry would form the Minnesota Brigade of the Northwest Indian Expedition.

The Eighth Minnesota first traveled to Paynesville, arriving early in the afternoon of May 22. They stayed in Paynesville for three more days, where they were joined by Companies A, C and D.[323] For the first time since the regiment was formed in 1862, all ten companies of the Eighth Minnesota were together in the same place. They would remain united as a regiment for the rest of the war.

Early in the morning of May 25, the regiment awoke and prepared for the day's march. For Company E it was a bittersweet moment. The men had mostly enjoyed the last year stationed in Paynesville. At 6:15 a.m., Company E left Paynesville for the last time.[324]

The Eighth Minnesota was not alone as it departed for Fort Ridgely. Accompanying the regiment was one company of the Second Minnesota Cavalry. In addition,

---

321 A pony is smaller than a horse but capable of carrying riders. Indian ponies were descendants of horses brought to the New World by the Spanish. Over several generations, those Spanish horses developed into smaller, leaner, yet strong ponies that could survive in the wild on the dry western plains.

322 Bertram, *Reminiscences*, Dec. 7, 1878, MNHS.

323 Washburn, *Diaries*, May 24, 1864.

324 Ibid., May 25, 1864.

the company wagons and seventy-five ox carts went with them to carry all the necessary gear.[325]

For the next four days, the Eighth Minnesota traveled south over the west-central Minnesota plains. Many of the men were shocked by the desolation of the region. There were barely any trees. "It was clean prairie in every direction as far as the eye could extend."[326] Nothing much was to be seen on the prairie but grass and the occasional bones of dead buffalo.

The unit reached Fort Ridgely at about Noon on Sunday, May 29. The fort was located on bluffs on the north side of the heavily wooded Minnesota River valley. Edson Washburn recalled how nice it was to see timber again.[327] Fort Ridgely itself, however, was not particularly impressive. John Strong from Company A observed that "There was no stockade around the place to make it deserve the name of a fort."[328]

At Fort Ridgely, the Minnesota Brigade was further expanded with the addition of forty-five scouts, ninety-three six-mule wagon teams and twelve ambulances. The wagons carried thirty day's rations consisting of hardtack, pork, beans, and coffee.[329]. That would be enough to get the brigade to the Missouri River where it would meet up with Sully's force and be resupplied by river boat.

The Eighth Minnesota and the rest of the Minnesota Brigade spent the next eight days at Fort Ridgely preparing for their trip to Dakota Territory. The officers thoroughly inspected each of the soldiers. Everything in their knapsacks was examined and anything that was not part of their issued gear was removed by the inspecting officers.[330]

On Monday, June 6, 1864, the Minnesota Brigade of the Northwest Indian Expedition started out from Fort Ridgely towards the Missouri River far to the west. The force now included the Eighth Minnesota, four companies of the Second Minnesota Cavalry, and some artillery from the Third Minnesota Battery. Once they reached the Missouri River and met up with General Sully, the brigade would be joined by Brackett's battalion of cavalry.

---

325 John Henry Strong, *A journal of the northwestern Indian expedition under General Sully, 18641865.* May 25, 1864, Dakota Conflict of 1862 Manuscripts Collections. Minnesota Historical Society.

326 Doud, *Diaries,* May 28, 1864.

327 Washburn, *Diaries,* May 29, 1864.

328 Strong, *A journal of the northwestern Indian expedition,* May 29, 1864. MNHS.

329 Washburn, *Autobiography,* p 7.

330 Strong, *A journal of the northwestern Indian expedition,* June 5, 1864. MNHS.

GENERAL ALFRED H. SULLY

Sully's Expedition

May 24 to July 27, 1864

Alfred Sully

General Alfred Sully was perhaps the most qualified commander to lead the Northwestern Indian Expedition due to his experience with the Plains Indians. Born in Philadelphia in 1820, he was the son of the well-known portrait artist Thomas Sully, who had gained notoriety for his paintings. Among his subjects were many celebrities of the time, including Thomas Jefferson, John Quincy Adams, Queen Victoria, and the Marquis de Lafayette.[331]

Young Alfred inherited some of his father's talent. As a youth, however, he preferred painting landscapes to portraits.[332] His father believed Alfred's talents would best be used as a draftsman or in engineering. Using his connections, Thomas Sully was able to secure Alfred an appointment to the U.S. Military Academy at West Point, where he could pursue those interests.[333]

Lieutenant Alfred Sully graduated from West Point in 1841. His first assignment was to Florida, where his unit played a small part in the war against the Seminole Indians. He had hoped to prove himself in combat, perhaps to earn glory and a promotion.[334] However, his unit was only involved in a few skirmishes. After returning from Florida, Lieutenant Sully spent the next five years in garrison or on recruitment duty.[335]

---

331 Most readers will be familiar with at least one of Thomas Sully's works. He painted the portrait of Andrew Jackson that appears on the $20 bill.

332 Langdon Sully, *No Tears for the General: The Life of Alfred Sully, 1821-1879*, Palo Alto, California, American West Publishing Company, 1974, 19.

333 Ibid.

334 Ibid at 22.

335 Ibid at 23.

Sully's next opportunity to gain combat experience came with the Mexican War. In 1847, he participated in the short siege at the Battle of Veracruz. The war ended, however, before he was able to engage in any serious fighting and he returned to the U.S.

From late 1848 until 1853, Sully was posted in California. While stationed there, he married the popular daughter of a prominent California family, and they had a child. Tragically, both his wife and infant son died within two weeks of each other.

In 1853, Sully returned home. After a few months in the East, he was assigned to frontier duty. There he led patrols through Minnesota, Dakota, and Nebraska territories. The following year, Sully was assigned to command Fort Ridgely. The fort had been established in 1853 to oversee the Sioux reservation established by the Treaty of Traverse de Sioux. Fort Ridgely was still under construction and Sully oversaw completion of the work.

Sully remained at Fort Ridgely until May 1855, when he was ordered to take a unit of soldiers and assume command of Fort Pierre, which was then in Nebraska Territory.[336] A year later, Sully was ordered to assist with the construction of Fort Randall, which was located on the Missouri River just above the present-day border of Nebraska and South Dakota.

It was at Fort Randall that Sully met and married the daughter of a Yankton Sioux chief. They soon had a child, a daughter they named Mary Sully. Mary was also given a Yankton name, "Soldier Woman."

When the Civil War broke out in 1861, Sully went to Washington in the hope that he might be appointed to command one of the regiments. Sully approached fellow West Point graduate, General George B. McClelland, seeking his support. Although Sully was several years older than McClelland, the two had both served in the Mexican War and were acquainted through their army service.

Sully served under McClelland in Virginia. He distinguished himself as colonel of the First Minnesota Volunteer Infantry Regiment during the Peninsula Campaign and was promoted to brigadier general.

In May of 1863, Sully was sent west so his experience with Indians on the plains could be put to use in Sibley's Expedition. Now in 1864, Sully was in full command of the Northwestern Expedition against the Sioux.

The Expedition Begins

The 1864 plan was for Sully to lead a brigade of troops north along the Missouri River and rendezvous with the Minnesota Brigade about July 1. The combined force would then proceed against any concentrations of Sioux.

---

336 Fort Pierre (pronounced "peer") was on the Missouri River in the center of present-day South Dakota. The city of Pierre became the state capitol.

Sully's brigade would leave Sioux City, Iowa and travel up the Missouri. He would bring with him the Sixth Iowa Cavalry, three companies of the Seventh Iowa Cavalry, two companies of the First Dakota Cavalry, an independent company of Nebraska Cavalry, a battery of light artillery and Brackett's Battalion.[337]

Brackett's Battalion was, at the time, a detached cavalry unit from Minnesota. The unit had significant combat experience. For a portion of the war, Brackett's Battalion was attached to the Fifth Iowa Volunteer Cavalry Regiment and saw action at Fort Donelson, Tennessee in 1862. The regiment later participated in actions throughout Tennessee and Mississippi.

Of all the Minnesota units formed during the civil war, Brackett's Battalion had the distinction of having served the longest. It was formed at Fort Snelling in August 1861 and not mustered out until June 1866.[338]

The battalion was commanded by Major Alfred Brackett from St. Paul. Brackett had been a deputy U.S Marshal prior to the war. He enlisted as a private but soon rose in the company ranks and eventually was in command of a battalion, which consisted of four companies.

Sully's brigade moved out from Sioux City on June 4, 1864. Along with the cavalry, Sully brought about twenty Indian soldiers, who were known as the "Dakota Scouts." The scouts would travel ahead of the main body of troops to identify the best route and pick the campsites.

Traveling West

On June 6, 1864, the Minnesota Brigade set out from Fort Ridgely for the Missouri River. The path would take them along the Minnesota River towards Big Stone Lake, which formed the border with Dakota Territory. Then they would go cross-country to the rendezvous point on the river about 175 miles straight west.

On the second day of the trip, Tuesday, June 7, the Minnesota Brigade arrived at a site named Camp Pope, where they would spend the night. There, the soldiers were met with an unwelcome surprise – about 250 civilians with 160 wagons and mule teams, accompanied by a variety of livestock.[339] The Minnesota Brigade received orders to escort these civilians across Dakota Territory to Montana.

337 A. M. English, *Dakota's First Soldiers*, South Dakota Historical Collections, Vol. IX, Hipple Printing Company, Pierre, South Dakota, 1918. 241, 273.

338 *Minnesota in the Civil and Indian Wars: 1861-1865*, vol. 1, 572.

339 Judge Nicholas Hilger, "Campaign of General Alfred Sully Against the Hostile Sioux in 1864, as transcribed in 1883 from the Diary of Judge Nicholas Hilger," *Contributions to the Historical Society of Montana*, vol. II, 314, State Publishing Company, Helena Montana, 1896. The number of emigrants and wagons varied significantly in recollections by different soldiers who participated in the expedition. However, as a member of the emigrant party, Hilger's number is probably the most accurate.

The soldiers referred to the civilians as the Idaho emigrants. The emigrants were headed to the gold fields of Montana, then part of Idaho Territory, to seek their fortune as miners. The federal government needed all the gold it could get to finance the war, so it provided a military escort to protect the emigrants as they crossed lands occupied by hostile Sioux.

Neither Colonel Thomas nor General Sully particularly welcomed the idea of having such a large group of civilians join the military expedition. At the very least, escorting the emigrant train would slow down Sully's pursuit of the Sioux. Protecting the emigrants would also require troops that Sully needed if the Sioux gave him battle on the plains. Nevertheless, the commanders had to follow orders and the Idaho emigrants joined the procession to the west

During the first few days on the march, the Minnesota Brigade passed through the Sioux agencies and the battlefield at Birch Coulee. The men saw firsthand the results of the Uprising—burned buildings, graves of the casualties and even the skulls of some who had been killed. They were not always sure whether the skulls were those of Indians or whites.

Within a few days, the Minnesota Brigade was past the scene of the Uprising and into wide-open country. At that point, they began to make good progress on their march to the Missouri River.

Each day on the march tended to be the same. A bugle sounded reveille at about 2 a.m. The men would tend to the animals as others prepared a breakfast and coffee. The breakfast was far from gourmet fare. In many cases it was the same as lunch or dinner—fried salt pork or bacon with hardtack soaked in the fat.

Sometime between 5 a.m. and 7 a.m., the troops would begin the day's march. There were frequent breaks. The standard practice was to march for fifty minutes and then rest for ten. That way the men and horses got a little rest each hour.

When fully spread out, the train of wagons, including those of the emigrants, extended for several miles. To shorten that distance and make the train easier to protect, the emigrants were moved up into two lines of wagons in the center. Soldiers rode farther out to protect the flanks of the train, with some assigned to the guard the rear.[340]

Traveling across the hot, dry Dakota plains was not pleasant for those near the center of the train. The hooves of horses, mules, and cattle, along with the wagon wheels, kicked up thick dry dust. "The earth was parched and was soon worked into an impalpable dust, which aggravated our thirst and filled our eyes and nostrils." Recalled David Kingsbury.[341]

340   *See*, generally, Cambell, *Personal Reminiscences*, 24.

341   Kingsbury, "Sully's Expedition Against the Sioux In 1864," 453.

The soldiers on the flanks had it much better. They were usually a few hundred yards out from the concentration of wagons and livestock. That was far enough away to avoid the choking dust.

The monotony of these marches could be mind-numbing as well as exhausting. Some of the men learned to sleep in the saddle or take quick naps during the short breaks. Otherwise, they occupied themselves with idle chatter and occasional singing.

At about 2 p.m. the march would come to a halt for the day and the soldiers would make camp. Each overnight camp was named, usually after an officer or some other honoree. For example, on June 23, they set up Camp Murphy in honor of the regimental surgeon John H. Murphy.[342]

After stopping at the designated campsite, the troops would then picket their horses. This was accomplished by driving a foot-long iron pin with a ring on top into the ground. The soldier would then tie his horse to the pin with a twenty-foot rope. The animals were then free to graze on whatever grass was available.

For the rest of the afternoon and evening the troops would ready equipment for the next day's march, tend to their animals and eat dinner. As darkness approached the troops would turn in to get as much sleep as they could before the same routine began again in the wee hours of the next morning.

Sully's Progress

As the Minnesota Brigade worked its way west, Sully's brigade continued north along the Missouri River. Sully's troops had access to plentiful supplies while on the march, thanks to several steamboats that unloaded cargo at pre-designated spots along the route.

Within a few days, Sully's forces had passed into country where attacks from hostile Indians became a real possibility. Pickets were posted around the camps each night to keep watch. As it turned out, Sully's troops were indeed under surveillance.

The Indians in Dakota Territory had good reason to keep a close eye on Sully's Expedition. The previous year, Sibley's Expedition had attacked the Dakota Sioux Indians even though they had nothing to do with the 1862 Uprising in Minnesota. Now, Sully was back in force and the Indians had to again prepare to defend their tribes and families.

The Indians drew the first blood that summer. On June 29, 1864, Captain Fielner, a topographical engineer assigned to Sully's command, set out ahead of the brigade with two Indian soldiers from the Dakota Scouts. They were riding about

---

342   Paxson, *Diary*, June 23, 1864 39.

five miles ahead of Sully's main force to locate good ground for the next night's encampment.

After a while, Captain Fielner and the two escorts reached the edge of the Little Cheyenne River, which was really nothing more than a creek at that point. However, it did provide a suitable location for Sully's Expedition to camp that night. They decided to picket their horses and then sit down to wait for Sully's force to arrive.[343]

With no Indians in sight, the men were not particularly cautious. It was a hot summer's day, so Fielner decided to go to the creek for a drink of cold water. As he made his way through the grass, three Indians suddenly rose from the brush and fired their weapons. The bullets found their mark. The captain fell mortally wounded with multiple shots through his arm and lungs.[344]

Meanwhile, the two Dakota Scouts had wandered off on their own. The sound of shooting made them realize that the Indians were between them and their horses. The Indians made a dash for the horses, but the animals reared up and pulled their picket pins from the ground. They galloped off onto the prairie chased by the three Indians.

When word of the attack reached the main column, Sully ordered a detachment of the Dakota Cavalry to go in pursuit. The soldiers chased the Indians for almost fifteen miles before they got within range.

As they closed on the Indians, the cavalry troops watched them ride into a ravine. The soldiers encircled the area and managed to trap all three of the Indians in a buffalo wallow.[345] The visibility was poor due to the vegetation. Soon a close-quarters fight began in which all three Indians were killed by the Dakota Scouts.[346]

Sully was no stranger to the Indian ways, he was, after all, married to a Yankton Sioux woman. He was intimately familiar with their sometimes gruesome methods of war and decided to send the Indians a message he thought they would understand.

When the successful chase party returned, Sully ordered them to go back and retrieve the heads of the dead Indians. The soldiers returned to the scene to perform the grisly act.

---

343 This portion of the story was set forth in Frank Myers, *Soldiering in Dakota Among the Indians in 1863-4-5*, Huron, Dakota Territory, 1888, 11. (Reprinted by State Historical Society, Pierre, S. Dak., 1936),10.

344 Ibid., 11; English, *Dakota's First Soldiers*, 276.

345 A buffalo wallow was a shallow bowl-shaped depression on the prairie formed over time by buffalo rolling in the dirt, perhaps to cool off or get rid of biting bugs. The wallows could collect water and often served as small ecosystem on the dry prairie. Dakota Territory was once covered with buffalo wallows. The remnants of some of these ancient wallows can still be seen from the air today. *See, Bison Bellows: What's Wallowing All About?*, https://www.nps.gov/articles/bison-bellow-1-28-16.htm, accessed Aug. 6, 2020.

346 Myers, *Soldiering in Dakota*, 11. See also, English, *Dakota's First Soldiers*, 278.

When the soldiers returned, Sergeant A.M. English of the Dakota Cavalry brought the heads to General Sully. English later recalled "Gen. Sully directed me to hang the heads on poles on the highest hill near the camp as a warning to all Indians who might travel that way."[347]

The Expedition Unites

On the evening on June 29, 1864, scouts from Sully's Brigade reached the Minnesota Brigade's camp. The following day, the expedition united along the banks of the Missouri River. There, the two brigades would have a chance to rest for a few days.

The rest was sorely needed, especially for the Minnesota Brigade. There had been little water along the route for the last few days of the march and almost no grass for the animals. Some were already suffering as a result with the expedition not even started.[348]

Many of the men were suffering from various ailments as well, especially from the effects of the alkaline waterholes they encountered along the way. Intestinal distress, such as dysentery or just diarrhea, was a common affliction. It dehydrated and exhausted the soldiers who fell victim to it but there was little the doctors could do for them.

For the next three days the soldiers remained in camp. Then, on Sunday, July 3, Sully's Expedition set out to the north along the Missouri River.

One of Sully's missions on this expedition was to locate a suitable location for a fort to act as a base of operations. The fort would also serve as a show of force to help maintain peace with the Indians. Sully finally found a suitable location on July 7 on the west bank of the Missouri River. The spot was a flat piece of bottom land where Long Lake Creek flows into the river.

Soldiers' Attitudes Towards the Indians

As the Eighth Minnesota rested, they had the opportunity for a small Fourth of July celebration. The soldiers created a makeshift stage out of some boxes so they could have an orator provide entertainment for the day. The man selected for this duty was an Eighth Regiment soldier by the name of Harris, who was also an Adventist preacher.[349]

---

347 English, *Dakota's First Soldiers*, 278.

348 Paxson, *Diary*, June 29, 1864 at 40. He noted that his horse nearly gave out.

349 Hodgson, "Recollections of the Sioux War No. 20," *Dakota County Tribune*, July 17, 1890. This was probably John A. Harris from Company C. He appears to be the only Harris that served with the Eighth Minnesota according to the roster published in *Minnesota in the Civil and Indian Wars: 1861-1865*, vol. 1, 401-415.

Harris covered all the patriotic themes that would be expected of any Fourth of July speech. What captivated the audience, however, was his vilification of the Sioux Indians and advocacy for their extermination. Thomas Hodgson described Harris's views and the crowds' reaction:

> *The more barbarous the speech became the more the boys applauded. There were no prisoners to be taken – even children and women were to be butchered if we ever got at them.*[350]

Another minister, probably Chaplain Lauren Armsby, stood up and rebuked Harris for the un-Christian nature of his speech.[351] Harris responded that Christian methods were not suited to warfare with the Indians and that the Old Testament method was the only practical way of dealing with them. Harris was quoted as saying:

> *"When God sent Saul down to destroy Amelek, He instructed him to destroy them utterly, root and branch. They had forfeited their right to live and hence were justly condemned to death."*[352]

After the exchange between Harris and Armsby, Thomas Hodgson recalled "It is plain the boys were in favor of the Old Testament method of dealing with enemies."[353] This should not have been surprising at the time as most of the soldiers looked back with anger at the Indian attacks during the 1862 Uprising.

Not all of those present agreed with Harris. There were certainly soldiers among the regiment that had some sympathy for the plight of the Indians. While they understood the logic of driving the hostile Sioux on to reservations to protect their families and friends in Minnesota, they also recognized the injustices committed against the Indians that caused the conflict.

As previously noted, George Doud of Company F appeared to fix blame for the Uprising squarely on unscrupulous traders.[354] William Houlton of Company E didn't appear to harbor ill-will against the Indians generally and may have sympathized with their unjust treatment. In a school composition assignment some years before the Uprising, Houlton wrote of the Indians:

---

350   Hodgson, Ibid.

351   Ibid.

352   Ibid.

353   Ibid.

354   *Doud Diaries*, 110; see Note 176.

*The places that we now love they loved just as well, and it was by
the law of might, not right, that they were driven from them.*[355]

Nevertheless, even those few soldiers who bore no particular animosity towards
the Indians were prepared to do their duty. The time would come for them to do so
within a few short weeks.

The Masonic Funeral

The Minnesota Brigade was able to grab a day or two of rest while the riverboats unloaded materials for the construction of the new fort. As they did so, the
troops witnessed a small gathering that appeared to have a significant impact on
some of the soldiers.

One of the civilians who worked on the riverboats died the same evening that
Sully's Expedition reached the site of the new fort. The deceased, Charles Clark, was
originally from somewhere out east. He had contracted tuberculosis and moved to
Saint Anthony, Minnesota hoping the weather would help keep the deadly disease in
check. His condition seemed to improve but after six months he thought it best to try
a dryer climate. For this reason, Clark volunteered to serve on one of the steamboats
that would supply Sully's Northwest Indian Expedition.[356]

As the steamboat traveled up the Missouri River towards the rendezvous with
Sully and the Minnesota Brigade, Clark was not feeling well. He determined that it
would be best if he took the first boat back to Minnesota after they delivered their
supplies.

Clark never did get the opportunity to catch a boat back to Minnesota. On the
night of July 7, 1864, about the same time the steamboat arrived at the rendezvous,
Clark suddenly and unexpectedly died of his ailment.

The thought of dying on the Expedition and being buried alone on the prairie,
without friends or family in attendance, haunted many soldiers. Clark, however, was
a Freemason. When other Freemasons on the Expedition learned that one of their
Brethren had died, they quickly organized a Masonic funeral. None of the Masons
on the Expedition had met Charles Clark, but he was their Brother nonetheless and
they had an obligation to see that he was buried properly.

On Saturday, July 9, a boat loaded with Masons from the Expedition escorted
the body of Brother Clark across the Missouri River to a patch of land that would

---

355 William Houlton, *The Indian*, Oct. 1856, William H. Houlton and Family Papers, MNHS.

356 *The Weekly Pioneer and Democrat*, Aug. 12, 1864.

later become the Fort Rice Cemetery. There, the assembled men held a Masonic funeral and then buried Charles Clark with Masonic Honors.[357]

The attention paid to Clark's burial by his brother Masons likely impressed other soldiers and perhaps gave them some comfort. It may be no coincidence that after this exposure to Masonic principles in practice, more soldiers decided to join the fraternity. Several did so immediately after they returned to Minnesota following Sully's Expedition.[358]

Crossing the Missouri River

The same day that the Masons laid Brother Clark to rest, the steamboats began ferrying the rest of the expedition across the water to the flat plain where Sully had chosen to build a new fort. Sully christened the site Fort Rice in honor of General James C. Rice, who had been killed at the Battle of Spotsylvania two months earlier.[359]

There were seven riverboats available at the landing to take the Expedition across: *Peoria, Isabella, New Caty, Gen. Grant, Tempest, Island City* and *Yellowstone*.[360] Not only did the boats need to take across more than 4,000 soldiers and about as many horses, but also nearly 500 army supply wagons, their mule teams and a few hundred head of beef cattle. Once that was done, then the emigrant train, including another 250 people, 160 wagon teams and their livestock, could begin to cross.

The crossing was slow. The riverboats had space limitations. Each boat could only hold two wagon teams at a time.[361] A few soldiers and horses could sometimes squeeze in with the wagons, but it was still a slow process. It took the seven riverboats three full days to ferry the army and emigrant train across the Missouri.[362]

Construction of Fort Rice

After reaching the western side of the Missouri River, the Expedition had eight days to rest while General Sully worked with his engineers to design the fort and begin its construction. Sully assigned the task of constructing Fort Rice to the 800

357 Paxson, *Diary,* July 9, 1864. *See also,* James B. Atkinson, *James Benton Atkinson Diary, 1864,* Dakota Conflict of 1862 Manuscripts Collections. Minnesota Historical Society, July 9, 1864.

358 Frank Parcher from Company E, for example, joined Clearwater Lodge #28 immediately upon his return from Dakota Territory while on French Leave from Fort Snelling (see Chapter 12).

359 *The Weekly Pioneer and Democrat,* Aug. 12, 1864.

360 Paxson, *Diary,* July 9, 1864.

361 Doud, *Diaries,* July 9, 1864 at 158.

362 Hilger, "Campaign of General Alfred Sully Against the Hostile Sioux in 1864," 314; Washburn *Diaries,* July 12, 1864. Edson Washburn recorded that the Idaho emigrant train crossed on July 12.

men of the Thirtieth Wisconsin Infantry.[363] The regiment began the initial construction work on July 12.

Work proceeded quickly and Fort Rice soon enclosed an area of 510 feet by 500 feet. When completed it was surrounded by a stockade made of cottonwood logs, which were plentiful along the banks of the Missouri River. To guard the northeast and southwest corners of the stockade, the Thirtieth Wisconsin constructed two log blockhouses.[364]

While the Thirtieth Wisconsin was busy with construction duties, the Minnesota Brigade spent its time preparing for the travels to come. The soldiers also found time for hunting and a little exploring. Some were surprised to find outcrops of iron ore and coal veins exposed on the prairie.

It was also clear to the soldiers that the climate was getting drier. While grass for the horses was plentiful along the Missouri River bottoms, those who explored farther out found the landscape "covered with cactus and prickly pears."[365]

Looking for a Fight

The Thirtieth Wisconsin made rapid progress on the construction of Fort Rice, so Sully decided it was time to get back to his mission—finding the Indians and escorting the emigrant train to the Yellowstone River. On July 19, 1864, Sully's Expedition left Fort Rice, first heading south to the Cannonball River, and then following it to the west.

By Friday, July 22, the Expedition had traveled approximately sixty miles west of Fort Rice. That day, two scouts returned to camp and reported that a large Indian village consisting of 1,800 lodges was located to the north near the Heart River.[366]

The report by the scouts was exactly what General Sully wanted to hear. He would take his force in pursuit of the Indians. The next morning, the expedition set out to the north in the direction of the Heart River.

The Heart River Corral

On Sunday, July 24, 1864, Sully's Expedition set out at 5 a.m. and marched twenty miles to a campsite along the Heart River, south of present-day Richardton, North Dakota. The march was not pleasant. One soldier described the day as "sultry

363   Hilger, "Campaign of General Alfred Sully Against the Hostile Sioux in 1864," 314.

364   *See*, Fort Rice Historical Site, North Dakota Historical Society, https://www.history.nd.gov/historicsites/rice/index.html, accessed May 17, 2020.

365   Doud, *Diaries*, July 11, 1864.

366   Paxson, *Diary*, July 22, 1864.

hot" and there was no timber along the way for shade.[367] The heat was hard on both men and animals—twenty-one oxen died during the march that day.[368]

The lack of grass and good water since leaving Fort Rice was already taking its toll on the expedition. The drought-stricken grass at the camp site was thin and dry but at least there was plenty of water. The expedition would lay over at this spot for a day of much-needed rest from the rigors of the march.

As the troops were setting up camp, some of Sully's Indian scouts arrived with urgent news. A large Sioux encampment was spotted roughly sixty miles to the northwest near a group of hills known as the Killdeer Mountains. Sully quickly decided to advance on the Indian encampment and either force them to surrender or fight. He immediately ordered the troops to prepare for a fast march to the location of the reported sighting.

The next morning preparations for the trip to the Indian encampment began in earnest. Sully wanted to travel light and fast, carrying a minimum of supplies. With this goal in mind, the plan was to take only what supplies the men could carry on their horses.

The taskforce also appropriated mules from the wagon teams and outfitted them with pack harnesses. These animals would carry additional food and ammunition.

Tents and other comforts would be left behind. The soldiers were to march with only the essentials. They would have to sleep under the stars. The men were even ordered to leave behind all their clothing, except what they wore.[369]

The emigrant train would remain at the Heart River with the wagons, animals and supplies that were not needed for the foray to Killdeer. Sully decided to leave a force of 800 men behind to protect what became known as the "Heart River Corral."[370] These included all of the emigrants and those soldiers who were not in good enough physical condition to make the arduous journey or participate in the expected fight.

Even though it was the height of summer, a significant number of soldiers were sick. Illness was a constant problem for the army during the Civil War and so it was for Sully's troops. Many were suffering from diarrhea or other stomach ailments brought on by the bad water. Typhoid, typhus, and other illnesses were present as well. The trip to Killdeer could prove fatal for these already sick men. Therefore, Sully decided to leave them behind at the Heart River to recover.

---

367 Gardner B. Colwell, Gardner B. Colwell *Diary* and certificate, 1864, May 8-1865 July 20; 1898, July 24, 1864, Minnesota Historical Society.

368 Ibid.

369 John E. Robinson to Libbie Robinson, Oct. 11, 1864, *John E. Robinson biographical memorabilia, 18591865*, Dakota Conflict of 1862 Manuscripts Collections. Minnesota Historical Society.

370 Nathanial Pope, Contributions to the Historical Society of Montana at 329.

Those with injuries or other physical ailments were also left behind to guard the emigrant train. Traveling over rough country with heavy wagons and thousands of large animals was dangerous work and inevitably led to everything from sprains to broken bones. Spending so much time in the saddle each day could also cause physical issues that limited a soldier's fighting ability.

Edson Washburn was one of those who was unable to make the trip to Killdeer. For almost two weeks he had been suffering from severe leg pain. He described it as "rheumatism" in his leg.[371] Based on his description, it may have been a pinched nerve or sciatica aggravated by sitting in the saddle during the long days on the march.

Edson must have been in pure misery with every step his horse took. Walking was just as bad. By the time Sully's Expedition reached the Heart River, he could do little more than limp around and cook for the company. Even that little bit of work was hard for him, and he paid for it at night with a very painful leg.[372]

Nevertheless, Edson was disappointed at being left behind. It would separate him from his brother Elbridge and the other soldiers of Company E, with whom he was close.

The soldiers and emigrants that remained at the Heart River realized that they were vulnerable to a surprise attack while Sully was gone with most of the expedition's strength. On the morning of Tuesday, July 26 those who were staying behind crossed the river to set up in a stronger defensive position. The new site would better enable the group to ward off any attack the Indians might attempt while the rest of the troops were gone.

The chosen location was on a patch of level prairie covering about a quarter-mile square. It was surrounded on three sides by a loop in the Heart River, which would protect much of the camp. At that point, the river was about fifty feet wide and would make it difficult for Indians to attack from that route. Thus, the troops would only need to defend a quarter mile-long land approach to keep the camp secure.

The location was also surrounded by good lookout points from which scouts could spot approaching danger. Less than a mile to the south across the river, a high hill provided the scouts with an excellent vantage point from which they could see for many miles in all directions. Scouts were stationed on this hill to watch for hostile Indians.[373]

Upon reaching the new campsite, the emigrant wagons and the bigger army supply wagons were formed into a wide circle that served as a corral for the large

---

371 "Rheumatism" was a general term used to describe a wide variety of physical ailments affecting the joints and connective tissues.

372 Washburn, *Diaries*, July 26, 1864. Remnants of the entrenchments are still visible today, although the depressions in the soil are difficult to spot when the grass is high.

373 Some carved their names into the rocks. The carvings can still be seen, but by 2017 weathering has made them almost unreadable.

number of cattle, horses, and mules that remained behind. The corral would double as a defensive perimeter, the proverbial circled wagons to ward of an Indian attack. The emigrants, invalid soldiers, and others left to guard the camp would remain at the Heart River Corral until Sully's force returned. None had any idea how long that might be.

That same morning, Sully's troops finished loading up and set out for the reported site of the Indian encampment. The taskforce, however, didn't get very far. The mules wouldn't move and proved almost useless as they rebelled against the unfamiliar pack harnesses.[374]

Sully was forced to turn the troops around and come up with an alternative to using pack mules. He pressed several private light wagons of the emigrants into service.[375] To ensure that the wagons could move rapidly, they were loaded only with essential supplies. Each wagon was teamed with four mules and carried 1,000 pounds of ammunition and provisions.[376] The taskforce finally set out about 3 p.m.

Within a half hour of departure, Sully's scouts spotted a party of approximately twenty-five Sioux warriors in their path ahead. Although the scouts had the Indians outnumbered, they did not attack. The captain in charge was allegedly drunk. One of the scouts reported that the captain "Kept fooling here and there let all the Indians get away."[377] Nevertheless, the scouts alerted the main force ten miles to their rear.

Upon learning of the small Indian scouting party up ahead, Sully ordered Brackett to send part of his battalion after them. Brackett's men soon found the Indians' camp and took them by surprise. A sharp but quick fight ensued in which the soldiers drove off the Indians. Only a few members of the Indian scouting party, however, were in camp at the time. The Indian casualties were reportedly three dead and three of their ponies were also killed.[378] The rest escaped.

Brackett's detachment fared much better in the skirmish. There were only two minor casualties. One soldier suffered a wound to the knee and a horse was shot in the neck with an arrow.[379]

374 Report of Brig. Gen. Alfred Sully, July 31, 1864, *Official Records*, series 1, vol. 41, part 1, 142.

375 Ibid.

376 Jared Daniels, Reminiscences Ch. 6, "Kill-Deer Mountain Battle," 1, MNHS; Report of Brig. Gen. Alfred Sully, July 31, 1864, *Official Records*, series 1, vol. 41, part 1, 142.

377 Charles Dugas to his parents, Fort Rice, Dakota Territory, Sept. 11, 1864, Charles F. Dugas letters, 1864, Dakota Conflict of 1862 Manuscripts Collections. Minnesota Historical Society.

378 Doud, *Diaries*, July 26, 1864.

379 Ibid.

In their haste to get away the Indian scouting party left behind a variety of belongings, which the soldiers quickly grabbed as spoils of war. These goods reportedly included a spyglass, four buffalo skins, moccasins, leggings, and one Enfield rifle.[380]

The engagement with the Indian party may have bolstered the troops' confidence but it also cost Sully's force the element of surprise. The Indians that escaped before Brackett's battalion arrived at their camp quickly made their way north to the Killdeer Mountains. There, they alerted the large Sioux encampment of the approaching army.

The skirmish north of the Heart River also put Sully's command on edge. The troops spent that night sleeping on the ground—they had no tents—with their horses saddled.[381] That way they were ready for prompt action if attacked. The men were also ordered not to make any campfires that would give away their position.[382] Hence, the men went without hot food or coffee to prepare for the coming day.

It was a short night with little rest for the troops. The bugle sounded early on the morning of July 27. The command struck their tents at 2:30 a.m. and were on the march an hour later. It was well and good that they got an early start. That enabled them to get a good distance in the relatively cool morning air. After the sun came up, one soldier described the day as "hot as thunder." [383]

It must have been a tough march in the rising heat. There was little drinking water and not much grass for the animals. Nevertheless, Sully's troops made almost thirty-five miles before stopping to make camp on the west side of the Oak River.[384]

Meanwhile, back at the Heart River Corral, the day was just as brutally hot. Edson Washburn recorded that the mercury reached 106 degrees Fahrenheit.[385] There was almost no shade and little wind to provide relief from the relentless heat. Despite the unpleasant and even dangerous conditions, the men at the corral went to work, spending the day digging entrenchments and setting up other defenses.[386] Then they waited for word from Sully's force.

---

380   Atkinson *Diary*, July 26, 1864; Doud, *Diaries*, July 26, 1864.

381   Doud, *Diaries*, July 26, 1864.

382   John Robinson to Libbie Robinson, Oct. 11, 1864, MNHS.

383   Atkinson, *Diary*, July 27, 1864.

384   Doud, *Diaries*, July 27, 1864.

385   Washburn. *Diaries*, July 27, 1864.

386   Ibid.

Battle of Killdeer Mountain

July 28, 1864

Sully was in a hurry to get started, so he ordered the bugle to sound at midnight on July 28, 1864. The men made coffee, tended to the animals, and prepared their equipment for what they all expected would be a momentous day. Soon the command was ready. The morning sky in western Dakota Territory began to show the first hints of light shortly after 3 a.m. A half hour later, the final march to the Indian encampment began.

As the sun rose, the morning quickly grew warm. The day promised again to be intensely hot and dry. At 9 a.m., after traveling fifteen miles, the command stopped for a short breakfast break. As was usually the case in the treeless Dakota Territory, there was no shade for the men or animals.

Nevertheless, it was not the unrelenting sun that made the most lasting impression of the breakfast site that morning. The troops would long remember that the resting spot was next to an exposed coal vein twelve feet thick.[387]

As the men made more coffee and gnawed on hardtack, Sully's scouts arrived with word that the large Sioux encampment was only seven miles ahead at the foot of the Killdeer Mountains.

The Dakota name for the Killdeer Mountains is Ta-ha-kouty, which means "The place where they kill deer." Deer thrived in the area thanks to plentiful water, woodland, and deep ravines with thick brush for cover. The Indians had long recognized this as a good location for successful deer hunting.

---

387 Doud, *Diaries*, July 28, 1864. Twelve feet may have been an exaggeration. One other soldier described the vein as five feet thick, which still must have been an impressive sight. Colwell, *Diary*, July 28, 1864.

Excitement began to mount as the men finished their short break. They prepared their equipment and gathered plenty of ammunition from the supply wagons.[388] Some braced themselves for the coming battle with a healthy shot of whiskey, while others preferred to rely on their "native courage."[389]

It took less than an hour of marching before the men first laid eyes upon the massive Indian camp at the base of the Killdeer Mountains. The encampment was still more than three miles away. Nevertheless, the men were astounded at its size.

The Indian camp appeared to be about a mile long, stretching roughly east to west along the south side of the Killdeer Mountains. Various eyewitnesses claimed that the camp consisted of somewhere around 1,600 lodges. If that estimate was correct, that meant Sully's troops might face between 5,000 and 6,000 warriors.[390]

The Indian camp was on good defensive ground. Colonel Thomas later reported that "A better position for defense and safety could not be found."[391] The front of the encampment faced south towards a long rolling prairie. On either side, the approaches to the encampment were protected by deep ravines filled with timber. To the encampment's north, more ravines and thickets provided an escape route into the Badlands.

At nearly the same time Sully's taskforce spotted the Indian camp, Indian scouts spotted the soldiers. Instantly there was great excitement on both sides as they began to prepare for battle.[392]

The Indians had advance warning that soldiers were on the way. The scouts had already alerted the encampment to Sully's movements following the skirmish with Brackett's cavalry troops two days earlier. They were surprised, however, that Sully's force managed to get so close so fast and undetected.

Despite the sudden appearance of the soldiers, the Sioux were confident in both their position and fighting ability. The Sioux warriors had Sully's force outnumbered. They had no intention of surrendering. In fact, the Sioux were so confident of victory that the women and children made no preparations for a retreat. Instead, as recalled by David Kingsbury, they "assembled in front of the camp to witness our annihilation, which their braves led them to believe was certain."[393]

---

388 John Robinson to Libbie Robinson, Oct. 11, 1864, MNHS.

389 Ibid.

390 These estimates were probably exaggerated. In all likelihood, each tipi held no more than 2 warriors. Even so, this would mean the army faced a substantial force of up to 3200 enemy combatants.

391 Report of Col. M.T. Thomas, Aug. 13, 1864, *Official Records*, series 1, vol. 41, part 1, 168-.

392 *Minnesota in the Civil and Indian Wars: 1861-1865*, vol. 1, 390.

393 Kingsbury, "Sully's Expedition Against the Sioux In 1864," 454.

Sully had to determine how best to attack the enemy. The rough terrain leading up to the camp made a mounted charge next to impossible.[394] He decided that the best option was to have the soldiers dismount and attack from the ground as infantry.

The troops were deployed in a long line facing north towards the Indian encampment. The First Brigade formed the right side of the line. Six companies of the Sixth Iowa Cavalry, along with three companies of the Seventh Iowa Cavalry were dismounted with every fourth man staying in the rear to hold the horses for the other three.

On the right flank were four companies of Brackett's Battalion. They would guard the advancing troops from flanking attacks. An element of the Third Minnesota Battery, under the command of Captain Jones, followed the right side of the line to provide artillery support under the protection of four companies from the Sixth Iowa Cavalry.

The Minnesota Brigade formed the left side of the line. Six dismounted companies of the Eighth Minnesota consisting of approximately 325 men formed the line of battle. The soldiers followed the standard cavalry and mounted infantry practice of having every fourth man hold his horse and the horses of the previous three men as they advanced. They were lined up from east to west about three or four paces apart, making a line that extended nearly a mile.

Companies B and D of the Eighth Minnesota were held back to provide a rear guard for the entire advancing force. These companies were also dismounted. They were spread out at three paces apart, making the line approximately two thirds of a mile long. Their mission was to follow behind the advancing troops in case it was necessary to remount.

Four companies of the Second Minnesota Cavalry provided protection for the Minnesota Brigade's left flank. Another element of the Third Minnesota Battery, under the command of Captain Pope and guarded by two companies of the Dakota Cavalry, were in the center following the line of advance. Company C of the Eighth Minnesota was held back in reserve to protect the artillery.[395] The train of supply wagons followed farther behind the line of advance, guarded by Company C of the Second Minnesota Cavalry.

Once the troops were in position, Colonel Thomas gave a speech, reminding the men to keep their place and obey orders.[396] Then, the entire force began a long slow advance towards the Indian village up ahead.

---

394   Report of Brig. Gen. Alfred Sully, July 31, 1864, *Official Records,* series 1, vol. 41, part 1, 142.

395   Report of Col. M.T. Thomas, Aug. 13, 1864, *Official Records*, series 1, vol. 41, part 1, 170.

396   Hodgson, "Recollections of the Sioux War No. 20," *Dakota County Tribune*, July 17, 1890.

Meanwhile, there was much activity in the Indian village. The men armed themselves while the women gathered bundles of their belongings.[397] Among those preparing to fight were Inkpaduta, leader of the Spirit Lake Massacre in 1857 and veteran of the Battle of Whitestone Hill the previous year, and a young thirty-something Indian leader named Sitting Bull.

As Sully's force began to slowly move forward across the broken terrain, the warriors formed their own line of battle between the soldiers and the encampment.[398] The warriors slowly rode out towards the advancing troops. They came nearly to within gunshot range of the soldiers as they made their reconnaissance. Some of the Indians would ride out and give a demonstration of their bravery to the advancing troops but they did not engage, at least not at first.[399]

When the line of soldiers reached a point almost a half mile from the Indian village at about 12:30 p.m., everything changed. A shot rang out, which was immediately followed by gunfire all along the line of nervous army troops.

It is not entirely clear who fired the first shot. Many of the soldiers' accounts claim the Indians fired first. However, these accounts were contradicted by Lieutenant Colonel John Pattee of the Seventh Iowa Cavalry. He provided the following account of what he claimed were the first shots as they approached the Indians:

> *They seemed to be in no hurry to meet us, but held back. This was the most formidable array the Dakota Indians had ever seen and they took a good look at us. About this time an Indian very gayly dressed, carrying a large war club gorgeously ornamented appeared in front of the 6th Iowa cavalry and called loudly to us and gesticulated wildly about one-half a mile away. When discovered, Major Wood, chief of cavalry, approached my position and said, "The general sends his compliments and wishes you to kill that Indian for God's sake." I dismounted and called out two men from Company K and one from Company L, 7th Iowa cavalry, who I knew were marksmen and the only men who carried Springfield rifle muskets and directed them to take the best aim possible and fire while I watched closely to see if the ball struck the ground between us and the hill on which the Indian stood, but the balls all passed over the*

---

397 Benjamin Witherell Brunson, "Reminiscences of Service With the Eighth Minnesota Infantry," *Glimpses of the Nation's Struggle*, Fifth Series, 365, 368, Military Order of the Loyal Legion of the United States, Minnesota (MOLLUS-Minn.), Saint Paul, 1908.

398 Ibid.

399 *Minnesota in the Civil and Indian Wars: 1861-1865*, vol. 1, 390.

hill. The Indian stood with his left side toward us and immediately stretched himself out flat along the horse's back and plied his left heel vigorously against the flank of his pony and disappeared from my sight over the hill. But the general was some distance to my right and upon much higher ground and afterwards told me that the Indian fell from his horse when nearly down the hill and was put on his horse by other Indians who were on foot and held there till they reached the mountains, then about four miles away.[400]

The Eighth Minnesota's Springfield rifles came into action after the first shots. The firing quickly became general along the Eighth Minnesota line.[401]

The units guarding the rear of Sully's force also heard the gunfire. Due to the broken terrain, they could not see what was happening in the front line. The rear guard quickly set up on a low rise of ground from which they could see the action. There, they noticed Indians popping their heads up from behind hills and ridges all around them.[402] The Indians, however, did not immediately attack.

The entire formation of troops continued to slowly advance towards the Sioux encampment. The warriors rode back and forth in full view of the soldiers, sometimes turning towards the line, coming closer each time.[403] They would ride up, fire, and then wheel back to reload out of range.[404] As they did so, the warriors would use their own ponies as cover. A bold Indian rider would "Swing around in a half circle and return, hiding himself all the time behind his horse with nothing but one leg and one arm exposed to our fire."[405]

The Indians quickly discovered that they were at a disadvantage due to the range of the soldiers' Springfields. About half of the Sioux warriors were armed only with bow and arrow. While these were effective close quarters weapons, the long-

---

400 John Pattee, "Dakota Campaigns," *South Dakota Historical Collections*, vol. 5, State Publishing Company, Sioux Falls, South Dakota, 1910, 308. Multiple sources indicate the first shot came from the Indians. Atkinson claimed the first shot was about 12:30, Atkinson *Diary*, July 28, 1864. George Doud also claimed the Indians fired the first shot at 12:45. Doud, *Diaries*, July 28, 1864. Gardner Colwell of Company F also recalled that "the Indians fired upon us first." Colwell *Diary*, July 28, 1864.

401 Brunson, "Reminiscences of Service With the Eighth Minnesota Infantry," 369.

402 John Robinson to Libbie Robinson, Oct. 11, 1864, MNHS.

403 William E. Seelye, *Narrative of the past and experiences and adventures of which the writer, W. E. Seelye, took part*, October 22, 1937, Dakota Conflict of 1862 Manuscripts Collections. Minnesota Historical Society, 6.

404 Ibid.

405 Hodgson, "Recollections of the Sioux War No. 21," *Dakota County Tribune*, July 31, 1890. Other soldiers were impressed by the Indians' skill at using the horses for protection during the battle. *See*, Cambell, *Personal Reminiscences*, 25; John Robinson to Libbie Robinson, Oct. 11, 1864, MNHS.

range accuracy of the army Springfield rifles forced the warriors to stay back. Any attempt to get close enough to use their bows would have been suicide in the open country. This frustrated some of the troops who were anxious to have a decisive engagement. Private Thomas Hodgson later wrote:

> *"It was in my judgment a misfortune for us that the Indians were so poorly armed. In the manner of arms and ammunition they were vastly inferior to us and as a matter of course were afraid to give us battle.*[406]

Being outgunned, it became clear to the Indians that they could not stop the advancing troops. Moreover, once the firing started, Sully brought the artillery into action. The cannon began shelling any concentrations of the enemy warriors, which quickly scattered them and diminished their effectiveness.

Some of the cannons were turned on the encampment itself, which created panic among the women and children. They had been so confident of victory that they hadn't made an effort to save the camp until it was too late.[407] The terrified residents hurriedly began to fold up the tepees like umbrellas, but had to abandon them under the artillery fire. The women and children had no choice but to flee for the safety of the Badlands, which lay beyond the ravines behind the camp.

Once the warriors realized that their families were in imminent danger the fighting became much more desperate. To buy time as the women and children fled, several hundred warriors slipped around the Eighth Minnesota's left flank through a gap between the hills and the Second Minnesota Cavalry. Their intent was to attack in the rear and draw the troops back.[408]

The flanking attack could have turned into a disaster for the Eighth Minnesota. The troops holding the horses had not advanced at the same speed as the dismounted soldiers. As a result, a gap had opened between the front line and their horses. The flanking maneuver threatened to cut off the rear guard, along with the supply wagons.

Realizing the threat on the flank, the artillery turned their guns away from the encampment and began firing on the Indians behind them. The rear guard, companies B and D of the Eighth Minnesota and Company B of the Second Cavalry, also

---

406 Hodgson, Ibid.

407 *Minnesota in the Civil and Indian Wars: 1861-1865*, vol. 1, 390.

408 Hodgson, "Recollections of the Sioux War No. 21," *Dakota County Tribune*, July 31, 1890.

opened up on the attacking Sioux warriors and repulsed their attack.[409] The Indians on the flank scattered and the threat was averted.

By this point, some of the troops began to sense that the enemy was getting more desperate. George Cambell realized that "All that the Indians were fighting for was to give their squaws and papooses time to get over the bluff and into the badlands where they would be safe."[410]

The action now shifted to the right side of the line where the dismounted Iowa cavalry troops and Brackett's Battalion were advancing. Many warriors had concentrated in the wooded ravines near the east side of the encampment. From there, they intending to launch an attack to slow the troops' advance and thereby gain more time for their families to escape.

One white woman witnessed the scene from the Indian perspective. Fanny Kelly, who had been captured and held prisoner by the Sioux for several months, watched Brackett's Battalion charge as she fled with the Indian women and children. She later described the action that took place, "General Sully's soldiers appeared in close proximity, and I could see them charging on the Indians, who, according to their habits of warfare, skulked behind trees, sending their bullets and arrows vigorously forward into the enemy's ranks."[411]

Seeing the growing threat on the right, Brackett ordered his men to charge into the ravines. Brackett led his mounted troops, who were armed with carbines, pistols, and sabers. The thick brush in the ravine provided the Indians with good cover where they could fight in close quarters. As a result, brutal hand-to-hand fighting ensued.

The woods and thickets of the ravine provided enough cover to help even the odds somewhat for the Indians. The close quarters fighting enabled them to use their bows and otherwise inferior firearms more effectively. Yet, it was still a rout. Brackett's men killed twenty-five to thirty-five warriors in that charge. It was difficult to count the true number of casualties as the Indians would pick up their dead and wounded, then ride off.

Brackett's charge drove the Indians farther into the woods and ravines, where they attempted to make a stand. The artillery then opened fire into the ravines. Overwhelmed by the power of cannons, the Indians had no choice but to retreat.

The threat on the right flank had been neutralized so Pope's battery returned to firing on the encampment. The troops continued to advance toward the camp,

---

409   Report of Col. Minor T. Thomas, Aug. 1, 1864, *Minnesota in the Civil and Indian Wars: 1861-1865*, vol. 2, 537.

410   Cambell, *Personal Reminiscences*, 28.

411   Kelly, *Narrative of My Captivity Among the Sioux Indians*, 99.

which by then had descended into total chaos. With shells exploding among them, the Indians and their families had to abandon the camp and all their worldly goods.

The firing on both sides let up as the Eighth Minnesota line neared the encampment at about 3 p.m. When the first troops entered the village, they found it wholly abandoned. The Indians could be seen swarming through the ravines and up the hill, out of reach of the soldier's guns.[412]

Sully did not want the Indians to get away. He ordered Major Camp to take companies E, F, H, and I of the Eighth Minnesota, have them remount and pursue the Indians to cut off their retreat into the Badlands.[413]

The soldiers found the pursuit very difficult. The Indians fled through narrow paths that were thick with brush. It was difficult to see more than a few feet in any direction.[414] The heavy brush provided such good cover that the troops were worried about being ambushed.[415]

Fortunately for the soldiers, no ambush materialized. The four companies of the Eighth Minnesota scoured the thickets, skirmishing with the Indians' rear guard as they went. The troops pushed ahead for about six miles until they arrived at the top of the bluffs. There, the advance of the Eighth Minnesota was halted by a band of 250-300 Indians.[416]

A short battle took place at the top of the hill until the Indian warriors pulled back. The soldiers opened fire with their rifles at the fleeing Indians, shooting so rapidly in the excitement that they continued firing even after being ordered to stop.[417]

Nightfall put an end to the shooting. There was no point in pursuing the Indians further, so the soldiers were ordered to return to camp. The exhausted men, who had been marching and fighting continuously for the past twenty-four hours, collapsed on the campground, hoping for some much-needed sleep.

Outcome of the Battle

By any measure, the battle had been a victory in favor of Sully's troops. Although the Indians outnumbered the soldiers, they did not have the firepower to effectively defend themselves against the well-armed adversary. David Kingsbury

412 Houlton, *Speech*.

413 Report of Lieut. Col. Henry C. Rogers, *Official Records*, series 1, vol. 41, part 1, 171, *Minnesota in the Civil and Indian Wars: 1861-1865*, vol. 1, 390.

414 Hodgson, "Recollections of the Sioux War No. 21," *Dakota County Tribune*, July 31, 1890. at 30.

415 Ibid.

416 Report of Maj. George A. Camp, *Official Records*, series 1, vol. 41, part 1, 172.

417 Hodgson, "Recollections of the Sioux War No. 21," *Dakota County Tribune*, July 31, 1890.

of Company E later remarked that the outcome would have been far different if the Indians had better arms.[418]

Most of the Indians defending the village were armed only with bows and arrows, which were effective weapons at short range. However, in the open fields on which most of the battle took place, the Indians could not get close enough to use the bows effectively. The extended range of the soldiers' Springfield rifles kept the Indians too far away to inflict casualties.

Even those Indians who had guns stood little chance against the troops. Most of the Indian firearms consisted of shotguns, trade muskets or inferior rifles. These were not much more effective than the bow and arrow, especially considering the range at which the soldiers could shoot accurately with their Springfields.

The Indian method of warfare also contributed to the one-sided outcome. The Sioux tended to focus on individual displays of bravery in battle. Hence, there was little coordination among the warriors. Their adversaries, the soldiers, were trained to function as a unit, which made them much more effective through concentrated strength in numbers. The combination of inferior arms and obsolete tactics could have led to heavy casualties for the Indians. It was difficult for the soldiers to estimate the actual number of enemy dead and wounded. Numerous accounts claim that the Indians picked up their dead and wounded whenever possible, leaving few bodies behind on the battlefield.

The actual number of Indian casualties may have been light under the circumstances. Soldiers and Indians alike heard the constant angry buzz of bullets whizzing by during the fight. Few of the rounds found their mark, however, and there was little damage inflicted on either side.

The soldiers' Springfields were accurate to a couple hundred yards or more. Nevertheless, the accuracy would have been limited because the soldiers had nothing upon which they could steady their weapons to aim as they advanced. Even if they paused and knelt to fire, resting an elbow on the knee to steady their aim, the soldiers were full of adrenaline and in the midst of chaos. Accurate fire at long range under such conditions would be difficult for even the best marksman. It was only when Brackett's men charged into the ravine that the opposing sides were close enough to inflict any real damage on each other.

Another factor that brings casualty counts into question is the tendency for a combatant to overestimate the enemy killed and wounded. Throughout history soldiers have claimed to have inflicted far more casualties than were actually the case. Examples from more recent conflicts include World War II fighter pilots often

---

418 Kingsbury, "Sully's Expedition Against the Sioux In 1864," 456.

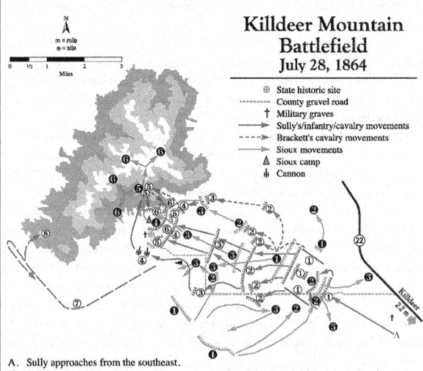

Killdeer Mountain Battlefield
July 28, 1864

⊕ State historic site
--------- County gravel road
† Military graves
━━➤ Sully's/infantry/cavalry movements
- - - ➤- Brackett's cavalry movements
━━➤ Sioux movements
△ Sioux camp
⫚ Cannon

A. Sully approaches from the southeast.
① Sully's forces form a phalanx, advance across a flat plain towards higher ground to the west.
❶ Sioux confront the phalanx on the front and flanks.
❷ Sioux attack the phalanx from the front and rear, abandon flanks.
② Rear guard of phalanx confronts Sioux; forward section of phalanx presses Sioux line back; Brackett's Cavalry breaks towards the northwest to flank the Sioux.
❸ Sioux abandon advance on rear guard, probe south flank; forward line retreats slowly towards village.
③ Sully's forces continue a steady advance; Brackett confronts Sioux at eastern foothills.
❹ Sioux retreat to village.
④ Sully's forces begin to encircle the village, artillery flanks the village from the south and begins shelling.
❺ Sioux begin to abandon the village.
⑤ Sully's forward line continue to envelope the village, Brackett and other forces move around to rear of village to cut off Sioux retreat.
❻ Sioux retreat into Killdeer Mountain ravines.
⑥ Brackett and outlying forces return to join Sully's encirclement of the village.
⑦ July 29, 1864—Sully skirts the mountain trying to cut off Sioux retreat into the badlands to the west—remaining troops destroy the village.
⑧ Sully's July 29th observation post.

claiming far higher numbers of planes shot down than could be confirmed, or the inflated body counts of the Vietnam War.

Calculating the Indian casualties based on the eyewitness accounts and anecdotal claims that the bodies were carried off caused casualty estimates for the Battle of Killdeer Mountain to vary widely. Lieutenant Benjamin Brunson of Company K estimated up to 600 Indians were killed in the battle. However, that was almost certainly far too high. Other participants in the battle placed the number killed much lower, somewhere in the seventy-five to one hundred.[419] Sully officially reported casualties of between 100 and 150 Indians.[420]

In fact, most eyewitnesses reported seeing only the twenty-five to thirty bodies of warrior dead in the ravine where they clashed with Brackett's Battalion.[421] Consequently, the Indian casualties were probably on the lower end of the estimates.

It is also difficult to determine the number of Indians wounded during the fight. Some estimates claim that 600 or more were wounded in the engagement. That number could be overestimated as well. Regardless, it is likely that a number of the Indian wounded would have died at a later time.

The casualties for Sully's force were only a fraction of those experienced by the Indians. The soldiers emerged from the fight with only two dead and eight wounded. Both of the men killed in action were from Brackett's Battalion.

Sergeant George Northrup from Company C of Brackett's Battalion was killed during the charge on the ravine. He fell with at least eight arrow wounds, including one through his heart. Northrup was one of the few men in the ranks that was actually familiar with the Dakota Territory. He had spent much time in the area prior to the Civil War and was sometimes referred to as the Kit Carson of the North.

Another soldier from Brackett's Battalion, Horatio Austin of Company D, was killed during skirmishing in the ravines. There were no other serious casualties among the soldiers engaged in the battle. The Eighth Minnesota came through nearly unscathed.

After dark, the troops quietly buried Northrup and Austin without ceremonial drums, bugle, or lights of any type. After finishing the burial, the graves were leveled out. On departure, the entire command marched over freshly turned earth to obliterate any trace of the graves.[422]

---

419 Hodgson, "Recollections of the Sioux War No. 22," *Dakota County Tribune*, Aug. 7, 1890.

420 Report of Brig. Gen. Alfred Sully, July 31, 1864, *Official Records*, series 1, vol. 41, part 1, 143.143.

421 Gardner Colwell, for example, recalled seeing only 27 bodies of fallen Indians in the ravine. Colwell *Diary*, July 28, 1864.

422 *Minnesota in the Civil and Indian Wars: 1861-1865*, vol. 1, 390.

The troops did not want to draw attention to the graves out of fear the Indians would dig them up and mutilate the bodies. The troops had no doubt heard reports Indians digging up victims' graves during the 1862 uprising and desecrating them. In one such example, a soldier in the Ninth Minnesota Volunteer Infantry Regiment described how his unit found the bodies of fourteen people killed by the Indians near Breckenridge, Minnesota. Soldiers from Fort Abercrombie had previously come across these victims and buried them. The Sioux later returned, dug up the graves and then drove stakes through the bodies into the ground.[423]

Ironically, the Sioux had to be just as afraid of whites desecrating Indian graves and corpses. One incident that occurred when the Sioux surrendered following 1862 uprising illustrated the hypocrisy that existed in some cases.

In November 1862, troops were assigned to escort the surrendered Sioux from along the Minnesota River to Fort Snelling, where they would be held until the government decided what to do with them. Along the route, angry white settlers tried to attack the helpless Indians with poles, pitchforks, and axes.[424] Occasionally, the settlers succeeded in striking one of the Indians. Some died as a result.

The troops tried to protect their prisoners from the assaults. At night, the Indians camped close together around a fire, while the soldiers camped in a circle around them for protection. In one case, after an Indian had died from blows inflicted by white settlers, the soldiers scraped their nightly campfire aside and buried the unfortunate man under it to prevent the whites from finding and presumably desecrating the body.[425]

In fact, some of the Eighth Minnesota troops who helped secretly bury Northrup and Austin were themselves guilty of desecrating Indian graves. On June 6, 1864, the Eighth Minnesota camped along the Minnesota River about twelve miles upriver from Fort Ridgely, having just completed the first day's march of the Northwestern Indian Expedition. The camp was located near the spot where the Dakota had first attacked army troops during the early days of the 1862 Uprising.

Some soldiers from Company H found the graves of two Indians near the camp. Those soldiers proceeded to dig up the bodies and kick them around, an act

---

423   One such example was witnessed by James Shotwell of Sauk Centre, a soldier in the 9th Minnesota Volunteer Infantry Regiment. Shotwell described how they came across the bodies of 14 persons killed by the Indians near Breckenridge, Minnesota. Soldiers from Fort Abercrombie had previously come across these victims and buried them. The Sioux later returned, dug up the graves and then drove stakes through the bodies into the ground. James A. Shotwell to son, Jan. 15, 1898, Dakota Conflict of 1862 Manuscripts Collections. Minnesota Historical Society.

424   Frances Densmore, *A Sioux Woman's Account of the Uprising in Minnesota*, circa 1934, Frances Densmore Papers. Minnesota Historical Society, 7.

425   Ibid.

that outraged and offended many of those who witnessed the disgusting spectacle.[426] George Doud of Company F angrily noted that their company commander failed to take "Any notice of their horrid acts."[427]

Destruction of the Indian Camp

The soldiers got little sleep the night after the Battle of Killdeer Mountain. In the darkness, the Indians were able to work their way in close to the campsite. They fired occasional rifle shots into the camp and harassed the pickets and scouts with arrows. They even got close enough to exchange words with Sully's scouts, some of whom were themselves Sioux.

The Indians complained to the scouts that it had not been a fair fight because most of their number were away from the encampment out looking for the troops. They promised to call in all their warriors and meet the soldiers again.[428]

At 1 a.m., the bugle called for the command to saddle up. Sully was determined to chase after the Indians who had fled the encampment the previous afternoon. The troops set out before first light to try and find a way around the mountains and cut off the Indians' path of retreat.

The troops could not pursue along the same route the Indians used the day before because they simply were not acquainted with the tangled map of bluffs, ravines, hills, and wallows to keep up with the Indians.[429] Moreover, the troops couldn't get over the mountains with artillery and wagons.[430]

It didn't take long for Sully to realize that it was no use to follow the Indians. The country was too rough, being cut up with deep wooded ravines. Some of those ravines were 100 feet deep with perpendicular sides. After making no more than eight miles in the chase, Sully called it off. The troops returned to the site of the encampment, arriving about 11 a.m.

Not long after the soldiers returned to the encampment, Sully may have missed an opportunity to avoid further conflict. A small delegation of Indians appeared on a nearby hillside and planted a white flag. It may have been an attempt to negotiate

426 Both Edson Washburn of Company E and George Doud of Company F were appalled and described the act using the term "brutal" in their respective diary entries. Doud, *Diaries*, June 6, 1864; Washburn diaries, June 6, 1864.

427 Doud, *Diaries*, June 6, 1864.

428 *Minnesota in the Civil and Indian Wars: 1861-1865*, vol. 1, 391.

429 Houlton, *Speech*.

430 Report of Col. M.T. Thomas, Aug. 1, 1864, *Official Records*, series 1, vol. 41, part 1, 165.

a truce. A few of the soldiers, however, fired on the Indians and they retreated. Sully did not see the flag until it was too late.[431]

Turning his attention to the encampment, Sully had to determine what to do with the vast amount of supplies the Indians had left behind. In their haste to abandon the camp, the fleeing Indians could only take whatever supplies they could carry, which wasn't much. They had abandoned the rest of their possessions on the campsite.

Even what little the Indians managed to carry away proved too much to haul through the ravines, especially when they were trying to dodge the deadly cannon shells. Unable to take the goods with them, the Indians tried to hide whatever they could in the thick vegetation.[432]

The Indians left behind substantial stores of everything they had prepared to carry them through the coming winter. The loss of these supplies was a severe blow to the Indians and, as the soldiers believed, probably irreplaceable.

The troops found huge amounts of food the Indians had preserved for the winter. This included tons of dried buffalo meat, which was stored in partially tanned buffalo hides, and huge quantities of dried berries stored in calf skins.

The Indians were forced to leave behind far more than food. They lost their shelter. Nearly all their tepees were still on the field. Many had collapsed during the battle from the impact of shells or been folded up in a vain attempt to drag them away before the troops arrived. The troops had to deal with all the buffalo hide tepee coverings and thousands of lodge poles, which had supported the coverings.

The men also found large quantities of household goods scattered about the encampment. These included brass and copper kettles, some of which were quite large. There were also mess pans and riding saddles. The Indians even abandoned many of their animals, including dogs and some ponies.

The soldiers discovered thousands of buffalo and antelope skins bundled and ready for market, as well as numerous buffalo robes. There was far too much material left in the camp or discarded in the nearby ravines for the troops to take with them. Sully did not want to let it fall back into the hands of the enemy.

Unable to remove all the Indians' property, Sully ordered his troops to destroy everything. For this task he detailed one of the Iowa Regiments and four companies of the Eighth Minnesota, including Company E.

For the rest of the day, the men labored to collect and destroy all the material left behind by the Indians. Some of the soldiers were sent into the ravines to recover

---

431 Report of Brig. Gen. Alfred Sully, July 31, 1864, *Official Records*, series 1, vol. 41, part 1, 144.

432 Strong, *A journal of the northwestern Indian expedition*, July 28, 1864. MNHS.

goods discarded by the fleeing Indians. They struggled to drag the bundles back to camp through the heavy brush and timber.[433]

Meanwhile, other soldiers were busy dealing with what remained behind in the encampment. All the lodge poles, food, tepee coverings and anything else of potential value to the Indians were piled up in stacks throughout the encampment. Then the soldiers set the stacks on fire. George Cambell recalled that they burned a pile of buffalo robes bigger than a meeting house.[434] The smoke and stench of burning leather so permeated the men's clothes and hair that they still smelled of it when they returned to the Heart River Corral some days later.

Soldiers also picked up relics from the battlefield as souvenirs.[435] Many of the buffalo robes slated for destruction were beautifully beaded with Indian artwork. These attracted the attention of many soldiers, who decided to appropriate the robes for themselves as spoils of war.

The challenge for those who wanted a buffalo robe was how to transport it back home. Buffalo robes were large and heavy. The troops, however, found an ingenious way to solve the problem. They would use the robes as saddle blankets by day and bed blankets at night.[436] Most of the soldiers took a buffalo robe in this matter, but some managed to take two or three.[437]

The officers also helped themselves to the spoils of war and were better able to store them for the return trip.[438] Officers could appropriate space in the wagons that by then had lots of room due to consumption of ammunition and food rations.

The smell of burning buffalo robes wasn't the only thing that followed the men back from the Indian encampment. The burned hides and the troops' newly acquired buffalo robes were infested with lice. These pests were quick to find a new home on the bodies of the soldiers.

The men were soon itching and scratching at the vermin. The lice did not discriminate between officers and the ranks, nearly everyone suffered. It was even worse than their prior battles with this foe because on the dry Dakota prairie, there was no

---

433 John Robinson to Libbie Robinson, Oct. 11, 1864, MNHS.

434 Cambell, *Personal Reminiscences*, 29.

435 A discarded powder horn retrieved by one of the soldiers is now in the possession of the Minnesota Historical Society.

436 Hodgson, "Recollections of the Sioux War No. 22," *Dakota County Tribune*, Aug. 7, 1890.

437 John Robinson to Libbie Robinson, Oct. 11, 1864, MNHS. It is unclear how many of the robes made it back to Minnesota as the command began to run short of horses and mules for transportation during their March to the Yellowstone River a week later.

438 Hodgson, "Recollections of the Sioux War No. 22," *Dakota County Tribune*, Aug 7, 1890.

water they could use to boil the lice out of their clothes. They would have to suffer through the lice infestation for quite some time.[439]

As the soldiers were clearing out the Indian encampment, an incident allegedly took place that disturbed many of the soldiers that learned of it. As they were gathering the property abandoned by the Indians, or so the story goes, the men came across two small papooses, which is what the soldiers called young Indian children. Their mother was either killed in the shelling or separated from her children during the chaos.

The soldiers set the tiny children on buffalo robes, where the men enjoyed entertaining the little ones and feeding them hardtack. Then, Sully's Winnebago scouts arrived on the scene.

The Winnebago tribe was no friend of the Sioux. The two tribes had fought over territory for generations. As the soldiers played with the youngsters, one of the scouts suddenly pulled out his tomahawk and sank it deep into the head of each child. Both children were killed instantly. The scout turned to the horrified soldiers and justified the cold-blooded murders by saying "Nits make lice."[440]

The killing of the Indian children in camp may or may not have occurred. It has many of the hallmarks of an urban legend.[441] It does not appear that any of the men who recorded the incident actually witnessed it. They also gave very different accounts. Benjamin Brunson from Company K of the Eighth Minnesota claimed the scouts killed two children with a tomahawk. David Kingsbury of Company E later wrote that only a single child was killed with a pistol shot.[442] Kingsbury, however, did not say that he witnessed the killing.

Withdrawal from Killdeer

On the afternoon of July 29, Sully's troops finished the destruction of the Indian supplies. Then they saddled up and began the return trip to rendezvous with the soldiers and emigrants left behind at the Heart River Corral. They didn't have

---

439 Cambell later wrote that they carried these lively reminders of the Indian camping grounds all the way to the Yellowstone River, which they would not reach until 2 weeks later, on August 12, 1864. Cambell *Personal Reminiscences*, 29.

440 Brunson, "Reminiscences of Service With the Eighth Minnesota Infantry," 371. "Nits" refers to a louse's eggs or to young lice.

441 An urban legend is defined as "an often lurid story or anecdote that is based on hearsay and widely circulated as true. Merriam-Webster at https://www.merriam-webster.com/dictionary/urban%20legend, accessed June 27, 2019.

442 Kingsbury, "Sully's Expedition Against the Sioux In 1864," 456.

time to go far due to the late departure but at least got a four-mile start on the return trip before breaking for the evening.

Bands of Indian warriors shadowed Sully's command as it moved south. The troops were aware of the surveillance and knew it would be important to establish a good defensive position when they camped for the night. Nevertheless, it was difficult to do so.

Because the grass was so thin, Sully set up a much larger perimeter than would normally be the case. This would ensure that there was enough grass within the perimeter for the horses and mules to forage. He ordered Major Camp to set up between twelve and fifteen picket posts approximately three miles out from the encampment.

The troops detailed to picket duty were sent out in groups of three men. One of the three men would always be mounted and ready to ride back to camp if it was necessary to sound the alarm. The mounted soldier would then ride to the right or left until he met the next picket post, then turn around and ride the other way. While this was going on, the other two men could try to nap.

The soldiers would rotate through the roles while on picket duty. One would ride as the other two rested. When the rider returned, one of the other soldiers would take his place. The men who got to rest would keep their horses tied to their wrists so they would be ready in the event of trouble.

On this evening, the picket posts were established while it was still light. Each post was set up about three miles from the camp on the highest ground available. As a result, these posts were within full view of the Indians, who were watching from cover and looking for weaknesses.[443]

Three men from Company D of the Second Minnesota Cavalry were detailed to take one of the picket posts. One of the soldiers promptly took the first shift riding the circuit between the picket posts to the right and left. As it was not yet dark, the other two men, privates David LaPlant and Anton Holzgen, sat down to rest and play cards. While they did so, they kept an eye out for approaching threats from the prairie.

As darkness began to fall, the picket rider suddenly heard an arrow whiz by his head.[444] Turning, the soldier was shocked to see that six Indians had infiltrated between him and the encampment and were now shooting at him with their bows. The soldier quickly rode into camp and raised the alarm.[445]

At about the same time, between fifty and one hundred warriors dashed at the picket post, intent on stampeding their horses and stealing the animals if possible.

443 *Minnesota in the Civil and Indian Wars: 1861-1865*, vol. 1, 546.

444 Cambell, *Personal Reminiscences*, 30.

445 Ibid.

Within moments, LaPlant and Holzgen were in the fight of their lives. However, the soldiers were too far from camp and the other picket posts to get any help. The Indians quickly overwhelmed them.

As the shooting began there was a great commotion in camp. At the time, 1,500 horses were out grazing, making them vulnerable to being run off by the Indians.[446] The horses were quickly tied up to prevent a stampede. The officers formed the soldiers into a line of battle around the camp to defend against the attack. There they waited into the night expecting an attack at any moment. However, the attack never came.

Meanwhile, the exposed picket posts remained vulnerable to Indian attack. Sergeant Campbell of Company D, Second Minnesota Cavalry took charge of the situation and began working the pickets back toward the camp.[447] It took several hours for the pickets to find their way because it grew so dark that they couldn't see the camp. All the campfires had been extinguished at the first shots as a precaution. Nevertheless, all the pickets, except LaPlant and Holzgen, eventually managed to make it back.

The following morning, Sunday, July 31, the soldiers were roused at 2 a.m. to prepare for the day's march. After the usual preparations, Sully's force was ready to set out for the Heart River Corral by 4:30 a.m.

Before the taskforce departed, Company E of the Eighth Minnesota, being on rear guard for the train, was ordered to go out and find LaPlant and Holzgen. They found both men dead at their post, one with fourteen arrows stuck in his body. The Indians had taken everything of value from the dead soldiers, including their carbines, revolvers, cartridge boxes, sabers and their horses.[448] The bodies, however, were not mutilated. The Indians had been in too much of a hurry and probably didn't want to spend time looking for them in the dark after making their charge towards camp.

As with the casualties at Killdeer Mountain, LaPlant and Holzgen were buried on the prairie. The signs of their graves were obliterated so the Indians would not find them. It was a sad and moving occasion for the men. Years later, Corporal William Houlton would recall his feelings upon leaving the grave site. "I don't know how the rest of you felt, but when I saw those men sticking full of arrows crowded into shallow holes without enough dirt to save them from the next wolf that came along, hundreds of miles from home, I felt a more sickening and cowardly sensation than I ever did in the army or anywhere else before or since."[449] Another soldier observed

---

446 Colwell *Diary*, July 29, 1864.

447 *Minnesota in the Civil and Indian Wars: 1861-1865*, vol. 1, 546.

448 Strong, *A journal of the northwestern Indian expedition*, July 30 1864. MNHS.

449 Houlton, *Speech*.

that it was hard on the soldiers "For them to be murdered while they were standing guard over us."[450]

The heat continued to be oppressive. Without much food or water, the mule teams and horses were beginning to give out. It was hard on the men as well. Nevertheless, they pressed on. Even under such rough conditions, the troops still managed to cover the thirty-eight miles to their destination near the Heart River Corral by 5 p.m.[451] There, the soldiers set up camp for the night.

The troops were thrilled to be back. In just six days, Sully's force had traveled over 170 miles and fought a significant battle, and they had done so with little water, minimal rations, and scant forage for the animals.

Because of all of this, the men returned from the trip utterly spent. By some estimates, the troops had slept no more than fourteen hours since leaving the Heart River. The lack of sleep combined with the oppressive heat, dehydration, and reduced food rations, had completely exhausted them[452].

The troops were also relieved to find the occupants of the corral safe and sound. The feeling was mutual. Ever since Sully and his force departed, those left behind had been under unrelenting stress. There were frequent reports circulating throughout the corral of nearby Indians, leaving the defenders constantly on edge.

Fearing that their small numbers could be easily overwhelmed due to inadequate firepower, the defenders even fashioned a cannon out of wood and metal bands. It was fired a few times, which they hoped would make the Indians think twice about attacking. As it was, nearly all the alleged Indian sightings were probably either false alarms or nothing more than small scouting parties that had no intention of attacking a well-defended fixed position.

Sully was anxious to continue in pursuit of the Indians he had engaged at Killdeer. He wrote a report for his superiors and stated that he intended to march for the Yellowstone River in two days and overtake the fleeing Indians along the way.[453]

The following morning, Monday, August 1, Sully's force moved its camp to within the defenses of the Heart River Corral. Only then did the officers discover that the commissary at Fort Rice had made a terrible miscalculation and underestimated the supplies that would be required for Sully's Expedition. As a result, the Expedition had at most only six day's rations left.[454]

---

450   John Robinson to Libbie Robinson, Oct. 11, 1864, MNHS.

451   Doud, *Diaries*, July 31, 1864.

452   John Robinson to Libbie Robinson, Oct. 11, 1864, MNHS.

453   Report of Brig. Gen. Alfred Sully, July 31, 1864, *Official Records*, series 1, vol. 41, part 1, 144.

454   Kingsbury, "Sully's Expedition Against the Sioux In 1864," 457.

The lack of rations put Sully in a bind. His force lacked enough supplies to pursue the Indians as they continued their flight from Killdeer. If he returned to Fort Rice, the Indians would have plenty of time to escape. Doing so would amount to abandoning any further action against the Sioux for the year.

If Sully continued towards the Yellowstone River as he originally planned, the Expedition could be resupplied from steamships. But there was one big problem with that plan. Between the Heart River Corral and the Yellowstone River lay the Badlands.

The Badlands were a significant obstacle, covering an area of over a hundred miles from north to south and about twenty miles across. The land is made up of rough and broken terrain with deep canyons, making the area nearly impassable for the wagon trains. Moreover, there were no maps of the area to show a path through the desolate landscape. It appeared that crossing the Badlands would be all but impossible.

Battle of the Badlands

August 1 to August 17, 1864

To Cross the Badlands

To determine the options for continuing the Expedition, Sully assembled his Indian guides, explained the situation, and consulted with them regarding the best route to the Yellowstone.[455] The guides told Sully it would be impossible for wagons to cross the Badlands and suggested returning to the southern route they had been traveling before they were diverted to attack the Indian village at Killdeer.[456]

The southern route, however, would take at least two and possibly three weeks longer than across the Badlands. The Expedition didn't have anywhere near enough rations for such an extended march, so taking such a wide detour was out of the question.

Then one Indian scout, a young lad barely eighteen years old, stepped forward. He was a member of the Blackfoot tribe and claimed that he had been through the Badlands with a war party years earlier.[457] He was sure that he could get wagons across the Badlands by digging paths through the ravines.[458]

---

455   Report of Brig. Gen. Alfred Sully, Aug. 13, 1864, *Official Records*, series 1, vol. 41, part 1, 144.

456   Ibid.

457   Some sources describe the young man as a Blackfoot and others as a Yankton.

458   Ibid.

THE NORTH DAKOTA BADLANDS IN THEODORE ROOSEVELT NATIONAL PARK. THIS WAS TAKEN IN THE SAME GENERAL AREA WHERE THE EIGHTH REGIMENT SOLDIERS WOULD HAVE FIRST SEEN THIS UNUSUAL LANDSCAPE. TAKEN BY THE AUTHOR IN 2018.

This was exactly what General Sully wanted to hear. He decided to trust the young scout and take the direct route to the Yellowstone River. There, Sully would replenish his supplies and continue in pursuit of the Indians.[459]

The soldiers themselves were looking forward to a few days' rest at the Heart River. By this time word of the ration shortage was circulating among the troops and some soldiers assumed that they might have to turn around and return to Minnesota. Those hopes were quickly dashed when General Sully addressed the troops assembled within the corral. Sully first complimented the men on their performance over the past few days. Then he informed the troops that they would continue their pursuit of the Sioux and set out for the Yellowstone River the next day.[460]

The march would not be easy. The men and animals were already in rough shape. Now they would have to travel almost 150 miles over some of the most rugged terrain in Dakota Territory before they had any hope of resupply. To make matters worse, the brutal heat, lack of water, and barren landscape would almost certainly take a toll on men and animals.

For the rest of the day on August 1, the troops prepared for their march west to the Yellowstone River. They were well aware that they would be exposed to the

459 Ibid.

460 John Robinson to Libbie Robinson, Oct. 11, 1864, MNHS.

enemy for most, if not all of that time. Therefore, they cleaned their guns and prepared for the possibility of further Indian encounters.[461]

That evening, fifteen Indian ponies were spotted running loose near the corral. This was a surprise as Sully's scouts had not seen any hostile Indians in the area. The troops supposed these were scattered horses that had either run away from the Indians during the battle at Killdeer Mountain or from the skirmish that the scouts had with the Indians on the evening of July 26 just after Sully first set out for Killdeer.[462]

Some of the troops, including men from Company E, went out after the ponies. They managed to catch at least six. David Kingsbury came back with one very nice animal. The Indian ponies were prized because they were in much better shape than the army issued horses, which some troops recalled were nothing more than a bag of bones to begin with. The horses only deteriorated the longer they remained in Dakota Territory.

Under the best conditions it would take well over a week to reach the Yellowstone River. With such rough terrain ahead and hostile Sioux potentially awaiting them, nobody knew how long the march would take. Even if the trip took no longer than expected, there was a very real risk that the Expedition would exhaust their supplies well before they reached the Yellowstone River. The officers, therefore, ordered that the men immediately be placed on reduced rations. From then on, the men would receive only a one-third ration of bread and a half-ration of meat.[463].

The long march ahead and lack of food were not the only issues facing the expedition. It was the hottest time of year on the northern plains. Temperatures were reaching into the triple digits and there was no shade from the unrelenting sun. The region was also experiencing an ongoing drought so it would be difficult to find any fresh water for the troops or the animals.

To make matters even worse, a plague of grasshoppers struck Dakota Territory that summer. Between the drought and the grasshoppers, there was nary a blade of green grass anywhere to feed the horses and mules. To top it off, there were potentially thousands of angry Indian warriors in the area that might attack at any point along the way. It would not be a pleasant journey.

West to the Badlands

On Wednesday, August 3, 1864, reveille sounded at 3 a.m. The troops struck their tents, tended to the animals, and made their coffee for the march. By 5 a.m. they

---

461 Doud, *Diaries*, Aug. 1, 1864.

462 Ibid.

463 Kingsbury, "Sully's Expedition Against the Sioux in 1864," 457.

were on their way across the plains with both brigades and all the emigrants. The day quickly grew hot, and the still air provided no relief. It must have been terrible for the men who had no shelter from the sun and even worse for the animals.

Sully's command proceeded twenty miles that day, following along the north side of the Heart River. They made camp for the night along the river, where they found some good grass for the animals. However, the water was bad.[464] That part of the river barely ran at all and was thick with mud. The few stagnant water holes that the Expedition came across on the prairie were often strongly alkaline, which was unpleasant for men or animals to drink if they could drink it at all.

The next morning, August 4, the expedition again started on the march by 5 a.m. and proceeded northwest. The day started out cloudy and was much cooler than it had been, giving a bit of relief to the men and animals.

Passing just south of present-day Dickenson, North Dakota, the men were astonished to see what appeared to be large sand dunes in the distance to the south.[465] In fact, these were actually large hills of exposed dolomite clay that glistened white in the burning sunshine. The hills covered an area of several square miles and rose above the surrounding terrain.

The force camped not far from the "sand dunes" that night and set out again on the morning of August 5. That day, the Minnesota Brigade was in front. As they traveled over the gently rolling plains, the soldiers could see little else but drought-stricken grass. The only breaks in the vast expanse of prairie were a few tall hills that rose over the landscape. The march on August 5 was just more of the same, but towards evening the soldiers first came across a sight unlike anything any of them had seen before – the Badlands.

Into the Dakota Badlands – "Hell with the Fires Put Out"

The Badlands had once been on the edge of an ancient shallow sea. Different sediments, volcanic ash from the Yellowstone super volcano, and decayed plant matter built up in layers over millions of years. Eventually, heat and pressure turned the various deposits into rock and clay.

Over time, the Little Missouri River had eaten away at the plains around it, cutting deep ravines and crevasses through the rocks. Some of winding canyons reached down more than 200 feet from the surrounding landscape, often with near vertical

---

464 Doud, *Diaries*, Aug. 3, 1864.

465 Both Edson Washburn and George Doud recorded the sight in their diaries. The formations that they saw that day are still clearly visible on Google Earth. They are also visible on the horizon about 8 miles south from Interstate 94 midway between Dickenson and Benfield near the small town of South Heart. Doud, *Diaries*, Aug. 5, 1864; Washburn, *Diaries*, Aug. 4, 1864.

walls. Wind and rain further eroded away the softer rock and clay, leaving an astonishing vista of hills in all shapes and sizes. The canyon walls and hillsides display brilliantly colored alternating bands of bluish-gray, red, white, black, and other hues.

Down in the Badlands were other interesting formations. Some of the black bands in the hills were formations of lignite coal. Lightning strikes and grass fires occasionally set an exposed coal vein on fire. The heat escaping from these coal fires would bake the surrounding rocks and clay, turning them into a red, brick-like rock called a "clinker." Clinkers are much harder than the surrounding rocks and protect the softer materials directly below from erosion. As a result, clinkers may be seen as a type of capstone that protects some of the buttes from wearing away.[466]

The resulting landscape is now and was then a stunning example of nature's beauty. None of this was visible to the approaching soldiers, however, until they were nearly to the edge. The Badlands lie below the horizon of the surrounding plains.

Many of these men were from New England or the Midwest, where they were accustomed to flat farmlands, shallow green river valleys, or forested hillsides. Now before them was a spectacular panorama of a barren, but colorful landscape unlike anything they had ever seen.

For many of the soldiers, their first views of the Badlands were just glimpses between the gentle rolling hills of the plains as they approached the rim of the canyons. George Cambell recalled that he could see the men riding ahead of him "standing in their saddles, craning their necks, very much interested.[467] Each file of soldiers, as they reached the same place, imitated them exactly.[468]

Their first view of the Badlands captivated the soldiers. For a short time, they forgot about everything else, including the Indians, and focused on the magnificent landscape below. One soldier wrote that "the scene before us surpassed the power of speech to describe."[469]

One of the emigrants wrote:

At every step of the advance we would be excited by new sights of what seemed to be towers, cones, monuments, etc. of every con-

---

466 *Coal Vein, A Guided Nature* Trail, National Park Service, U.S. Department of the Interior, Theodore Roosevelt National Park, https://www.nps.gov/thro/planyourvisit/upload/CoalVeinShort.pdf, accessed May 5, 2019.

467 Cambell, *Personal Reminiscences*, 20.

468 Ibid., 21.

469 Hodgson, "Recollections of the Sioux War No. 23," *Dakota County Tribune*, Aug. 14, 1890.

ceivable description, which so impressed all that but few words were spoken.[470]

A soldier from Company F of the Eighth Minnesota provided more details:

There stretching to the front on either side of us lay a country that seemed to have sunken to some mighty earthquake – as if after the earthquake vast chasms have opened in checkered forms that the rains and storms of centuries had washed the chasms wider and wider leaving all shapes of fluted hills and pinnacles, some of them worn to a point at the top, some still had a little green spot of herbage on their tops, some had been clean washed away and boulders and petrified bones were strewed over the ground that had once been a hill.[471]

Not everyone was quite so impressed with the Badlands. Edson Washburn called it the "hills of desolation."[472] General Sully wrote that he "became alarmed, and almost despaired at ever being able to cross it."[473] He remarked to his officers that it was "Hell with the fires put out."[474]

Darkness began to fall as the Expedition reached the eastern rim of the Badlands. The lead elements made camp on the edge and had a spectacular view of the sun setting over the colorful geologic structures below. Distracted by the expansive scenery, some of the Expedition forgot to look for water, food, and fuel as they set up camp.[475]

Sully's scouts did locate a small pool of muddy water that afternoon about a mile and a half away from the camp. It was the only available source of water that day, so it was quickly depleted. The 3,000 soldiers had to compete for the precious liquid

470   Hilger, "Campaign of General Alfred Sully Against the Hostile Sioux in 1864," 315. Nicholas Hilger was one of the emigrants traveling to what is now Montana. He had served as captain in the militia at Henderson, Minnesota following the Dakota uprising in 1862. In 1864, he resigned his commission and joined the group of emigrants traveling to Idaho territory to go into the mining business. He settled in what is now Helena and spent the rest of his life in Montana.

471   Hodgson, "Recollections of the Sioux War No. 23," *Dakota County Tribune*, Aug. 14, 1890.

472   Washburn, *Diaries*, Aug. 5, 1864.

473   Report of Brig. Gen. Alfred Sully, Aug. 13, 1864, *Official Records*, series 1, vol. 41, part 1, 144.

474   Various versions of the statement were recorded. See e.g., Kingsbury, "Sully's Expedition Against the Sioux In 1864," 457 and English, *Dakota's First Soldiers*, 284.

475   Hilger, "Campaign of General Alfred Sully Against the Hostile Sioux in 1864," 315.

with nearly as many horses and mules.[476] Even what little water the soldiers managed to retrieve consisted of nothing more than thin mud.[477]

The wagon train, which had been spread out for miles, continued to file into the encampment for some time. It was well after dark before the last teams arrived. The latecomers found setting up camp a bit difficult in the dark. There was barely a quarter moon that night and it didn't rise until after 11 p.m. Campfires and stars provided the only illumination.

It was so dark that away from campfires a soldier could not see his hand in front of his face. This led to a tragic incident. Some of the cavalry soldiers who made up the rear guard had camped close to the cliffs to get a better view of the Badlands in the setting sun. After dark, one of those soldiers, blinded by the campfire, accidently stepped off the cliff edge and fell more than 200 feet to his death.[478] His unrecogniz-able and broken body was located by his comrades the next morning. They buried him on the spot where he was found.[479]

The cavalryman wasn't the only casualty of the darkness that night. Three other soldiers who were also camped along the ravines backed up to avoid the heat of the campfire, fell over the bluff and were badly hurt.[480]

The following morning, Saturday, August 6, the men rose to a meager breakfast of bacon and hardtack. There was no water left for coffee. They set out at 4:30 a.m. and began the long winding descent into the Badlands below. Sully's Indian guides led the way. A large pick and shovel brigade was organized to follow behind the Indian guides and cut a road wide enough for wagons to pass.[481]

The Expedition train slowly uncoiled down into the valley like a long snake as it moved around all the geologic features of the landscape. The going was dif-ficult. Descending into the valley required a very circuitous route and sometimes required traveling back uphill. "We zigzagged around the buttes and frequently went three miles to gain one," recalled George Cambell.[482] One of the emigrants was aston-ished when, more than two hours after the head of the column had disappeared into

476   John Robinson to Libbie Robinson, Oct. 11, 1864, MNHS.

477   Ibid.

478   Hilger, "Campaign of General Alfred Sully Against the Hostile Sioux in 1864," 315.

479   Hilger at 315.

480   Cambell, *Personal Reminiscences*, 21.

481   Hilger, "Campaign of General Alfred Sully Against the Hostile Sioux in 1864," 316.

482   Cambell, *Personal Reminiscences*, 22.

the valley below, he saw it coming back toward him from another direction farther down.[483]

Clearing a path was no easy job. The "pioneers," as the pick and shovel brigade were called, leveled the road, made bridges, and put down corduroy.[484] The pioneers were followed by the soldiers, who helped get the wagons and artillery pieces up and down the ridges.

The ridges the train had to cross were often so steep that the brakes on the wagons were useless. The soldiers had to use ropes to control the wagons and artillery pieces in the descent when going downhill and pull them up by ropes when traveling on a steep uphill course. This effort required a lot of manpower. "Often it would take nearly a company to draw a gun up one ridge and then let it down the other side."[485]

The horses, mules and emigrant's livestock had trouble with the steep inclines as well. The animals were difficult to control and one man from Company H was injured by stampeding horses.[486] The Expedition made only eleven miles that day.

Despite the hardship of travel through the Badlands, the men were awed at the beauty of their surroundings, and many took the opportunity to do a little exploring. They found plenty of colorful scenery, petrified wood, and exposed coal veins. A few soldiers amused themselves by trying to ignite the coal veins. George Cambell recalled that the coal veins were easy for the soldiers to light on fire, but difficult to put out.[487]

Members of Company E who later worked on the Northern Pacific Railroad, claimed that those veins were still burning after twenty-five years.[488] The claim is credible. A coal vein fire burned in Theodore Roosevelt National Park, which includes much of the North Dakota Badlands, for twenty-six years from 1951 until 1977.[489] Moreover, tracks put down by the Northern Pacific Railroad in the 1880s ran very close to the path followed by Sully's Expedition twenty years earlier. Smoke from the coal fires would likely have been visible from passing trains.

---

483 Hilger, "Campaign of General Alfred Sully Against the Hostile Sioux in 1864,"315-316.

484 "Corduroy" refers to laying logs side by side across a road to permit wheels to pass over rutted or pockmarked ground.

485 Cambell, *Personal Reminiscences*, 22.

486 Washburn, *Diaries*, Aug. 6, 1864.

487 Cambell, *Personal Reminiscences*, 24.

488 Ibid.

489 *See, Coal Vein, A Guided Nature Trail*, National Park Service, U.S. Department of the Interior, Theodore Roosevelt National Park, https://www.nps.gov/thro/planyourvisit/upload/CoalVein-Short.pdf, ,accessed May 5, 2019.

There was also wildlife to be seen in the ravines. Antelope were plentiful and there were signs of buffalo, although they didn't see any at the time.

The soldiers also realized that they were being shadowed by Indians. As they traveled through the Badlands, small Indian raiding parties constantly tried to infiltrate the train to kill the whites and steal horses.

The Indians were very adept at concealment and could get in close to the Expedition without being detected. In one case an emigrant's wagon had broken down within hailing distance of camp. The man told the rear guard to go ahead because he would be following in just a minute. They were within sight of the campfires and could clearly hear the talking of soldiers already in camp, so the rear guard thought it safe to leave him.

After about five minutes, there was no sign of the emigrant, so a sergeant took his squad to go and help him. They quickly located the man. He was dead and scalped right where they left him a few minutes before. The Indians had silently killed the man and stolen his horses within full view of the camp.[490]

After a hard day of traveling through the rough terrain throughout August 6, the Expedition reached the banks of the Little Missouri River. This tributary of the Missouri lies in a valley with steep bluffs on each side. There were large cottonwood trees along its banks but little grass for the animals. The water was very muddy, a result of the eroded clay and other materials being carried by the current to the Missouri River. George Cambell claimed that there was two inches of mud in every pail of the river water.[491]

The river was also somewhat alkaline. Between the mud and the alkalinity, the water was unpleasant to drink. Nevertheless, compared to the dry barren country they had just crossed, it was a veritable paradise.[492] The men and animals tried to make the most of it. However, the brief opportunity to rest was suddenly broken when large numbers of Indian warriors began to arrive.

The Battle of the Badlands Begins

As dusk began to fall on the evening of August 6, the men went to work pitching their tents. Suddenly, three or four Indians rode into view on a steep bluff just

---

490   Cambell, *Personal Reminiscences*, 32.

491   Cambell, *Personal Reminiscences*, 33.

492   Kingsbury, "Sully's Expedition Against the Sioux In 1864," 458.

yards away from the soldiers' camp.[493] The soldiers fired a few shots at the small band, who quickly wheeled their horses and ducked out of sight.[494]

That same day, the young Blackfoot scout identified an exit going west from the Little Missouri River bottoms. It consisted of a dry creek bed that ran through a deep and narrow canyon. The floor of the canyon sloped upwards gently for a few miles. It would take a lot of work, but the canyon could be dug out to create a road just large enough for wagons to pass.

Early on the morning of Sunday, August 7, the pick and shovel work crew was organized for the day. The size of the crew was increased to between 600 and 700 men for the hard work ahead. The work detail's objective was to build a road from the camp to the canyon and then up to the rolling plains above. Company I of the Eighth Minnesota and Company H of the Second Minnesota Cavalry accompanied the work crew to provide protection.

By mid-morning the work detail had cut a road along the west side of the river and was already working their way up the canyon. As they progressed, the crew cut into the canyon walls and filled holes so wagons could pass.[495] Even with all the men and labor, they could only widen the path just enough for a single wagon to pass through. Slowly but steadily, the work crew inched ahead.

The soldiers that remained behind in camp that morning were allowed some time to rest on the east side of the river. A few soldiers, including several from Company F, took advantage of the break to lead their horses into the woods beyond the picket lines in search of better grass. They did so without orders and apparently without the knowledge of their officers. Not yet realizing that large numbers of Indians were nearby, most of the Company F soldiers left their saddles and rifles behind in camp.[496]

The small group traveled down river about a mile, where they tethered the horses.[497] As the horses grazed next to the river, three Company F soldiers, John Webb, Bob Moore, and James Wilson used the time to take a swim.

493   John Robinson to Libbie Robinson, Oct. 11, 1864, MNHS.

494   Ibid.

495   Strong, *A journal of the northwestern Indian expedition*, Aug. 7, 1864. MNHS.

496   Report of Brig. Gen. Alfred Sully, July 31, 1864, *Official Records*, series 1, vol. 41, part 1, 145. Sully did not mention the specific unit involved but from various other sources it was almost certainly Company F of the Eighth Regiment, including Thomas Hodgson of Co. F, who mentioned leaving their guns behind as they went out to graze horses. Hodgson, "Recollections of the Sioux War No. 23," *Dakota County Tribune*, Aug. 14, 1890. Likewise, Gardner Colwell of Company F noted that "we carelessly left our guns in camp. Colwell *Diary*, Aug. 7, 1864.

497   Hodgson, "Recollections of the Sioux War No. 23," *Dakota County Tribune*, Aug. 14, 1890.

Another Company F soldier, Thomas Hodgson, had also gone down river with several horses. He tethered them not far from the others so they could graze. Then Hodgson laid down in grass nearby to rest and read a poetry book.[498]

At about 7:30 a.m., as the soldiers were enjoying a swim in the refreshingly cool Little Missouri River, Webb realized something was wrong. His horse began acting strangely alarmed. Webb tried to convince his skeptical companions that the horse's behavior meant they were in danger. Webb got out of the water and dressed. As he mounted his horse to take a look around, he spotted an approaching Indian raiding party.[499]

With the Indians closing in there was no time for Moore and Wilson to get their horses. Both grabbed their clothes and ran for their lives. Webb galloped up to Hodgson and raised the alarm. Hodgson quickly rounded up the horses he had tethered and tried to get them back to camp. The horses, however, didn't want to move. They were reluctant to leave the good grass.[500]

As the fleeing soldiers tried to collect the rest of the horses, they found another small raiding party of maybe seven Indians cutting the tether lines.[501] A few of the soldiers had revolvers and began exchanging fire with the Indians. Suddenly, many more Indians emerged out of the underbrush on both sides of the river. Fearing that they were about to be surrounded, the soldiers abandoned the rest of the horses and sprinted for the safety of camp.

At the same time another raiding party of Indians tried to steal some horses closer to the camp. A number of shots were exchanged but it did not appear that there were any casualties. Nevertheless, the Indians managed to capture two more horses from Sully's Brigade.[502]

The sound of the gunfire instantly alerted the soldiers in camp. Soldiers from Company F quickly gathered their rifles and, without orders, set out to rescue their comrades. By the time they arrived the Indians had already fled with their captured horses. However, a vigorous pursuit by Sully's scouts caused the raiding party to abandon all but two of the animals, those stolen from Moore and Wilson.[503]

Meanwhile, the pioneer brigade suddenly realized they too were in imminent danger. While the pioneers had been focused on constructing the road, a band of

---

498 Ibid.

499 Ibid.

500 Ibid.

501 Ibid.

502 Doud, *Diaries*, Aug. 7, 1864.

503 Hodgson, "Recollections of the Sioux War No. 23," *Dakota County Tribune*, Aug. 14, 1890.

Indians had worked their way into position on the heights overlooking the canyon. At about 10 a.m., the Indians opened fire, pouring down bullets and arrows on the work crew.

One of the pioneers later recalled "From every point, cliff, hole or cave the Indians fired upon us."[504] The pioneers panicked and, along with their guards, fled back to camp.[505] While many of the pioneers claimed to have narrowly escaped with their lives, there were miraculously no casualties.

When the gunfire first erupted, the entire Expedition in camp saddled their horses and hitched up the wagons in preparation for an attack. After the initial commotion died down, Sully decided that since everyone was ready, the Expedition would break camp and follow the road cut by the pioneers across and upriver for about three miles. As the Expedition moved out, the soldiers found themselves under constant surveillance by the Indians.

Upon reaching the canyon where the pioneers had been working, Sully realized that would take too long to complete the road to the top. As a result, Sully ordered the Expedition back across the river to camp for the night in a spot that promised better grass for the animals.[506] As the train proceeded back across the river, they were fired on by Indians in the nearby hills. The troops returned fire, perhaps hitting three or four of the enemy. At the same time the Third Minnesota Battery fired some cannon shells at them after which the Indians quickly disappeared.[507]

The Indians did not leave, however, but simply went out of sight. Company B of the Sixth Iowa Cavalry was placed on the northeast corner of the camp. As the sun went down, the troops noticed some Indians on the cliffs 200 feet above their heads. "We momentarily expected them to take advantage of their position to fire, or roll some large boulders down upon us," recalled Private Frank Myers.[508] Fortunately, before the Indians could take action, they came under cannon fire and fled.

The Sioux did not go far. From their positions in the hills overlooking the camp, the Indians taunted the soldiers well into the evening. Some of the Sioux were multilingual and they demonstrated their mastery of English vulgarity by pouring forth a steady stream of profanity aimed at the soldiers.

The Indians claimed to have 10,000 warriors a short distance off and that the soldiers were surrounded on all sides. The Sioux proposed to take the troops pris-

---

504 Hilger, "Campaign of General Alfred Sully Against the Hostile Sioux in 1864," 317.

505 Myers, *Soldiering in Dakota*, 20.

506 Report of Brig. Gen. Alfred Sully, July 31, 1864, *Official Records*, series 1, vol. 41, part 1, 145.

507 Doud, *Diaries*, Aug. 7, 1864.

508 Myers, *Soldiering in Dakota*, 20.

oner, after which they would force the officers to eat the enlisted men. The Indians also claimed to have a white woman as a prisoner and invited the soldiers to try and free her.[509]

The skirmishing went on well into the evening. Lieutenant Colonel Pattee of the Seventh Iowa Cavalry recalled that at least 3,000 shots were fired that night.[510] The soldiers were ordered to saddle the horses at midnight and then further ordered to stay outside near the pickets in case of Indian attack.[511] The exhausted troops had little opportunity to sleep. "What little chance we got to lay down during the night, we had to do so with our revolvers and sabers buckled to us and guns in our hands."[512]

Across the Little Missouri

At daylight, on Monday, August 8, the troops realized they had been camped on a flatland that was ordinarily part of the riverbed. Much of the area consisted of quicksand.[513] That made their third crossing of the Little Missouri all the more treacherous. To make matters worse, an estimated 3,000 Indians conducted isolated attacks as the troops began crossing at about 9 a.m.[514]

The entire Expedition had to follow their young Blackfoot guide through the narrow canyon the pioneers had opened the day before. It was no more than thirty feet wide and at points not much wider than a single wagon. The sides of the canyon were between thirty and forty feet high. The path followed a dry creek bed which cut through the hills at a gentle slope for quite a distance.[515]

The Indians had been reinforced after the Battle of Killdeer Mountain. They now had Sully's force completely surrounded. Nevertheless, they kept their distance. As at Killdeer, most of the Indians were armed only with bows and arrows.[516] Only a few had firearms and those had nowhere near the range of the soldiers' Springfields.

---

509 Ben W. Brunson reminiscence, undated manuscript, 8, Dakota Conflict of 1862 Manuscripts Collections. Minnesota Historical Society. In fact, the Indians did have a white woman with them as their prisoner, Fanny Kelly.

510 Pattee, "Dakota Campaigns," 312.

511 Washburn, Diaries, Aug. 8,1864.

512 Myers, Soldiering in Dakota, 20.

513 Strong, A journal of the northwestern Indian expedition, Aug. 8. 1864 MNHS.

514 Colwell, Diary, Aug. 8, 1864.

515 The length of the dry creek bed is in dispute. Strong's diary from Aug. 8, 1864 claimed that the creek bed was only a mile long. Frank Myers of the 6th Iowa Cavalry claimed they followed it for 4 miles. Based on measurements taken using Google Earth®, it appears that 4 miles is the closest approximation.

516 Colwell, Diary Aug. 81864.

The Indians had one advantage, however. From the bluffs above the dry creek bed, they could fire down on the train at short range. This they proceeded to do.

To protect the train, the Eighth Minnesota dismounted half of its men with the other half holding the horses. The dismounted men were ordered to scale the steep bluffs on the north of the canyon to clear away the Indians shooting into the train. The Second Minnesota Cavalry did the same on the south side of the canyon to guard the train's left.[517] For the next several miles of travel, the troops were engaged in a running gun battle with thousands of Indians.

At about 11 a.m., as the lead element of the train emerged from the canyon onto a more gentle rolling plain, an Indian rose out of the grass and fired at the Blackfoot guide. The bullet struck the Blackfoot in the chest and exited his back just below his shoulder blade.[518] As the young guide fell to the ground it appeared that Sully's Expedition was going to be lost in the Badlands.[519]

The troops were not lost for long. The wounded young Blackfoot was instantly picked up by Sergeant Richard Hoback from Company H of the Second Minnesota Cavalry. Hoback carried the guide back to an ambulance where his wound was dressed.[520] The wound, as it turned out, was not quite so serious as it first appeared. The Blackfoot guide returned to the front of the train after a short stay in the ambulance.

At about the same time the Blackfoot guide was shot, large numbers of Indians rose up with a war whoop around the front of the train and commenced firing.[521] A sharp skirmish ensued with the Indians quickly being pushed back.

The troops continued to forge ahead, clearing the Indians from within shooting range of the train. By this point, the wagon train was spread out for almost four miles, making it difficult to for the soldiers on the flanks to guard it effectively.

As more of the train emerged from the canyon, the troops that scaled the bluffs were able to remount their horses. They spread out from each side of the train to push the Indians farther out of range of the wagons.

The soldiers and the mounted Sioux warriors played a cat and mouse game for hours in the hot sun. During this time, the Indians' horsemanship skills were on display. Watching the Indians ride left the soldiers, many of whom had only learned to ride over the previous year, astounded at their capabilities. George Cambell mar-

517 Strong, *A journal of the northwestern Indian expedition*, Aug. 8. 1864 MNHS.

518 Myers, *Soldiering in Dakota*, 21.

519 Benjamin Witherell Brunson, *Ben W. Brunson reminiscence, undated*, Dakota Conflict of 1862 Manuscripts Collections. Minnesota Historical Society, 10.

520 Hilger, "Campaign of General Alfred Sully Against the Hostile Sioux in 1864," 318.

521 Brunson, *reminiscence, undated*, 10.

veled at how the Indians could escape up what appeared to be nearly vertical bluffs: "...their way of getting up hill was to slip off behind, catch hold of the tail of the pony, and go up the steepest hill they could find."[522]

As at Killdeer, the Indians suffered many times more casualties than the soldiers and emigrants. Only a handful of soldiers received wounds, most of which were minor. The Indians on the other hand sustained numerous dead and wounded. The exact number of casualties was difficult to determine because the Indians tried to take away the bodies of those who fell.

As the day wore on, the men began to suffer from the effects of heat and dehydration. There was no water for them along the way. Nor had they been able to eat. The constant battle with the Indians gave the soldiers no time for nourishment.

To make matters worse, the area had little, if any grass for the horses and mules. Nor was water easy to find. The mules and horses suffered terribly as the battle raged through the heat of the day.

CONE BUTTE, WHICH RISES APPROXIMATELY TWO HUNDRED FEET OVER THE BATTLEFIELD AROUND SULLY'S MUD HOLE. THE BLUFFS IN THE FOREGROUND ARE ABOUT THIRTY FEET TALL. TAKEN BY THE AUTHOR IN 2018.

522 Cambell, *Personal Reminiscences*, 22.

The Mud Hole

The going had been so rough that Sully's Expedition only managed to make about ten miles on August 8. At about 3 p.m., the train had reached a small water hole which offered some hope of refreshment and a good campground.

The site was at the eastern entrance of a valley less than a half mile long and maybe 250 yards wide. Steep hills lined the north and south sides of the valley. Those hills rose sixty feet from the valley floor to flat bluffs from which Indians could oversee the campsite. On the west end of the valley the ground rose more gently, which would allow the train of wagons to exit onto open plains. Less than 500 yards to the northwest of the camp site, a distinctive 200-foot-tall cone-shaped butte overlooked the entire valley.

The water hole itself was described as a pool of stagnant rainwater about fifty feet across and four inches deep. It sat atop from ten to eighteen inches of mud.[523] As the train pulled into the site, thirsty horses and mules, desperate for water, made a rush for the water hole. It took everything the men had to keep them out and prevent the animals from trampling the whole thing into mud.[524]

Those efforts turned out to be in vain. The water was already muddied. The first soldiers to reach it had ridden their horses straight in, churning up the mud for all that followed.[525]

By this time, the troops had been fighting for almost ten hours in blistering hot sun without access to any water except what they had in their canteens. At first, it seemed like the shallow mud hole was a godsend. Then they realized that plenty of buffalo had made use of the isolated water hole and left it befouled with their excrement.[526] William Houlton described it as "about as pleasant as the drippings of a common barn yard."[527]

The exhausted and parched soldiers had little choice, they could drink the putrid water or possibly die of dehydration or heat stroke. About all they could do was boil it to brew coffee, which at least made it safe to drink. However, as one soldier later recalled, "The strongest coffee we could make would not kill the taste."[528]

523 Hilger, "Campaign of General Alfred Sully Against the Hostile Sioux in 1864," 318.

524 Ibid.

525 Myers, *Soldiering in Dakota*, 22.

526 Hodgson, "Recollections of the Sioux War No. 24," *Dakota County Tribune*, Aug. 21, 1890.

527 Houlton, *Speech*.

528 Hodgson, "Recollections of the Sioux War No. 24," *Dakota County Tribune*, Aug. 21, 1890. Sadly, this was not the worst coffee the men would endure during their service. *See*, Chapter 16, Major Camp and the Coffee.

SULLY'S MUD HOLE LOOKING SOUTHWEST FROM THE BLUFFS NEAR CONE BUTTE. THE ONLY STANDING WATER IS LOCATED IN A PUDDLE SURROUNDED BY THE THREE TREES IN RIGHT CENTER OF THE PHOTO. TAKEN BY THE AUTHOR IN 2018.

Despite the unpleasantness of the water, the troops and horses made full use of it. "We used it all up clean or dirty rather before we marched the next morning" recalled James Robinson, a private in Company B of the Second Minnesota Cavalry.[529]

The troops found themselves surrounded yet again. Large numbers of Indians lined the flat bluffs surrounding the mud hole encampment in full view of the troops. From the high ground they fired into the camp, although the long range prevented accurate targeting. They also occupied Cone Butte. Although out of rifle range, the Cone Butte position gave the Indians a good view of the entire area.

Near dusk, a band of Indians collected on a ridge not far from the soldiers' encampment. Suddenly, several hundred of them charged downhill towards the camp. This panicked the emigrants, who had camped on the east side of the mud hole. The women and children ran for the soldiers' camp.[530]

The soldiers responded quickly. Every man in camp grabbed his weapons and went out to meet the attacking Indians.[531] At the same time, the cannon opened up on the attackers. The artillery quickly caused the Indians to scatter and retreat.

---

529 John Robinson to Libbie Robinson, Oct. 11, 1864, MNHS.

530 Myers, *Soldiering in Dakota*, 21.

531 Ibid.

As the sun sank behind the horizon and darkness slowly fell over the battle-field, the fighting began to taper off. Sully's Indian scouts out on the perimeter were again close enough to the Sioux warriors that they were able to exchange words with one of their leaders. Sitting Bull shouted back and forth with Sully's scouts, asking why they helped the soldiers and threatening "we have to kill you."[532]

The soldiers had suffered light casualties during the day. None were killed in the fighting, and only about seven men were wounded and then only one seriously. The Indians, on the other hand, again suffered a disproportionate number of dead and wounded. Throughout the day, soldiers managed to capture at least twenty-five riderless Indian ponies, many of which had blood in their saddles indicating the former occupants had been shot from their mounts.[533] Some estimates placed the Indian casualties at over 300 warriors.

Even though things grew quieter on the evening of August 8, the already exhausted soldiers would get little rest. One cavalier recalled that "Every soldier in the whole command, not on the sick list, was put on guard, either picket or camp guard, and we got but little or no sleep."[534]

The fitful slumber of those soldiers who did manage to doze off was cut short at 12 a.m., when the troops were ordered to saddle up and get ready for the day's march. After preparing their horses and gear, the men were then ordered to lay down on the ground with their arms to get a little more rest.

At 2 a.m. on the morning of August 9 the men were again roused to prepare breakfast so they would be ready to move out at daybreak. There wasn't much available to satisfy their hunger. Rations were running low, and the supplies of some essential items had already been exhausted. Lieutenant Lewis Paxson noted that there was no coffee for breakfast that day.[535] Considering how important coffee was to keep the troops moving, that must have been a terrible blow. For most of the soldiers, breakfast consisted of nothing more than perhaps a little bacon and some fried hardtack.[536]

At 3:30a.m., just as the sky was lightening in the predawn hours, the shooting picked up again. At first the engagement involved just a few of the deployed skirmishers. By 5 a.m. there was heavy firing all along the lines surrounding the camp.

532 *See*, Robert M. Utley, *Sitting Bull: The Life and Times of an American Patriot*, New York, 1998, 58-59.

533 Doud, *Diaries*, Aug. 8, 1864.

534 Myers, *Soldiering in Dakota*, 22.

535 Paxson, *Diary*, Aug. 9, 1864 at 43.

536 Washburn, *Diaries*, Aug. 8, 1864.

However, soldiers from Company F learned that morning from the scouts that there was a deep gully about a half mile from camp in which a basin had been cut out of the surrounding clay by a small waterfall. Even though the stream was dry, the basin was sheltered and held water all summer long. As this was mostly rainwater, it was drinkable, unlike the alkaline ground water.

For the men of Company F, the promise of delicious rainwater was too much to pass up. It was dangerous to travel out to the water basin with so many Indians about. The men decided to send half the company first while the rest kept a lookout for the enemy. Then the second half of the company would be able to fill their canteens while the first half stood guard.

The first half of Company F returned from the water basin without incident. The second half of the company had just climbed down into the gully when two of the lookouts, Privates Elijah Houck and Thomas Hodgson spotted a band of Indians approaching at full gallop. They gave the alarm and ran for camp.[537]

It appeared that the Indians would cut off Houck and Hodgson from the camp and overtake them. However, members of Company F and others in camp had witnessed the developing attack and more than 200 men quickly went to their rescue. There was an exchange of fire, and one Indian was shot from his horse. At this, the others retreated. As a result, Houck and Hodgson escaped and safely returned to camp.[538]

At 6 a.m., the Expedition began to move out to the west. The shooting picked up as approximately 500 warriors continued to skirmish along the flanks of the slowly moving wagon train. The soldiers, however, were able to keep the Indians far enough away from the wagons to prevent any serious casualties. The Third Minnesota Battery used their cannon to scatter any concentrations of Indians. They also used the cannons at the back of the train to prevent Indians from attacking the rear as it traveled west.

At about noon, after hours of fighting, the Indians suddenly disappeared and the shooting stopped.[539] It soon became apparent why the Indians abandoned the fight. In the path of the train was a large but now deserted Indian camp.

The Abandoned Indian Camp

The camp belonged to the Indian refugees who had fled from Killdeer Mountain almost two weeks earlier. This camp was where they stopped to regroup. Clearly,

---

537 Hodgson, "Recollections of the Sioux War No. 24," *Dakota County Tribune*, Aug. 21, 1890.

538 Doud, *Diaries*, Aug. 9, 1864.

539 Ibid.

it was not intended to be occupied for any length of time. One soldier observed "I cannot say they were in camp, for they were wholly tentless."[540]

As Sully's troops approached, the Indians, no doubt wishing to avoid another Killdeer-like disaster, fled. "Their fires were yet burning; and many of their effects, including the undisposed-of bodies of dead warriors, were left in the camp to tell of the hasty and unexpected flight."[541] The warriors who had been skirmishing with the troops earlier that morning had withdrawn to protect their families as they retreated. The Indians split up in smaller groups and headed toward the Missouri River.

The now vacant camp was so large that it took Sully's Expedition an hour and a half to pass through it.[542] Its size was estimated as about three miles long, from north to south, and three-fourths of a mile wide.[543]

Near this camp, some soldiers noticed a Sioux burial, which appeared to confirm that these were the same Indians they had encountered at Killdeer Mountain.

> As we were passing near by where a child had been buried, I rode up to see it. The manner of their burial is this, they take five or six sticks and place one end of each on the ground in a circle around and fasten the other ends together about eight feet from the ground, they suspend a sort of a basket underneath in which they place the corpse after having wrapped it in numerous blankets and buffalo robes. This child had wrapped up with it all its playthings such as it had played with and such as I suppose they thought it would want on its arrival at the "Happy Hunting Ground." The child I should judge to be five or six years old and to all appearances it was one that we had killed in our first fight as there was a wound in its temple looking like a bullet wound.[544]

The Expedition moved about three miles past the large Indian camp before it halted for the night. There the commanders took stock of their situation. The men were utterly exhausted after three days of constant fighting in the merciless heat and without adequate food, water, or sleep. The running battle had been even harder on the animals. The horses and mules were already suffering from poor water and lack

540 Brunson, "Reminiscences of Service With the Eighth Minnesota Infantry," 374. The Indians had left all their lodges behind when they fled from Killdeer Mountain and had not yet be able to replace them.

541 Hilger, "Campaign of General Alfred Sully Against the Hostile Sioux in 1864," 319.

542 Strong, *A journal of the northwestern Indian expedition*, Aug. 9. 1864 MNHS.,

543 Hilger, "Campaign of General Alfred Sully Against the Hostile Sioux in 1864," 319.

544 John Robinson to Libbie Robinson, Oct. 11, 1864, MNHS.

of forage when they arrived in the Badlands. The fighting over the past few days only made matters worse. One by one, the animals were giving out.

With supplies running low and no prospect of resupply there was little choice but for the Expedition to push on until it reached the Yellowstone River, approximately sixty miles to the northwest. There, the Expedition would reach the supply boats that Sully had arranged to have waiting.

Nevertheless, this would be no easy march. Thanks to the grasshoppers the entire route was devoid of any greenery for the horses and mules. Nor would the drought-stricken landscape offer much water for men or animals. What little water they would find was likely to be heavily alkaline and undrinkable.

There was great concern for the welfare of the mules and horses. Without them the Expedition would have to abandon wagons with what little supplies they had left. As horses died, more soldiers would have to walk, placing the weakened and dehydrated men at further risk of heatstroke and possible death. Furthermore, the Expedition was still at risk of attack.

Despite the disappearance of the Indians, the men were again ordered to saddle up the horses about midnight and to sleep with their arms handy for the rest of the short Dakota summer night. This proved to be a wise decision as it turned out that the Indian danger was not yet over.

On the morning of Wednesday, August 10, the Expedition began preparations for the day's march. As dawn spread over the Dakota prairie, gunfire suddenly erupted from the pickets outside the campground. A small band of Indians had attacked the troops on picket duty and had driven them back into the camp. The troops, having their arms within reach all night, were quick to respond. The soldiers rushed out of camp and skirmished with the Indians for a short time. The Indians quickly withdrew and were not seen again.

March to the Yellowstone

When the Expedition finally set off about mid-morning, the soldiers were astonished to find a landscape entirely devoid of vegetation. "There was not a green thing to be seen" recalled Private Thomas Hodgson of Company F.[545] The grasshoppers had consumed every bit of grass down to the dirt as far as the eye could see. "We marched over a rough, rolling country, with no grass on the prairie, the hills and prairie looking more like chalk than ground."[546]

---

545 Hodgson, "Recollections of the Sioux War No. 24," *Dakota County Tribune*, Aug. 21, 1890.

546 Myers, *Soldiering in Dakota*, 23.

The going was slow. There were many ravines and gullies to cross. In some cases, the soldiers had to build makeshift bridges that the train could only cross in single file. In all, the Expedition managed to make only fifteen miles that day.

As they marched in the brutal heat, the condition of both men and animals quickly deteriorated. The horses and mules had not eaten much of anything for three or four days at that point and were sorely lacking for water. Thomas Hodgson described the situation: "It was intensely hot, and our horses died off like rotten sheep."[547]

Company E was detailed to rear guard and ordered to shoot any animals that could not continue the march rather than leave them to starve or fall into the hands of the Indians. Sadly, the Company E soldiers stayed busy shooting the dying horses and mules all day.

The soldiers were not in much better than the animals. They were extremely dehydrated. Those that had given in to temptation and drank the alkaline waters were paying the price as it wreaked havoc on their gut. Moreover, the last of the hardtack was gone. The men would have to go without food until they reached the Yellowstone River.

The Expedition camped for the night near Beaver Creek. The risk of Indian attack was still fresh in the mind, so the officers again ordered their troops to lay with their arms and equipment from midnight forward.[548]

It was another sleepless night for many of the troops. It was not Indian attacks that disturbed their slumbers but the constant neighs and brays of the animals. One of the Iowa cavalry soldiers recalled "Our horses had gone so long without water and feed that they pawed the earth and kept up considerable noise all night, preventing many from sleeping in their sympathy for the poor dumb brutes."[549]

On Thursday, August 11, the Expedition rose early as usual and set out at 5 a.m. There were two deep ravines that the train had to cross, which slowed the progress considerably. On the other side of those obstacles the landscape became gently rolling, which allowed the train to travel more easily across the open country.

That day, however, would prove the hardest day of the Expedition for the animals. Many had reached the breaking point, and when they did the horse or mule simply laid down and refused to move. If an animal would not get back up after a short time, the troops were ordered to shoot it.

547   Hodgson, "Recollections of the Sioux War No. 24," *Dakota County Tribune*, Aug. 21, 1890.

548   Washburn, *Diaries*, Aug. 10, 1864.

549   Myers, *Soldiering in Dakota*, 24.

One member of the Eighth Minnesota noted that "our road of today will be marked with their skeletons."[550] Another feared that "two days more of such travel and we will all have to go on foot."[551]

The prospect of walking the rest of the way back did not appeal to the soldiers. The men did what they could to try and save the animals, both for humanitarian purposes and for their own survival. Private Frank Myers of the Sixth Iowa Cavalry recalled:

> *While the horses belonged to the government, the men were just as anxious to save them as though they had been their own, and would frequently walk miles rather than allow the worn-out beasts to carry them. Besides, we were getting a long way from civilization, which materially increased the value and services of our horses.*[552]

George Cambell made a similar observation regarding the Company E horses: "we could not ride our horses so we led them."[553] Some even divided their rations with their horses in an attempt to keep them alive.[554]

Despite the desperate efforts of the soldiers, many of the animals died or had to be shot. Frank Myers of the Sixth Iowa Cavalry estimated that his unit had to shoot about seventy-five horses that day.[555] The story was the same in other units as well. George Doud from Company F of the Eighth Minnesota noted that sixty-three horses and mules gave out.

The dehydrated soldiers suffered mightily as well in the heat. "By two o'clock in the afternoon the tongues of many of the men would be so swelled that they could not talk."[556] David Kingsbury later recalled that:

> *Men and animals were nearly exhausted from fatigue, short rations and bad water or none. I was so weak that, on our last day's march to the river, I fell from my horse twice, and such was the condition of many.*[557]

---

550 Strong, *A journal of the northwestern Indian expedition*, Aug. 11. 1864 MNHS.

551 Atkinson, *Diary*, Aug. 11, 1864.

552 Myers, *Soldiering in Dakota*, 24.

553 Cambell, *Personal Reminiscences*, 33.

554 Houlton, *Speech* 9.

555 Myers, *Soldiering in Dakota*, 23.

556 Hilger, "Campaign of General Alfred Sully Against the Hostile Sioux in 1864," 327.

557 Kingsbury, "Sully's Expedition Against the Sioux In 1864," 459.

The Expedition managed to make nearly thirty miles on August 11, even with the toll the march took on the men and animals. They were fortunate to find a campground with at least some grass for the horses. It wasn't very good grass, being described as "swamp grass, as dead and dried up as grass would be in Iowa in the month of' December.[558] Nevertheless, the horses and mules ate it with relish.

The next morning, Friday, August 12, the march was delayed a few hours while the troops continued to graze the animals on what little grass was available. Before setting out at 10 a.m., welcome news arrived. Scouts reported that the train would reach the Yellowstone River by nightfall. With renewed spirit the train moved out.

Sioux in the Aftermath

After abandoning their camp west of the Badlands on August 9, small groups of Indians began to regroup back at the Missouri River. When they were safe and Sully's forces were no longer in pursuit, the warriors trickled in to rejoin their families. It was then that the Indians began to realize the scope of their losses. Fanny Kelly, the Sioux prisoner, described what she witnessed:

> "...a scene of terrible mourning over the killed ensued among the women. Their cries are terribly wild and distressing, on such occasions; and the near relations of the deceased indulge in frantic expressions of grief that cannot be described.[559]

There was good reason besides their casualties for the Indians to pull back. They were already suffering terribly after losing all their food following the battle at Killdeer Mountain. Fanny Kelly later recalled that "Hunger followed on the track of grief; all their food was gone, and there was no game in that portion of the country." Furthermore, "...the country through which we passed for the following two weeks did not yield enough to arrest starvation."[560]

The Indians had simply had enough. They had suffered too many casualties and lost so much of their critical supplies for them to continue the fight, at least until the following year. Instead, the Indians fled to the southeast, away from Sully's forces, and focused on survival for the coming winter.

---

558 Myers, *Soldiering in Dakota*, 25.

559 Kelly, *Narrative of My Captivity Among the Sioux Indians*, 106.

560 Ibid.

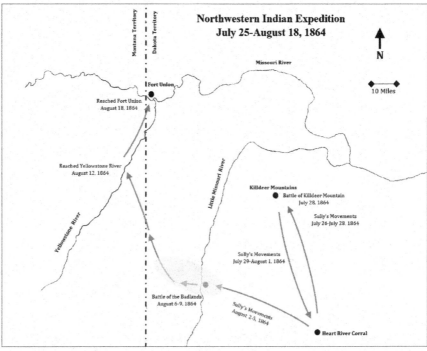

MOVEMENTS OF SULLY'S EXPEDITION FROM ARRIVAL AT THE HEART RIVER CORRAL UNTIL IT REACHED FORT UNION MORE THAN THREE WEEKS LATER. THE SHADED PORTION INDICATES THE AREA IN WHICH THE EXPEDITION AND THE SIOUX ENGAGED IN A THREE-DAY RUNNING BATTLE ACROSS THE BADLANDS FROM THE EAST SIDE OF THE LITTLE MISSOURI RIVER TO ALMOST THE BORDER WITH MONTANA TERRITORY.

Refresh and Return

August 12 to October 13, 1864

In the early afternoon of August 12 the lead elements of the Expedition came within sight of the Yellowstone River. At about the same time, one of Sully's Indian scouts arrived carrying a small chip of wood.

> *It did not need words to tell what that chip meant; it had been cut by our steamboat men and was floating down the sweet, cool waters of the longed-for Yellowstone. An orderly carried that little fresh-cut chip down the weary, straggling line, and as the burning, bleary eyes of the men beheld it, their strength came back and with a desperate energy the speed was rapid and unflagging to the river.[561]*

The Yellowstone River flows through a flat low plain near the present-day Montana border with North Dakota. The first view of the river the men found encouraging. Both banks were lined with big shady groves of cottonwood trees, which were teeming with elk, bear, deer, and antelope. There were also bushes full of mouth-watering berries and choke cherries.

Within a short time, the Expedition reached the banks of the river. The river was about 250 yards across and flowed in a strong, tricky current. George Cambell recalled that it was like no river he had ever seen; "the water seemed to have two

---

561 Col. Thomas, quoted in *Minnesota in the Civil and Indian Wars: 1861-1865*, vol. 1, 393.

motions – down stream and from bank to bank."[562] The water was slightly yellowish in color, perhaps due to sediment from the rocks that gave the river its name. However, it was eminently drinkable to the delight of both the men and their animals.

> *And when the bank of the beautiful river was reached, for the moment all discipline was forgotten; men and animals rushed into the stream and swallowed the life-inspiring fluid, and joy and happy shouts took the place of misery in the command.*[563]

After satisfying their thirst, some soldiers grabbed their rifles and went hunting while others set up camp for the night. The hunters were successful, returning with deer, elk, and antelope. Soon, the smell of fresh venison steaks wafted from the campfires. The meat was a godsend for the starving troops. James Robinson of the Second Minnesota Cavalry wrote in a letter home that "the antelope was the best eating of any meat I think I ever tasted."[564]

Two of the steamships, the *Alone* and the *Chippewa Falls*, soon arrived to resupply the troops. They had been a few miles downriver when the Expedition arrived. Sully had ordered the cannons fired to alert the ships to their location. By nightfall the soldiers had full rations again, plus the delicious game they had hunted.

There was supposed to be a third steamship, the *Island City*, which had traveled up the Missouri with the *Alone* and *Chippewa Falls*. However, it had snagged on an obstruction near Fort Union and sank. This was a common peril facing all river steamships.

The only problem with the east bank of the Yellowstone was the lack of grass for the horses and mules. The troops expected that the steamships would bring a good supply of corn, oats, and other forage for the animals. In fact, generous supplies of nutritious animal feed had been sent with the steamships. Unfortunately, nearly all of it was loaded on the *Island City*. Those were among the supplies lost when the ship sank.[565] The horses and mules would have to make do with the limited grass along the riverbank.

Sully had planned to resupply the Expedition from the steamships and then turn back to the northeast to resume pursuit of the Indians. The loss of the *Island City* dashed any hope Sully had to continue the chase. The animals had already gone several days without food. The horses and mules, so essential to the Expedition, simply could not endure another grueling march without the precious grain that was

---

562   Cambell, *Personal Reminiscences*, 34.

563   *Minnesota in the Civil and Indian Wars: 1861-1865*, vol. 1, 393.

564   John Robinson to Libbie Robinson, Oct. 11, 1864, MNHS.

565   Kingsbury, "Sully's Expedition Against the Sioux in 1864," 459.

now on the river bottom. Moreover, the water level in the river was dropping rapidly, as normally occurred in late summer. Soon, the water would be too low for steamships to travel, making any resupply all but impossible.[566]

Under the circumstances, Sully had no choice but to change his plans and return to Fort Rice. As a first step, Sully decided to cross the river in search of better grass. Then, the Expedition would make a slow thirty-five-mile march up the west bank to Fort Union. The crossing would not begin until the following afternoon. That gave the soldiers time to lay around for a while and graze the animals.

A sizeable number of soldiers, animals, and military baggage would have to cross to the far bank of the wide and strong river. The emigrant train would need to cross as well. With only two steamboats, moving the entire Expedition across the Yellowstone would take a very long time. To speed up the process, scouts located a place just shallow enough for the wagons to ford the river.

The officers quickly developed a plan for the crossing. Most of the mounted soldiers would cross with the baggage as passengers on a steamship. Every fourth man would swim his horse and three others across the river. The army wagons and the emigrant train would have to cross at the ford.

It would nevertheless be a treacherous crossing, whether it be by swimming the horses across in the current or driving the wagons across the shallow ford. The ford was not a straight path. It followed a crooked sandbar, where any misstep could cause the unfortunate wagon drivers to drop into deeper water and be swept away by the swift current. To help keep the wagons on the sandbar, stakes were placed in the water along the safest path.

The Minnesota Brigade began crossing at 9 p.m. Those selected to swim the horses across were not always enthusiastic about the assignment. It would be a perilous job. Some of them realized the danger and paid others to take their place. The rest, including Edson Washburn, simply got on with the job.

The soldiers' fear of the river crossing proved well-founded. When it came time to ford the river some of the mules got scared and tried to swim or even climb into the wagons. In a few cases, the panicked mules dragged their load off the staked path and were swept away by the current in a tangled mess with their wagons and drivers. The army lost a few wagons in the process, as did the emigrants. Several mules and two men were swept away by the strong current. All tragically drowned.[567]

---

566 Report of Brig. Gen. Alfred Sully, August 13, 1864, *Official Records*, series 1, vol. 41, part 1, 147-148.

567 The various accounts of the crossing generally agree that two of the emigrants drowned. The accounts disagree somewhat on the number of mules that were swept away. George Cambell recalled that three or four six-mule teams were swept away, which means twenty-four mules may have drowned. Cambell, *Personal Reminiscences*, 35. George Doud recorded a smaller number. He noted in his diary for that day that twelve mules drowned.

Once a wagon, team and driver were taken away by the current there was little that the bystanders could do to save them. George Cambell described one rescue attempt:

> *I remember particularly we tried to save one poor fellow, followed him half a mile on the shore, throwing sticks for him to use to keep himself up. The current would roll a man under in spite of himself; and, when we would think he was coming near shore, he would suddenly disappear and come up further out in the stream.*[568]

Those soldiers who had to swim horses across the river in the middle of the night had one unexpected and unpleasant experience when they were done. Although it was the middle of August and the days were still fiery hot, the nights were now cooling off drastically.[569] Those soldiers coming out of the river soaking wet would have found themselves freezing in the chilly night air. The unfortunate men no doubt made a beeline for the nearest campfire to warm up and dry out. Even those who stayed dry by crossing on the steamships were wearing their overcoats and blankets by morning.[570]

After the all-night crossing of the Yellowstone, the Expedition spent the rest of the day looking after the animals, hunting, and resting. The hunters were again successful, owing to the abundance of wild game. As a result, the Expedition was well supplied with fresh meat.

At 8 a.m. the following morning, Monday, August 15, the Expedition picked up the march again. This time, they were heading almost due north, following the west bank of the Yellowstone River. Their destination was Fort Union.

Stops at Fort Union and Fort Berthold

Fort Union was located on the north side of the Missouri River about three miles west of the confluence with the Yellowstone.[571] Fort Union was older than most other forts in DakotaTterritory. It had been built in 1828 by the American Fur Company as a trading post. Indians from several area tribes brought their furs and buffalo hides to the fort where they could exchange them for a variety of trade goods.[572]

---

568 Cambell, *Personal Reminiscences*, 35-36.

569 Edson Washburn noted how chilly it was that night. Washburn, *Diaries*, Aug. 14, 1864.

570 Doud *Diaries*, Aug. 14, 1865.

571 The reconstructed fort site, which is now owned by the National Park Service, sits just on the North Dakota side of the border with Montana. In fact, the parking lot, which is only 100 yards from the fort, is in Montana.

572 https://www.nps.gov/fous/learn/historyculture/index.htm, accessed March 10, 2019.

PART OF SULLY'S EXPEDITION CAMPED NEAR FORT BERTHOLD.

The expedition arrived on the Missouri about a mile downstream from Fort Union late in the day on August 18. The steamships began ferrying the men and equipment across the river that night. The soldiers again swam the horses across the river, which was narrower and less treacherous than the Yellowstone had been four days earlier. This time, the crossing was made without the loss of a single man or beast.[573]

At Fort Union, the troops had a chance to rest the horses and mules, which were all in very rough shape. There had been no green grass since the troops crossed the Yellowstone. Between the drought and grasshoppers, all that was left for the animals to eat was willow brush.[574]

For the next couple of days, the men prepared for the return trip to Fort Rice. They spent the time loading wagons and caring for the horses, mules, and livestock that would accompany the Expedition on the march.

At Fort Union, most of the emigrant train split from Sully's Expedition and continued west. A few of the emigrants, discouraged by the hardships they had

573 Kingsbury, "Sully's Expedition Against the Sioux In 1864," 460.

574 Strong, *A journal of the northwestern Indian expedition*, Aug. 19. 1864 MNHS.

experienced during the previous weeks, decided to return with the soldiers to Minnesota.[575]

The Expedition was due to depart for Fort Rice on Sunday, August 21. As the soldiers were preparing for the march, Company E was called up for a special assignment. It had been reported that the Idaho emigrants may have stolen some government horses and cattle before they split off from Sully's force and were perhaps harboring some deserters. [576] At about noon that day Company E was ordered to overtake the Idaho emigrant train and search it for the stolen goods[577] and the deserters. Meanwhile, the rest of Sully's force would set out for Fort Berthold, which was on the Missouri River about 110 miles to the east southeast.

Company E was ordered to travel light. They were not to take any rations for the men or horses. It was expected that they would quickly overtake the Idaho train, complete their mission, and then catch up with the rest of the troops by breakfast the next morning.[578]

The company set out on its mission by mid-afternoon. However, the emigrant train had a much greater head start than expected. Company E went only a short distance and then camped for the night.

The company set off again at daylight the next morning. They started out at a trot, hoping to catch the emigrant train before it went too much farther. After only a few miles, however, they had to slow the pace to save the horses. Company E finally caught up with the Idaho train at about 10 a.m. on August 22, thirty-five miles from their starting point.

As ordered, Company E proceeded to search the emigrant's wagons for government property. William Holton recalled that "We found nothing of value except some horses and they were too poor to stand the trip back to camp."[579] Consequently, the officers decided to abandon the horses. There was no sign of the deserters, but the soldiers did find some army cattle and took them back before permitting the Idaho emigrants to continue on their way.[580]

---

575 Hilger, "Campaign of General Alfred Sully Against the Hostile Sioux in 1864," 320. The emigrant train eventually made it to the base of the Rocky Mountains. There they settled at a mining camp called "Last Chance Gulch." That camp soon grew into a city that is now Helena, Montana.

576 Strong, *A journal of the northwestern Indian expedition*, Aug. 21. 1864 MNHS.

577 Washburn, *Diaries*, Aug. 21, 1864.

578 Houlton, *Speech.*

579 Ibid.

580 Strong, *A journal of the northwestern Indian expedition*, Aug. 22. 1864 MNHS. Strong recorded that Company E returned with some cattle, but no deserters.

After finishing their business with the Idaho emigrants and taking some time to rest and graze the animals, Company E set out to catch up with the rest of the Eighth Minnesota. It was after 9 p.m. before the men rode into camp. By then, they were completely exhausted.

The men had gone thirty hours without food and with little rest. The soldiers were pleased when, despite the late hour, they found pans with stacks of "go dogs" that had been prepared for them. All the go dogs were quickly devoured by the hungry men.[581] Some of the men were simply too exhausted to enjoy the meal. Edson Washburn recorded that he went to bed without supper that night.[582]

While the trip to search the emigrant train was hard on the Company E soldiers, it was perhaps even harder on their horses. Poor grazing and bad water had already taken a toll. The largely wasted trip after the Idaho emigrants left horses as "thoroughly worn out and so weak they could hardly wiggle" by the time Company E caught up with the rest of the regiment.[583]

For the next six days Sully's force continued towards Fort Berthold. Along the way, scouts occasionally saw a few buffalo and shot some to provide food for the troops. The horses, however, still suffered. The animals grew weaker by the day. Many more horses gave out and had to be shot along the way.

On Sunday, August 28, 1864, Sully's Expedition finally reached the vicinity of Fort Berthold. Like Fort Union, it began life as a trading post and was reinforced over time for military purposes. Fort Berthold was located on the north bank of the Missouri River.[584] The troops camped about three miles away from the fort.

Nearby the encampment were villages of the friendly Mandan and Ree Indians. These were comparatively small tribes with a combined total of maybe 600 warriors. They were terribly afraid of the Sioux. The Sioux had been in a state of constant war with these smaller tribes and would kill their women and children if given a chance.[585] Consequently, the Mandan and Ree stayed close to Fort Berthold for protection.

Many of the soldiers were impressed with the Indian settlements around the fort. They lived in large lodges, some sleeping from twenty-five to fifty people. The

581 Houlton, *Speech*. "Go dogs" may have been a reference to wieners. The term "dog" was already in use to refer to small sausages by the mid-nineteenth century. It was not until well after the Civil War, however, that those sausages were mated with a bun and condiments into the form we know today as "hot dogs."

582 Washburn, *Diaries*, Aug. 22, 1864.

583 Houlton, *Speech*.

584 In 1953 the Missouri River was dammed to form Lake Sakakawea, which now extends more than 125 miles from the Garrison Dam west to Williston, North Dakota. The site of Fort Berthold now lies beneath the surface of the lake approximately 20 miles west of the dam.

585 Doud, *Diaries*, Aug. 29, 1864.

tribes farmed approximately 7,000 acres of corn along the river in well-kept fields.[586] They appeared quite industrious,[587] which was viewed favorably by the soldiers of New England stock who had grown up with the Protestant work ethic.

General Sully held a council with the chiefs that afternoon. The chiefs complained that they could not hunt buffalo because of the hostile Sioux and that had caused them to go hungry. Sully promised to send more troops the following summer to fight the Sioux. He also asked the chiefs to join him in that fight.

After the council, the troops and Indians had a chance to mingle. These were very different tribes than the Sioux bands many of the soldiers had known in Minnesota before the Uprising. These Indians seemed genuinely happy to have the soldiers around. The Indians even put on a show and serenaded the troops.

A few of the soldiers engaged in a bit of horse trading with the Indians. Several were still in possession of horses captured from the Sioux at Killdeer Mountain or in the Badlands. These they traded at Fort Berthold for other Indian ponies. The soldiers tended to be satisfied with the bargains, but at least one mused that "the Indians generally got the best trade."[588]

The Indians also sold food, mostly corn and squash, to the soldiers. What the men were most interested in, however, were the various crafts the Indians had for sale or trade. The soldiers bought plenty of them.[589] The trinkets were popular, and the soldiers continued to trade them amongst themselves.[590]

There is evidence the soldiers participated in some other activities that were less documented and perhaps not consistent with good military order and discipline. Some of the men in Sully's command slipped by the guards and went up to the fort. There it is likely that they enjoyed whiskey, gambling, and other pleasures that could be had there.

Those pleasures may have included a bit of frolic with the Indian women. William Houlton would later make a veiled reference to something that went on there in a speech given at the Company E reunion in 1878, saying "Some got something at Fort Berthold they afterwards wished they had not."[591] He left to the imagination what that "something" might be.

---

586 Atkinson, *Diary*, Aug. 29, 1864.

587 Ibid.

588 Ibid.

589 Ibid; Strong, *A journal of the northwestern Indian expedition*, Aug. 29. 1864 MNHS.

590 Atkinson, *Diary*, Aug. 29, 1864.

591 Houlton, *Speech*. From the context, this suggests one or more soldiers contracted a sexually-transmitted disease.

The Buffalo Herds

After leaving Fort Berthold on August 31, the Expedition moved rapidly toward Fort Rice. On the that day alone, the Expedition marched twenty-one miles south along the Missouri River before it camped for the night.

Continuing the next day, the men first laid eyes upon what must have been one of the most astonishing sights of the nineteenth century – massive herds of buffalo grazing on the plains. The troops started seeing buffalo that morning "at first in small groups and later in immense herds of countless numbers."[592]

The sight must have been breathtaking for those who witnessed it. There were tens of thousands of these magnificent creatures spreading out as far as the eye could see. James B. Atkinson of Company D, Second Minnesota Cavalry recorded that he "never saw so many buffalo in his life."[593] George Cambell described seeing buffalo by the thousands "in droves a mile square."[594] Edson Washburn recalled there were doubtless 500,000 of them.[595]

At first blush, it may seem as though Washburn's number was a bit exaggerated. Perhaps it was, but some estimates claim that North America once supported as many as 60,000,000 buffalo.

By 1864, the wild bison herd was much smaller than at its peak. There were multiple factors that reduced the bison numbers. The two greatest factors were disease and hunting. Wild horses left behind by the Spanish and other livestock imported by European settlers brought diseases that affected the bison numbers. In addition, the trade in buffalo hides took its toll. Cow buffalo hides were especially prized for leather. Hunters, therefore, focused on killing females. Unfortunately, the uncontrolled hunting of cows had a much greater impact on the reproduction capabilities of the herd than the killing of bulls.

Despite the shrinking buffalo population, there were still plenty of the animals in the wild when Company E crossed the Dakota plains. An estimate from 1865 placed the number somewhere around 15 million animals, most of which would have been on the great plains stretching from Texas north through Dakota Terri-

---

592 Kingsbury, "Sully's Expedition Against the Sioux In 1864," 460.

593 Atkinson, *Diary*, Sept. 1, 1864.

594 Cambell, *Personal Reminiscences,* 37. Cambell noted in his reminiscence that the buffalo were extinct at the time of his writing. That was about 1890, barely 25 years after the buffalo had free reign of the plains. While that statement was mostly true, there were still a few hundred buffalo left alive at that time. All of the buffalo in North America today are descended from that small number.

595 Washburn, *Autobiography,* 4.

tory.[596] If that 1865 estimate was correct, Edson Washburn's claim of seeing a half million animals in one herd could have been plausible.

The sight of so many buffalo was not only awe inspiring, it could be frightening as well. These were the largest mammals roaming North America at the time. A mature bull could grow up to nine feet long, stand six feet tall at the shoulders and weigh more than 2,000 pounds. Moreover, these animals could run at speeds of up to forty miles per hour, faster than a man or horse.

With such size and speed, even a single buffalo could inflict great damage on men, animals, and wagons. That was especially the case when such a beast was wounded or otherwise provoked. That capability was demonstrated on September 1 when a member of the Second Cavalry shot a bull buffalo from horseback. He rode up for a closer look at the downed animal. Much to the surprise of the cavalryman, the bull was not quite done. It turned and charged, breaking the horse's hips, and leaving the dismounted cavalryman to "skedadle for his sweet life."[597] [sic].

The soldiers were certainly wary of the damage that a single angry buffalo could inflict. It was the threat of an uncontrollable stampede, however, that most terrified the troops.

Stampedes were a very real risk, not just to the men but to the buffalo themselves. When a large herd got spooked, the great mass animals could crush anything in their path, even other buffalo. David Kingsbury of Company E later described what he saw on the plains.

> When one of those vast herds, often numbering thousands of animals, got started in any given direction, nothing could stop them except a cliff or a river, and then only after hundreds had been killed by being forced over the precipice or into the water. I saw more buffaloes than I could count lying dead, or dying, at the foot of a high bluff, they having been forced over the brink during a stampede; and at another time a sand-bar, evidently quicksand, in the Missouri river, was seen covered with dead buffaloes, the stench from which was terrible.[598]

The Indians used the buffalo stampedes to their advantage when hunting. They would frighten the buffalo and force the herd to run in the direction of a cliff. There,

---

596 James H. Shaw, "How Many Buffalo Originally Populated Western Rangelands?" *Rangelands*, vol. 17, no. 5, Oct. 1995, 148.

597 Doud, *Diaries*, Sept. 1, 1864.

598 Ibid.

by the sheer weight of numbers behind them, the leading buffalo would be forced over the edge of the cliff and fall to almost certain death or great bodily injury. The Indians could then safely deal with the dead and dying buffalo at the bottom where they fell.

These spots were known as "buffalo jumps." In fact, the Expedition camped near the bottom of one such buffalo jump on the night of September 5. From the large number of the bones scattered at the cliff bottom, it appeared to be a successful hunting practice of the Indians.[599]

Drinking water for men and horses continued to be scarce along the route back to Fort Rice. Consequently, the availability of water holes dictated where the brigade camped each day.[600] On the afternoon of September 1, the brigade came across a small lake and decided to camp there for the night. The thousands of buffalo grazing nearby on the plains all but ignored them, at first.

As evening approached, the scattered buffalo began to collect in a herd and then move closer to the Expedition's camp. The animals evidently sought to drink from the same waterhole that was then within the camp.

As the herds approached, the pickets began to fire at the buffalo in an attempt to scare them away, but without success. All the gunshots did was panic the buffalo in the rear of the herd, driving the mass forward. Within moments, the herd descended upon the camp.[601]

The men instinctively realized the danger. They ran out of their tents and wagons, shooting in all directions at the buffalo. Soon, buffalo were running everywhere throughout the camp. For the next twenty minutes, the men put up a valiant defense. "The balls flew around us thicker and faster than they did in the Indian fights" recalled one soldier.[602]

Eventually the buffalo retired, leaving behind somewhere between fifty and a hundred of their number dead. The carcasses were scattered everywhere about the camp, even among the officer's tents. Colonel Thomas later recalled that "a tremendous old bull slept his last sleep as my nearest neighbor that night.[603]

The battle with the buffalo had one important side benefit—there was more than enough meat to feed the thousands of men on the Expedition. For the next sev-

599 Strong, *A journal of the northwestern Indian expedition*, Sept. 5. 1864 MNHS.

600 Cambell, *Personal Reminiscences*, 37.

601 *Minnesota in the Civil and Indian Wars: 1861-1865*, vol. 1, 394.

602 Strong, *A journal of the northwestern Indian expedition*, Sept. 1. 1864 MNHS.

603 *Minnesota in the Civil and Indian Wars: 1861-1865*, vol. 1, 394.

eral days the men feasted on an ample supply of buffalo rumps, steaks, and tongues.[604] The buffalo meat was far better than anything in the quartermaster's rations. The men couldn't get enough of it. A few days later, when a buffalo ran into camp and was shot, one soldier claimed there were "about 100 men standing ready, knife in hand, to cut out a steak."[605]

During the next couple of days on the march, the Minnesota Brigade had to remain constantly vigilant to prevent the ever-present buffalo from causing further damage to men, horses, and wagons. For the most part, the buffalo ignored the train of wagons and soldiers. In some cases, the buffalo were even so bold as to wander inside of the units guarding the flanks of the wagon train.[606] These animals posed a risk to the soldiers, especially if they were startled. It got so perilous that to keep the buffalo out the soldiers frequently had to corral the Expedition's camp at night as a precaution.[607]

On Saturday, September 3 the Expedition settled into camp by a chain of small lakes. The water wasn't good. It was so salty or alkaline that even the horses wouldn't drink from one of the lakes.[608]

While the water wasn't the best, the next day was Sunday and the Expedition would rest. The march to Fort Rice would resume on Monday, September 5. The troops didn't even care that the break was due primarily to the needs of the exhausted horses and mules, not those of the men.[609]

The men tried to make the most of their day off. They still had to tend to their animals, but there was plenty of time for rest and relaxation.

This was the first Sabbath the troops had off since the Minnesota Brigade met up with Sully's Brigade back in June. Edson Washburn of Company E, along with some other men, took advantage of the opportunity. They held a prayer meeting that morning.[610] After that, the men spent the rest of the day sleeping and tending to the needs of their horses.

---

604 Kingsbury, "Sully's Expedition Against the Sioux In 1864," 460.

605 Strong, *A journal of the northwestern Indian expedition*, Sept. 5. 1864 MNHS.

606 Strong, *A journal of the northwestern Indian expedition*, Sept. 2. 1864 MNHS.

607 Kingsbury, "Sully's Expedition Against the Sioux In 1864," 460.

608 Atkinson, *Diary*, Sept. 4, 1862.

609 Strong, *A journal of the northwestern Indian expedition*, Sept. 4. 1864 MNHS.

610 Washburn, *Diaries*, Sept. 4, 1864. Washburn, a deeply religious man, no doubt was grateful for the chance to attend the prayer meeting. However, on that day he wished "I were home to go to church with those I love."

Nearby, other troops took advantage of their day off to participate in a time-honored pursuit of soldiers – poker and gambling. Private Doud of Company F noted with irony "preaching and gambling only 20 rods apart."[611]

Another popular activity that day was hunting. Many of the men went out in pursuit of the nearby buffalo. They had beautiful weather for it. The day began cloudy but quickly turned sunny and unseasonably warm for September. The hunters managed to bag several buffalo, ensuring a steady supply of fresh meat.

Reveille sounded early on the morning of September 5 and the Expedition was on the march by 4:30 a.m. The weather had turned chilly and damp overnight. The Expedition still traveled a good distance that day in spite of the weather and herds of buffalo that sometimes obstructed their way. That evening, one buffalo ran right into camp and was killed within feet of the tents.

The weather the following day was even worse. It was foggy with a cold hard rain that fell all day and into the evening. The men were miserable.

The train was surrounded by buffalo most of the day and had to hold up at times due to the size of the herds. The troops struggled to keep the buffalo out of the train. At one point a herd got spooked and ran right through the column.[612] George Cambell later wrote that "the buffalo paid no attention whatever to us and we were so wretchedly cold that we would not pull our guns out from under the blankets to fire at them."[613]

The nasty weather on Tuesday, September 6 was not only hard on the men, it was hard on the animals. The condition of the animals had constantly deteriorated since the Expedition had reached the Yellowstone. The animals were already suffering from malnutrition due to lack of grain for feed. Moreover, they had been drinking the alkaline water for days.

The steady cold rain that day was the final straw. Horses and mules began to give out. Some dropped dead. Others had to be shot. In the neighborhood of forty to fifty horses and mules perished in the rain that day.[614] And that was just in the Minnesota Brigade. Sully's Brigade reportedly lost 100 mules in the same manner.[615] So many teams of animals gave out that the Expedition had to make camp earlier than usual that day.

---

611 Doud, *Diaries*, Sept. 4, 1864. A rod is 16 ½ feet. As a result, 20 rods equals approximately 100 yards.

612 Kingsbury, "General Alfred Sully's Indian Campaign of 1864," 460.

613 Cambell, *Personal Reminiscences*, 38.

614 Atkinson *Diary*, Sept. 7, 1864

615 Doud, *Diaries*, Sept. 6, 1864

The soldiers made camp in a hollow along a small ravine, which had good fresh water springs running from the sides. That night, the wet, cold miserable men were issued whiskey rations. While many of the troops were no doubt already well acquainted with the consumption of spirits, a number of the Company E men were abstainers. Still, after enduring the cold, numbing rain all day, a healthy ration of whiskey had to be quite appealing. William Houlton recalled "...I and I think some others tasted liquor for the first and only time in the Army."[616]

The soldiers continued to hunt buffalo each day to feed their ranks. Hunting was a welcome diversion, and the men were eager to try their hand at bagging a big buffalo. In fact, some of the Eighth Minnesota soldiers complained that the cavalry and scouts were doing all the hunting and not leaving any fun for them.[617]

Return to Fort Rice

The Expedition reached Fort Rice on September 9, 1864. The Thirtieth Wisconsin had been busy while Sully was on the march. When the Expedition left the site on July 19, it was simply a flat piece of grassland along the west bank of the Missouri River. By the time the Expedition returned, the site had been transformed into a real fort. Fort Rice now covered a rectangular area of approximately 200 by 175 yards, and several buildings were already in place.

The Minnesota Brigade made camp on the east side of the Missouri River opposite the fort. Orders were waiting for the Eighth Regiment to return to Fort Snelling, which elated the men. They would finally get to go home. First, there would be a welcome five-day pause. This was the longest opportunity the men and animals had to recover since they first set out from Fort Rice almost two months earlier.

The extended rest was desperately needed. Many of the men returning from the Expedition were sick from disease or from the effects of drinking the alkaline water they encountered on the march. Several men from the Eighth Minnesota were still in the hospital at Fort Rice, having been too sick to even accompany the Expedition. These included Company E soldiers Franklin Clifford from Clearwater and John Felch from Elk River.[618]

All the Company E men eventually recovered from their maladies. Not everyone on Sully's Expedition was so lucky. Four soldiers from the Eighth Minnesota

---

616 Houlton, *Speech*. It might not be surprising that Company E had so many abstainers. There was strong support for the temperance movement around Wright County and Lynden Township in Stearns County from which Company E was recruited.

617 Strong, *A journal of the northwestern Indian expedition*, Sept. 20. 1864 MNHS.

618 Washburn, *Diaries*, Sept. 10, 1864.

died of disease at Fort Rice that summer. Others from the Second Minnesota Cavalry and Brackett's Battalion succumbed to disease as well.

Not all the Eighth Minnesota men, however, would have the opportunity to rest on the riverbank by Fort Rice. While Sully's Expedition was crossing Dakota Territory, another train of emigrants bound for the Montana gold fields arrived at the fort guided by Captain James Fisk.

Rather than follow the same path as Sully's Expedition, Captain Fisk decided to lead his emigrant train on a more southerly route, which would largely avoid the Badlands. The emigrants had already traveled more than 200 miles west of Fort Rice by the time Sully's command returned.

Isolated on the great plains, the emigrant train made an appealing target. Hostile Sioux ambushed the train and killed several of the guards. Lacking protection, Captain Fisk circled the wagons into a corral for defense.

That night, two volunteers took their horses and slipped out of the wagon corral. For the next several days they hurried back to Fort Rice, arriving almost at the same time as Sully's Expedition.

To save Fisk's emigrant train, Sully issued orders for each company in the Eighth Minnesota to select twenty men for a rescue mission. The march to relieve Fisk would be no picnic. The Eighth Minnesota's horses were in such rough shape that they could not make the trip. The soldiers would have to march the 200 miles to Fisk's position on foot. Only the cavalry troops assigned to the Fisk rescue mission would be mounted. They were given their choice of the best horses available.

The rescue mission set out on September 11, 1864. The 200 Eighth Minnesota troops that participated would catch up with the rest of the regiment later at Fort Snelling.

For the next few days, the Minnesota Brigade stayed busy preparing for the return trip to Fort Snelling. In addition, they received both their back pay and mail.

The soldiers were anxious to get moving. The water at Fort Rice wasn't much better than the caustic alkaline water that the men had endured on the march. It was so bad that more and more men were getting sick on it. Moreover, with the approach of autumn the weather was getting very cold at night. All the men looked forward to the trip home.

They got their wish on Thursday, September 15. At noon that day, the Eighth Minnesota, minus the troops allocated to the Fisk rescue, began the march back to Fort Snelling with the rest of the Minnesota Brigade. Their route would take them to Fort Wadsworth, which was near the eastern edge of Dakota Territory, and from there to Fort Ridgely.

Homeward Bound

The return trip got off to a tragic start. Only a mile or so into the march, DeWitt Slater, a forty-six-year-old private in Company F, stopped to rest. He died suddenly a few minutes later. The cause of death was determined to be heart failure. This shocked the men in the Eighth Minnesota because Slater had been in good health up to that time and shown no indications of illness.

Later that same day, another forty-something private, Jacob Arth of Company K, died on the march. The Eighth Minnesota was still close to Fort Rice so the bodies of both men were sent back there for burial under military escort.[619]

Both of the deceased men had survived the brutal heat, lack of food and water, not to mention battle with the Indians. To lose their lives just as the ordeal was ending struck their surviving comrades hard. The unexpected deaths of the two soldiers cast a gloom over the camp that night.[620]

The Minnesota Brigade continued its course towards Fort Wadsworth for the next several days. It was not always a comfortable trip. The weather continued trending colder. The strong autumn winds on the open prairie penetrated the soldiers' thin clothes, chilling them to the bone as they marched. One night, the regiment camped next to a small lake and awoke to find it covered with a half inch of ice. The freeze also killed nearly all the remaining green grass that the horses might eat.

There were some welcome distractions to relieve the mind-numbing monotony of the daily rides. The soldiers spoke with each other about rumors that they would be sent to Atlanta to join Sherman's army.[621] Occasionally, the soldiers practiced making the Sioux war whoops at the top of their lungs in case they might want to emulate their former foe when engaged in battle with the rebels.

The troops continued to see buffalo and the scouts had a chance to do some hunting. Others, not wanting to miss out on the fun, also tried their hand at buffalo hunting. One of these was the regimental surgeon, Doctor John H. Murphy.

On September 19, Dr. Murphy, perhaps bolstered with some liquid courage, decided to try his hand at buffalo hunting. He grabbed his pistol and set out on horseback in pursuit of the giant beasts.

Army-issued pistols were generally either .36 or .44 caliber. While effective against a human-sized target at close range, these weapons would be of questionable

---

619 Doud, *Diaries*, Sept. 15, 1864.

620 Washburn, *Diaries*, Sept. 15, 1864.

621 In fact, the army chief-of-staff, General Halleck, wanted to assign the Thirtieth Wisconsin and Eighth Minnesota to General Sherman in Atlanta. Halleck to Pope, Sept. 21, 1864, *Official Records*, series 1, vol. 41, part 3, 296.

effect on a one-ton buffalo. Such a pistol was more likely to annoy a large buffalo than to kill it. And that was exactly what happened when Dr. Murphy found his prey.

Murphy set his sights on a large bull. Riding at full speed beside the galloping buffalo, he fired his pistol at the animal. The shot had no apparent effect on the angry bull. It did, however, spook Dr. Murphy's horse. The startled equine threw him to the ground directly in front of the charging bull. Once Dr. Murphy hit the ground, he was utterly helpless. The enraged bull didn't even slow down as it gored him in the groin and trampled him.[622]

After effortlessly tossing Dr. Murphy aside, the bull continued on after the horse. History does not record whether the horse got away. Dr. Murphy, however, obviously did not. He was badly injured.

When the men of Company E reached Dr. Murphy, he was unconscious and bleeding. They formed a stretcher with their rifles and carried him back to the hospital wagon. Years later, Andrew Bertram jokingly commented of the good doctor that "he wasn't as successful killing buffaloes as men."[623]

Dr. Murphy survived his encounter with the large bull and was even able to joke about it. When asked what was the matter, he responded "Oh, nothing, only I took a horn too much"[624] which was perhaps a pun on the use of a buffalo horn as a drinking vessel. While Murphy may have been able to joke about it, his wounds were severe enough that he would need a long time to recover. He did not rejoin the regiment for its later service in the South.

By Sunday, September 25, the Minnesota Brigade was nearly out of rations. Fortunately, Fort Wadsworth was nearby. After spending two days at the fort to replenish its supplies, the Minnesota Brigade set out again. The next few days were uneventful as the brigade pushed forward, sometimes making over twenty-five miles a day. At long last, on October 8, the brigade reached Fort Ridgely, the point from which they had started on Sully's Expedition more than five months before.

The troops were able to rest at Fort Ridgely on Sunday, October 9 in preparation for the last leg of their march to Fort Snelling. It must have seemed like heaven. It was a comfortable layover. The food was plentiful and of much wider variety than they had in Dakota Territory. Edson Washburn was thrilled to finally have some real vegetables for the first time in many months.[625]

---

622 Doud, *Diaries*, Sept. 19, 1863.

623 Bertram, *Reminiscences*, Dec. 7, 1878, MNHS.

624 Hodgson, "Recollections of the Sioux War No. 19," *Dakota County Tribune*, June 26, 1890.

625 Washburn, *Diaries*, Oct. 9, 1864.

On Monday, October 10, the Minnesota Brigade disbanded, and the Eighth Minnesota set out for Fort Snelling. Taking the "Fort Road",[626] the regiment proceeded to St. Peter. From there, it turned north to follow the Minnesota River towards Henderson. Along the way, the soldiers visited every house they passed to buy fresh bread and butter, which to them were luxuries compared to the hardtack they had to eat while on the Dakota plains.

The regiment passed through the small town of Henderson on October 12 and traveled north another two-and-a-half miles before setting up camp along High Island Creek. There, the parents of one soldier showed up and were briefly reunited with their son. The rest of the soldiers looked forward to seeing their own families soon.

The following morning the regiment continued along the west side of the Minnesota River and set up camp by the town of Carver. The men were only two days' march from Fort Snelling. Excitement was beginning to build. On reaching the fort the men were fully expecting a furlough home before they shipped out again for the south.

---

626 The Fort Road was the main thoroughfare between St. Peter to Fort Ridgely. It is still known by that name and follows nearly the same path as in the 1860s.

French Leave

October 14 to November 3, 1864

For the men of Company E, their long trek in pursuit of the Sioux was finally coming to an end. On Friday, October 14, the regiment set out at 5:30 a.m., passing through the small settlements of Chaska and then Shakopee.

A lot of trade passed between Shakopee and Fort Snelling. Consequently, there was a good road between the village and fort, which made for much easier travel than what the men had been experiencing. That evening, the regiment camped on Nine Mile Creek, which, as the name implies, was a mere nine miles from Fort Snelling and hopefully a furlough home.[627]

Starting early in the morning as usual, the regiment finally arrived at Fort Snelling shortly after 9 a.m. on Saturday, October 15. They knew the Northwestern Indian Expedition was finally over when the Eighth Minnesota was ordered to turn in their horses.[628] A few friends and relatives had come down from Monticello and were already waiting to give Company E a warm welcome. The men enjoyed this brief taste of home before being called in to organize their equipment and arrange their quarters.

By the time the Eighth Minnesota arrived at Fort Snelling, orders had been issued for the regiment to join the Twenty-Third Corps in Nashville, Tennessee.[629] The Twenty-Third Corps was part of Sherman's Army of the Tennessee and commanded by General John Schofield. The Eighth Minnesota was assigned to the Third Brigade of the Twenty-Third Corps, First Division.

---

627 The location of the camp was in present day Bloomington, Minnesota. Old Shakopee Road, which runs from near the Mall of America to the western edge of Bloomington, approximates the route of the old road between Fort Snelling and Shakopee. The regiment probably camped in the area near the current intersection of Old Shakopee Road and Thomas Avenue.

628 Strong, *A journal of the northwestern Indian expedition*, Oct 15. 1864 MNHS.

629 Pope to Halleck, Oct. 11, 1864, *Official Records*, series 1, vol. 41, part 3, 799. In most sources from the Civil War era, the corps designation was made using Roman numerals. In that format, the Eighth Minnesota was assigned to "XXIII Corps." For readability, it is written out.

Colonel Minor Thomas, in recognition for the fine work he did leading the Minnesota Brigade during Sully's Expedition, was assigned command of the Third Brigade. Lieutenant Colonel Henry Rogers therefore assumed command of the Eighth Minnesota.

Knowing that they would shortly be called upon to go south, and that they were unlikely to return home until their three-year enlistment was up, all the men looked forward to a furlough. Colonel Thomas was receptive to the idea of sending the Eighth Minnesota home on furlough. He knew very well what a toll Sully's Expedition had taken on the men. He thought that they had performed admirably under adverse conditions and earned the right to go home for a short while. Thomas did not doubt that the leave would be forthcoming. He expected there would be plenty of time for the men to go home before the regiment went south.

Even General Pope recognized the contribution of the Eighth Minnesota on Sully's Expedition:

> *In parting with the Eighth Regiment Minnesota Volunteer Infantry, which is ordered South, the major general commanding avails himself of the opportunity to bear testimony to the high reputation for discipline and efficiency maintained by that regiment during its whole service in this department. The uncomplaining and soldierly fortitude with which it has borne the hardships of service on the frontier, and has sacrificed strong inclinations to join the armies in the South, and to exhibit its high qualities on a wider field and a more prominent theater, is beyond all praise. Its record in this department warrants the confident belief that its course hereafter will be attended with all the fame and honor which its most ardent friends could devise.*[630]

One factor that favored granting furloughs was that the regiment's departure for the south would almost certainly be delayed by the absence of the 200 men who were assigned to the Fisk rescue. The rescue force made up almost one third of the Eighth Minnesota's combat strength. Therefore, it was unlikely the regiment would leave until they returned.

It would take time to get those men back to the regiment. The plan was for the Fisk rescue force to travel with Sully by steamship down the Missouri River to St. Louis. From there, the Eighth Minnesota men would ride a steamship back up the Mississippi to Fort Snelling.

630   General Orders No. 37, Oct. 12, 1864, *Official Records*, series 1, vol. 41, part 3, 826-827.

Colonel Thomas believed that the Eighth Minnesota would not leave for the south until all the soldiers who remained with Sully could rejoin the unit. He expected that the regiment would be waiting at Fort Snelling for several days before the remaining 200 soldiers arrived.[631]

Prior to leaving Fort Ridgley for the march to Fort Snelling, Col. Thomas had wired General Sibley's adjutant to request that the Eighth Minnesota receive furloughs until the soldiers assigned to the Fisk rescue arrived at Fort Snelling. That would allow plenty of time for leave, even for the soldiers who lived the greatest distance from the fort.[632]

The Eighth Minnesota had a lot to do at Fort Snelling before the men could leave for home. They had to go through the process of turning in their horses and surplus equipment from Sully's Expedition. They also needed to set up their tents and organize the camp. These tasks took the rest of the day on October 15. The men worked quickly to ensure they were ready to leave when the furloughs were handed out.

At roll call that evening, however, the soldiers' hopes of seeing their friends and family were crushed. The officers announced that no furloughs were to be granted before the Eighth Minnesota shipped out for the south. Apparently, General Sibley did not agree with Colonel Thomas on the need for furloughs.

The announcement enraged the entire regiment. The soldiers' anger and disappointment were on full display that night and throughout Sunday, October 16. The troops were incensed at the unfairness of it all. George Cambell later wrote "You would have thought you were in a hornet's nest and that there were a thousand of them."[633]

The Fort Snelling officer corps may have noticed that the grumbling died down as darkness fell Sunday evening. Perhaps they believed that the soldiers had grudgingly accepted the decision to withhold furloughs. From their perspective, it was just another crisp quiet October night.

However, as it turned out, the fort's officers would be in for quite a surprise the next day. Having reached the conclusion that the good of the service did not require their presence until the regiment was ready to move South, Company E and nearly the entire Eighth Minnesota had skedaddled during the night.[634]

631 Seelye, *Narrative*, 10-11. As it turned out, the members of the Eighth Regiment that rescued Captain Fisk would not return to Fort Snelling until after the war. Instead, they traveled down the Missouri by boat to Sioux Falls and from there by wagon to Cedar Rapids, Iowa. There, the Eighth Regiment men were able to board a train to the east. They eventually reunited with the rest of the regiment at Murfreesboro Tennessee.

632 Thomas to Olin, Oct. 15, 1864, *Official Records*, series 1, vol. 41, part 3, 903.

633 Cambell, *Personal Reminiscences*, 41.

634 Houlton, *Speech*.

As the officers called the roll the next morning, the scope of the incident first became apparent. The camp was almost deserted. At most, only the officers and a few men from each Eighth Regiment company answered the roll call. Even the non-commissioned officers, sergeants and corporals, had abandoned their posts and gone home.

The company officers likely turned a blind eye to what transpired the previous evening. They certainly did not try to stop it. Most of the officers probably realized that they could not prevent their troops from leaving anyway. [635] To interfere at that point likely would have harmed the bonds of trust they had earned in the eyes of the troops they were expected to lead in battle. In fact, the officers probably sympathized with their men. They were human after all, and the company officers had also looked forward to furloughs.

The regimental officers claimed that they had no idea of what was happening that night. George Cambell, however, recalled of Company E's departure in the darkness that "as we passed the colonel's tent, he was standing in the door looking at the sky trying to forecast the weather for the next day, I suppose."[636] It was unlikely that the mass exodus of several hundred men from the regiment's camp could have gone unnoticed by Colonel Thomas and the other regimental officers. Private Strong of Company A described it as a "general stampede."[637]

Word quickly spread throughout Fort Snelling that the Eighth Minnesota had taken "French leave." That term originated from British and French social conventions of the mid-eighteenth century. At first, the phrase referred to a guest leaving a social gathering without saying goodbye to their hosts. By the time of the Civil War, it came to mean going absent without leave or AWOL.

It was not unusual during the Civil War for soldiers to take French Leave. Unlike deserters, those who took French leave usually returned to their units. And while it was a serious offense, going AWOL normally involved individuals or small groups of soldiers. The offense was generally addressed at the company or regimental level. Little notice of such incidents was taken by higher-level commanders. A whole regiment going AWOL, however, was a different story.

The Eighth Minnesota soldiers who took French Leave that cold October evening probably were not aware of the trouble it would cause for the officers who remained behind. Not that they would have cared. The reaction by the generals commanding the Department of the Northwest was swift and intended to be severe. This was, after all, a serious breach of military discipline.

---

635   Cambell, *Personal Reminiscences*, 41.

636   Ibid., 41-42.

637   Strong, *A journal of the northwestern Indian expedition*, Oct. 17. 1864 MNHS.

General Sibley, commander of the District of Minnesota, telegraphed news of the incident to General Pope. Sibley informed Pope that "Through remissness or connivance of the guard nearly half of some companies of the Eighth Minnesota left camp last night and have gone home. They are determined to see their families before leaving."[638] Sibley also reported that it would take a week to collect the stragglers. He claimed that not more than 250 men remained in camp.

In fact, Sibley may have overstated the number of men who stayed behind. Most of the companies in the regiment were already well below their full complement of 100 troops. Additionally, 200 men, twenty from each company, were absent because they were still on their way back from Dakota Territory with General Sully. In all likelihood the number that remained behind was perhaps ten or twelve from each company.

Those who chose to remain in camp did not necessarily do so out of a sense of duty or fear of the consequences. Company E, for example picked a few men to stay and guard their comrades' rifles and equipment.[639] They did so out of a sense of loyalty to their fellow soldiers, not devotion to the army.

General Pope was furious with the Eighth Minnesota's antics. After he had heaped praise upon the regiment, they now made him look the fool.[640] His anger rolled through General Sibley to the fort commanders, regimental commanders, all the way down to the company officers. Pope immediately ordered General Sibley to arrest the guards and officers implicated in the plot. Pope especially wanted the names of those officers involved who should be recommended for dismissal.[641]

General Sibley promptly appointed his adjutant, Captain R.C. Olin, to carry out General Pope's orders. Olin was given authority to investigate the departure of the Eighth Minnesota and arrest any officers involved. Colonel Thomas was ordered to cooperate and take whatever steps were necessary to recall those absent without leave.[642] Sibley then sent an update to Pope, again stating it would take several days to round up the missing soldiers.

Colonel Thomas must have been greatly embarrassed at having his entire command go AWOL, even though he could not have missed them sneaking away in the night. Edson Washburn of Company E, who was by nature not a rule breaker and stayed behind to guard the company's equipment, was one of the few who saw the

---

638   Sibley to Pope, Oct. 17, 1864, *Official Records,* series 1, vol. 41, part 4, 63.

639   Cambell, *Personal Reminiscences,* 41.

640   *See,* General Orders No. 37, Oct. 12, 1864, *Official Records,* series 1, vol. 41, part 3, 826-827.

641   Pope to Sibley, Oct. 17, 1864, *Official Records,* series 1, vol. 41, part 4, 63.

642   Sibley to Olin, Oct. 18, 1864, *Official Records,* series 1, vol. 41, part 4, 102.

232 | Sherman's Woodticks

colonel at roll call that Monday morning. In perhaps the greatest understatement of that day he wrote "Col. feels very bad about the boys leaving the fort."[643]

Meanwhile, the Eighth Minnesota soldiers quickly set off for home. Company E traveled with some members of Company A, who were from the Anoka area. Anoka was along the Mississippi River north of Minneapolis, and the route home for most of the men from Company E ran through the town.

After leaving the fort, the soldiers traveled on foot through the night. At sunrise on Monday, October 17, they had already made it past Minneapolis, crossed the Mississippi River at Saint Anthony and covered several more miles to the north. The army had, after all, whipped them into shape for long hard marches.

Their haste was not to avoid any pursuit by military authorities. There was almost nobody left in camp to give chase. Instead, they were simply in a hurry so they could maximize their time at home. To that end, they hired some local farmers and their teams, who carried them by wagon the rest of the way. By nightfall, nearly all the Company E men were back at their homes in Monticello, Clearwater, and nearby rural areas.

Coincidentally, William Bell Mitchell, who had purchased the St. Cloud Democrat in 1863 from his aunt, Jane Swisshelm, had been at Fort Snelling on Saturday, October 15 to interview Colonel Thomas, Lieutenant Colonel Rogers, and other commanders of the Eighth Minnesota on their return from the Indian Expedition. Colonel Thomas told him that they hoped to visit St. Cloud, but could not obtain furloughs as the regiment was under orders to go South.[644]

Mitchell left St. Anthony late on October 15 for the return to St. Cloud.[645] He may or may not have been surprised to run into the group of forty to fifty Company E men north of St. Anthony. Regardless, he knew a good story when he saw one. Mitchell decided to travel with them, as they were all headed in the same direction.

Mitchell described his fellow travelers as "packed on and in" two coaches and a wagon. The men were thrilled to be going home and shared their exuberance with all those they saw along the way with happy waves and good-natured banter.

In addition, the soldiers made clear to everyone they passed who they preferred in the upcoming presidential election. "Three cheers for Uncle Abraham!" was the salutation given to onlookers throughout the trip.

One might assume that the soldiers would have preferred Lincoln's opponent, the former general George B. McClellan. However, that was clearly not the case. Despite General McClellan's popularity with his troops early in the war, the Com-

---

643   Washburn *Diaries*, Oct. 17, 1864.

644   St. Could Democrat, Oct. 20, 1864, 3.

645   Mitchell went on to write the *History of Stearns County*.

pany E men told Mitchell that not more than five men in the whole regiment would vote for McClellan.[646]

Colonel Thomas was now left with the problem of rounding up those who had gone AWOL so he could put the regiment back together in time to depart for the south. Pursuant to orders from General Pope, Thomas ordered the company officers to get their men back by evening roll call on Sunday, October 23 or they would be considered deserters.[647] This was no small matter for the Eighth Minnesota men. Deserters could be court-martialed and shot.

To comply with the Colonel's orders, Captain Brookins considerately ordered Edson Washburn and the other Company E enlisted men who remained in camp to go home, round up the fifty or so missing soldiers from Company E, and bring them back to the fort.[648]

That order was obviously made with a wink and a nod. It was simply absurd to expect a handful of lowly privates to subdue approximately fifty men and march them back to Fort Snelling against their will. All Brookins did was ensure that Washburn and the others got their own unofficial furloughs.

Washburn indeed hurried straight home to Otsego Township, not far from Clearwater. There he did most of his "searching" at his parents' home while socializing with family, his fiancée, and a variety of friends. He even spent some time helping neighbors with farm work.[649] Somehow, he never spotted any of the dozens of Company E men openly walking the streets of Monticello and surrounding area. Not surprisingly, Washburn returned to Fort Snelling on October 23 without having captured a single man.[650]

Beginning on Saturday, October 22, the scattered men of the Eighth Minnesota left their homes for the return to Fort Snelling. The Company E men had as far to travel as those of any other company. Still, many didn't leave until the last minute.

Edson Washburn and his mother set out together from their home near Monticello on the morning of October 22. They stopped for dinner at about 1:30 p.m. in the small Mississippi River town of Champlin. There, Washburn found 130 men, mostly from Company E and Company A, who had likewise stopped for dinner

646   St. Could Democrat, Oct. 20, 1864, 3.

647   Ibid., 1.

648   Washburn, *Autobiography*, 4.

649   Washburn, *Diaries*, Oct. 18-23, 1864.

650   Ibid., Oct. 23, 1864.

during their journey back to the fort.[651] Washburn and his mother spent Saturday night at his sister's house in Minneapolis before he returned to Fort Snelling.

Throughout the day on Sunday, October 23 the Eighth Minnesota's soldiers trickled back into camp at Fort Snelling. They came from their unauthorized leave singly and in small groups. About ten Company E men from the Clearwater area, including George Cambell and Charlie Gibbs, traveled back together. They hired Charlie's father Seth to take them back to Fort Snelling with this wagon team.

Seth Gibbs was glad to accommodate. He was a former Republican state senator from Clearwater and a staunch supporter of the Union cause.[652] Furthermore, he was a partner in the furniture business with none other than First Lieutenant Thomas Tollington.

Having been busy relaxing for several days, the Clearwater men lost track of the time. They got a late start. Mr. Gibbs had to drive the team quickly to make it back to Fort Snelling by evening roll call on October 23. George Cambell was especially concerned because his last name began with "C", which made his name one of the first names that would be called.

The Gibbs wagon pulled into the fort at a trot, where the men found the roll call for Company E was already underway. Just as the sergeant shouted "Cambell," George jumped from the wagon, ran up behind the company and yelled "HERE!" It was a very close call.[653]

Sure enough, by the end of roll call, nearly the entire Eighth Minnesota had returned, including every man in Company E. General Sibley later telegraphed the news to Major General Pope after the regiment had already embarked for the South. Sibley noted that the men appeared ashamed of their actions.[654]

In reality, the men of Company E had no shame whatsoever for doing what they thought was just. To the contrary, they were unrepentant and proud of standing up for their rights. The men saw their actions as nothing more than correcting a fundamentally unfair denial of their furloughs. In their later years, veterans of Company E would fondly recall their episode of French leave as having been a statement against army injustice.

It did not take long for Captain Olin to complete his investigation of the incident. His report conveniently cleared all the Eighth Minnesota's officers. Sibley telegraphed headquarters to alert them that the full report would soon be delivered. He

651 Washburn, *Diaries*, Oct. 22, 1864

652 He served only one term after it was alleged he didn't live in the senate district he represented.

653 Cambell, *Personal Reminiscences*, 42.

654 Sibley to Pope, October 17, 1864, *Official Records*, series 1, vol. 41, part 4, 261.

also assured headquarters that the plans for French leave had been kept secret from officers and instead blamed the feeble response of the guards.[655]

The fallout from the French leave incident continued for a time, even after the Eighth Minnesota shipped out for the south. When the regiment reached Murfreesboro, Tennessee, Colonel Thomas ordered Captain Brookins to report in writing the names of all non-commissioned officers of Company E who absented themselves without leave for reduction to the ranks, or to explain in writing why they should not be so reduced.

The non-commissioned officers chose to respond themselves. They drafted a statement to explain why they felt justified in going absent without leave and delivered it directly to Colonel Thomas. There was a tone of defiance in their statement:

> After five months constant marching we returned to Fort Snelling and found orders for the _South_ awaiting us. We were ready cheerfully to comply with this, supposing that we should, as all before us had, first receive a short furlough or leave of absence. But when we were assured that it was not within the power of any Officer of this Department to grant this, and that though within a few hours ride of home, we were to be sent South for the balance of our time without being permitted to go home, we felt justified in absenting ourselves _without_ leave.[656]

Regarding punishment for taking French leave, the statement almost dared the colonel to punish them:

> Conscious of no wrong, we have no apology to offer, for though _soldiers_ we do not forget that we are also men. If in your opinion it is necessary that we should be made examples of, it is not within our province to say why you should not.[657]

The statement was signed by James Ambler, William Houlton, Timothy Desmond and H.W. Fuller, all sergeants and corporals. What, if any response Col. Thomas made to the Company E non-commissioned officers has been lost to history,

---

655   Ibid., at 125.

656   Answer to Col. Thomas, Nov. 6, 1864, Houlton Papers, MNHS. William H. Houlton is likely the primary author as he was very articulate and served as company clerk.

657   Ibid.

but that appears to have been the end of the French leave matter. There is no record of any man in the Eighth Minnesota ever being officially disciplined for the incident.

On to Tennessee

The Eighth Minnesota learned upon their return to Fort Snelling on Sunday, October 23 that they would ship out for the South in two days. The next day was a flurry of activity at Fort Snelling as the soldiers drew new clothing and equipment, cleaned their weapons, and prepared for departure.

The trip would require the regiment to march from Fort Snelling to the riverboat levee in St. Paul. There, the regiment would load onto riverboats and barges. From St. Paul, they would travel down the Mississippi River to Winona. Then, the Eighth Minnesota would board a train on the Wisconsin side of the river and travel by rail to their final destination, Murfreesboro, Tennessee.

The troops were ready to go by the appointed time on the morning of Tuesday, October 25. There was only one problem. The boats that were to take them downriver from St. Paul had not arrived. As a result, the men of the Eighth Minnesota had nothing to do but stay at Fort Snelling and lay around all day.[658]

Reveille was sounded at 3a.m. the following morning. The troops formed up and set out at daybreak for the seven-mile march to the levee in St. Paul where they would board the riverboats. Most of the march was uneventful. However, the soldiers were in for an unpleasant surprise when the Eighth Minnesota entered St. Paul.

As the troops marched through St. Paul to the levee, they began hearing taunts from some of the townsfolk, such as "Boys, you will never get back" and "You will leave your bones down there."[659] The dedicated volunteer soldiers were naturally offended and angered at these venomous barbs, which they attributed to the Copperheads.[660]

"Copperhead" was a political term that meant a northern Democrat who was in favor of letting the South secede. There were plenty of them in Minnesota. Democratic party strongholds, such as St. Paul and St. Cloud, had many residents who could be classified as Copperheads. They had no love for the Minnesota soldiers that volunteered to fight for the Union, and the feeling was mutual.

The Eighth Minnesota arrived at the St. Paul levee about 10:30 in the morning and waited for the arrival of their boats. They had to wait until 2:30 p.m. before The *Albany* arrived at the levee. The *Albany* had been engaged in the Minnesota River

---

658 Washburn, *Diaries*, Oct. 25, 1864.

659 Cambell, *Personal Reminiscences*, 43.

660 Ibid.

trade since 1861.[661] The boat was far too small to fit the entire Eighth Minnesota. However, it arrived towing two barges, one tied to each side of the boat. The boat and barges combined had enough space to accommodate the regiment.

Company E, much to the soldiers' disappointment, was assigned to ride in one of the barges. The conditions were terrible. The barges were loosely covered with a thin canvas roof, which did little to keep out the rain and drizzle that had been falling all day. As the troops boarded, they discovered that an inch of mud covered the floor of the barges. Moreover, even if the floor had been dry, there was not anywhere near enough room for men to lay out and sleep.

Even worse, the barge was so crowded that there was no place for the men to so much as sit. Edson Washburn wrote "Our accommodations are nearly as good as a pigsty."[662] The conditions were so bad that some of the soldiers openly wondered whether this was their punishment for taking French leave.[663]

After traveling in the barges for the better part of two days the men were cold, wet, and tired. They were covered in mud splattered about the barges and very hungry because there had been nothing to eat but hardtack and river water.[664] Needless to say, the men were in a foul mood.

When the officers informed the miserable passengers that due to a storm raging outside, they would have to stay in the barges for another day, it was just too much. Company E and the other troops confined to the barges went into open rebellion. Several hundred voices began to chant "go ashore, go ashore, go ashore!" Some loudly threatened to cut the barges loose. Other soldiers began giving the Indian war whoop they had learned in Dakota Territory and pounded up on the floor of the cabin above.[665]

The officers took the hint. The *Albany* and barges tied up for the night at Lake City on the Minnesota side of Lake Pepin, a large lake formed by a widening in the Mississippi River. There the men disembarked and slept in a warehouse.[666]

Before first light the next morning, Friday, October 28, the men loaded back on the boat and barges for the last seventy miles of their river journey. The Eighth Minnesota arrived at La Crosse, Wisconsin later that day and transferred to a train. The passenger cars of the train must have seemed luxurious compared to travel by barge.

661 George Byron Merrick, *Old Times on the Upper Mississippi: The Recollections of a Steamboat Pilot from 1854 to 1863*, Cleveland, OH, Arthur H. Clark Company, 1909, 258.

662 Washburn, *Diaries*, Oct. 26, 1864.

663 Houlton, *Speech*.

664 Washburn, *Autobiography*, 4.

665 Houlton, *Speech*; Cambell, *Personal Reminiscences*, 44.

666 Washburn, *Diaries*, Oct. 28, 1864.

The soldiers spent the rest of the day in the railroad cars as they crossed Wisconsin. They traveled through Milwaukee and then south to Chicago, where the Eighth Minnesota arrived at about 3 a.m. on the morning of October 29.

Upon arrival, the men grabbed their gear and marched to a nearby soldiers' rest camp. For the rest of the day and most of the next, the soldiers were able to get some sleep and good meals. The men also enjoyed comforts that had been absent during their time in Dakota Territory. A group from Company E even managed to make it to the theater on the evening of October 29.[667]

It was well and good that the Eighth Minnesota enjoyed its time in Chicago. The next leg of the trip to Nashville would not be so pleasant.

On the evening of Sunday, October 30, the Eighth Minnesota assembled and marched back to the railyard. What they found waiting for them was shocking to say the least. The regiment was ordered to board freight cars that had last carried cattle and had not been properly cleaned out.[668]

As was the case when they were loaded on to the barges in St. Paul, the Company E men concluded they were again being punished.[669] Sure enough, the rebellious nature of Company E reappeared when the men perceived that the army was treating them unfairly. They turned up their noses, fell in line and said they couldn't go.[670] The defiance of Company E caused a significant delay. Only after the officers reasoned with them did the men decided they had made their point and proceeded to board the freight cars.

The railroad crews tried to crowd forty or fifty soldiers into each of the narrow freight cars. Company E was having none of it. As on the barges, packing the cars to such capacity would not permit the men to sit, much less lie down.

As they boarded, the soldiers began mooing and "Bellowing like a crowd of bulls."[671] They also discovered a way to obtain more space in the cars. The first men on board did not proceed to the ends of the car. Instead, they remained crowded around the open door. This gave the appearance that the car was fuller than was actually the case. The railroad workers responsible for the loading process couldn't make an accurate headcount in the darkness and had to take their word for it when the troops said the car was full.[672]

---

667 Cambell, *Personal Reminiscences*, 44.

668 Cambell, *Personal Reminiscences*, 44.

669 Houlton, *Speech*.

670 Cambell, *Personal Reminiscences*, 44.

671 Houlton, *Speech*.

672 Cambell, *Personal Reminiscences*, 44-45.

The mini rebellion of the Eighth Minnesota didn't end there. When the engine got up to steam and started to move forward the engineers realized that only one car was attached. Someone had pulled all the linchpins that connected the remaining freight cars.

For the next two hours the train crew and railroad officials fussed around trying to get the linchpins back from the Eighth Minnesota troops but to no avail. Finally, the railroad officials "said they were very sorry but that was the best they could do for us and it was very necessary we should go south immediately."[673]

While not entirely satisfactory, it seems that the troops realized this was the best they were going to get, and they would have to be satisfied with a moral victory. "We got into the cars, the linchpins came back, and off we went."[674]

At least the troops managed to find some straw to put down over the floor while they were waiting for the situation to be sorted out. The straw covered the filth left by the previous occupants of the cattle car and gave the men a softer place to sleep.[675]

Even though the cars were not carrying as many troops as intended, there were still too many for all the men to lie down comfortably. The cars were only eight feet wide. Fortunately, they quickly arrived at a solution called "heads to points."[676] In this position, the men would lie down across the car alternating with their heads pointing to opposite side walls and their legs dovetailed.[677] It wasn't the most comfortable position, but it allowed the men to get some sleep despite the crowded conditions.

The troop train passed out of Chicago and south through Indiana. The railroad was not in the best of shape and the going was slow. In the wee hours of Tuesday, November 1, the traveling soldiers were rudely awakened by a sudden shaking. The train had ground to a halt.

As the soldiers jumped out of the cars to see what happened, they were greeted with a shocking sight. The locomotive had derailed and was lying on its side. The shaking they experienced was caused by the freight cars leaving the tracks and bouncing over the railroad ties.[678] Fortunately, none of the freight cars had turned over like the locomotive so there were no injuries among the troops.

---

673 Houlton, *Speech*.

674 Ibid.

675 Cambell, *Personal Reminiscences*, 45.

676 Ibid.

677 Washburn, *Autobiography*, 5.

678 Houlton, *Speech*.

Hearing the commotion of the derailment, an old woman who lived next to the track came out to see what happened. Upon finding the derailed freight cars, the concerned woman inquired whether any of the cattle had been hurt. The troops assured her that the "cattle" were just fine.[679]

The derailment occurred near New Albany, Indiana, a small town just across the Ohio River from Louisville, Kentucky. The troops waited around the wreck until daylight. Then they retrieved their gear and proceed to march the two miles to town. From there, they crossed the Ohio River into Louisville and set up camp for the night.

In the finest tradition of Company E, George Cambell decided to have a little fun with the system while assigned to guard duty the night of November 1. At the evening roll call, the colonel gave a pointed lecture about the need for strict obedience to orders. When Cambell reported for guard duty at 8 p.m., he was ordered to allow nobody from the Eighth Minnesota to leave camp without a written permit from the commanding officer.

Cambell knew the order to confine the *entire* Eighth Minnesota to camp wasn't quite correct. These routine orders normally applied only to enlisted men. Officers were free to come and go as they pleased. However, Private Cambell decided to take the colonel's earlier lecture to heart. After all, it wasn't his job to correct such mistakes.

Cambell had great fun stopping the commissioned officers who tried to pass through his post and then sending them back for permits. Before long, Lieutenant Colonel Rogers showed up and began writing the permits for the officers on the spot. Cambell later recalled that "When I was relieved, you may be sure I got new orders."[680]

On the evening of November 2, the Eighth Minnesota again loaded into freight cars for the trip from Louisville to Nashville. One member of Company E did not join the men on the train. Private John Ponsford had taken ill and was left behind in hospital at Louisville. He would have to catch up to the Eighth Minnesota when he recovered.[681]

The train traveled through the night. It was again slow going due to the condition of the track. Further delays resulted from another train that derailed up ahead. It was 8 p.m. on Thursday, November 3 before the troop train finally pulled into Nashville. There they camped for the night to await the last leg of their trip to Murfreesboro.

---

679 Ibid.

680 Cambell, *Personal Reminiscences*, 46-47

681 Ponsford never rejoined the unit. He died in hospital at Louisville on Nov. 22, 1864. He was only 20 years old.

Fortress Rosecrans

November 4 to December 6, 1864

At dawn on Friday, November 4, 1864, the regiment began the final day of its journey to Murfreesboro. As usual, the day started for the soldiers with the obligatory coffee. Then the regiment set out for the railroad depot where they would board a train for the thirty-mile trip to Murfreesboro. After hours of delays, the train finally left the station at 3:30 p.m.

The trip was not pleasant for many of the troops. The train consisted mostly of open flat cars, which provided no protection from the weather. And that protection was sorely needed. It rained off and on all day. The soldiers riding on those open cars were fully exposed to the elements and it made them miserable.

The wet tracks also made the going very slow. The railroad line had not been well-maintained during the war. It was worn out. Moreover, it ran mostly uphill. The engine's wheels slipped on the wet tracks along the steeper grades, slowing the train to a crawl. The wheels slipped so much that they had to send soldiers out ahead to place sand on the tracks so the engine could gain traction. Never missing the humor in such situations, George Cambell recalled those walking alongside the train jokingly shouted at the soldiers to "get out and push." [682]

The regiment's train finally reached Murfreesboro in the evening darkness at about 9:30 p.m. It was a short march to the regiment's assigned camps site, which was on a hillside along the Shelbyville Pike just outside the western edge of Murfreesboro. Due to the late hour, the regiment spent the night sleeping on the damp ground. [683] It was a cold, wet, and miserable night for the men.

---

682 Cambell, *Personal Reminiscences*, 47.

683 Washburn, *Diaries*, Nov. 5, 1864.

The following morning, the regiment began setting up what would be their home for the next few weeks. The men were pleased with the location of the camp. The site had a supply of good fresh water, which the men must have greatly appreciated after their experience in Dakota Territory.

As the soldiers set up camp, the day quickly turned sunny and warm. This gave the men an opportunity to get caught up cleaning their guns, washing clothes and the other mundane but necessary aspects of camp life.

Looking over their surroundings, the men of the Eighth Minnesota really saw for the first time what this war had wrought on the landscape and people. There had been plenty of hard fighting in and around Murfreesboro since the war began and the countryside showed it.[684] There were new graveyards around the area where the war dead had been hastily buried. In addition, James Davison of Company F noted that old cannon balls, broken bayonets, and discarded guns could be picked up anywhere in any direction.[685]

The most recent large-scale engagement near Murfreesboro had been the Battle of Stones River, which spanned three days from December 31, 1862, to January 2, 1863. It pitted the Union Army of the Cumberland under General William Rosecrans against the Confederate Army of Tennessee, commanded by Braxton Bragg. The battle was a bloody one, resulting in almost 25,000 casualties among the 78,000 men engaged from both sides.

Fortress Rosecrans, which was approximately a mile north of Murfreesboro, had been built in 1863 following the Battle of Stone's River. It was the largest fort built by the Union Army during the Civil War and enclosed more than 225 acres. Within its walls were several large supply depots and warehouses that were used to support Sherman's army during the Atlanta campaign.

As its name implies, the fortress was named after General Rosecrans, who led the Union forces in the Battle of Stones River. It presented a formidable defensive position. The fortress was built of thick earthen walls and was surrounded by a ten-foot ditch with pointed spikes to repel any Rebel attacks. In addition to all the supply houses contained within the walls, the fortress could also hold more than 13,000 troops.

There was also a smaller battle that took place at Murfreesboro in the summer of 1862 that had special significance for the men of Company E and the rest of the Eighth Minnesota. On July 13, 1862, Confederate units under the command of

---

684 James Davison to Sister Ina, Murfreesboro, Tennessee, Nov. 28,1864, Charles E. Davison and family papers, 1852-1864. MNHS.

685 Ibid. George Cambell also noted that there were plenty of relics to be found on the old Stones River Battlefield. Cambell, *Personal Reminiscences*, 47.

then Colonel Nathan Bedford Forrest attacked the Union garrison at Murfreesboro. Among that garrison was the Third Minnesota Volunteer Infantry Regiment.

Nathan Bedford Forrest would become perhaps the most feared Confederate cavalry general during the Civil War. Forrest himself had humble beginnings. He was born the son of a blacksmith in a small Tennessee cabin in 1821. He went into business at a young age and managed to build a fortune in various business ventures, including as a slave trader, and through farming. He eventually acquired several plantations near Memphis and settled there.

When the Civil War began, Forrest, by then one of the richest men in the South, enlisted as a private. He soon used his own wealth to outfit a regiment of cavalry, after which he was promoted to lieutenant colonel. By the time Forrest engaged the Minnesota troops at Murfreesboro, he was a full colonel in charge of a brigade of cavalry.

Many of the men in Company E had friends and family among the Third Minnesota. Andrew H. Bertram's father George was a private in Company H of the Third Minnesota and Capt. Brookins' brother, also named George, was a corporal in Company I of the same regiment. Numerous other soldiers in the Third Minnesota were known to the men in Company E and the citizens of Monticello.[686]

In June of 1862, Union General Don Carlos Buell was ordered to drive out the rebels and capture Chattanooga. At the time, Buell's Army of the Ohio was camped 180 miles to the west at Corinth, Mississippi.

Such a long march required substantial supplies for the troops. The Army of the Ohio was dependent on supplies from the Nashville quartermaster and commissary. It was of vital importance that the Nashville and Chattanooga Railroad, which ran through the towns of Murfreesboro and Stevenson, remain in operation to supply Buell's forces.[687]

The Confederates learned of Buell's planned attack on Chattanooga. Realizing that the Chattanooga forces were inferior to Buell's, the Confederates ordered Forrest to take three regiments of cavalry, about 1,400 men, to Murfreesboro. His mission was to sever Buell's lines of communication and otherwise delay Buell's movements until reinforcements could arrive at Chattanooga.[688]

Murfreesboro had a Union garrison that numbered less than 1,000 troops. While together that number might have been enough soldiers to make an even fight with Forrest's troops, the Union troops were spread out. They had been placed in smaller groups around the town. This allowed the soldiers to cover a larger defensive

---

686   *The North-Western Weekly Union*, Aug. 9, 1862.

687   *Minnesota in the Civil and Indian Wars: 1861-1865*, vol. 1, 151.

688   Ibid.

line. However, it would also allow Forrest's cavalry to isolate the smaller pockets of defenders and overwhelm them.

There were 250 men of the Ninth Michigan Infantry Regiment about three quarters of a mile east of town. Near the Ninth Michigan were eighty men from the Seventh Pennsylvania Cavalry and another eighty-one men of the Fourth Kentucky Cavalry. Nine companies of the Third Minnesota, consisting of approximately 500 men, were camped a mile away on the western edge of Murfreesboro.[689] Supporting the Third Minnesota were four guns and sixty-four men of Hewitts' Kentucky Field Artillery.

When Forrest's cavalry attacked the garrison at Murfreesboro on the morning of July 13, 1862, he directed the bulk of his force to attack the Ninth Michigan and cavalry units on the eastern side of town. The Ninth Michigan put up a good fight. They inflicted considerable casualties on the attacking Confederates and killed a colonel in the process. However, outnumbered and having suffered significant losses of its own, the Ninth Michigan was quickly pushed back into the town.

By Noon the Ninth Michigan had lost almost half its strength, eleven dead and eighty-nine wounded. With so many casualties, the regiment had no option but to surrender. At that point, the Confederates moved in and occupied Murfreesboro.

Hearing the large volume of gunfire coming from the east side of town, the Third Minnesota troops quickly formed a line of battle. Supported by Hewitt's battery, the regiment began advancing towards Murfreesboro.[690] They promptly ran into about 300 troops from Forrest's cavalry brigade. Hewitt's artillery was quickly brought into action and the Confederates scattered.

The Third Regiment found itself in a commanding defensive position along the Nashville Pike. Skirmishers were ordered out into the woods that extended from their position to the edge of Murfreesboro. Artillery was positioned to cover the Nashville Pike and other places the Confederates might congregate for an attack. Then they waited for the expected attack.

The Confederates only made one attempt to attack the Third Regiment. A Georgia regiment formed for a charge, but they were quickly driven off. This only boosted the confidence of the Minnesota men and made them look forward to more fighting.

Meanwhile, the Third Minnesota commander, Colonel Henry C. Lester, learned what had happened to the Ninth Michigan. At about the same time, firing could be heard coming from the Third Minnesota camp, which was out of sight about a mile away.

A skeleton crew of about twenty men had been left behind to guard the camp. They had been attacked by Forrest's troops. All the Minnesota soldiers were either

689   Ibid at 152.

690   *Minnesota in the Civil and Indian Wars: 1861-1865*, vol. 1, 152-153.

captured or killed. The rebel cavalry proceeded to burn and loot the officer's tents, and then they quickly retreated.

Concerned at the gunfire back at camp, Colonel Lester repositioned the regiment in an even stronger defensive position to the rear of the Murfree house (presumably the town's namesake or a relative thereof). There, the regiment had a chance for a break to get food and coffee. By early afternoon, the men were again in good spirits, well-armed, and eager for a fight.[691]

Soon, confederates approached under flag of truce. They carried a letter with a request for Colonel Lester to meet with Confederate Colonel Duffield in town. Colonel Lester accepted the invitation and followed the confederates into Murfreesboro. Little did Lester know, but Forrest had lined the route in and out of town with an ostentatious display of troops, giving the appearance of much greater numbers than the Confederates really had.

Forrest's ruse had the intended effect. What Lester saw in Murfreesboro convinced him that the rebels were present in overwhelming force. He believed that further resistance was futile and would certainly result in defeat with great loss and no possibility of escape. In reality, Forrest had fewer than 1,000 men. That would almost certainly not be enough of a force to defeat the Third Minnesota, which was heavily armed and in a strong defensive position.

After returning from the meeting with Duffield, Lester called his officers together to describe what he saw in town. Lester was deeply concerned and raised the possibility of surrender. After some discussion, Lester decided to put the matter to a vote of his commanders. The officers voted in favor of continuing the fight.

Convinced that they were outnumbered and without hope of reinforcements, Lester reopened the discussions. This time he was more persuasive. When he put it to another ballot, the vote for surrender prevailed.

The men of the Third Regiment had held their own during the fighting that day and were confident they could prevail against further attacks by Forrest's troops. So, it was with dismay and astonishment that the men received orders to surrender.[692]

When news of the surrender reached the other Minnesota regiments it was a blow to morale. Officers and enlisted men alike considered the surrender a disgrace, and a stain upon the honor of every Minnesota soldier.

Now, on November 5, 1864, the men of the Eighth Minnesota found themselves setting up camp on nearly the same ground that their comrades in the Third Regiment had occupied almost two and a half years before. The irony could not have

---

691 Ibid at 154.

692 *Minnesota in the Civil and Indian Wars: 1861-1865*, vol. 1, 155.

been lost on them. Perhaps, they even hoped to encounter General Forrest again so they could even the score.[693]

The warm sunny weather that the regiment enjoyed during their first day at Murfreesboro was not to last. The following day again turned cold and rainy. Rain continued almost constantly for the first seven days. The men were yet again wet and miserable. George Cambell recalled that "every stitch of clothes we had were soaked through."[694]

Soldiers from Company E who had formerly been farmers or mechanics were accustomed to improvising solutions to camp problems, especially when it came to their comfort. In no time, they got their hands on some metal pipe and conduit, which they used to rig makeshift stoves. Before long, the men were enjoying lots of comfort in their warm, dry quarters.[695]

For the next couple of weeks, the Eighth Minnesota troops spent most of their time on guard or police duty. They also used the time for drill and inspections, even in the wet nasty weather.

At that time, troop trains were constantly passing through Murfreesboro to reinforce Union Army elements that were in pursuit of General John Bell Hood and his Confederate Army of Tennessee.[696] This was a critical mission for the Union. Hood intended to cut off the supply lines feeding Sherman's army.

Hood had moved up from the south along roads to the west of Murfreesboro. Aware of the danger this posed, troops stationed in and around Fortress Rosecrans began preparing to defend against an attack and possibly a siege.

Fortress Rosecrans was not yet ready if the rebels should surround it. Despite the warehouse space, supplies were low. Food rations has already been scaled back. Edson Washburn noted on November 14 that "Our rations are not enough for us to eat."[697]

If the Confederates attacked, it would become necessary for the troops in and around Murfreesboro to draw into the fortress. To make room for these units, the Eighth Minnesota was ordered to construct additional quarters within the fortress. Starting on November 9, groups of ten men from Company E were detailed to go out and cut timber to be used for building fortifications and quarters. This could be hazardous duty as Confederate guerillas were known to be operating in the area. For that

693 Nathan Bedford Forrest was promoted to brigadier general only days after his forces engaged the 3rd Minnesota. He was a major general by the time the Eighth Minnesota arrived at Murfreesboro in 1864.

694 Cambell, *Personal Reminiscences*, 48.

695 Ibid.

696 The confederate armies were generally named after states or regions, such as the "Army of Tennessee" or "Army of Northern Virginia." The Union armies were named after rivers, such as "Army of the Potomac." As a result, the clashes around Nashville were between the Confederate Army of Tennessee and the Union Army of the Tennessee, referring to the Tennessee River.

697 Washburn, *Diaries*, Nov. 14, 1864.

reason, some additional members of Company E went along to stand guard. The work details continued to go out each day to cut the timber required for construction. They tried to do some foraging to supplement the rations, but there was little food to be had.

On November 16 the troops who participated in the rescue of Lieutenant Fisk's ill-fated expedition in Dakota Territory finally caught up with rest of the Eighth Minnesota. It was a happy reunion.

A few days later, Confederate guerillas and regular cavalry managed to cut the supply lines to Murfreesboro. Rations for the troops stationed in and around Fortress Rosecrans had to be further reduced as a result. Even worse for the morale of the men, no mail was able to get in or out.

Union commanders finally decided that it was growing too risky to leave troops camped outside the walls of Fortress Rosecrans. They were too vulnerable to attacks by the nearby Confederates. On Thanksgiving Day 1864, the Eighth Minnesota was ordered to move into quarters within Fortress Rosecrans.

Edson Washburn received some good news the following day. He, William Dallas, and Lewis Goyette were all promoted to corporal. Each was placed in charge of a squad of between six and eight men.

However, the weather continued to be dismal. Thomas Hodgson of Company F described just how bad it was:

> It was constant rain, sleet or snow. The weird winds were constantly moaning and howling. It froze at night and thawed in the middle of the day, and the mixture of mud and snow was fearful. To stand guard for two hours at a time in the darkness of those cloudy nights and walk a beat in cold driving rain was to make one night seem like a month.[698]

Throughout the last couple weeks of November, troops continued to arrive in the area. Rumor had it that the Union forces were now up to 80,000 men.[699] The tension was growing, and the men sensed that there would soon be a clash between the opposing forces.

First Rebel Encounter – Overalls Creek

On November 30, 1864, the Union and Confederate armies clashed at Franklin, Tennessee, which was about twenty-five miles west of Murfreesboro. The Eighth Minnesota remained in Fortress Rosecrans but the men were well aware of the battle

698 Hodgson, "Recollections of the Sioux War No. 28," *Dakota County Tribune*, Dec. 4, 1890.

699 Washburn, *Diaries*, Nov. 29, 1864.

raging nearby. The troops could clearly hear the booms of the cannon and other sounds of fierce fighting.[700] As the battle carried on into the evening, the flashes of exploding shells lit the night sky. The troops in Fortress Rosecrans could even see the arc of shells traveling through the air.[701]

The Battle of Franklin proved a decisive victory for the Union. Hood's army suffered more than 6,000 casualties, which were a serious blow to the Confederate force. Despite emerging victorious, the Union forces pulled back towards Nashville after the fight to defend Sherman's supply lines.

With the Union withdrawal, Confederate forces were left in control of the countryside surrounding Fortress Rosecrans. The railroad lines and turnpikes were no longer safe to travel with Confederates in the area. As a result, several Union regiments that were bound by train for Nashville became stranded in Murfreesboro.[702]

Defenders within Fortress Rosecrans welcomed the added troop strength. There was one problem, however. The stranded regiments had to eat. The additional mouths to feed placed greater strain on the already meager supply of rations stockpiled at the fort. The quartermaster had to cut the troops down to quarter rations and they were ordered to prepare for a siege.[703]

Hood and his troops were headed northeast towards Nashville in pursuit of the Union army. As the Confederates began to move, Hood ordered General Forrest to take his troops and attack the rail line between Murfreesboro and Nashville. Forrest had taken up a defensive position on the outskirts of Nashville on December 2 and was within sight of the capitol. When Hood's infantry arrived to relieve his troops, Forrest took his cavalry south along the Nashville-Murfreesboro railroad to attack several fortified blockhouses that protected the rail and telegraph lines.

In addition to his cavalry, General Forrest was also in command of General Bate's infantry division and other units from Cheatham's Corps. Forrest ordered those units to carry out similar attacks on blockhouses along the Murfreesboro rail line.

During one of these attacks, the Eighth Minnesota had its first serious encounter with the Confederates. On December 4, Bate's troops attacked blockhouse No. 7, which guarded a railroad bridge just over four miles to the northwest of Fortress Rosecrans. The troops in the fort could see the smoke and hear the gunfire as the attack got underway. The Thirteenth Indiana Cavalry was sent out to investi-

700   Washburn, *Diaries*, Nov. 30, 1864. Washburn mistakenly thought the fighting took place at Columbia.

701   Hodgson, "Recollections of the Sioux War No. 28," *Dakota County Tribune*, Dec. 4, 1890.

702   Ibid.

703   Ibid.

gate. Upon discovering the battle, the unit sent a call for reinforcements back to the fortress.

Blockhouse No. 7 sat on the south side of Overalls Creek. It was located near a small railroad bridge, just to the west of the rail line that angled to the northwest towards Nashville. The Thirteenth Indiana Cavalry promptly set up a defensive line on the south side of the creek to protect the blockhouse as they awaited reinforcements. For the next few hours, the Indianans skirmished with rebel sharpshooters on the north side of the river.[704]

General Rousseau, the commander of Fortress Rosecrans, ordered General Milroy to take reinforcements to the scene. General Robert H. Milroy was a lawyer from Indiana before the war. When hostilities began with the South, he raised a company of Indiana volunteers and was elected captain.

Milroy rose rapidly through the officer ranks. He was first appointed colonel of a regular army regiment. He later rose to brigadier and then major general following the second Battle of Bull Run. It looked like Milroy was destined for greater things. And then came the Gettysburg Campaign.

Milroy was headquartered at Winchester, Virginia in June 1863 when General Lee's Army of Northern Virginia moved north towards Pennsylvania. With almost 7,000 men under his command, Milroy was confident he could hold out against any Confederate attacks launched against his position. He convinced his superiors that his troops should remain in place instead of withdrawing out of the Confederates' path.

On June 15, 1863, the Confederates attacked. Milroy escaped but the rebels captured 3,000 of his men and nearly all his supplies. Milroy was initially blamed for the loss of men and material. A court of inquiry into his actions was later held and he was ultimately found blameless. Nevertheless, Milroy was from then on viewed with disfavor. He had been reassigned first to recruiting duties and later to defending the railroad lines in Tennessee.

It was the protection of the railroads that brought Milroy to Fortress Rosecrans in the late fall of 1864. He no doubt viewed the opportunity to lead troops against Forrest's command as a way to redeem his reputation.

Milroy gathered a brigade, consisting of the Eighth Minnesota, 174th Ohio and the Sixty-First Illinois infantry regiments, along with a section of the Thirteenth New York Artillery.[705] With this force, Milroy set out to defend against Bate's attack.

Milroy arrived at the scene with the brigade early in the afternoon. His first order was to place the artillery on a bluff above the creek. From there, the artillery

704 Report of Maj. Gen. Robert H. Milroy, Dec. 6, 1864, *Official Records*, series 1, vol. 45, part 1, 615.

705 Ibid.

engaged the enemy's cannon, which were located on a hill about 900 yards away on the other side of the creek.

Next, Milroy ordered the Sixty-First Illinois to advance as skirmishers, followed by the 174th Ohio. These units were to advance towards a highway bridge about a quarter mile to the west where they would cross the creek. At the same time, Milroy sent the Eighth Minnesota to the blockhouse and ordered them to cross the creek if practicable and flank the rebel artillery.[706]

The Sixty First Illinois made it across the highway bridge under heavy fire. Once the Illinois regiment drove back the rebel sharpshooters, Milroy sent the 174th Ohio into the action. The Ohio troops also made it across the bridge despite intense rifle fire. Together, the Illinois and Ohio infantry regiments managed to push Bate's forces back from the bridge.

Meanwhile, the Eighth Minnesota was having no luck in its attempts to cross the creek. As pickets looked for a ford, the rest of the regiment stayed in place to defend the artillery as they exchanged fire with the rebel batteries. This was the first time that the regiment had been under real fire from a trained and organized foe. "We had shells to dodge, and grape, canister and musketry to face," recalled Lieutenant Benjamin Brunson.[707]

The Minnesota troops were itching to get into battle but were ordered to stay in place. While guarding the artillery at Overalls Creek was less dangerous than engaging in the full battle, having the rebel shells scream in and burst over their heads tested the Eighth Minnesota's courage.[708] The frustrated troops only direct contact with the enemy infantry that day was limited to exchanging rifle fire with Confederate sharpshooters stationed along the north side of the creek.

As darkness fell, the firing dropped off. The Confederate forces pulled back approximately five miles to the north. Milroy had the 174th Ohio and Sixty-First Illinois return to the south side of the creek, along with the Thirteenth Indiana Cavalry, and take up a defensive position with the Eighth Minnesota. At 9 p.m., Milroy, not hearing any sign of the enemy, decided to withdraw to the safety of Fortress Rosecrans.[709]

The Union casualties from the engagement amounted to approximately sixty-four killed and wounded. Most of those were in the 174th Ohio. Only one soldier from the Eighth Minnesota was wounded and then only slightly. The rebel casualties

706 Ibid.

707 Brunson, "Reminiscences of Service With the Eighth Minnesota Infantry," 378.

708 Hodgson, "Recollections of the Sioux War No. 28," *Dakota County Tribune*, Dec. 4, 1890.

709 Report of Maj. Gen. Robert H. Milroy, Dec. 6, 1864, *Official Records*, series 1, vol. 45, part 1, 616.

were impossible to know. Milroy reported that he saw eight or ten Confederate dead and the troops captured twenty prisoners.[710]

To Edson Washburn of Company E, the Battle of Overalls Creek seemed like a victory for the Union troops.[711] Others were not so sure. Private Thomas Hodgson of Company F later wrote "There was no victory, and we retired to camp late in the evening without having accomplished anything definite."[712]

On the day after the battle at Overalls Creek, Monday, December 5, Companies E and F were assigned to leave the safety of Fortress Rosecrans and cut timber. The Eighth Minnesota had been detailed to help construct an abbatis[713] to provide additional protection against rebel attack. Thomas Hodgson of Company F described the process for building such a fortification:

> This is done by digging a trench two feet wide by about two and one-half feet deep, then laying sharp pointed rails a foot apart in the trench leaning outward. The trench was then filled and the rails were thus firmly held in place with the points to the foe. This is effectual against any direct and rapid charge by cavalry.[714]

Construction of an abatis required the troops to venture out from the fort and cut hundreds of wood rails. It was common for the work crew go out four miles or more from the safety of the fortress into cedar swamps, where they could find the best trees. The cut wood was hauled back to the fortress by wagon teams running back and forth all day. Most of the men driving the wagon teams, "teamsters," were recently freed blacks.

Companies E and F set out early and spent the entire day on December 6 cutting wood. The teamsters made multiple trips out to haul the loads of rails from where the soldiers were working in the swampy woods back to the fortress. The wagons would proceed down a narrow road through the woods to where the crew was working, then once loaded up with wood, it was difficult to turn around so the wagons would continue down the road until they emerged on the pike road on the

710 Ibid.

711 Washburn, *Diaries*, Dec. 4, 1864.

712 Hodgson, "Recollections of the Sioux War No. 28," *Dakota County Tribune*, Dec. 4, 1890

713 Hodgson, "Recollections of the Sioux War No. 28," *Dakota County Tribune*, Jan. 15, 1891 (No. 28 appears to have been used twice by mistake in both the Dec. 4, 1890 and Jan. 15, 1891 editions of the paper). An abbatis was a type of defensive fortification made of branches or felled trees pointed at the enemy and interlaced using ropes. It formed a crude barrier but was effective at slowing advancing troops. By World War One, the abbatis had largely been replaced by barbed wire.

714 Ibid.

other side of the woods.[715] Then they would return to the fort on the wider, and more improved pike, creating a circular route of transport.

At about 3 p.m., the wagons returned to pick up the last load of the day. The soldiers loaded up the wood and were about to leave for the return trip to the fortress when the alarm was given that they were being surrounded by rebel cavalry.[716] The Confederates had emerged from the timber and were leisurely advancing down the very road that the work detail was planning to take back to the fort.[717] "Sure enough, we could see them riding on the roads each side of the swamp."[718]

The Eighth Minnesota men were terrified of being captured by the rebels. They had no doubt heard stories of the abominable conditions in Confederate prison camps such Andersonville and Libby Prison.[719] It was also possible that the enemy were Confederate guerrillas, who might not be inclined to take prisoners. Under the circumstances, the men knew that capture meant starvation, disease, and often death.

Whatever treatment the white soldiers could expect as prisoners, the black teamsters would have it far worse. The best they could hope for if captured was to be pressed into service as slaves for the rebel army. There was a distinct possibility they could be shot outright for aiding the Union.

The teamsters had good reason to be scared. Just eight months earlier, General Forrest's cavalry troops had captured Fort Pillow on the Mississippi River not far from Memphis. Most of the fort's 600-man garrison, which included a large number of African American soldiers from an artillery unit, surrendered after a brief fight.

The Confederates refused to treat the African American soldiers as prisoners of war. Many were shot or bayoneted to death at the hands of their captors in what became known as the Fort Pillow Massacre. News of the massacre had been widely reported in the north so the teamsters hauling rails for the Eighth Minnesota solders would have heard the story.

Wagon teams could not turn around on the narrow road through the woods. Nor could the wagons proceed to the pike road where the rebels were passing in force. Without other options and fearful of being captured, the teamsters mounted the lead mules from each team, cut the animals free from their harnesses, and then

---

715 Ibid.

716 Cambell, *Personal Reminiscences*, 50.

717 Hodgson, "Recollections of the Sioux War No. 28," *Dakota County Tribune*, Jan. 15, 1891.

718 Cambell, *Personal Reminiscences*, 50.

719 At least 12 men from Company B of the 9th Regiment perished in Confederate prisons at Andersonville and Milan Georgia after being captured near Memphis in June 1864. Company B was raised in the same area and at about the same time as Company E of the Eighth Regiment. Many of the men in Company E would have known at least some of the captured soldiers.

made a beeline for the fortress.[720] The wagons, with the remaining mules still harnessed to them, had to be left behind.[721]

At first, Captain Aldrich, commander of Company F, organized the troops in a line of battle to protect the wagons. The objective was to hold the rebels off long enough to extricate the teams.[722] Company E was on the left and Company F on the right of the line.[723]

The troops waited for what must have seemed like an eternity for the rebels to attack. As they waited, it became clear that the two Minnesota companies were greatly outnumbered. Moreover, the rebels were mounted. Thomas Hodgson recalled "Just why the rebs did not make a dash on us and gobble us up was at that moment a mystery. It seemed to us that they could have done so with the utmost ease."[724]

Realizing their vulnerability under the circumstances, the officers formed the soldiers into a column and double-quick marched them out after the teamsters. "And it was double-quick with a vengeance."[725] It instantly turned into a stampede as the men tried to escape before the rebels closed a small gap in the shrinking perimeter. According to George Cambell, the gap was so narrow it "was not half gun shot from the rebel cavalry on each flank."[726]

Sentries at Fortress Rosecrans had also seen the rebel cavalry and raised the alarm. Union cavalry was quickly dispatched to protect the wood cutting detail as they ran for the fortress. The order was given to shell the rebels with heavy artillery and a battery of cannon was run out to provide cover fire for the returning teamsters and soldiers.[727]

The artillery and cavalry presence apparently discouraged the rebels from engaging further and the Eighth Minnesota men managed to make it safely into the fort. George Cambell later learned that the rebel cavalry were not guerillas, but elements of General Nathan Bedford Forrest's cavalry brigade.[728]

---

720 Cambell, *Personal Reminiscences*, 50.

721 Hodgson, "Recollections of the Sioux War No. 28," *Dakota County Tribune*, Jan. 15, 1891

722 Ibid.

723 Ibid.

724 Ibid.

725 Ibid.

726 Cambell, *Personal Reminiscences*, 51.

727 Ibid.

728 Cambell, *Personal Reminiscences*, 51.

The following morning, Tuesday, December 6, rebels were again seen in the area. The Eighth Minnesota was ordered out on patrol to find them. The regiment set out on the Lebanon Pike.

Lebanon Pike was described as "a very handsome street with a row of trees in the centre for shade."[729] The Eighth Minnesota was marching up a gentle hill about two miles from town where the pike ran straight. Suddenly, the rebels appeared with cannon at the top of the hill and began firing six inch shot down the road.[730]

The Eighth Minnesota immediately took to the ditches on both sides of the road and began to withdraw back towards Murfreesboro. As they did so, the rebel artillery continued to send shot down the street. George Cambell described the effect of the cannon on the trees in their path: "The balls made a nice smooth six inch hole in one side but they slivered up the place the size of a peck measure on the other."[731] Cambell didn't appreciate what the rebels were doing to those beautiful old shade trees in the middle of the pike. He recalled that "the way the Johnnies put the cannon balls through the trees was scandalous."[732]

Despite the rebel cannon fire, the Eighth Minnesota returned unscathed from its march. So far, the regiment had been lucky. In its first close encounters with the rebels over the past three days, not one soldier from the regiment had been killed, seriously wounded, or captured. Alas, their good fortune was not to continue.

---

729   Ibid., 49.

730   Ibid.

731   Ibid. A peck is a dry measure equal to two gallons or ¼ bushel. A basket the size of a peck measure that Cambell described would have been somewhere between 10" and 12" in diameter.

732   Ibid.

The Deadliest Day

December 7, 1864

Following the Battle of Overalls Creek, General Rousseau decided that he needed better intelligence about the number of rebel troops surrounding Fort Rosecrans. Rousseau ordered General Milroy to make a reconnaissance of the area. Specifically, Rousseau wanted to know the strength and composition rebel forces in the vicinity and whether they were determined to stand and fight. It would not take long to learn the answers.

Early on the morning of December 7, 1864, Milroy gathered his forces for the reconnaissance. It consisted of seven regiments of infantry and one six-gun battery of artillery. These Milroy formed into two brigades. The First Brigade was placed under the command of Colonel Thomas of the Eighth Minnesota.

In addition to the Minnesota troops, the First Brigade included a six-gun battery from the Thirteenth New York Artillery, the 174th Ohio, the 181st Ohio, and the Sixty-First Illinois Infantry. As Thomas was now in charge of the entire First Brigade, Lieutenant Colonel Henry Rogers took command of the Eighth Minnesota.

The Sixty-First Illinois was a battle-hardened unit that had seen action at Shiloh in 1862 and participated in the siege at Vicksburg. However, casualties and illness over the previous two years had reduced the regiment's numbers to about a quarter of its original size. Due to its diminished strength, Milroy assigned the Sixty-First Illinois to act as skirmishers.[733]

Milroy's Second Brigade included the 177th and 178th Ohio infantry regiments, plus the Twelfth Indiana Cavalry. In addition, Milroy brought along a small unit of the Fifth Tennessee Volunteer Cavalry to serve as scouts. The entire reconnaissance force included just over 3,300 men, divided between 2,000 troops in the First Brigade and 1,300 in the Second Brigade.

---

733 On the advance, skirmishers acted much like pickets around a camp. They generally consisted of light infantry who moved four or five hundred yards outside the main body of troops. Their job was to detect enemy threats that might be engaged by the main force. *See*, generally, Daniel Butterfield, *Camp and Outpost Duty for Infantry*, New York, Harper & Brothers, 1863, 82-83.

GENERAL ROBERT S. MILROY CA. 1862

The Eighth Minnesota was up early and soon heard the "long roll" of the regiment's drums, which meant they were going to battle.[734] The two brigades set out from the fortress at first light, heading south for the Salem Pike. Milroy deployed the Tennessee Cavalry in advance, followed by the Sixty-First Illinois. The First and Second brigades followed with the artillery.

The previous evening, the enemy had been busy. General Forrest had ordered one brigade of troops to dig in on a hilltop with a clear view of the Salem Pike. From that position, Confederates immediately observed Milroy's force as it moved out onto the road. The Confederates quickly reported the activity to General Forrest, who realized from the size and composition of the advancing Union troops that Milroy intended to make battle.[735] Forrest welcomed the opportunity and eagerly prepared for the coming fight. Forrest ordered his troops to withdraw from along the Salem Pike and moved them about three miles to the north. There, they took up a position along the Wilkinson Pike, which ran west from Murfreesboro. The new position offered good defensive ground and would be an ideal location to lure Milroy's force into a trap. There, the rebels began building hasty fortifications in anticipation of the upcoming battle.

Meanwhile, Milroy's force continued down the Salem Pike. It wasn't long before it encountered the enemy. The first contact was with rebel mounted sentries only a half mile beyond the Union picket lines surrounding Fortress Rosecrans. The outnumbered rebels quickly rode off.

Another 300 rebel cavalry troops were waiting a couple miles farther west. Milroy's force encountered them near a crossing at Stone's River. Milroy put the New York artillery into action and began shelling the small enemy force. The Confederates took the hint and disbursed. Milroy's troops proceeded across the river and down the Salem Pike.

---

734 Hodgson, "Recollections of the Sioux War No. 28," *Dakota County Tribune*, Jan. 15, 1891. Drums were often used to communication commands to the troops. The Long Roll meant to attack and was sure to get the adrenalin flowing for the soldiers.

735 Report of Maj. Gen. Nathan B. Forrest, Jan. 24, 1865. *Official Records,* series 1, vol. 45, part 1, 755.

Milroy's force advanced about two miles down the pike past the Stone River crossing. During a brief stop at the Spence Farm, which sat along the pike, Milroy learned that some rebel cavalry units were lying in wait only a mile further down the pike. He also received word that a strong rebel force was concentrated to the north near Wilkinson Pike. Unbeknownst to Milroy, this troop concentration was the trap General Forrest hoped to spring on the Union troops.

Wilkinson Pike was just a few miles to the north of and ran roughly parallel to Salem Pike. At this point, Milroy faced a choice, either pursue the rebel cavalry to the west or turn north towards the larger entrenched rebel force. He chose to go after the stronger force to the north.

Before moving towards the rebels' reported position, however, Milroy ordered a small contingent of troops to escort sixty fine hogs found on the Spence Farm back to Fortress Rosecrans. This would conveniently prevent the hogs from falling into rebel hands. Whether the hogs survived their stay among the hungry federal troops within the fortress is lost to history.

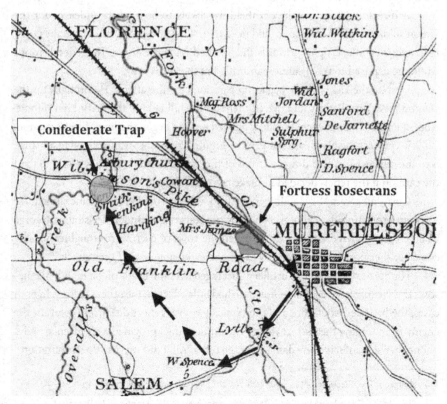

MILROY'S MOVEMENTS ON THE MORNING OF DECEMBER 7, 1864.

The Trap Springs and Fails – The Cornfield

As Milroy guided his troops north, he seemed to meander a bit and eventually turned back to the east towards the fortress. Some of the soldiers assumed that that Milroy was having trouble finding the enemy and instead was taking them back.[736] However, he suddenly turned the force back to the north. Leading the way, the Sixty-First Illinois skirmishers reached the edge of a cornfield, where they found the enemy waiting.

Forrest's Confederate troops were dug in at the top of the hill on the other side of the cornfield. The cornfield straddled a deep valley just south of the Wilkinson Pike. The rebels were in an ideal defensive position: they held the high ground and had fortified their line while waiting for the federal troops to arrive. In addition, rebel cannon could cover the entire cornfield.

General Forrest's troops outnumbered Milroy's forces. The dug-in Confederate forces in position above the cornfield included four brigades of infantry, a battery of four cannon and a brigade of cavalry.[737] In total, Forrest had nearly 3,700 Confederate troops to face Milroy's force of 3,300 men.

A direct attack across the cornfield was likely to be a costly endeavor for the Union soldiers. Milroy's forces would need to first advance downhill across the cornfield and then attack uphill towards the fortified rebel positions. The federal troops would be exposed to rebel cannon and rifle fire the entire way.

Despite the risk, Milroy began preparations for the attack. He brought up the six-gun New York Battery and placed them on the hill behind the Sixty-First Illinois. Almost immediately, the rebel artillery opened fire and began shelling Milroy's cannon.

To protect the New York Battery, the Eighth Minnesota was ordered to advance into the cornfield and lie down in front of the cannon. This way, they could defend the cannon if the rebels decided to make a ground assault.

Cornstalks were still standing in the field, which provided some concealment for the men protecting the cannon. However, the stalks also hindered visibility. George Cambell remembered that the men wished the rows of corn were straighter so they could see the approach of the enemy as far out as possible should they attack.[738]

For the next half hour an artillery duel raged over the heads of the Eighth Minnesota. The shelling from each side, however, had little effect on the other's battery. In both cases, the batteries would fire and then quickly move a short distance to prevent the enemy from finding the correct range. The artillery duel provided a spectacular sight, but neither side inflicted any damage on the other. All it did was use up ammunition.

---

736 Hodgson, "Recollections of the Sioux War No. 28," *Dakota County Tribune*, Jan. 15, 1891.

737 The size of a Confederate brigade in 1864 was comparable to the size of a Union regiment.

738 Cambell, *Personal Reminiscences*, 52.

As the artillery exchange went on, Milroy realized what Forrest was up to and decided not to fall into the trap. The rebel position was too strong for a head-on assault. An attack by the federal troops through the cornfield was exactly what the rebels wanted. Advancing by that route would cost the attacking troops dearly. Moreover, Milroy did not want to engage an enemy of unknown strength without the security of Fortress Rosecrans in his rear should his force need to fall back.[739]

Milroy decided to make a reconnaissance and gather more information before taking any further action. He dismounted and, accompanied by a few skirmishers, set out on foot to scout the enemy positions. Using the thick brush that surrounded the cornfield for concealment, Milroy worked his way around the right side of his lines. There, he discovered that the enemy's left flank ended at an open cotton field.

From the edge of the cotton field the rebels had a marvelous view. They could see any approaching danger from that direction well in advance. That gave the rebels a sense of security and perhaps left them overconfident. Consequently, that avenue of approach remained only lightly fortified.

Milroy returned from his reconnaissance just as the New York Battery ran out of ammunition. The battery had set out that morning with only fifty rounds per gun in their limber chests.[740] The artillery unit failed to bring additional supply wagons with reserve ammunition. Without ammunition, the big guns were useless. Milroy, therefore, ordered the battery back to Fortress Rosecrans so they could reload.

At about the same time, Milroy ordered his troops to sneak quietly out of the cornfield. The Eighth Minnesota made it to the trees on the south edge of the field where the troops were no longer within view from the rebel positions. Using the trees for cover to mask their movements, Milroy's force moved to the east at the double quick.[741]

Milroy had decided to attack the rebel positions across the cotton field and hit their exposed left flank. He placed the First Brigade in the lead with the Sixty-First Illinois out front as skirmishers. The Eighth Minnesota was on the right, the 174th Ohio in the middle and the 181st Ohio on the left. Milroy held the Second Brigade in reserve. Upon seeing the federal troops leave the cornfield, the rebels initially thought they had given up the fight and were withdrawing back to the fortress. Before long however, the rebels realized that Milroy was in fact reforming his troops for an attack across the cotton field aimed at the rebel's exposed left flank.

While Milroy and Colonel Thomas organized the First Brigade for the attack, the Eighth Minnesota was ordered to stand at parade rest. As they stood in place,

---

739   Report of Maj. Gen. Robert H. Milroy, Dec. 6, 1864, *Official Records,* series 1, vol. 45, part 1, 617.

740   A limber chest was a box affixed to a horse-drawn cart that carried the ammunition for the cannon. The cart was then attached to the cannon and both pieces were pulled by horses.

741   Washburn, *Autobiography,* 5.

the rebels turned their cannon towards the concentration of troops and opened fire. It was a bit unnerving for the soldiers on the receiving end of the artillery barrage. George Cambell recalled "it tries any one's courage to stand leaning on his gun and watch the Johnnies fire shells at him."[742]

The rebel cannon continued firing, although not inflicting any casualties. Dense smoke from the cannon soon obscured the regiment's view of the battery. While standing and awaiting orders, looking toward the rebel cannon, George Cambell recalled that the cannonballs were clearly visible as they flew out of the cloud of gun smoke. "One can see the balls as plainly as a base ball can be seen in a game."[743] The soldiers watched each projectile emerge from the smoke cloud and then speculated as to whether it would strike before hitting them, tear through the ranks, or pass overhead.[744]

The Sixty-First Illinois, advancing as skirmishers, came within sight of the enemy battery. Leander Stillwell looked at the artillery pieces and saw "a large, fine-looking man, mounted on an iron gray horse," near one of the cannons. The man appeared to be intently watching the troops advance across the field. Stillwell believed this man had to be a high-ranking Confederate officer. Although the range was long, Stillwell managed to take two well-aimed shots at the man. Neither found its mark. The man remained steady in his saddle after each shot and eventually galloped off. Stillwell later learned that the man was General Forrest himself.[745]

The commanders continued to organize the troops for the imminent assault on the rebels. It took only a few minutes, but it seemed like an hour or more for the troops who had to stand defenseless against the artillery barrage. The rebels were slowly getting the range and the missiles were coming closer and closer.[746]

It also seemed like the rebels were concentrating their artillery fire on the Eighth Minnesota to the exclusion of all others. The 174th Ohio, for example, was completely ignored by the rebel cannon.[747]

At last, the order was given to charge the enemy and the Eighth Minnesota moved forward. The order to charge did not necessarily mean to advance at a full run. It could be at the pace of a brisk walk. The troops were expected to maintain their line and ranks during the charge, so a slower pace was often necessary.

742 Cambell, *Personal Reminiscences*, 53.

743 Ibid.

744 Ibid.

745 Leander Stillwell, *The Story of a Common Soldier of Army Life in the Civil War*, Erie, KS, Press of the Erie Record, 1917, 134.

746 Hodgson, "Recollections of the Sioux War No. 29," *Dakota County Tribune*, Feb. 5, 1891.

747 Ibid.

The troops of each company were arranged in four lines, or ranks, one behind the other. In this formation, the ten companies of the Eighth Minnesota formed a line approximately 250 yards wide from its right to left flanks.

Almost simultaneously with the order to charge, a cannonball struck the dirt about thirty feet in front of the first rank of troops, just to the right of Company E. What happened next was horrific. The ball "rose again and with demonic energy tore through the ranks of Company F."[748] A few yards away, William Houlton of Company E heard the ball strike his fellow soldiers. He recalled that the sickening sound "was like striking an ax into a beef creature."[749]

After bouncing up from the ground, the ball first struck the gun of Private Samuel Higgins of Company F and then passed straight through his body. Fragments of the rifle flew with such force that they were believed to have killed another soldier, Private James Payton.[750] Looking at the carnage caused by the shot, Private Thomas Hodgson of Company F was surprised to see that the ball which caused the damage lay in the open just a few feet beyond his dead and mangled comrades "as harmless as the cold clay it had just made."[751]

There was some question as to how many casualties that cannon shot inflicted. George Cambell of Company E saw the ball take out four men at once.[752] Other witnesses saw up to six men fall when the ball struck.[753] Cambell's account seems to be more accurate.

Thomas Hodgson of Company F later wrote that "four out of the six who were carried out of the ranks by the cannon ball recovered, having only been stunned by the concussion of the missile."[754] Official reports indicate that Company F suffered only five casualties total that day, including the two men killed by the cannonball.[755]

Immediately after the deadly shot, the double-quick charge turned into a run. It wasn't even clear that the commanders had issued the order to advance so quickly.

---

748 Ibid.

749 Houlton, *Speech*.

750 Hodgson, "Recollections of the Sioux War No. 29," *Dakota County Tribune*, Feb. 5, 1891. The unfortunate soldier's last name was also sometimes spelled as "Peyton."

751 Ibid. The "cold clay it had just made" meant turning live bodies into corpses that would return to the soil.

752 Cambell, *Personal Reminiscences*, 53.

753 Private Thomas Hodgson saw six men fall, Hodgson, "Recollections of the Sioux War No. 29," *Dakota County Tribune*, Feb. 5, 1891, while Corporal William Houlton of Company E saw the ball take out 5 men. Houlton, *Speech*.

754 Hodgson, "Recollections of the Sioux War No. 30," *Dakota County Tribune*, March 5, 1891.

755 *Minnesota in the Civil and Indian Wars: 1861-1865*, vol. 1, 408-410.

The word was passed from soldier to soldier, and it seemed like the right thing to do. The men of the Eighth Minnesota simply ran towards their objective. "We rushed forward like demons, giving the Indian yell for which our regiment was noted."[756]

The Deadly Pause

By this time, the Eighth Minnesota had advanced so quickly that it outran the supporting regiments. Being too far out in front placed the regiment in danger of being flanked should the rebels attack. When the Eighth Minnesota reached a point only about 200 yards from rebel fortifications along the wood line, the troops were suddenly ordered to halt so the officers could reform the lines.

The Confederates, seeing the Eighth Minnesota standing still and exposed, let loose with everything they had. Cannon boomed and rifles cracked all along the Confederate line. This was the first time the Eighth Minnesota had truly been engaged face-to-face in battle with a veteran, trained and organized enemy. It was a far different experience than Indian fighting. Lieutenant Brunson from Company K noted that they would have rather fought Indians for a whole year than those rebels for an hour.[757]

At first, the Eighth Minnesota stood in place, but it was immediately apparent that the troops in this position were sitting ducks. The officers quickly ordered the troops first to drop to their knees, then to lay down and hold their fire. The result was that the entire regiment was laying headfirst on a downward slope towards the enemy. In this position the troops made perfect targets for the enemy in the woods. With orders not to fire back, Company E and the rest of the Eighth Minnesota were utterly defenseless.

Firing from the rebel lines was fast and furious. Bullets smacked into the ground all around the four ranks of soldiers. Thomas Hodgson of Company F noted that the rebel fire was so intense that "the cotton stalks were all cut off just as if a hailstorm had swept them."[758] Looking back years later, William Houlton recalled "It always seemed a miracle to me that any of us ever got out of that hail of bullets alive."[759]

One of the reasons that the Eighth Minnesota survived the heavy rebel gunfire was that many of the rebel bullets went high. This was a common problem for both sides during the Civil War. The heavy large caliber bullets fired from Civil War era muzzle-loading firearms traveled in a broad arch, much more than the flatter path of bullets fired from modern firearms. In battle, soldiers tended to misjudge the trajec-

756 Hodgson, "Recollections of the Sioux War No. 29," *Dakota County Tribune*, Feb. 5, 1891.

757 Glimpses, page 381.

758 Hodgson, "Recollections of the Sioux War No. 29," *Dakota County Tribune*, Feb. 5, 1891.

759 Houlton, *Speech*.

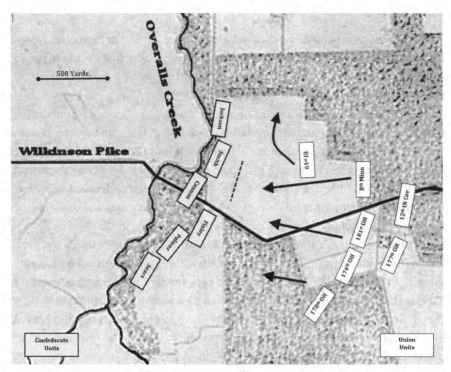

MAP OF THE ENGAGEMENT ON WILKINSON PIKE, DECEMBER 7, 1864. THE DASHED LINE SHOWS ROUGHLY WHERE THE EIGHTH MINNESOTA WAS ORDERED TO HALT AND LAY DOWN IN FULL VIEW AND RANGE OF THE ENEMY FOR APPROXIMATELY 15 MINUTES.

Adapted by author from map of Stone's River Battlefield that showed the location of woods and fields during the Civil War period. Weyss, J. E, and N Michler. Topographical sketch of the battle field of Stone River near Murfreesboro, Tennessee, December 30thto January 3d 1863. Position of the U.S. troops on the 2d of Jan. 1863. [S.l, 1863] Map. https://www.loc.gov/item/99448527/.

tory of the bullet and aim too high. As a result, many bullets sailed overhead of the intended target, striking harmlessly into the earth beyond. George Cambell claimed that this tendency was the salvation of the regiment. "If they had fired at first as they did afterward, low down, not one man would have escaped."[760]

As the firing went on, the rebels began to find their range. Soon, Company E started to take casualties. Captain Brookins was one of the first. Leading from the front, the captain went down severely wounded by a bullet to his chest. A bullet struck recently promoted Corporal Lewis Goyette square in the body.[761] He winced in pain and dropped hard to the ground. William Houlton, who was standing next to him, was certain Goyette was dead.[762]

760 Cambell, *Personal Reminiscences*, 54.

761 *List of Killed and Wounded of Co. "E" Eighth Minn. Inf., Dec. 7, 1864*, Gibbs Family Papers, Wright County Historical Society. The list appears to have been written by Charlie Gibbs but is undated and unsigned.

762 Houlton, *Speech*.

Under the hail of bullets, it didn't take long before the Eighth Minnesota troops began to disregard the order to hold their fire. The men instinctively began to return shots at the rebels whenever targets exposed themselves peeking over their fortifications along the tree line.

For what must have seemed like an eternity, the Eighth Minnesota lay under fire in the cotton field. In reality, the pause lasted no more than fifteen to twenty minutes.

A short distance away, the Confederates continued taking aimed shots at the exposed troops. Bullets continually kicked up geysers of earth, showering the federal soldiers with dirt. Although it must have been terrifying to be under such heavy fire, the men of Company E kept their cool. Soon they were concentrated on returning fire. Some of the soldiers were even able to find dark humor in the close calls. William Dallas took a bullet through the forearm as they were lying in the cotton field. Smiling through the pain, he held it up to show George Cambell, who was lying prone a short distance away. Cambell yelled back through the deafening sounds of battle that he "would take one like that and call it square with the Johnnies."[763]

Cambell also recalled seeing William McPherson, who was three ranks behind him, crawl forward to a nearby stump. McPherson was one of the youngest men in Company E but had earned a reputation as an excellent shot. He used the stump both for cover and to steady his gun. Spotting a target, McPherson carefully took aim and fired. He must have hit his mark because he turned around with a big smile on his face, apparently quite pleased with himself. However, he was surprised to see the company laughing at him through the gunfire. In the heat of battle, McPherson failed to notice that a rebel bullet had passed through the front of his forage cap and exited out the top, pulling a tuft of his long hair with it. The sight of McPherson's hair sticking straight up out of the bullet hole was too much for his nearby comrades. They roared with laughter despite the deadly rain of rebel bullets.

Just behind Cambell, a bullet struck Private Joseph Locke in the upper thigh near the hip. He was told to go to the rear. Although he was able to walk, his gait was much affected by the wound. To the other soldiers it was a comical sight. Cambell later wrote "It was no laughing matter to him but we had to laugh to see him go off, for all the world like a pair of compasses, drawing his gun behind him.[764]

The Company E men might not have found the situation as funny if they had realized what a toll the Confederate fire was taking on them during the pause in the cotton field. Brookins, Goyette, Dallas, and Locke were all wounded and out of the fight. More casualties were to come.

---

763 Cambell, *Personal Reminiscences*, 55.

764 Cambell, *Personal Reminiscences*, 59.

The intense firing continued, and the list of Company E casualties grew. Elbridge Washburn was shot and killed instantly as his horrified brother Edson lay at his side. Corporal Henry Fuller suffered a severe wound in his wrist. Thomas Anderson took a bullet in the thigh. John Albright and Alonzo Bryant both were wounded in the arm.

As seconds slowly ticked by, more men were hit, including Sam Kriedler and Elisha Sabin, who both suffered hand wounds. George Wedgewood joined the list of casualties when he was struck in the shoulder by a bullet.

Many other Company E men had close calls. Cramer Swartout suffered a slight scratch from a bullet. Charles Vorse was hit four times. The bullets ripped through his clothes, canteen, and haversack, but miraculously none touched his skin.[765]

Into the Woods

At long last the other regiments caught up to the Eighth Minnesota. By that time, there were indications that the rebel line was wavering. It appeared that some units of the rebel infantry were slowly falling back. Colonel Rogers saw an opportunity and ordered Companies C and K, which were at the far left of the Eighth Minnesota line, to advance into the woods. Just as Rogers gave the order, a bullet slammed into him, shattering his arm and knocking him from his horse.

Rogers, however, was not out of the fight. Instinctively, he knew that the men's courage could only stand the murderous fire from the Confederate positions for so long. If any of the companies wavered in resolve or fell back, others might follow. The result could be a mass retreat and with it defeat. Rogers was determined not to let that happen.

Despite his wounds, he rose from the ground and stood by his horse in full view of the troops, hoping it would inspire them to stay in the fight. In that, Rogers was successful, for none of the Eighth Minnesota companies faltered. The wound must have been terribly painful, but Rogers remained at his post until the battle ended.

Lieutenant Brunson of Company K, following Rogers' order, quickly led his men in a charge to the trees where Finley's Florida Brigade was dug in behind hastily prepared fortifications. Finley's Brigade was a battle-hardened unit that had seen plenty of action throughout the Civil War.

As Company C and Company K rose to charge, something remarkable happened. Although Rogers had ordered only the two companies forward, the entire Eighth Minnesota rose as one and charged forward to the woods. The most probable explanation for this event was that officers along the line saw Company K rise to charge and, not being able to hear in the noise, smoke, and chaos of the battlefield, assumed the entire

---

765   Ibid.

regiment was ordered to move forward. Consequently, the officers, not wanting to be left behind in the open, led their own commands forward as well.

By this point the troops in the cotton field had had enough. Anything was preferable to sitting still as stationary targets for the enemy. William Houlton recalled that the most welcome order he ever received in the army was when Lieutenant Tollington, having taken command after Brookins was wounded, shouted "forward Company E!"[766]

Within moments Company E joined the charge for the woods. As they did so, the entire regiment again let loose with "Indian war whoops" which they had learned on the Dakota plains and since practiced for just this moment.

The use of the "Rebel Yell" by Confederates during the war has been well-documented. The Rebel Yell often unnerved the Union soldiers who heard it during a Confederate attack. At the same time, it gave confidence to the Confederates as they charged. It is not known exactly what the Rebel Yell sounded like, but whatever it was sent chills down the spine of those who heard it.

Now, the rebel troops under Forrest's command were on the receiving end of a similar cry. The use of a war cry from Union troops was unusual. The Eighth's war whoop must have been a shock to the rebels as the dark figures rose and came charging out of the smoke and haze of the battlefield.

Indeed, use of the war whoop at that critical moment may have saved many of the Minnesota soldiers' lives. When the cry rose at once from the entire Eighth Minnesota it caused the Confederate fire to slacken noticeably at a time when the attackers were most vulnerable. They were at close range and in the open field. The lull was brief, but it bought the men of the Eighth Minnesota precious seconds to reach cover in the woods.

The casualties for Company E continued to mount. Just as Tollington ordered the men forward, a Confederate bullet smashed into Ellett Parcher's head, killing him instantly. Moments later, William Ponsford was hit in the head by a bullet and dropped motionless to the cold Tennessee soil.

With almost superhuman resolution, the Eighth Minnesota charged forward, crossing the 200 yards of open ground to the edge of the woods in about a minute. Leander Stillwell of the Sixty-First Illinois, watching from the far right of the Union line, described what he saw: "The whole line went forward with a furious yell, and surged over the Confederate works like a big blue wave, - and the day was ours."[767]

Upon reaching the woods, Company E instinctively employed the lessons gained from their Indian fighting experience. Instead of advancing through the timber as they crossed the cotton field, in organized ranks that would make them

766 Houlton, *Speech.*

767 Stillwell, *The Story of a Common Soldier*, 136.

easy targets, they individually advanced from tree to tree, using them for both concealment and protection.[768] "We slipped from tree to tree whooping like Indians"
recalled Edson Washburn.[769]

George Cambell was one of the first to reach the edge of the woods and quickly
took cover behind a big tree. Looking back, he was shocked at the number of dead
and wounded soldiers laying in a line on the cotton field. It appeared to him like they
had lost half the regiment.

Undeterred, Cambell peeked around the side of the tree trying to find a target
for his Springfield. This was no easy task. For one, he was admittedly not a very
good shot. Perhaps more importantly, finding any target under the circumstances
would be difficult. The butternut color of the Confederate uniforms provided excellent camouflage for the defenders. Their uniforms almost exactly matched the color
of the dead leaves still clinging to the trees during this early part of winter. The fog
of gun smoke hanging in the woods further obscured the Confederate soldiers. As a
result, it was hard for Cambell and the other troops to distinguish the Confederate
targets in the low visibility of the battle.

Nevertheless, Cambell eventually picked out three rebel soldiers standing
nearby. Knowing his limitations with the rifle, Cambell figured it best to aim his shot
for the man in the middle. He took careful aim, fired... and missed. The startled rebels instantly turned their attention to Cambell. Three bullets slammed into the tree
just as he pulled back to reload.

Attempting to move forward, Cambell realized that those three rebel soldiers
were now after him. He sprinted for the next tree and sure enough three more bullets
slammed into the bark just as he reached cover. He later commented that "It gives a
fellow a peculiar feeling down his backbone when they are hunting for him that way."[770]

More and more Eighth Minnesota soldiers made it into the woods despite the
intense firing from the Confederate works. A few more did not.

Frank Parcher was running for the woods desperately calling out "Ellett!" as he
searched for his brother, not knowing that Ellett lay dead in the cotton field behind
him. Just before he reached the tree line, Frank took a bullet squarely through his
shoulder, which dropped him in his tracks.

Gunshot wounds to the shoulder in movies and TV are often depicted as minor injuries. In fact, a bullet wound to the shoulder, especially when made with a heavy soft lead
Minne ball, wreaked havoc on the body, shattering bones and ripping away flesh. A soldier
with such a wound could almost always expect to be disabled for the rest of his life.

768 Cambell, *Personal Reminiscences*, 57.

769 Washburn, *Autobiography*, 5.

770 Cambell, *Personal Reminiscences*, 57.

Meanwhile on the left of the line, the men of Companies C and K charged forward directly at the rebel cannon that had made life so miserable for the regiment over the past half hour. The rebels suddenly realized that the cannons were in danger of being overrun and went into action. The gunners quit firing to retrieve their teams of horses to pull the cannon to safety.

Seeing what the rebels were doing, Lieutenant Brunson of Company K took advantage of the opportunity. He ordered his men to ignore the enemy soldiers and aim for the horses. This they did, killing one horse after another until the rebels were forced to abandon both cannon and flee.

The Minnesotans continued to press on the Confederate line. Suddenly, the center of the rebel line crumbled. To the great surprise and dismay of General Forrest, Finley's Florida Brigade, which had been defending the center to the right of the cannons, broke and fled to the rear.[771] Moments later, the troops in Smith's Brigade fled from their position just to the left of the cannons.

Further back in the Confederate lines, the rebel soldiers saw the dark figures coming at them through the smoke. Now the lack of visibility worked against the Confederates. They mistook the rapidly approaching figures for Union troops and fired a volley into the Floridians' ranks. The friendly fire created chaos amongst the Floridians, and they fled at a full run. The panic was contagious and other Confederate troops began to break and flee behind the Floridians.

Seeing his lines crumble, General Forrest tried everything he could to reform his troops but without effect. Finally, an enraged Forrest drew his pistol and ordered a fleeing color bearer to stop. When his order was ignored, Forrest shot the man dead.[772] Taking the dead soldier's flag, Forrest rode up and down the line trying to rally his troops but was unable to stop the rout.[773] Before long he realized that the position was untenable, and Forrest ordered his troops to withdraw.

Many of the fleeing confederate soldiers were cut off by the rapid Union advance. These men had little choice but to surrender or die fighting. Most chose to surrender.

George Cambell heard the shout "Surrender or I will blow your brains out!"[774] He turned to his left to see a fellow soldier of diminutive stature pointing his rifle at a rebel lieutenant and eleven men who had been hiding behind a log. The rebels promptly put down their weapons and gave up.

---

771 John Allan Wyeth, M.D., *Life of General Nathan Bedford Forrest*, New York & London, Harper & Brothers, 1899, 551. Finley's Florida Brigade was a veteran unit that had distinguished itself at Gettysburg

772 Ibid., 552.

773 Forrest included this incident in his report, but omitted any mention of shooting his own soldier. *Official Records*, series 1, vol. 45, part 1, 755.

774 Cambell, *Personal Reminiscences*, 57.

Cambell chuckled at the sight. The young man appeared not even as tall as his rifle (the Model 1861 Springfield measured only fifty-six inches). Nevertheless, the soldier declined the offer of assistance with his prisoners, saying "I can manage them."[775] The soldier Cambell observed may have been Gilbert McNutt of Company F, who, as Thomas Hodgson later recalled, captured eleven rebels as he sprang upon a log.[776]

Perhaps McNutt had the right idea by taking charge of his own prisoners. That ensured he would receive credit for their capture. Not every soldier received the recognition to which he was entitled. Edson Washburn later described what followed when he captured some rebel soldiers:

I had the satisfaction of capturing three rebels from behind a log, sending them to the rear where someone who had skulked during the first of the fight took them in to the Fort and claimed the honor of capturing them. (Such is fame).[777]

Union troops chased the retreating Confederates northward through the woods for about half a mile. The Eighth Minnesota halted only when they reached the back edge of the trees. Major Camp, who had taken command of the regiment after Lieutenant Colonel Rogers fell, wanted to press the advantage, and continue the pursuit.

Chasing the fleeing enemy seemed the natural choice. However, lacking cavalry and artillery, there was little chance that the Eighth Minnesota would catch up with the rebels. Moreover, there was still plenty of fight left in them. With limited daylight remaining, Milroy decided to consolidate his gains and ordered a halt.

The men of Company E who made it through the charge now had a little time to pause and take in the destruction of the battlefield. George Cambell came across a wounded rebel who begged him for water. The man's leg was broken from a gunshot wound. Cambell obliged and shared his canteen. After taking a hearty draught, the wounded man, having heard the war whoops, turned to Cambell and asked "Are you'ns Indians?"[778]

As the battle ended and the adrenaline wore off, the men paused to take stock of the situation. Edson Washburn had watched as his brother Elbridge was killed at his side in the cotton field. Yet, Edson still charged with his regiment. Now, as he had a brief time to reflect on what had just happened, the exuberance from surviving the intense battle quickly gave way to devastation at the loss of his brother.

775 Ibid.

776 Hodgson, "Recollections of the Sioux War No. 30," *Dakota County Tribune*, March 5, 1891.

777 Washburn, *Autobiography*, 6.

778 Cambell, *Personal Reminiscences*, 58.

Other victorious soldiers began to take measure of their opponents. Searching through Confederate soldiers' abandoned knapsacks, the men were shocked to find no food other than raw shelled corn. That was all the rebels had to eat.

Many of the dead Confederates were barefoot, even though it was already winter. Their feet were thick with callouses and almost black with dirt, "with the skin wrinkled and corrugated to the extent that it looked like the hide of an alligator."[779] The men found it hard to believe that their enemy could fight in such conditions. Many in the Eighth Minnesota expressed a newfound respect for their foe.

CONFEDERATE GENERAL NATHAN BEDFORD FORREST

About that time supply wagons caught up with the troops. Milroy had the men replenish their ammunition from the wagons in case they needed to hold their position through the night. However, that turned out to be unnecessary.

While the Union commanders were focused on the battle along the Wilkinson Pike, Confederate cavalry had used the opportunity to attack Murfreesboro itself. They penetrated well into the town but quickly withdrew.

The threat to Murfreesboro, so close to Fortress Rosecrans, was of great concern to General Rousseau. Rather than allow Milroy to press the attack, Rousseau decided to order Milroy to retreat into the fortress.[780]

Just as the troops were preparing to march back to the fort, the artillery unit returned with a full load of ammunition. In the aftermath of the battle a large contingent of enemy cavalry had remained within view but at a distance. They were keeping watch on Milroy's movements. Without artillery there was little Milroy could do about the onlookers. When the battery returned, Milroy seized the opportunity and ordered the artillery to fire on the rebel cavalry. The enemy promptly scattered.

After all the momentous action of the day, the march back to the fort was largely uneventful. The entire force was back within the walls of Fortress Rosecrans by dusk.

---

779 Stillwell, *The Story of a Common Soldier*, 137.

780 Wyeth, M.D., *Life of General Nathan Bedford Forrest*, 553.

Aftermath

December 8, 1864 to January 17, 1865

The troops defending Fortress Rosecrans could hear the battle raging along Wilkinson Pike the afternoon of December 7. Messengers had already returned with news of the Eighth Minnesota's charge and subsequent victory over Forrest's rebel troops. Many among the garrison's troops left the fort to line the road and cheer as the Eighth Minnesota, or the "Indian Regiment" as they came to be called, marched back into the fort. While the cheer helped raise the spirits of the men for a time, the soldiers soon had to deal with the loss of their friends and brothers.

That evening was especially somber around Company E's quarters. That company, along with Company F, had taken the brunt of the fire. As a result, both companies suffered a disproportionate number of killed and wounded. William Houlton recalled that the night quickly turned gloomy as the men began to realize the extent of the casualties, observing that "few and low were the words spoken that night."[781]

Edson Washburn had an exceptionally rough time. He returned to an empty tent. The other three occupants were gone. His brother had been killed at his side just a few hours earlier. William Dallas was in the hospital with the arm wound he sustained that afternoon. The last occupant of the tent, James Ambler, was already in the hospital due to an illness and did not accompany the rest of Company E that day.[782] Washburn's tent must have seemed like the loneliest place on earth in the growing darkness.

Some of the Clearwater men, including George Cambell, went to check the army wagons returning from the battlefield with dead and wounded. They were hoping to find the body of their friend Ellet Parcher. Passing one wagon, Cambell heard a muffled cry "Oh, for God's sake, take him off of me!"[783]

---

781 Houlton, *Speech.*

782 Washburn, *Autobiography,* 6.

783 Cambell, *Personal Reminiscences,* 60.

Investigating further, the soldiers discovered a very much alive but severely wounded Confederate soldier. The wounded man must have been unconscious when he was found and mistaken for dead. He had been tossed into the wagon with the corpses collected on the battlefield. Cambell and his friends moved enough bodies to pull the man out. The unfortunate rebel had been shot through the legs.

Cambell wondered whether it was the same rebel who had shared his canteen after the fight.[784] He also tried to imagine what horror the man must have endured when he came to, perhaps believing he had been buried alive in a trench. Trenches were often used as mass graves for enemy casualties. Being buried alive was a common fear in the nineteenth century. Medical science was still primitive compared to modern standards, which sometimes made it difficult to determine with certainty whether a person was truly dead.

Private Thomas Hodgson recalled that one member of Company F had been buried in Dakota Territory after he appeared to suffer a heart attack while on the march. The man was relatively young and appeared to be in excellent health when he suddenly died. Years later, some of his comrades still believed that it was a case of suspended animation and he had been buried alive. Hodgson noted "While this is not likely it is terrible to think of its being a possibility."[785]

Company E paid a heavy price in the victory on Wilkinson Pike. Nearly one third of those who participated in the battle fell as casualties. Most of the casualties occurred during the short time the men were halted in clear view of the enemy in the old cotton field.

Two of their number were dead, Ellet Parcher and Elbridge Washburn. Both left behind brothers in the company. Another thirteen were wounded in the engagement, several seriously.

Most of those wounded in the battle would never rejoin Company E. The wounds caused by the large caliber bullets fired from Civil War era rifles were devastating, leaving behind destroyed flesh and shattered bones. Doctors had limited ability to deal with such wounds. It would be a long road to recovery for them.

Nevertheless, there was some good news that night. Contrary to William Houlton's initial assessment, Lewis Goyette had survived his wound and was brought back on a hospital wagon. Likewise, William Ponsford, who had taken a bullet to the head, was found still breathing on the battlefield just as darkness fell that night. The bullet must have bounced off his head, knocking him out cold. He remained unconscious

---

784 Ibid., 60.

785 Hodgson, "Recollections of the Sioux War No. 28," *Dakota County Tribune*, Dec. 4, 1890. Hodgson's account referred to the death of DeWitt Slater from Company F, who had dropped dead shortly after departing Fort Rice for the return to Minnesota on September 15, 1864.

as he was loaded onto the hospital wagon and then placed in hospital. He would not awaken until two days after the battle.

The following day, December 8, Company E remained in camp. Many of the soldiers visited their wounded friends in the hospital. Others had a more somber duty that day. Edson Washburn, for example, had to view the corpses of those killed the previous day to identify the body of his dead brother.[786]

Two days later, on December 10, a funeral was held for the Eighth Minnesota dead. They were buried together just outside of Fortress Rosecrans.[787] After that there was little for the men to do but wait for further orders.

Waiting

The battle on Wilkinson Pike, while a victory for the Union, did not break the siege at Fortress Rosecrans. Confederate troops remained in the area as the bulk of Hood's army closed in on Nashville. The day after the battle, General Forrest received a communication from Hood with orders to drive the Union forces back into Murfreesboro. However, Hood specifically cautioned Forrest not to construe the order "as to mean to attack the enemy's works at Murfreesborough" (meaning Fortress Rosecrans).[788]

The Confederate cavalry continued to attack the railroad lines and keep reinforcements from reaching Murfreesboro. As a result, food rations were not making it to the troops defending Fortress Rosecrans. With thousands of troops at the fort and no end to the siege in sight, the food supplies soon began to dwindle. Hodgson wrote that for the week after the battle "we fasted and growled at 'Pap' Thomas for his slowness at Nashville."[789]

The "Pap" Thomas mentioned by Hodgson was General George H. Thomas,[790] commander of the federal troops defending Nashville against Hood's Confederates. General Thomas had developed a reputation for being slow and deliberate. Until Thomas's troops moved against Hood, the siege at Fortress Rosecrans would continue.

Not that the army didn't try to get supplies to Fortress Rosecrans. On Tuesday, December 13, 1864, a supply train was dispatched to the fortress from Chattanooga. It didn't make it. About four or five miles from the fort, the rebels set up a trap. They

---

786 Washburn, *Diaries*, Dec. 8, 1864.

787 After the war, the bodies were disinterred and reburied in individually marked graves in the Stone's River National Cemetery on Old Nashville Highway northwest of the fortress.

788 Mason to Forrest, Dec. 8, 1864, *Official Records*, series 1, vol. 45, part 1, 666.

789 Hodgson, "Recollections of the Sioux War No. 30," *Dakota County Tribune*, March 5, 1891.

790 No relation to Col. Minor Thomas of the Eighth Minnesota.

removed rails where the tracks went through a cut,[791] which wrecked the engine. As the escort troops jumped from the train, they found themselves under the guns of the Confederates lining each side of the cut. They had no choice but to surrender. Some, however, must have escaped for news of the attack soon reached Fortress Rosecrans.

The rebels promptly set to work looting the train. It turned out to be a profitable attack for the ill-supplied Confederates. They made off with fifteen carloads of badly needed bacon and hardtack.[792]

Four regiments, including the Eighth Minnesota, were promptly sent to the relief of the supply train. When they arrived after dark, the troops found the Confederates had carried away everything except for a few pieces of hardtack scattered on the ground.[793]

The relief force pursued the Confederates for a few miles but had to give up the chase. On their return to the fort, the troops gathered corn and raided farm smokehouses along the way. The foraging didn't provide much relief. What little food they did find could not make up for that which was lost to the Confederates.

The troops were not the only ones who suffered for lack of food during the siege at Fortress Rosecrans. There was little feed for the thousands of mules and horses that supported the army. These animals had to be regularly fed so they would be strong enough to haul cannon, conduct cavalry operations and all the other critical functions of the army's animals.

For the next two weeks the Eighth Minnesota had little to do. The Confederates had severed communications lines, including mail delivery. The men lacked the energy to do much anyway. Hunger was beginning to take its toll.

Company E continued to be sent out of the fortress on missions to cut wood or forage for food. They didn't come back with much. The hunger was beginning to drive the men to go after food wherever they could find it. George Cambell, perhaps feeling somewhat remorseful, later admitted:

> I was guilty of stealing corn from the mules and parched the same to help me out. Of course, mules having to work and draw loads must have something to eat whether the soldiers did or not.[794]

Being tired, bored, and hungry, and confined within the muddy fortress, some of Company E men became a bit cranky. On December 14, Sergeant Dan Desmond

791   A railway cut was a passage dug through hills to keep the tracks mostly level.

792   Colwell, *Diary*, Dec. 12, 1864.

793   Brunson, "Reminiscences of Service With the Eighth Minnesota Infantry," 381.

794   Cambell, *Personal Reminiscences*, 51.

and Private Nick Flynn got into some sort of kerfuffle, either between themselves or, more likely, with officers from another unit. Whatever happened, both men found themselves under arrest.

The following day, Privates Ed Woodworth from Clearwater and William Lane, the "little drummer boy" from Minneapolis, got into a scrape with the colonel of the Third Michigan Cavalry and were placed under arrest.[795] It appears that all four men were quickly released with little or no punishment. With rebels all about, the army simply couldn't waste good fighting men.

Finally, on December 15, 1864, federal forces under General George H. Thomas engaged Hood's Army of Tennessee just outside of Nashville. Over the next two days, Thomas's army soundly defeated the Confederates.

The troops within Fortress Rosecrans could clearly hear the booming of the cannon twenty-five miles away to the northwest. Hopes began to build that fighting would soon lift the siege, enabling the troops within Fortress Rosecrans to again receive food rations.

The defeat at Nashville forced Hood to withdraw. What was left of the Confederate force retreated to the south and west towards Franklin, pursued by federal cavalry. After reaching Franklin, the Confederates continued their retreat south towards Columbia, Tennessee.

News of the Union victory at Nashville reached Fortress Rosecrans on December 17.[796] This brightened the spirits of the men, who expected supplies to reach them within a few days. Perhaps more importantly to men like Edson Washburn, the mail would resume again.[797] A supply train finally made it through on December 21 and Washburn got his mail.

The Eighth Minnesota had little time to share in the provisions that arrived on that supply train. The next morning, the regiment received news that they would leave Fortress Rosecrans and march towards Columbia to assist in the pursuit of Hood's forces. For the next two days the Eighth Minnesota engaged in frenzied preparations for the march.

Pursuit of Hood's Army

After two weeks of confinement in Fortress Rosecrans, the Eighth Minnesota finally set out at 9:00 a.m. on December 24, Christmas Eve, to give chase to the

---

795 Washburn, *Diaries*, Dec. 14-15, 1864.

796 Washburn, *Diaries*, Dec. 17, 1864.

797 Ibid.

retreating Confederates.[798] The men were exhausted before they even set out. They had been on reduced rations for so long that they were terribly weak, and many were sick. Worse yet, the weather was cold and icy. By the time the regiment stopped for the night, the troops were all freezing and hungry.

Throughout the march that day, the troops had looked out with envy at the Tennessee countryside, which was rich in farm produce.[799] George Cambell noted "I wish you could just imagine about six thousand men, hungry as bears, going to a plantation where pigs and chickens were plenty."[800]

It did not take long before men began to break off from the march and help themselves to the local bounty of farm products. The soldiers generally didn't feel bad about doing so. They considered the locals to be southern sympathizers. After all, Tennessee had seceded from the Union. Under such conditions, the soldiers rationalized that it wasn't really stealing. It was foraging.

George Cambell wasn't entirely comfortable with this 'foraging'. It seemed to him "very queer."[801] While the whole concept of foraging seemed rough to Cambell, he later noted that perhaps it "had to be to show the Southern people what a hateful war they had compelled us to engage in."[802]

The commanders had issued strict orders against foraging. These were widely ignored. The company officers, and often the regimental officers were less than enthusiastic about enforcing the orders and ignored violations as their troops scavenged the countryside for food and fuel.

Major George Camp appears to have been one officer who willfully overlooked the actions of his men. With Colonel Thomas now leading a brigade of three regiments and Lieutenant Colonel Rogers severely wounded, Major Camp had assumed command of the Eighth Minnesota. It was his duty to enforce the orders against foraging that had come down from higher-ranking officers. He faced serious consequences if he failed to obey. Nevertheless, Major Camp tended to put his men first. Soldiers' accounts indicate that Camp would look the other way when his troops helped themselves whatever food they could obtain from nearby plantations.

George Cambell recalled one such episode. In one of his first foraging attempts he set out with a group of the Company E men to a large mansion they had passed on the road. There, they found a smokehouse. Cambell was able to grab a pail of apple

798   Ibid., Dec. 22-24, 1864.

799   Cambell, *Personal Reminiscences*, 62.

800   Ibid.

801   Ibid., 64.

802   Ibid., 64-65.

butter and a small ham. Others picked up anything they could. Then they returned to their unit as it rested nearby during a break from the march.

As Cambell and the others returned to the ranks, Major Camp rode up on horseback. He reminded the ranking Company E officer present, Thomas Tollington, who was acting captain since Brookins was wounded, that strict orders had been issued against foraging. He then asked Tollington to report any men of his who were absent. Tollington replied "Major, I think my men are all here, sir."[803] Cambell looked around and saw only about twelve of the men in Company E, perhaps a quarter of its number.

Major Camp was a well-respected officer and sharp as a tack. There wasn't much that could escape his attention. Nevertheless, in this case he didn't say a word about the thin ranks. If fact, he didn't even appear to notice the soldier standing behind a rail fence a few feet away holding a live pig by the nose to keep it from squealing. Instead, he turned away from Tollington and slowly rode off with a very broad grin.[804]

In another case Major Camp rode by Company F, which was resting by a rail fence next to a field during a break in the march. Looking out into the field, Major Camp saw a number of pigs. Camp then remarked to the Company F men that it was against orders to kill any animals and such an offender would be punished.[805] "Still," Camp continued, "it is better to kill one of those pigs than to let them bite you."[806]

The Company F men got the hint. Within ten minutes, nearly every bayonet in the company had on it a chunk of pork.[807]

By the end of the first day on the march it seemed like everyone was caught up in the idea of foraging, which led to some comical sights. Years later, William Houlton recalled seeing Alphonso Nickerson, a forty-year-old private in Company E, chasing an old goose around a barn, trying to kill it with the ramrod from his rifle. He was evidently determined to turn that goose into Christmas supper.[808] There is no record of whether Nickerson succeeded, but, him being one of the oldest men in the company, it is quite likely the goose managed to elude him and his ramrod.

As could be expected, the locals did not take kindly to having their food confiscated by the federal troops. In one incident, Sergeant Timothy Desmond led a group of Company E men up to the yard of a large southern house where a group of

---

803   Ibid., 63.

804   Ibid.

805   Hodgson, "Recollections of the Sioux War No. 30," *Dakota County Tribune*, March, 1891.

806   Ibid.

807   Ibid.

808   Houlton, *Speech*.

domesticated turkeys had taken refuge. Several women were standing in front of the house warily watching the troops.

Sergeant Desmond, a former New England lumberman of Irish descent, was an imposing figure. He was muscular from his lumbering days and stood over six feet tall. Yet, he was always polite. He took off his hat and asked the ladies if they would be kind enough to let him have one of the turkeys. When one of the women promptly said "no," Desmond drew his pistol and shot a turkey, which fell dead at his feet. He then picked up the bird and thanked the woman is if she had freely given it to him.[809]

The enraged woman told Desmond that "if my lover were here, he would kill you." Desmond, no longer amused, responded "Lady, I saw your lover as he has gone North from Nashville for his health."[810]

William Houlton recalled the incident differently. "She told him (Desmond) she had a fella in the rebel army and she would send him after him." Desmond allegedly responded to this taunt with "no you won't for we just killed them up at Murphy's up to Murfreesboro."[811] Regardless of the true story, to George Cambell the whole episode "seemed fearfully rough."[812]

Throughout history it seems that one man in every military unit became adept at scrounging. So it was with Company E. Private Randolph Holding, one of the men who had enlisted from Clearwater, quickly proved to be a master at the art of foraging. He disappeared early on the first day of the march and wasn't seen again until evening. When he caught up with Company E, Holding brought along two horses and three liberated slaves, all of which were loaded down with food.[813]

George Cambell and several other Company E men accompanied Holding on a foraging mission the following day. They walked into a house and found a woman ironing clothes. They asked the woman if she had anything to eat. She replied "no." The men had a look around and quickly discovered a barrel of apple butter, dried apples, and a sack of flour.

After using some of the newly-ironed clothes to wrap up the foodstuffs, Holding asked the woman if she had any salaratus, a leavening agent similar to baking soda. She did. Private Holding then asked if she would bake them some biscuits. She adamantly refused to do anything more for the men that had just confiscated

809 Cambell, *Personal Reminiscences*, 64.

810 Ibid. The phrase probably suggested that the woman's lover was either a prisoner of the federals or dead.

811 Houlton, *Speech*.

812 Cambell, *Personal Reminiscences*, 64.

813 Ibid., 65.

her food. Undeterred, the troops simply went to the next house and had the biscuits baked there.[814]

Holding demonstrated his foraging skills on many other occasions. One night during the march in pursuit of Hood, he asked George Cambell to stand his turn at watch. In return, Holding promised him a very good breakfast. Cambell agreed.

Earlier in the day, Company E had marched past a large well-stocked plantation. It was marked with a yellow flag to indicate it was being used as a hospital. Consequently, the men left it alone and proceeded on down the road. Holding, however, learned from one of the liberated slaves that the master of the house had hung out the flag as a ruse to save his property. "There isn't a sick soldier on the place" the former slave told Holding.[815]

That night as Cambell took his turn at guard, Holding led a small force of Company E men back to the plantation. There they found plenty of poultry and cornmeal. As promised, the next morning Cambell enjoyed a good breakfast of turkey stew thickened with cornmeal.[816]

The foraging continued each day the troops were on the march. On December 26, 1864, Edson Washburn noted that the foragers returned that day with "sheep, hogs, hens and other stuff."[817] The troops marched along all types of food hanging from their rifles - "chickens, turkeys, meat, everything that could be found to eat in that country."[818]

Despite the foraged food, the march was still difficult for the Eighth Minnesota troops. Many were ill from the weeks of poor food, lack of warm shelter, and the cramped and unsanitary conditions in the fortress. Several men had dysentery or other digestive ailments. Like many others in Company E, Edson Washburn was suffering from diarrhea, which left him dehydrated and fatigued.[819]

After the first day of marching, the weather began to warm. The snow and ice that had accumulated over the past several days began melting. As a result, the roads quickly turned to mud. Marching in mud is much more exhausting than hiking across solid ground. The wet mud gripped the boots, adding weight and creating suction, which required much more energy for each step.

---

814 Cambell, *Personal Reminiscences*, 70. The incident didn't sit well with George Cambell. He never went foraging with Randolph Holding again, although he was happy to share in the spoils that Holding brought back from later foraging excursions.

815 Ibid., 68.

816 Ibid., 70.

817 Washburn, *Diaries*, Dec. 26, 1864.

818 Cambell, *Personal Reminiscences*, 63.

819 Washburn, *Diaries*, Dec. 26, 1864.

As a result of their exertions slogging through the mire, the troops found themselves getting hot and sweaty in their heavy blue greatcoats. In their fatigued and overheated state, many soldiers found the greatcoats too warm to wear and too heavy to carry. Soon the road was littered with discarded coats, blankets, and just about anything else that the troops thought they could do without.[820] Many would come to regret that decision.

It took the brigade four days to travel the forty-five miles over the muddy countryside to reach Columbia, Tennessee. They arrived late in the day on December 28. There, the Eighth Minnesota was ordered to stop and go into camp for a few days. The stop was welcomed by many of the men, especially those who were still suffering from various illnesses.

There wasn't much foraging to be done while the troops were confined to camp. Columbia and much of the nearby countryside had been devastated by the war. Consequently, the troops had to get by on their meager army rations of hardtack, beans, and other unappetizing fare.

The next day, December 29, the weather turned colder. The men huddled around the campfires to stay warm. Those who abandoned their greatcoats along the roadside during the previous days no doubt had second thoughts about dumping their apparel.

Nevertheless, the soldiers made good use of the time in camp. Edson Washburn, for example, took the opportunity to wash up, clean his gun and then find some medicine for his diarrhea. Unfortunately, the medicine proved ineffective.

New Year's Eve was much like the previous few days. Quiet but cold and windy. The soldiers divided their time between guard duty, sleep, and the general routine of army life.

At least the paymaster finally arrived. The Eighth Minnesota lined up and received their back pay. Edson Washburn spent the rest of the day mending his tent and preparing to stand guard that evening until the arrival of the new year.

As Washburn ended his shift at midnight, out of the darkness came the strains of "Old Hundred," a well-known hymn also known as "the Doxology."[821] A band had set up on a nearby snow-covered hill and rang in the new year with the solemn and beautiful music.

Upon hearing the music, many of the men paused to reflect on what the new year might bring and to think of their loved ones at home. Washburn noted in his diary "Hail to the new year may it be a happy one to us all. My dinner consists of dry hardtack. What do they have at home? Something good I bet."[822]

---

820 Houlton, *Speech*.

821 Edson Washburn noted that the band played the Doxology. Washburn, *Diaries*, Jan. 1, 1865. William Houlton later recalled it as the "Old 100." Houlton, *Speech*. Both were correct. It was the same hymn melody.

822 Washburn, *Diaries*, Jan, 1, 1865.

The Eighth Minnesota remained in camp near Columbia until Tuesday, January 3. That morning the regiment set out again in pursuit of Hood and marched about fifteen miles to Duck River, except for Companies D and E, which were ordered to wait behind until a train arrived from Spring Hill with supplies. They waited for it the rest of the day.

Before the rest of the regiment departed, however, the soldiers from Company E loaded their knapsacks onto the wagons. They thought they were lucky because that way they wouldn't have to carry the extra weight when catching up with the regiment after completing their assignment. Company E finally left Duck River at dusk. Rather than take the muddy roads, the men decided to take a shortcut across country. It was a good plan... in theory. What in fact happened was that Company E became lost in a swamp as they marched through the darkness.

With little food and no shelter – their tents, blankets, and other equipment were all traveling in the wagons – Company E spent a cold, hungry night marching through the countryside.

At 6 a.m. the next morning, the troops emerged from the woods and onto the road ahead of the train.[823] There was nothing they could do but wait. The hungry men sat and gnawed on the little hardtack they had brought with them. There was simply no other food to be had. Both armies had been over this ground recently and there was little to forage.[824]

At long last, the troop train reached the crossroads where Company E was waiting. The cold, hungry men retrieved their knapsacks and rejoined the march. During the day, the troops passed ex-president James K. Polk's country home and thought it splendid.[825]

By evening on January 4, the men of Company E were totally spent. They had been marching for two days, mostly without sleep due to their ordeal in the swamp the previous night, and with little to eat other than the miserable hardtack. When the order came to make camp for the night, many of the men were too tired to even pitch their tents. The men paired up, shared their two blankets and covered themselves with a large, rubberized cloth.[826]

Now warm and somewhat comfortable on the ground, the men of Company E quickly fell into a deep sleep. At some point during the night, George Cambell half woke and realized he was having difficulty breathing. At first, he thought it was the

823   Washburn, *Diaries*, Jan. 3, 1865.

824   Cambell, *Personal Reminiscences*, 66.

825   Both Edson Washburn and George Cambell were impressed with Polk's country home, probably his childhood residence, and mentioned it in their recollections.

826   Cambell, *Personal Reminiscences*, 66.

blanket covering his face. As he lifted it off, he looked out into the bright moonlight and was startled to discover that it had snowed.

The men of Company E were so tired from their travels that none woke as the snow fell. Now, to George Cambell, the place looked like a cemetery. There was nothing but a bunch of white burial-like mounds where the men were sleeping. "It seems that two inches of snow had fallen and hidden the whole company from sight."[827] To Cambell, it looked like he and his sleeping partner were the only ones left and the others had marched away.[828]

For the next two days, the brigade made slow progress in the chase for Hood. They made eight miles on Friday, January 6 and another ten on Saturday, January 7. It rained and snowed a bit each day, making the march more of a hardship.

As the train of soldiers moved into the site chosen for camp that night, Company E was placed on rear guard. Two soldiers from Company D had taken a break from the march to fix their feet, which had suffered mightily because the shoes issued to the Eighth Minnesota were all wearing out. They told the Company E men that they would be along in just a minute and not to wait for them.

The Company E rear guards went around a bend just out of sight of the two Company D soldiers. As they did so, the captain on duty heard about the men lagging behind and ordered a squad from Company E to go back and get them to hurry up.[829]

Only a few minutes elapsed between the time Company E marched from sight of the two sore-footed soldiers. Yet, when they returned, the two men had disappeared. The Company E squad shouted for them and traveled back down the road quite a way trying to find them. There was no trace.

Unbeknownst to the search party, the two men had been captured by Confederate guerillas who had seemed to appear out of nowhere. As the Company E squad desperately searched for the two soldiers, they were only about thirty-five feet away with two guns pointed at their heads to keep them quiet.[830]

The Company D soldiers would later escape their captors, but only after being robbed of money, watches, and good clothes. By the time they found the Eighth Minnesota days later, they had suffered a great deal from the cold and hunger. Cambell observed that from that time until the end of the war those two always kept inside of the rear guard.[831]

---

827 Ibid.

828 Ibid.

829 Ibid., 67.

830 Ibid., 68.

831 Ibid.

On Monday, January 9, the Twenty-Third Corps, still on Hood's trail, reached the Tennessee River. They were too late. Hood had already crossed the river and burned the bridges behind him. The commanders decided to break off the pursuit and ordered the troops into camp in a woodland near the Tennessee River. George Cambell described it as the nicest piece of oak timber that he ever saw.[832]

That stand of timber wouldn't last long. The men immediately went to work with axes and began building rough, dome-shaped log cabins. Before they left the camp several days later more than 160 acres of that oak timber had been cleared.[833]

For the next ten days, the men enjoyed relative comfort in their warm makeshift log cabins. Edson Washburn was still suffering greatly from his bout with diarrhea when Company E went into camp. However, after a few days in the more comfortable accommodations he began to feel better.

There was little for the men to do in camp but prepare for the next movement. Rumors were circulating that the Twenty-Third Corps would go to North Carolina and join Sherman's army, which was then moving north from Savannah. They used the time in camp to cut each other's hair and get their gear ready for the expected trip to the South.

On Saturday, January 14, riverboats arrived with supplies and, to the soldiers' delight, mail. Hearing from home always buoyed the troops' spirits. Company E also received word on the condition of their comrades who had been wounded in the battle on December 7. Most of the wounded were doing well. The one exception was Clay Helm. The news was that he was only expected to live a short time longer.[834]

With the mail came orders for the Twenty-Third Corps to proceed to North Carolina via Washington, D.C. The companies each drew five-days' rations from the riverboats to prepare for the trip. It turned out to be more of the same. Edson Washburn noted the recurring complaint that "We have not much of a variety to eat. Hardtack, pork and coffee."[835]

On Tuesday, January 17, 1865, the Eighth Minnesota left its comfortable quarters along the Tennessee River and made the short march to Clifton. At Clifton there were riverboats waiting to transport the Twenty-Third Corps upriver. There were not enough boats for all the troops, so the Eighth Minnesota was forced to camp for the night and wait for the riverboats that would transport the Second Brigade.

832 Ibid., 71.

833 Ibid.

834 Washburn, *Diaries*, Jan. 14, 1865.

835 Ibid., Jan. 15,1865

On to Washington

January 18 to February 21, 1865

The Eighth Minnesota spent most of the day on January 18, 1865 laying around and waiting for the arrival of the riverboats that would take them on the journey to Washington, D.C. The intended route would take them down the Tennessee River to Paducah, Kentucky. From there the steamships would travel up the Ohio River to Cincinnati and then on to Wheeling, West Virginia. At Wheeling, the troops would then transfer to rail cars and travel on to Washington D.C. The Eighth Minnesota would get a short break in Washington before shipping out to join Sherman's Army and the rest of the Twenty-Third Corps in North Carolina.

The riverboats arrived late in the day and the troops immediately commenced boarding. The Eighth Minnesota was assigned to the *Morning Star*, a large side wheeler, and the 178th Ohio on a sister ship. At about 10 p.m. on the night of January 18, the riverboats left Clifton.

Steamboat Races

At daylight the following morning, the two riverboats found themselves traveling alongside each other. Both ships were owned by the same line and were new enough that they had never been tested to see just how fast they could travel.[836] The boat crews began pushing each other. As one or the other moved slightly ahead, the other would speed up and try to sneak into the lead. This little competition quickly turned in to a full-fledged race and the soldiers on board loved it.

Since the earliest days of civilization men have enjoyed racing just about anything that moves, including each other, horses, dogs, and, more recently everything

---

836 Cambell, *Personal Reminiscences*, 71-72.

from automobiles to garden tractors. Whether as participants or spectators, races have always been an attractive pastime.[837] Riverboat races were just as captivating.

Riverboats during the Civil War were powered by steam engines, which functioned essentially in the same manner as the engines that powered railroad locomotives. Steam pressure would drive a piston back and forth in cast iron cylinder. The power generated from the piston would be transferred to a paddle wheel by a shaft attached to the piston rod.

Steam to power the engine came from water-filled cast iron boiler tanks. Each boiler tank sat over a firebox. The crew burned wood or less commonly coal in the firebox to heat the water in the boiler tanks. As the water boiled, it turned to steam. The steam pressure flowing from the boilers would drive the piston.

Steam pressure, however, could build to dangerous levels so the engines were equipped with safety valves that would allow excess pressure to escape. If the pressure got too high, the valve would blow and let off steam.[838] The safety valve served a useful purpose, but by limiting the steam pressure it also acted as a type of governor that restricted the power output of the engine.

Riverboat races prior to the Civil War were common, although they were rarely held for mere sport. There was a strong economic incentive to having the fastest boat. When two boats came together going the same direction, the faster boat would be the first to reach the next landing. This was important because the first boat to reach a landing usually secured the passengers and freight that were waiting for transportation and the accompanying profits.[839] The slower boat might find the landing empty and would have to proceed without the benefit of any additional revenue.

A riverboat's speed, and therefore its profit potential, depended on the steam pressure its boiler could generate. The higher the pressure, the faster the boat. Not surprisingly, crews developed creative techniques to raise the steam pressure when necessary to race their competition to the next landing. However, with added pressure came added danger.

The easiest way to build higher steam pressure was to disable the safety valve. This could be accomplished any number of different ways. One riverboat captain described seeing a safety valve held down by a line tied to a fifty-pound anvil. "The

---

837   Racing remains as popular as ever. The largest spectator sport in the United State in 2012 was NASCAR auto racing.

838   Hence the origin of the term "to blow off steam" or "to let off steam" which today generally refers to when a person releases pent up emotion or energy.

839   George Byron Merrick, *Old Times on the Upper Mississippi: The Recollections of a Steamboat Pilot from 1854 to 1863*, Cleveland, OH, Arthur H. Clark Company, 1909, 143.

boilers might have blown up a hundred times before the safety-valve would have acted."[840]

Crews would sometimes run the boilers with low water to increase pressure. This process allowed the walls of the boiler to glow red hot. When water was injected into the red-hot boiler it instantly flashed into steam. In some cases, this would cause the steam pressure rise so quickly that the pistons and safety valve could not release it fast enough. If the rise in pressure was more than the boilers could bear, the result was a boiler explosion. By one estimate up to eighty percent of boiler explosions were due to running the engine with low water in the tank.[841]

Crews also would blow more air into the firebox to increase the temperature, which would then result in higher steam pressure. There were probably many other tricks of the trade to increase the steam pressure and speed of the riverboats, but all the different methods employed to gain speed came with increased risk to life and property.

If the pressure got too high, the boiler and fuel in the firebox could explode in a huge fireball, turning the boilers into a bomb. Fortunately, boiler explosions accounted for a relatively small number of riverboat losses. Far more riverboats were destroyed due to striking an obstruction, running aground, ice damage, or fire than were lost to boiler explosions. Records indicate, for example, that only two out of seventy-three riverboats wrecked on the Mississippi between 1823 and 1863 between St. Louis and St. Paul were lost due to boiler explosions.[842]

Nevertheless, there were so many riverboats plying the nation's waterways in the nineteenth century that such disasters were a regular occurrence. Between 1829 and 1909 hundreds of vessels were destroyed by boiler explosions.[843]

Boiler explosions were feared because they were more devastating than other perils that could befall a riverboat. In many cases, when a riverboat got into trouble the captain could simply run the boat up to shore, where passengers and crew could safely leave the vessel. However, when a boiler blew, the resulting explosion generated a fireball and steam, which often killed or scalded the unfortunate passengers and crew. Even survivors of the blast were in great danger. George Merrick, a riverboat captain who worked on the Mississippi River from 1854 to 1863, later wrote:

When a boiler explodes, the boat becomes immediately helpless, so that it cannot be run ashore, which occasions the considerable loss

---

840 Ibid., 47.

841 Ibid., 39.

842 Ibid., 231.

843 Ibid., 39.

of life. In cases of explosion, also, the boat almost invariably burns in the middle of the river, and there is little chance for escape; for it is next to impossible to reach the life-boats carried on the roof, and if reached it is seldom found possible to launch them.[844]

In fact, it was a boiler explosion that caused perhaps the deadliest maritime disaster in U.S. history. On April 24, 1865, the *Sultana*, a large side-wheel riverboat, set out on the Mississippi River from New Orleans bound for St. Louis. Although the Sultana was designed to carry 376 passengers, it was overloaded with more than 2,000 Union troops, most of whom were recently released prisoners of war.

In the wee hours of the morning on April 27, as the Sultana was a few miles north of Memphis, Tennessee, the boilers exploded with great violence. The explosion and ensuing fire killed a significant number of soldiers and crew. Many more drowned as they jumped into the river to avoid the flames. In all, it is estimated that up to 1,700 soldiers and crew may have perished in the *Sultana* disaster.

Perhaps unaware of the danger, the soldiers of the Eighth Minnesota and 178th Ohio each cheered on their own riverboat. As the speed picked up, the troops began to congregate on the side facing the other riverboat so they could engage in good-natured heckling of the other regiment. Soon, the weight of so many troops on one side of each vessel caused the riverboats to list dangerously towards each other. The *Morning Star* tipped so much that it almost took the opposite wheel out of the water.[845] That drew the captain and mates out of the wheelhouse, swearing at the soldiers and trying to move the men about the boat to even out the weight. [846]

The riverboats went on and, although the soldiers had to stay disbursed to even out the weight, the race continued. The two boats did everything they could to keep up with each other. When one stopped for fuel, so did the other. The pressure was on for those who had to load the coal. Even that task was a race and a terror for those who lug it on board.[847]

Prior to the war, Private George Cambell had been a millwright and mechanic. He was intimately familiar with the steam engines used to power the mills. Out of curiosity, he went down to the *Morning Star's* engine room during the race to see how the crew were getting up to steam. He was shocked and dismayed to discover that the safety valve was held down with a crowbar.[848] Moreover, the crew were soaking the fire-

---

844   Ibid., 231.

845   Cambell, *Personal Reminiscences*, 72.

846   Ibid.

847   Ibid.

848   Ibid.

wood in oil to generate even more heat as it burned in the firebox. Cambell later wrote "I began to think it was dangerous and kept at the extreme end of the boat all I could."[849]

Finally, the officers realized that they were taking far too great a risk and put an end to the racing.[850] After all, a boiler explosion was likely to cause far more casualties on the Eighth Minnesota than the Indians or Confederates could ever dream of inflicting on the battlefield.

Cincinnati

In the wee hours of the morning on January 21, 1865, the steamships carrying the Eighth Minnesota and 178th Ohio arrived at Portland, Kentucky, which was a small riverboat landing just outside of Louisville. There, the brigade changed boats for the next leg of the trip to Washington. The troops had to disembark and then march about four miles through Louisville to where the new riverboats were waiting to take them to Cincinnati and then on toward Wheeling, West Virginia.

The weather began to deteriorate about the same time the ships left Louisville that morning. The temperature dropped and it turned foggy. The boats made only ten miles before they had to tie up for the night due to the reduced visibility in the fog.[851]

By daylight the next morning the visibility had improved, and the steamboats set out for their next stop in Cincinnati. When they arrived at about 10 p.m. on the evening of January 22 it had grown much colder. A considerable amount of snow fell overnight, making conditions miserable for the men sleeping on the open deck. The boats tied up at Cincinnati to wait for the weather to improve.

The weather did not get any better. By Tuesday, January 24, 1865, the temperature in Cincinnati had dropped to -10 degrees Fahrenheit. The troops still camped on the exposed decks were moved out of the cold into the already crowded interior of the boats. Meanwhile, the river quickly iced up in the sub-zero temperatures, making travel by boat almost impossible.

The cold snap continued into the following day. Some of the men from Company E were given permission to leave the boats for a trip into town. Edson Washburn used his short break to stop by the Sanitary Commission in town and buy gloves, pencils, and other miscellaneous items.[852]

---

849   Ibid. George Cambell later could see firsthand the results of a boiler explosion. In 1869, his brother Moses Cambell was partners in a small steam-powered sawmill not far from St. Cloud, Minnesota. One cold afternoon, the engine exploded, leveling the sawmill and injuring most of the workmen, including George Cambell's brother and nephew. Fortunately, only the engineer was killed.

850   Ibid., 73.

851   Washburn, *Diaries*, Jan. 21, 1865.

852   Ibid., Jan. 25, 1865. The United States Sanitary Commission was an organization that helped set up hospitals, ran rest homes and provided creature comforts to traveling soldiers.

A few members of the company used the trip into town for more nefarious purposes. The men's clothing was again in tatters from the fighting at Murfreesboro and their pursuit of Hood through Tennessee. The long marches had been tough on their shoes. To replace their apparel, some of the men resorted to creative theft.

One such example occurred where one soldier went into a shoe store and tried on a pair of cavalry boots. Those boots cost almost $20, which would be the equivalent over $300 today. As the soldier was admiring the boots, his accomplice came in. Pretending to be enraged, the accomplice said "Ah! I have found you, take that!" He then proceeded to give the soldier in the new boots a swift kick. The solder then chased his accomplice down the street in apparent wrath. Of course, neither of them ever came back.[853]

It seems that something about being in the army gave a few members of Company E the idea that dishonesty was acceptable, at least during their time in the service. However, the majority of Company E were likely appalled at the behavior of their few comrades. George Cambell recalled that it was a demoralizing influence on the company.[854] Fortunately, the dishonesty practiced by those few members of Company E ended with the war and their return home.[855]

Temperatures stayed cold, dropping to almost -20 degrees Fahrenheit. It became clear that the river would not open any time soon, so the officers made alternative travel arrangements for the two regiments. Just after dark on the evening of January 25, the troops boarded freight cars at the Cincinnati railyard. The train was bound for Columbus, Ohio and from there to Washington.

Yet again, the men were forced to travel in miserable conditions. None of the freight cars had stoves to protect the men from the bitter cold outside. Nor did the cars have any seats; they were empty except for loose straw. It was not pleasant, but the men suffered through the overnight trip until they finally arrived at Columbus the following morning.

At Columbus, the troops had most of the day off before the train was scheduled to leave for Wheeling. The men used the time to get out and about the town. Many went to the Sanitary Commission for coffee, which was not particularly good but at least it was hot. Thanks to that at least, the men spent the day in relative comfort.

On the evening of Thursday, January 26, the men re-boarded the train for the trip to Wheeling. The going was slow, and the Eighth Minnesota's misfortune with trains continued: the train had only gone about forty miles when there was a sudden screech as the cars ground to a halt.

---

853 The story is related in Cambell, *Personal Reminiscences*, 73-74.

854 Ibid., 74.

855 Ibid.

For the second time since leaving Fort Snelling, the Eighth Minnesota's train had derailed. The incident occurred just as the front of the train reached a bridge that spanned a deep ravine. George Cambell was one of the first men out of the car, and he was shocked to discover they were hanging over the side of the bridge.[856] Two wheels of the car went off the tracks at least eighty feet over the creek below.[857] Only the links and coupling pins prevented the car from falling into the chasm.[858]

Cambell recalled that "I dropped down on the bridge, saying nothing, and most of the rest followed."[859] One at a time, the men in that car had to climb out onto the bridge timbers and work their way back to safety. It was fortunate that nobody was killed and, despite the conditions, the men exiting the car were "glad to get off that cheap."[860]

The derailment on January 27 delayed the trip by a full day while a wrecker came forward to straighten the train and put it back on the tracks. During that time, the troops had to remain outside in the cold.

The day, however, was not all bad. The waiting troops spread out over the nearby countryside. Locals, alerted to the situation of the stranded troops, gathered food from all around and treated the men to a royal supper.[861] George Cambell found a good meal about a half mile away from the tracks. The cakes and other "eatables" were most welcomed by the grateful troops.[862]

That evening, the engineer sounded the locomotive's whistle to alert the scattered troops that the train was back on the track. The troops came streaming in from every direction and re-boarded the train, which then set off for Wheeling.[863]

For the next three days the train made slow but sure progress towards Washington, passing through Wheeling into Virginia. From there the train traveled through a corner of Pennsylvania on into Maryland and back down into West Virginia, not far from Washington, D.C.

Major Camp's Coffee Break

There were frequents stops for food and coffee along the way to Washington. To save time, the regimental quartermaster would usually wire ahead and arrange to

856 Cambell, *Personal Reminiscences*, 46.

857 Houlton, *Speech*.

858 Hodgson, "Recollections of the Sioux War No. 30," *Dakota County Tribune*, March 5, 1891.

859 Cambell, *Personal Reminiscences*, 46.

860 Ibid.

861 Hodgson, "Recollections of the Sioux War No. 30," *Dakota County Tribune*, March 5, 1891.

862 Washburn, *Diaries*, Jan. 27, 1865.

863 Cambell, *Personal Reminiscences*, 46.

have vendors brew coffee so it would be waiting when the train stopped. That way the men wouldn't have to pause and brew their own.[864] Upon arrival, the men would quickly get their coffee and a regimental officer would sign a receipt so the contractor could be paid by the army.

The coffee waiting for the men at the train stations, however, was not exactly the best. According to George Cambell, the vendors along the way brewed coffee in large iron kettles that were never washed, and it was so bad that those who dared consume it only knew it was coffee because the contractors told them so.[865] Thomas Hodgson of Company F claimed it was brewed from roasted rotten wheat.[866]

Nevertheless, bad coffee was generally better than no coffee. Major Camp had the quartermaster telegraph ahead to the commissary at the next stop in Martinsburg, West Virginia, the last stop before the train reached Washington DC. The quartermaster performed that duty and requested the commissary to have some food and hot coffee waiting when the regiment's train arrived.[867] The train pulled into Martinsburg at 7 a.m. on the morning of January 31, 1865. The soldiers of the Eighth Minnesota disembarked the train, with high hopes of what might be waiting for them.

Sure enough, the vendors were ready with soft bread and vats of hot coffee. This time, however, the coffee tasted especially disgusting and was almost undrinkable. Private Thomas Hodgson of Company F later wrote that the regiment had endured coffee made from water soaked in buffalo chips, a reference to the putrid mud holes of the Dakota plains, "but nothing ever struck us quite so rank as this."[868]

The soldiers complained to Major Camp, who was proven to have little patience for those who tried to cheat the government or otherwise take advantage of his troops. He first demonstrated this tendency while in command of Companies A, H and J of the Eighth Minnesota at Fort Abercrombie in 1863. There, he banished one settler from the safety of the fort in a dispute over a claim for the inflated value of a cow allegedly killed by one of the soldiers.[869]

---

864   Ibid., 72-73.

Ibid., 72.

865   Ibid., 72-73.

866   Hodgson, "Recollections of the Sioux War No. 30," *Dakota County Tribune*, March 5, 1891.

867   Ibid.

868   Hodgson, "Recollections of the Sioux War No. 30," *Dakota County Tribune*, March 5, 1891. Not everyone found the coffee so bad as to warrant complaints to the regimental commander. Edson Washburn mentioned having soft bread and coffee furnished to them at Martinsburg but made no mention of the quality of the beverage. Perhaps he had simply become accustomed to bad coffee by that point. Washburn, *Diaries*, Jan. 31, 1865,

869   The incident is mentioned in the town history: *A Century Together, A History of Fargo, North Dakota and Moorhead, Minnesota*, Fargo-Moorhead Centennial Corporation, June, 1975, 136.

George Cambell recalled that Major Camp was "foolish enough to drink a cup" of the beverage.[870] Whatever was in the cup certainly didn't meet the Major's definition of coffee. He was so disgusted by the vile liquid that he refused to sign the contractor's receipt for the provisions.

The coffee incident might have ended there, but the contractor complained to the commanding general. That happened to be Brigadier General William H. Seward, Jr., son of Lincoln's Secretary of State. General Seward was a decorated combat veteran and been posted to command a brigade based in Martinsburg after recovering from wounds sustained in battle the previous summer.

The general was in no mood to deal with what must have struck him as a trivial dispute. He ordered Major Camp to sign a receipt for the coffee. According to Thomas Hodgson, the major responded that he would be glad to sign a receipt for coffee when he got some.[871] In response, General Seward ordered Major Camp placed under arrest.

The arrest of Major Camp created a serious, but short-lived leadership problem for the Eighth Minnesota. Colonel Minor Thomas was serving in command of the entire brigade, and Lieutenant Colonel Rogers was in hospital recovering from the serious wounds he sustained at Murfreesboro. With Major Camp under arrest, none of the regimental commanders were available. Command of the Eighth Minnesota fell on the senior company captain.[872]

This was a bitter blow to the men, who generally despised the contractors. They viewed them as parasites, making money at the expense of the soldiers. Moreover, the men had a strong sense of fairness. To them, the arrest of Major Camp represented a great injustice.

The incident only raised the soldiers' respect for Major Camp. In the eyes of the men, "Major Camp was disciplined for one of the best acts of his military career."[873] Fortunately for the Eighth Minnesota, it appears that the matter was quickly resolved, and Major Camp returned to the regiment.

The troops left Martinsburg by train later that same morning. They passed through Harper's Ferry just before nightfall, a location that would have been well-known to the soldiers at that time. Harper's Ferry had been in the news since 1859, when John Brown led a raid on the federal armory located there to seize weapons with the hope of starting an armed slave rebellion.

870   Cambell, *Personal Reminiscences*, 73.

871   Hodgson, "Recollections of the Sioux War No. 30," *Dakota County Tribune*, March 5, 1891.

872   Cambell *Personal Reminiscences*, 73.

873   Hodgson, "Recollections of the Sioux War No. 30," *Dakota County Tribune*, March 5, 1891.

Harper's Ferry had also played a strategic role in the Maryland campaign of 1862 that ended at the Battle of Antietam, as well as during the following year in the events leading up to the invasion of Pennsylvania and the Battle of Gettysburg.

Sherman's Woodticks

After traveling through the night, the Eighth Minnesota awoke on the morning February 1, 1865, to find that their train had finally reached Washington D.C. They disembarked at New Jersey Station, where the soldiers visited a Sanitary Commission building to warm up and enjoy some breakfast and coffee.[874]

The men had a little free time, so several of them, including George Cambell and Edson Washburn, decided to wander over to see the Capitol. The imposing building was only a block away from the train station. The great dome was still unfinished and surrounded by scaffolding. Cambell later commented that it "seemed to us to be waiting to see whether we conquered the South before putting any more money on it."[875]

The Eighth Minnesota soon received orders to proceed by steamship south to join Sherman's army in North Carolina. There was only one problem: Washington was in the midst of the same cold snap that had dogged the troops since they arrived in Cincinnati. As a result, the Potomac River was frozen, and shipping had ground to a halt. No travel by river or sea from Washington would be possible until the river thawed. So began what one man from Company E recalled as the most disagreeable three weeks of their army service—truly a dramatic statement considering the extreme conditions the men had endured over the previous nine months[876]

They had survived the brutal heat, dehydration, and starvation rations during the Dakota campaign. They had also nearly starved on the reduced rations at Fortress Rosecrans, where they fought a significant battle and then, despite their weakened state, chased Hood's army across Tennessee in the snow and cold. For the men to consider Washington D.C. as even worse than all those hardships said a lot about the conditions there in early 1865.

After the short respite from their travels at New Jersey Station, Company E moved out with the rest of the regiment for their temporary quarters to await the thaw. They marched east down Pennsylvania Avenue and then across the Anacostia River to Camp Stoneman in Maryland.

---

874 Washburn, *Diaries*, Feb. 1, 1865. Although Washburn didn't mention the station by name, New Jersey Station was the primary railroad hub for Washington D.C. during the Civil War. It was only a block from the Capitol building.

875 Cambell, *Personal Reminiscences,* 75.

876 Washburn, *Autobiography*, 6.

The camp was on a flood plain about three miles from the Capitol building, which was clearly visible to the west.[877] Originally established as a cavalry depot, Camp Stoneman was then being used to quarter various Union Army units as they transited through Washington.

Upon reaching Camp Stoneman, Company E drew wedge tents and settled into camp. The wedge tents must have seemed like a luxury to the men compared to their tiny and uncomfortable dog tents. They were large enough to accommodate about four men with plenty of room to stretch out.

There were, however, some drawbacks to the wedge tent. The heavy canvas covering was not insulated, and the wind easily penetrated the fabric. When they arrived in Washington, the daytime temperatures were barely making it above freezing. It only got colder and windier after that, which made the men miserable.

To make matters worse, there was little wood available to burn for fuel at Camp Stoneman. The wood that was available consisted of green pine, which was difficult to light and, once burning, put out little heat. It was barely enough to cook food and certainly not enough to warm a leaky and uninsulated tent.

Company E had endured far colder temperatures while they were posted at Fort Ripley during the first winter of their service and at Paynesville during the second. The temperature there frequently dropped below zero, sometimes as cold as -40 degrees Fahrenheit. At Fort Ripley and Paynesville, however, the soldiers had the benefit of living in wooden buildings that were heated by heavy cast-iron stoves. Those stoves radiated generous amounts of heat throughout the barracks. Moreover, they had an unlimited supply of good wood for fuel. The accommodations at their previous winter quarters allowed the troops to spend the time in relative comfort. They were exposed to the cold only for portions of the day when standing guard, cutting wood or out on drill.

Camp Stoneman was altogether different. Even when the temperature warmed into the thirties the men were constantly freezing and at risk of hypothermia. It became almost unbearable as temperatures plummeted to near zero in mid-February. The constant cold winds forced their way through the thin tents, which retained almost no heat. The soldiers had only their clothes and blankets to insulate them against the elements.

To keep warm under such conditions, groups of soldiers would abandon their separate abodes and huddle together in one crowded tent all day while wearing their full clothing and boots.[878] Even then, many of the men's feet froze, although it doesn't

---

877 Houlton, *Speech*; Washburn, *Autobiography*, 6; Hodgson, "Recollections of the Sioux War No. 31," *Dakota County Tribune*, March 26, 1891.

878 Cambell, *Personal Reminiscences*, 76.

appear that any suffered serious frostbite. Edson Washburn noted at the time "It is enough to kill a person to have to stop in tents this cold weather."[879]

With so many men huddled together in close quarters, it was inevitable that sickness would spread within the camp. In no time it seemed like the whole company had come down with severe colds— and it wasn't just Company E. The entire regiment was soon suffering the effects of illness. In some cases, a cold or the flu led to life-threatening pneumonia.

Edson Washburn was one of those who caught a terrible cold and cough. He treated it with a bottle of cough syrup he obtained from the Sanitary Commission.[880] Others had more severe illness and some never recovered.

At least nine members of the Eighth Minnesota died of illness between the time they left Cincinnati and departed from Washington, D.C. almost a month later. One of those was from Company F. None of the deaths were from Company E, although a number of those men spent time in hospital for at least part of their stay in Washington. Other regiments were hit even harder with illness. The two Ohio regiments camped with the Eighth Minnesota each had more than 100 men in the hospital with illness.

The Eighth Minnesota suffered a great deal during their stay in Washington.[881] In a reunion speech given some years after the war, William Houlton described the three weeks Company E spent at Camp Stoneman waiting for the Potomac River to thaw as the most miserable weeks of their time in the service.[882]

Despite the awful conditions at Camp Stoneman, there were also occasional bright spots. On February 9, nine of the Company E wounded from Murfreesboro rejoined the unit in Washington. They reported the remainder of the company's wounded were doing well.[883]

The men were also able to leave camp on occasion for a look around the nation's capital. Passes were granted to each company for twelve men at a time. They would use the passes to cross the Anacostia River back into Washington and do some sightseeing. Among the most popular destinations were museums, the capitol building and the White House. One location of particular interest to some of the men was the

879   Washburn, *Diaries*, Feb. 9, 1865.

880   Ibid., Feb. 8, 1865

881   Houlton, *Speech*.

882   Ibid.

883   Washburn, *Diaries*, Feb. 9-10, 1865.

patent office. There they could see on display the model of a machine patented by a young Abraham Lincoln to lift steamboats over sandbars.[884]

While sightseeing in Washington, men of the Eighth Minnesota frequently encountered a Massachusetts regiment that was assigned as the provost guard. During the Civil War, the provost guard served in much the same role as the military police do in the modern army. It did not appear that the provost guard cared much for the Eighth Minnesota. The regiment failed to make a good impression when it arrived in dirty tattered uniforms. Neither the soldiers nor their uniforms had much opportunity to be washed since the unit left Murfreesboro more than a month before. As a result, the soldiers looked like a ragtag crew of frontiersmen from the backwoods.

Soldiers from the Massachusetts provost guard regiment seemed to pick on the grungy bunch of Minnesotans and derisively dubbed the Eighth Minnesota "Sherman's Woodticks."[885] It may have been intended as a derogatory term, but before the war was done, the Eighth Minnesota would be proud to be associated with Sherman's army.

In fact, the men of the Eighth Minnesota thought the Massachusetts soldiers, who had never served in combat and dressed in crisp clean uniforms, were just a pompous bunch of dandies who wanted to "put on style."[886] The Eighth Minnesota soldiers referred to those troops as the "paper command"[887] or "paper-collar regiment."[888]

Some men of Company E began to feel unjustly harassed by the provost guard while in Washington. As was their custom, Company E tried to make life difficult for those who played games with them. Rather than being intimidated by the Massachusetts provost guards, George Cambell and his comrades enjoyed teasing them by pretending to not have passes from camp. When subjected to hostile questioning by the provost guards, the Company E men played dumb and "put them to lots of trouble to get correct answers."[889] Only after they got the provost guards sufficiently worked up would the Company E men show their passes.[890]

884 Hodgson, "Recollections of the Sioux War No. 31," *Dakota County Tribune*, March 26, 1891. Lincoln held registered patent number 6,469. The model of the invention that Hodgson described is now housed at the Smithsonian Institution. Edson Washburn also visited the patent office to see the many curiosities and inventions. Washburn, *Diaries*, Feb. 15, 1865

885 *Minnesota in the Civil and Indian Wars: 1861-1865*, vol. 1, 396.

886 Cambell, *Personal Reminiscences*, 75.

887 *Minnesota in the Civil and Indian Wars: 1861-1865*, vol. 1, 396.

888 Cambell, *Personal Reminiscences*, 75. Paper collars were in style for suits and uniforms at the time because they always looked starched and were easily replaced.

889 Ibid., 76.

890 Ibid., 77.

Despite harassment from the provost guards, most of the men from the Eighth Minnesota had a good time while visiting Washington. As could be expected, the members of the regiment tried to catch a glimpse of their leaders, who would have been celebrities to the soldiers.

George Cambell described going over to the White House on a Sunday pass to see if he "could get a sight of 'Old Abe.'" The effort was probably for naught as he made no record of actually seeing the president.

Other members or the Eighth Minnesota had better luck. Thomas Hodgson, accompanied by soldiers from Company F, caught sight of General Grant while visiting the capitol building just outside the rotunda, then, as they left the building, the Company F men ran into a crowd of soldiers gathered around a carriage. After being informed that it was President Lincoln's, they decided to wait. They were not disappointed. A few minutes later, the president came down the stairs, nodded to the crowd and boarded his carriage. Hodgson later described his impression upon viewing the president:

> *Mr. Lincoln was very tall and dressed to make him look even taller than he really was. He wore a silk hat and an old fashioned overcoat such as are never seen in these days. The waist ran down to the hips, and from there it extended on down to the heels.*[891]

Lincoln appeared to Hodgson as exceedingly sad, almost like he had been weeping. Despite this lackluster impression, Hodgson was glad that he saw the face of the president because some day his descendants would brag that their great-grandfather saw President Lincoln.[892]

One experience all the men who went into Washington on a day pass encountered was the hoard of vendors selling everything imaginable, no doubt at inflated prices. The men from Company E tended to despise the street vendors and other suppliers who constantly tried to take advantage of the soldiers as they passed through. Edson Washburn observed "Peddlers thicker than toads after a shower."[893]

---

891 Hodgson, "Recollections of the Sioux War No. 31," *Dakota County Tribune*, March 26, 1891.

892 Ibid. The incident occurred only 2 months before Lincoln's assassination.

893 Washburn, *Diaries*, Feb. 13, 1865.

With Sherman

February 20 to April 18, 1865

Out to Sea

At long last, the ice finally went out from the Potomac. Company E rejoiced when the order came to move out for the South. On February 20, 1865, the men broke camp and marched six miles to Alexandria, Virginia, where the Eighth Minnesota was to board the Steamship *Ariel* for the trip to North Carolina.

Along the march, the men were amused by the vendors who sold various kinds of pies in the street. Many were southern sympathizers—they were perfectly happy to sell pies to the troops and wished the men well when they bought from them. However, if the passing men spurned their sales pitch, they would spew venom, such as "I hope you will never come back again; hope you will leave your bones in the South."[894] The men had heard similar taunts from the Copperheads as they left St. Paul for Tennessee months earlier. Despite their animosity towards the vendors, the men in Company E generally paid them little mind. However, they did occasionally amuse themselves by feigning interest in buying pies and then walking away to provoke the vendors.

The Eighth Minnesota Regiment boarded the *Ariel* that evening, along with elements of the two Ohio regiments that were also part of the third brigade. Even though all three regiments were far under their original strength, there were still well over a thousand men that had to crowd into the boat. Every available space was used. The Ohio regiments were allotted space in the middle deck and in the hold. The Eighth Minnesota on the other hand again found itself assigned to the open deck, where they sat exposed to the elements. Company E was allocated deck space not far from the wheelhouse.

The steamship *Ariel* was an ocean-going wooden hull vessel. It was propelled both with side wheels and sails. The ship was built in 1855 by Cornelius Vanderbilt

---

894   Cambell, *Personal Reminiscences,* 77.

as a mail carrier. When the Civil War broke out, Vanderbilt leased it to the federal government, where it was used mostly to run between Washington and Panama to transport California gold that was much needed for the war effort.[895]

In 1862 the *Ariel* made headlines when it was captured by the CSS *Alabama* near Cuba while on its way to Panama. At the time, the *Ariel* was transporting a contingent of 150 U.S. Marines, plus arms and ammunition, to the Pacific. The marines were ready to put up a fight rather than surrender to the Confederate ship and armed themselves for battle. However, the *Ariel*'s captain, recognizing that they were badly outgunned, ordered the marines to stand down.[896]After being held for three days by the Confederate ship, the *Ariel* was released for ransom in the form of a $228,000 bond and the marines aboard were paroled. However, the Confederates stripped the ship of all the weapons, ammunition and about $9,500 in cash.

After its return, the *Ariel* continued in the service of the Union Navy for the rest of the war. It resumed its runs to Panama and was sometimes used by the navy to shuttle troops down the Atlantic Coast.

Shortly after setting out from Alexandria on February 21, the *Ariel* came within view of George Washington's home and his tomb at Mount Vernon. The sight was profoundly moving for the soldiers. They had, after all, volunteered to save the Union that General Washington had formed. The men spontaneously began singing patriotic songs, one of which a soldier from Company F found years later:

LET WASHINGTON SLEEP.
By M. S. PIKE.

Disturb not his slumber, let Washington sleep,
'Neath the boughs of the willow that over him weep;
His arm is unnerved, but his deeds remain bright,
As the stars in the dark vaulted heavens at night,
Oh! wake not the hero, his battles are o'er,
Let him rest undisturbed on Potomac's fair shore;
On the river's green border with rich flowers dressed,
With the hearts he loved fondly, let Washington rest.

Awake not his slumbers, tread lightly around;
'Tis the grave of a freeman, —'tis liberty's mound;

895   *See,* The Ships List, http://www.theshipslist.com/ships/descriptions/panamafleet.shtml, accessed Sept. 2, 2018.

896   *New York Herald,* Dec. 28, 1862.

Thy name is immortal—our freedom it won—
Brave sire of Columbia, our own Washington.
Oh! wake not the hero, his battles are o'er,
Let him rest, calmly rest, on his dear native shore;
While the stars and the stripes of our country shall wave
O'er the land that can boast of a Washington's grave.[897]

The *Ariel* proceeded down the Potomac for several hours. As night began to fall it sailed into Chesapeake Bay, and Company E did the best they could to make themselves comfortable for the night on the deck.

As dawn broke on the morning of February 22. the men awoke to find themselves in the Atlantic Ocean. It was a beautiful sunny day with calm seas. Most of the Company E men had never been on anything larger than a riverboat, and only a handful had ever been out on the ocean. The men were overcome with the spectacle of the open ocean and endless horizons in all directions.

One major drawback to being crowded onto the deck of the steamer was there wasn't a place to make proper food. The men had nothing available for breakfast but an unappetizing meal of hard tack and fat boiled salt pork. Worse yet, they weren't even able to brew any coffee.[898]

As it turned out, the lack of food may have been a blessing in disguise. Despite the smooth seas, many of the soldiers were soon overcome with a most unpleasant sensation – seasickness. From his spot near the wheelhouse, George Cambell watched in amusement as his friends got up from their bedrolls that morning, seemingly well, and then suddenly dashed for the rails as they were hit with a bout of seasickness. They leaned over the rails to, as Cambell put it, "pay their tribute to Old Neptune."[899]

Cambell, however, didn't find seasickness funny for long. When he arose from his place on the deck that morning, he too, quickly succumbed. Cambell and most of his comrades in Company E spent much of the rest of the trip holding on to the rails. He later wrote "Of all the miserable sicknesses, that [seasickness] takes the lead."[900]

Apart from seasickness the trip wasn't all bad. As the ship traveled south it entered the gulf stream, a huge current of warm ocean water that travels north from

---

897 *Special Day, Programs and Selections for the Schools of Michigan*, State Superintendent of Public Instruction, 1908, 60.

898 Washburn, *Autobiography*, 6.

899 Cambell, *Personal Reminiscences*, 78.

900 Ibid.

warmer climates and wraps around the north Atlantic to Europe. From the ship, the men could see whales and porpoises following the warmer water.[901]

The ocean voyage was relatively short. They were at sea for only two days before the ship arrived at Fort Fisher, which stood about sixteen miles south of Wilmington, North Carolina. Fort Fisher had been a strong defensive position for the Confederacy. It guarded the sea approach to Wilmington. The fort had been captured after a brisk battle on January 15, 1865. It was intended that the Eighth Minnesota would disembark at the fort, then move north to join General Sherman's forces in the attack on Wilmington.

Shortly after the ship arrived, however, there was a change of plans. A dispatch boat, the *Eliza Hancock*, came out to greet the troopships with news that Wilmington had just fallen to Sherman's Army. An officer on board the dispatch boat reported that the troops were no longer needed at Wilmington and carried orders for the ships to head back north to Beaufort.[902]

It took only a few hours for the ships to reach Beaufort. The port town was less than 100 miles northeast of Fort Fisher. There, the Eighth Minnesota spent the next two days aboard ship awaiting their turn to disembark. It was not a pleasant wait. There was little to do apart from try to sleep on the cramped ship, and the food didn't make things any better. As always seemed to be the case, the soldiers were stuck with little more than hardtack, boiled pork, and coffee.[903] Finally, on the evening of February 25, the *Ariel* moved into a slip on the dock and the Eighth Minnesota began sending its baggage ashore.

Arrival at New Berne

It was about 2 a.m. in the morning of Sunday, February 26, 1865, when the soldiers were finally able to disembark from the *Ariel*. After doing so, the troops had to load all their gear onto rail cars. The Eighth Minnesota would go by rail to New Berne, North Carolina, a trip of about forty miles.

The regiment arrived at New Berne later that morning. It was a miserable day to set up their new camp as it drizzled and rained nearly the whole time, not letting up for the next several days.

Finally, on March 3, 1865, the Third Brigade received orders to move out. The Twenty-Third Corps would move west towards the town of Kinston where it would

---

901 Paxson, *Diary*, Feb. 22-23, 1864.

902 Washburn, *Diaries*, Feb. 23, 1865.

903 Ibid., Feb. 24, 1865.

unite with Sherman's forces. The combined force would then continue the attack against the rebels that had been driven out of Wilmington.

The Confederate forces facing Sherman's troops were under the command of General Joseph E. Johnston. Johnston was a Virginian who graduated from West Point and rose to the rank of brigadier general. When the war began in 1861, Johnston resigned from the U.S. Army and joined the Confederates.

Johnston successfully led his troops to victory as a brigadier general in the First Battle of Bull Run. His actions earned further promotions. By 1865, Johnston was a seasoned and effective commander. However, he was at a disadvantage when defending against Sherman's army. Sherman seemed to have an almost unlimited number of men and supplies. Johnston's forces were slowly and steadily shrinking due to attrition and were at risk of being overwhelmed.

It turned out to be a very difficult day of marching for the Eighth Minnesota troops. Constant rain over the past few days had turned the roads to mud. Marching in such conditions was exhausting and made even more challenging by the heavy equipment they carried. In addition to all the regular gear each man had been issued, including the nine-pound Springfield rifle, they were all issued three days' rations and seventy rounds of ammunition. The ammunition alone added more than six pounds to the heavy gear they were already wearing.

The weather was much warmer in North Carolina than the soldiers had experienced in Tennessee or Washington. The soldiers quickly overheated as they slogged through the mud. Some soldiers began to lighten their burden by throwing away anything they didn't need to lighten their burden. Soon, the road was littered with overcoats and other clothes discarded by the exhausted troops.[904] Unlike the last time this happened in Tennessee, the soldiers were unlikely to ever need the heavy overcoats again in the warmer southern weather.

The Eighth Minnesota struggled to travel ten miles per day over muddy roads under their heavy packs. The march paused on Sunday and Monday, March 5 and 6, for the men to rest and drill. On March 7, the regiment marched along railroad tracks to the town of Dover. From there, they could hear cannon and rifle fire erupting from a sharp battle at Kinston, eight miles away to the west.[905]

The rail line along which the troops advanced had recently been repaired by the Federals to supply Sherman's army as it pursued Johnston's forces. Johnston was moving north after the defeat at Wilmington and hoped to meet up with Lee's Army

---

904 Washburn, *Diaries*, March 3, 1865. Lieutenant Lewis Paxson made the same observation in his diary for March 3rd.

905 The Battle of Kinston, which took place from March 7 to 10, 1865 is also known as the Battle of Wyse Fork.

of Northern Virginia near Petersburg. This made the railroad a target. If the rail line could be taken and destroyed, it would hinder the resupply of Sherman's forces.

Confederate troops under General Braxton Bragg suddenly showed up in front of the advancing Federals at Kinston and attacked the First Brigade of the First Division, which was comprised mostly of Indiana infantry troops. The surprised Federal troops managed to stop the Confederate advance and fought back from hastily fortified positions.[906] The Confederates made repeated charges at the First Brigade but all failed to make a breakthrough.

It was the initial contact with Bragg's forces that members of the Eighth Minnesota heard late in the day on March 7. The Third Brigade, including the Eighth Minnesota, was called up but it did not join the fight. Instead, the regiment was ordered to put up breast works and defend the railroad line.

The Eighth Minnesota took up its position along the railroad and waited. Then, one after another, soldiers from the First Brigade came running down the tracks in a panic from the direction of the battle. Each claimed his regiment was wiped out. George Cambell described the scene:

> What impressed it on my mind was that every man was the last man of the regiment, all the rest had been killed. We thought there were hopes for that regiment yet as there were several hundred last men who survived.[907]

The fighting at Kinston went on for three days. Finally, Bragg's forces withdrew to rejoin Johnston. For the next few days, Company E and the rest of the Eighth Minnesota remained in and about Kinston as the rest of the Twenty-Third Corps arrived from the east. Then the corps set out for Goldsboro, twenty-six miles to the northwest, where they would meet up with Sherman's army.

The Eighth Minnesota arrived in Goldsboro on March 21 and set up camp. The next day, Sherman's troops began to arrive. The Eighth Minnesota had been called "Sherman's Woodticks" due to their tattered and dirty appearance following the siege at Murfreesboro and the pursuit of Hood. Yet, compared to Sherman's troops, the Eighth Minnesota might as well have been in dress uniforms.

Sherman's army had left Atlanta for its march to the sea cut off from the Union supply lines. The army had been forced to forage and live off the land as they fought their way from Atlanta south to Savannah. Sherman then turned to the north

---

906   *Minnesota in the Civil and Indian Wars: 1861-1865*, vol. 1, 397.

907   Cambell, *Personal Reminiscences*, 81.

and continued his march through South Carolina to Wilmington as his army chased Johnston's forces.

By the time Sherman's soldiers began arriving at Goldsboro, they had been on the march and fighting a running battle with Johnston's troops for more than four months. And they looked it. By their appearances, the troops had not drawn any clothes for some time[908]

Despite their ragged attire, Sherman's troops projected a certain bravado. William Houlton recalled:

> *Many of them were without hats coats or shoes and all dirty and rugged but tough and hearty as bears and feeling as proud and big as if every man weighed a ton and their self-satisfied air said plainer than words -this army will go where it pleases and it can't be whipped...*[909]

The men of the Eighth Minnesota were in awe of these battle-hardened troops. They brought with them all the spoils of war that they had collected along their march, including a number of old fancy carriages that the troops had confiscated from the first families of Georgia. Seeing Sherman's troops march past, George Cambell recalled "It was as good as a picnic and three circuses, and we did little else than stand and gap [sic] at them all day."[910]

Arriving as part of Sherman's forces were regiments of United States Colored Troops. If seeing African American soldiers was a surprise for the men in the Eighth Minnesota, none bothered to make note of it. The only surviving reference to the USCT regiments they encountered that day was by George Cambell, who simply observed "and one thing was for sure, they had good brass bands."[911]

Soon, General William Tecumseh Sherman himself arrived. On Thursday, March 23, 1865, the general reached Goldsboro and reviewed the Twenty-Third Corps. His appearance did not make a big impression on the Minnesota soldiers. Edson Washburn described Sherman as "a very plain and ordinary looking man."[912] William Houlton later recalled that "he rode down our line with an old slouch hat on and looking as messy as his army."[913]

---

908 Ibid., 82.

909 Houlton, *Speech.*

910 Cambell, *Personal Reminiscences,* 82. Cambell apparently meant to use the word "gape."

911 Cambell, *Personal Reminiscences,* 82.

912 Washburn, *Diaries,* March 23, 1865.

913 Houlton, *Speech.*

GENERAL WILLIAM TECUMSEH SHERMAN

Joining up with Sherman's forces allowed the Eighth Minnesota a few days' rest as the army organized for its next push to keep the pressure on Johnston's Confederates. This welcome break was made all the more joyous as the Fourth Minnesota was camped nearby. Several members of Company E had friends or family in the Fourth Minnesota. Soon, some of them stopped by to visit, including Joe Goyette, Lewis's brother.

On Saturday, March 26, 1865, Company E moved out again with the rest of the Eighth Minnesota. The day's march was easy and short, only about four miles to the east of Goldsboro. The following day, the unit continued the march until they reached the Wheat Swamp Church, just a few miles to the northwest of Kinston.[914]

The place name of "Wheat Swamp" had nothing to do with grain. According to local legend, its namesake was an Indian called Wheat, who hid in a swamp nearby where the church now stood.[915] This church would be the Eighth Minnesota's headquarters for up to a week. Therefore, the troops were ordered to fortify their position and they commenced building breastworks.[916]

The Eighth Minnesota remained at Wheat Swamp for the next few days. The men continued working on the fortifications. The rations were rather thin and the railroad from New Berne still wasn't fully operational, so the men made time to do some foraging about the neighborhood.

At 2 p.m. on March 31, Major Camp called up the Eighth Minnesota, along with about thirty cavalry troops, for a patrol towards the small nearby town of Hookerton. About three miles east of Wheat Swamp, the regiment encountered roughly ninety enemy troops. In the ensuing skirmish, the Eighth Minnesota captured four Confederates, including two lieutenants. The regiment spent the night camped on the road and returned to Wheat Swamp the next afternoon.

---

914 The church still stands.

915 Naomi Dail Holder, *History of the Wheat Swamp Christian Church Including the Conditions in Europe and the Colonies*, New Bern, NC, 1977, 3.

916 Washburn, *Diaries*, March 27, 1865.

For the next few days, the Eighth Minnesota remained in camp. There wasn't much for the soldiers to do, which led them into trouble. Moreover, the men sensed that the Confederacy was near collapse. A few began to slack off on their duties as it appeared their time in the army might be nearly up.

On the morning of Thursday, April 6, 1865, four soldiers of the Eighth Minnesota didn't bother to appear for roll call. Those men quickly discovered that army discipline was not letting up at all. The four men were ordered to carry heavy logs around camp as punishment for their offense.[917]

This was but one of many common punishments meted out to soldiers for minor offenses of army discipline, such as unauthorized absence from camp or missing roll call. The methods were all intended to be unpleasant at best and frequently involved pain, public humiliation, or both.

Later that same day, exciting and welcome news reached the Eighth Minnesota—Richmond had fallen.[918] The soldiers all realized that its capture meant the war was nearly over.

While the men had been disappointed by multiple false reports of the fall of Richmond over the past two years, this time it seemed different, and the men celebrated. Confirmation of this momentous event came in the following day. It was such an important development that the men could talk of little else.

The war, however, was not yet over. To the north, General Robert E. Lee was on the move with the Army of Northern Virginia, still trying to escape from Grant. Closer to the Eighth Minnesota in North Carolina, Johnston's army remained in the field.

Orders arrived for the Eighth Minnesota to move out from Wheat Swamp early in the morning on April 9 and head towards the North Carolina capitol of Raleigh. The troops made a twenty-six-mile march through Goldsboro into the country. The regiment made a similar march the following day.

Early on the morning of April 11, the Eighth Minnesota set out again. They had just started the march when the lead elements of the brigade came across three Union soldiers hung in a tree. They had probably been out foraging and been captured by rebel guerillas.

The sight of their fellow soldiers hanging in a tree along the road enraged the Union troops. They considered the hangings an act of murder, not a legitimate means of war. They also felt betrayed. The war was winding down. Many rebels had already laid down their arms and started for home.

---

917 Paxson, *Diary*, April 6, 1865.

918 Nearly all of the Eighth Regiment's diarists recorded this event on April 6, 1865.

George Cambell later recalled meeting lots of rebel soldiers on their way back home. In these encounters it had often been "Hail fellows, well met."[919] Many soldiers in the brigade even shared their rations with the starving rebels.

Now, as the men stared at three of their own strung up by the rebels, it became too much. From that moment on the troops in the brigade set fire to every house and building they came across in retaliation for the murders. Edson Washburn noted of the march that day that "Several splendid mansions burned on the way."[920] The only exception was for slaves' quarters, which were left standing.[921]

The situation became so bad that General Ruger, the division commander, issued strict orders against burning buildings. Furthermore, the general ordered that any man caught setting fire to a house should be summarily shot. That order, however, didn't seem to stop the fires.

In fact, Ruger's strict order was read to the Minnesota troops in front of a large two-story southern mansion with a piazza that ran clear around the house. After reading the order, General Ruger and the other officers made themselves comfortable on the piazza. While the troops laid down around the house, the officers placed guards at every door. One of the officers was heard to say "At least, this one house will be saved."[922]

The officer's statement turned out to be premature. As the officers sat on the piazza, smoke and fire began to shoot out of two peaks on the roof. Within a short time, the mansion was totally engulfed in flame.

Reflecting back years later, soldiers knew that burning those houses was wrong. In the moment, however, the anger at the senseless murders and resentment for the wealthy supporters of the southern cause overcame any moral reservations the soldiers had about destroying civilian property.

The Federal troops were not the only ones who resented the wealthy southerners. As the Eighth Minnesota paused to rest for a few days while waiting for bridge repairs, George Cambell was posted for twenty-four hours to guard a poor white family against foragers. The family consisted of the parents and seven daughters. Three of the daughters were married to Confederate soldiers and three others "were looking eagerly for the return of certain members of the Secession army."[923]

---

919 Cambell, *Personal Reminiscences*, 104.

920 Washburn, *Diaries*, April 11, 1865.

921 Cambell, *Personal Reminiscences*, 103-104.

922 Ibid., 104.

923 Ibid., 83. The family also had three sons who were serving at the time in the Confederate army.

Cambell was perplexed because aside from the family's daughters, there wasn't anything to guard. There was not enough food in the house to feed even one hungry soldier. He went on to describe his experience:

> *They were the poor white class who furnished the fighting men of the South. These young ladies concluded the war was about over and rejoiced, if such were the case, because Mrs. ----------- would lose her slaves and be no better off than they.*[924]

Cambell was also appalled at the poor white family's utter lack of education. "Not one of the whole nine people in the house could read and their conversation was about as intelligent as we could expect from school children seven or eight years of age."[925] This must have been astounding to Cambell for nearly all the members of his company, not to mention their friends and family back home, were well-educated and quite literate.

Some of the Union soldiers took advantage of the southerner's ignorance. In one such instance, soldiers had peeled labels from sarsaparilla bottles, which were printed on green paper that resembled "green-back" paper money issued by the U.S. Government, and passed them off to the local southerners as currency. Until the locals caught on, the soldiers were able to buy supplies readily with the labels.[926]

The Eighth Minnesota continued the march early in the morning on April 12, 1865. They did not yet know it, but they were about to receive the best news any of them had heard since they enlisted more than two and a half years earlier.

The End of Hostilities

As the Twenty-Third Corps continued its march towards Raleigh on the morning of April 12, a commotion arose at the rear of the column. George Cambell wrote that they could hear a "terrible uproar" and, looking up, "we could see hats and everything else that a fellow could throw in the air."[927] William Houlton recalled:

> *We could hear cheering, faint at first on account of distance but gradually growing louder and nearer. Wave after wave of cheers*

---

924 Ibid.

925 Ibid.

926 Ibid., 84.

927 Ibid., 88.

such as only regiments of soldiers give when they get out to enough raise you right off your feet.[928]

The cause of the excitement along the road soon became clear. An officer on horseback was riding down the road and delivering some sort of news to the head of each regiment. William Houlton described the situation:

> *Our curiosity was at its height when we saw a single horseman gallop towards us wildly swinging his hat. Both himself and his horse in a wash of sweat. He would stop at each Regiment and deliver a message and then that Regiment would explode in its men. When he reached our Regiment this was the message - Lee has surrendered with his whole army to General Grant!*

When the rider reached the Eighth Minnesota he was met by Major Camp, who then rode behind the man repeating for all to hear "Lee has surrendered!"[929] Although this news was not entirely unexpected, the soldiers rejoiced. "The men went wild with joy and singing John Brown's Body Lies A-mouldering In The Ground."[930] There was now no doubt that the end of the war was imminent.

The Eighth Minnesota was ordered to halt for a couple hours of rest and celebration. They stopped in a large orchard. As the men rested, the regimental bands marched up and down the rows of troops playing, in the words of Thomas Hodgson, "the sweetest music our ears ever heard."[931]

Fireworks

The orchard where the Eighth Minnesota stopped was near the town of Smithfield on the bank of the Neuse River. Nearby was a large turpentine factory.

Turpentine is a highly flammable liquid distilled from pine sap. It has long been used as a solvent, especially for oil-based paint. In the nineteenth century, it was also used for lamp fuel, medical purposes, and a variety of other applications.

One by-product of the turpentine distillation process is rosin, a hard glass-like substance that has a variety of industrial uses. Rosin begins to melt at about the boiling point of water and, like turpentine, is highly flammable.

928 Houlton, *Speech.*

929 Cambell, *Personal Reminiscences,* 88.

930 Washburn, *Autobiography,* 7.

931 Hodgson, "Recollections of the Sioux War No. 32," *Dakota County Tribune,* May 7, 1891.

The factory was full of tar, turpentine, and rosin and dry as powder.[932] George Cambell later noted that immense quantities of rosin were found at the turpentine factory.[933] He also recalled that "it didn't take long to apply a match to it."[934]

The resulting fire made for quite a spectacle that the men would remember the rest of their lives. William Houlton described the sight:

> Soon great masses of flame and black smoke were shooting up as from a volcano, to the height of several hundred feet. It would puff and puff, like a live monster writhing in pain. Soon the mass of inflammable pitch began to melt and run in streams, burning as it ran, spreading fire in all directions, and finally, running into a stream of water, furnished the novel spectacle of a river on fire. The whole scene was terrific beyond description.[935]

The heat of the fire was so intense that it shriveled nearby trees. It belched dense black smoke so high in the air that George Cambell was sure it could be seen for a hundred miles.[936] As the troops viewed the scene with great awe, many of the men repeated the same phrase to one another – "There goes the rebellion."[937]

The Lost Regiment

As the turpentine factory burned out, the Eighth Minnesota was ordered to continue its march towards Raleigh. The men, still elated from news of Lee's surrender and the spectacular turpentine factory fire, were looking forward to a short march to their designated position. There, they expected to set up camp early and get some rest. This, however, was not to be.

In celebration of the surrender, some of the field officers had cracked open what whisky could be found and got so drunk that they didn't know where they were going.[938] Their judgment being impaired by spirits, they led the regiment down the wrong road.

932 *Minnesota in the Civil and Indian Wars: 1861-1865*, vol. 1, 398. *See also*, Houlton *Speech*.

933 Cambell, *Personal Reminiscences*, 89.

934 Ibid.

935 *Minnesota in the Civil and Indian Wars: 1861-1865*, vol. 1, 398.

936 Cambell, *Personal Reminiscences*, 89.

937 Hodgson, "Recollections of the Sioux War No. 32," *Dakota County Tribune*, May 7, 1891.

938 Houlton, *Speech*. Curiously, the part about the officers being drunk didn't make it into the Eighth Regimental history published in *Minnesota in the Civil and Indian Wars: 1861-1865*, vol. 1. Houlton extracted the rest of the story almost word for word from his unpublished speech.

As a result, the Eighth Minnesota, lost in the blackness, marched much of the night under the weight of full gear and without any food. The foot-sore, exhausted, and hungry soldiers, who should have reached their destination several hours earlier, finally arrived in the middle of the night. Needless to say, they were in a foul mood. "The boys were as mad and ugly as a few hours before they bad been pleased and happy."[939]

There was to be little rest for the unfortunate troops of the Eighth Minnesota. No sooner did they get their tents set up than they were ordered out on picket duty. After stumbling a mile or more through the brush, the men reached their assigned positions. The scene they discovered simply added insult to injury. The picket position they occupied was just a few yards from where they began their ill-fated march the previous afternoon.[940]

In the morning, the Eighth Minnesota was ordered to pack up and continue on towards Raleigh. The already exhausted men marched another twenty-four miles that day before they could finally lie down and rest. Their burden perhaps seemed a little lighter with news of the surrender because that meant they would get to go home soon. Or so they thought.

Assassination

The Eighth Minnesota, along with the rest of Twenty-Third Corps, entered the North Carolina capitol unopposed late in the day on Friday, April 14, 1865. The arriving Union forces were met by the North Carolina governor and several other state officers, who sought and received army protection.[941] Sherman's whole army was there. It appeared that there were soldiers everywhere in and around Raleigh.

Early that evening, the Eighth Minnesota arrived at its designated camp on the outskirts of Raleigh. It had been a thirty-plus mile march that day and the soldiers were completely spent. Some were so tired that they didn't even have the energy to eat. Instead, they simply went to sleep.

Their sleep was shortly interrupted by a visiting party from the Fifth Minnesota Infantry. Many of the Eighth Minnesota soldiers had friends or family in the Fifth Regiment and were no doubt glad to see the visitors. Nevertheless, sleep was more important for many of the exhausted troops. George Cambell, who personally knew several of the visitors later wrote "I was too tired to make myself known or pay much attention to them."[942]

---

939 *Minnesota in the Civil and Indian Wars: 1861-1865*, vol. 1, 398.

940 Houlton, *Speech.*

941 Paxson, *Diary*, April 14, 1865.

942 Cambell, *Personal Reminiscences*, 86.

After the camp was fully set up the following day, the Eighth Minnesota soldiers finally had some free time. George Cambell and some others used the time for sightseeing. They went up to visit the North Carolina Capitol building.

There, in the front room of the capitol building, George Cambell saw General Sherman for the first time (he may have been in the hospital when Sherman reviewed the troops at Goldsboro). Sherman was in discussions with some Confederate officers, although Cambell was too far away to hear what they were saying.[943]

As it turned out, the Confederates Cambell saw were from General Johnston's staff and had arrived to negotiate a truce. Sherman and Johnston would meet at Durham, North Carolina, two days later to work out the final terms of surrender.

On the same day that Sherman's troops entered Raleigh, President Lincoln and his wife Mary decided to take in a play at Ford's Theater in Washington. As the President and First Lady watched "Our American Cousin" the actor John Wilkes Booth surreptitiously entered the President's box overlooking the stage and fired his derringer pistol point blank into the president's head.

A doctor at the scene quickly determined that the wound would be fatal. The president was carried to a house across the street from Ford's Theater and laid out on a bed to await the inevitable as his family and government officials gathered. At 7:22 a.m. on Saturday, April 15, 1865, President Abraham Lincoln died of his wound.

Reports of the assassination did not reach the Eighth Minnesota in Raleigh until April 17. When it did, the news was a terrible blow to the shocked and saddened troops. "We were absolutely horror struck – dazed as it were" recalled Thomas Hodgson of Company F.[944] Regimental Chaplain Armsby held a special service on the occasion, which was well attended by grieving soldiers.

Sorrow among the Union troops soon gave way to anger. "The citizens of Raleigh instinctively felt the change and hurriedly withdrew to their houses and shut their doors."[945] The fears of the local population were well-founded. In the Union camps angry soldiers spoke of taking revenge by torching the town. "It seemed as though every house would be burned" George Cambell later recalled.[946]

It was the quick thinking of some officers from Baltimore that prevented the burning of Raleigh. The officers told the troops, perhaps as a white lie or because they simply had their dates mixed up, that they were in Washington the day after

---

943 Ibid., 87.

944 Hodgson, "Recollections of the Sioux War No. 32," *Dakota County Tribune*, May 7, 1891.

945 Houlton, *Speech*.

946 Cambell, *Personal Reminiscences*, 87.

the date of the alleged assassination and that they saw Lincoln then alive and well.[947] Unsure of what to believe, the soldiers were divided on how to proceed.

The officers took advantage of the soldiers' uncertainty to march them all to camps outside the city. There, the commanders placed a double ring of provost guards around the troops to prevent any soldiers from entering the city.[948] Meanwhile, the newspapers of Raleigh published headlines begging the army not to hold the town responsible for the act.[949]

At some point, the confined Union troops would have learned they had been duped into camp and may have been planning to carry out their plans to avenge Lincoln's death at a later time. Fortunately, word soon arrived that Johnston had finally surrendered to Sherman on April 18, effectively ending the war. News of the surrender and the resulting peace quickly deflated the soldier's desire for revenge and the danger to Raleigh passed.

947 Ibid.

948 Ibid., 87-88.

949 Houlton, *Speech*.

Hardtack
No More

April 19, 1865, to August 21, 1865

With the surrender of Johnston, Sherman's army halted in place. For the next few days, the Eighth Minnesota remained in camp and awaited orders. During this time, the officers tried to keep the men organized. Newly breveted[950] General Minor Thomas reviewed the Eighth Minnesota on April 19. The following day General Sherman conducted a review of the entire Twenty-Third Corps, including the Eighth Minnesota. The rest of the time the men just sat around waiting for what would come next.

On April 26 the Eighth Minnesota received orders to break camp. Still uncertain of their destination, the men packed up their tents and gear in preparation for the march. Then, they waited. And waited. Later in the evening they were finally told to pitch their tents for the night without having gone anywhere.

The Eighth Minnesota continued to sit in place with little to do. Rumors constantly swirled through the camp regarding when the regiment would be sent home but nothing much seemed to happen.

It wasn't until May 2 that the Eighth Minnesota learned what would become of it. Now that the war was over, the mission of Sherman's army shifted from destruction to occupation. Regiments were to be disbursed throughout North Carolina to maintain order and defend against potential guerilla actions by die-hard Confederates. The Eighth Minnesota was one of those units assigned to occupation duty. It was ordered to pack up and march for Charlotte, where it would be stationed until time came for the regiment to go home.

---

950   A brevet is often an honorary promotion that comes without increased pay or responsibility. It was also used to support an officer who was commanding a unit higher than would ordinarily be the case for his rank. Col. Thomas had been commanding a brigade, both with Sully and in the 1st Division of XXIII Corps for nearly a year. The brevet rank of brigadier general reflected this service.

There was still a lot of marching ahead before the men could get to Charlotte. The first leg retraced the steps back to Greensboro. Little did the men know at the time, but the officers had placed bets on who would be the first to reach their destination. The wagon teams were giving out, so to avoid being slowed down waiting for them the men were each issued six-days' rations and 100 rounds of ammunition to carry along with their normal compliment of equipment.

It wasn't long after starting out on this "race" that the men realized there was no reason for them to carry such a load. "We could see no use for the ammunition, the war being over, so we threw it into the river" recalled George Cambell.[951] The soldiers soon littered their path with other unwanted items, including large amounts of hardtack and rotten food.

George Cambell recalled of the rations they had been issued that "the bacon was about strong enough to crawl off on its own."[952] It was a good thing they lightened the load as much as they could. The Eighth Minnesota traveled nearly twenty miles that day and they had a long way to go before reaching Charlotte.

Delays along the way had slowed the regiment's pace so much that it was ordered to conduct a night march. The soldiers were by that point very sleepy and utterly exhausted. Some of the Company E men decided the army could do without them until morning. About a dozen soldiers, including George Cambell and Charlie Gibbs decided to simply lay down, go to sleep, and catch up with the regiment in the morning.[953]

While enjoying a deep sleep, Cambell was rudely shaken awake by a hard push and a shout. His tormentor claimed to be the officer of the rear guard. An officer of the rear guard was responsible for making sure there was no straggling or foraging going on while the unit was on the march. These officers frequently wore a red sash in the same manner as a scarf as a badge of authority.[954]

Cambell, his normally calm temper roused by the rude awakening and having little patience for pesky officers from other regiments, responded angrily: "I don't see an officer of the guard!" The following exchange then ensued:

---

951 Cambell, *Personal Reminiscences*, 90.

952 Ibid.

953 Ibid.

954 *See*, generally, REVISED UNITED STATES ARMY REGULIATIONSI OF 1861. 4AN APPENIX1 CONTAINING THE CHANGES AND LAWS AFFECTING ARMY REGULATIONS AND ARTICLES OF WAR TO JUNE 25, 1863. WASHINGTON: GOVERNMENT PRINTING OFFICE. 1863, https://quod.lib.umich.edu/m/moa/AGY4285.0001.001?rgn=main;view=fulltext, last accessed Dec. 30, 2019.

Officer: You can look at me.
Cambell: I don't see any scarf.[955]
Officer: I don't have to wear a scarf.
Cambell: Then you don't have to be an officer of the guard.

The officer then placed Cambell under arrest. Cambell was forced to march back to headquarters, where he was brought before the general in charge. A new conversation followed:

General: What are you here for?
Cambell: I don't know.
Sergeant: He was arrested for sassing the officer of the day.
General to Cambell: Don't you know better than that?
Cambell: Yes, when an officer showed scarf and authority, I know better.

The general, apparently wishing to avoid further embarrassment, did not pursue the matter. Cambell soon found himself sent back to Company E.

The long marches took their toll on the men physically. They were exhausted much of the time. Soldiers in the war often learned to fall into a deep sleep anytime the opportunity presented itself, even if there was surrounding noise and commotion.

A soldier in such a deep slumber during the day presented too good an opportunity for the pranksters in Company E to pass up. George Cambell described what would happen when they found one of their comrades getting some sleep:

Now, to keep ourselves awake, we had to play some jokes on each other. One was to get a shovel from the vans and, when we found a man asleep, we would slip up, dig a hole along side of him, then roll him in. My! The expression on his countenance when rolled into the pit was laughable enough. It woke him up effectively, for that day at least.[956]

The Eighth Minnesota camped at Goldsboro until May 11. At about 3:00 that afternoon, they boarded railroad flatcars for the eighty-mile trip to Charlotte. The men were no doubt happy to be riding instead of making the march on foot.

---

955 An officer of the guard uniform included a red scarf.
956 Cambell, *Personal Reminiscences*, 92.

The rail trip, however, was not as comfortable as the soldiers may have hoped. Those on the flat bed rail cars were fully exposed to the elements. Unlike the previous few days, the weather turned cold. To top it off, heavy rain began to fall early in the evening and continued all night.

It was a long cold night for the soldiers. The train moved slowly because the southern railroad lines were in rough shape. Edson Washburn noted that it was so chilly and wet that he ached with the cold.[957] George Cambell jokingly referred to it as "a regular water-cure treatment."[958] The cold rain probably didn't do Cambell any good. He had been ailing for the previous couple weeks with what was probably dysentery or some other malady.

At about 10:00 a.m. on Friday, May 12, 1865, the train carrying the Eighth Minnesota pulled into Charlotte. The day was unseasonably chilly. The wet and tired soldiers quickly set up a temporary camp and spent the rest of the day sleeping or just resting.

The next day, things began looking up. The weather grew warmer, and the regiment moved to a permanent camp. It turned out to be a very nice location along the main road heading south through Charlotte. George Cambell described it as a "beautifully shaded hill."[959] There, the Eighth Minnesota fixed up their tents and made permanent bunks because they expected to stay put for a while.

By the time the regiment arrived in Charlotte, many of the men were physically in rough shape. The lack of proper food and sleep over the previous weeks had drained them. In their weakened state the soldiers were more susceptible to disease. Dysentery was common, as were fevers, colds, and other illnesses. Edson Washburn was one of those suffering from dysentery and noted in his diary that "Many of the boys have the diarrhea."[960]

Fresh Fruit at Last

To help the soldiers deal with their illnesses and general weakness, the regimental doctor recommended that they should eat lots of blackberries. George Cambell was one of those who followed the doctor's advice. He treated his lingering ill-

957 Washburn, *Diaries*, May 11, 1865.

958 Cambell, *Personal Reminiscences*, 92. George Cambell had spent his formative years helping his family run a water-cure establishment at New Lebanon Springs, New York from 1845 to 1855. The water-cure was what today might be called a spa treatment. It consisted of hot and cold baths in spring water and, when combined with a strict diet, was said to cure just about any malady.

959 Cambell, *Personal Reminiscences*, 93.

960 Washburn, *Diaries*, May 19, 1865.

ness with scalded condensed milk and blackberries.[961] Many other soldiers adopted a similar diet, following the doctor's orders.

Fortunately, there was an abundance of fruit growing in the area. There were abandoned fields near the camp that had been entirely overgrown with blackberries. Strawberries were also plentiful on some of the nearby farms. The soldiers began gathering fruit in large quantities to supplement their diet. Edson Washburn, for example, managed to pick three quarts of strawberries on his first outing.[962]

Berry picking was not without risk. Even though the Confederate army had surrendered, there were still bands of guerillas operating in the area. The soldiers had to go out in squads because the guerillas would rob a single soldier or worse if he was caught.[963] The Eighth Minnesota troops had no quarrel with the Confederate soldiers, who they viewed as honorable, but they feared the guerillas and held them in contempt.

On occasion, berry picking expeditions were used as traps to try and draw out the guerillas. A single man would move about carelessly to present an easy target for the guerillas. If they did try to rob the single soldier, they would be surprised by four or five others hiding nearby behind a fence or other cover.[964]

Guerillas were not the only danger for those out collecting produce. The locals were very protective of their gardens and fields. In one case, a former Confederate captain who had just returned from the war, shot a soldier from the 174th Ohio Regiment as the man was robbing his garden.[965]

Returning Confederates

The Eighth Minnesota was camped on the main road through Charlotte. Soon, thousands of paroled Confederate soldiers from Lee's and Johnston's armies were passing the camp on their way south. They were all on foot, having to walk hundreds of miles in some cases to get back home.

The Union troops were shocked at the cadaverous condition of their former enemies. The Confederate army had been almost without rations for months before the surrender and there was little to eat along the path home. Many of them had nothing but a little leftover cornmeal. As a result, the paroled soldiers were starving.

---

961   Cambell, *Personal Reminiscences,* 93.

962   Washburn, *Diaries,* May 15, 1865.

963   Cambell, *Personal Reminiscences,* 99.

964   Ibid., 100.

965   Paxson, *Diary,* June 14, 1865.

For the most part, the Eighth Minnesota soldiers treated their former enemies with respect and compassion. George Cambell recalled that "Their regular soldiers were brave and kindly men; such was our experience."[966] William Houlton later said, "I am sure there was no feeling on our part towards them but one of pity and often we divided our rations with them."[967] Houlton further described what impact the sight had on the men of Company E:

> When it was remembered that the Confederates, without pay or clothes, with health broken, their cause hopelessly lost, were returning to desolated homes, while the Union soldiers, comfortably clothed and paid, the wounded pensioned, and, more than all, were returning victorious to homes of comfort, the difference was too marked to inspire other than feelings of pity for the poor victims of the unholy ambition of leading traitors.[968]

Edson Washburn, whose brother Elbridge had been killed by the Confederates at Murfreesboro, echoed those sentiments when he later described spending time in camp:

> ...doing little but watch the poor dejected rebel soldiers as they wended their way home after making heroic sacrifices and fighting desperately for a bad cause, only to be beaten and return penniless, ragged and disheartened to their desolate homes. But such is war.[969]

Washburn did not appear to harbor any animosity towards the rebel soldiers. He also shared his hardtack and coffee with them.

Not everyone was quite so sympathetic to the returning rebels. There was occasionally some taunting of the beaten foe. William Houlton remembered that Lieutenant Tollington was mean enough once to ask a gaunt stoop-shouldered skeleton who was walking by how much pension he was going to get.[970] However, this type of incident seemed to be an exception to how the men of Company E dealt with the returning Confederates.

Ex-Slaves

---

966 Cambell, *Personal Reminiscences*, 99.

967 Houlton, *Speech*.

968 *Minnesota in the Civil and Indian Wars: 1861-1865*, vol. 1, 399.

969 Washburn, *Autobiography*, 7.

970 Houlton, *Speech*.

The ex-rebel soldiers encountered by the Eighth Minnesota were just passing through. They would grab a bite to eat and then be on their way. The occupying Union soldiers also had to deal with another large group that stayed put: former slaves. The Charlotte area had not been attacked by Union troops during the war. To keep their slaves out of Union hands, many plantation owners in the path of Sherman's army had sent them to Charlotte.

Former slaves began to arrive at the Eighth Minnesota's camp in large numbers. "The joy of those poor blacks at the approach of the Union army knew no bounds and found expression in many queer and touching ways."[971] William Houlton later recalled one such example:

> I remember one strong man coming in to ask if he really was free
> and then if his wife and his children were his own and, on being
> assured till he was convinced and the joyful fact come home to
> him, his bosom heaved with emotion and he by turns laughed and
> cried and all the while his streaming eyes turned heavenward and
> thanking the Lord.[972]

Freed blacks told the soldiers of their mistreatment at the hands of slave owners. They also informed the soldiers of the cruelty local home guards had inflicted on Union prisoners of war:

> One of them pointed out a little stream that ran by our camp
> where a hundred men, who had been taken prisoners, were halted
> while marching to Salisbury. "Here was where one man was shot
> while leaving the ranks to lie down and drink, and here another
> and another were shot dead and left lying in the water while the
> rest marched on." I tell you we had little use for the white men who
> stayed home or were home guards.[973]

Lauren Armsby, the regimental chaplain, began holding religious services for the freed slaves on the Eighth Minnesota's parade ground. Those services drew blacks from great distances. Some of these services included more than 3,000 former slaves in the audience.

---

971   *Minnesota in the Civil and Indian Wars: 1861-1865*, vol. 1, 398.

972   Houlton, *Speech*.

973   Cambell, *Personal Reminiscences*, 99.

The blacks were generally well-treated by the soldiers. The men had heard stories of how blacks had fed, sheltered, and guided northern prisoners who escaped from the rebels. Now, many of the blacks had nothing to live on. The regiment, therefore, put lots of the blacks to work and gave them all their spare rations.

While many of the soldiers certainly sympathized with the ex-slaves over what they had endured, few recorded any of their views regarding what was to come next, such as the issues of equal rights and citizenship for the freed blacks. There were certainly plenty of the soldiers who harbored racist views of the ex-slaves. Some resented going to war over the issue.

Camp Life in Charlotte

Now that the war was over, the men of the Eighth Minnesota had a little more freedom. The soldiers made frequent trips into Charlotte. There, they discovered that the young ladies of the town had nothing but contempt for the Union men. As they were walking down the sidewalk, the ladies would step off while the soldiers approached and hold their dresses out of the way.[974] It appears that this gesture was intended to convey much the same meaning as displaying the middle finger would do today.

The soldiers determined to do something about the situation. The next time it happened one of the soldiers said loudly "Did you see what dirty stockings that girl had on?"[975] That bit of public humiliation did the trick, and the local women stopped the practice.

Almost immediately after setting up camp in Charlotte, the attitude of the Eighth Minnesota men towards the army began to change. Their patience was wearing thinner as each day passed without orders directing the regiment to return to Minnesota. "We thought it was time we were at home and got all the fun we could out of soldiering with as little duty as possible" recalled George Cambell.

Much of that fun came at the expense of the army. The men of Company E quickly returned to one of their favorite amusements, tormenting the officers of other regiments. They had mastered this skill at Fort Snelling, Washington, and elsewhere.

The Twenty-Fifth Massachusetts Volunteer Infantry Regiment was stationed in Charlotte at the same time as the Eighth Minnesota. This regiment was formed in 1861 and spent much of the war stationed at New Berne, North Carolina.

Unlike the Massachusetts provost guard that harassed the Eighth Minnesota in Washington, the Twenty-Fifth Massachusetts was a veteran regiment. It had taken part

---

974 Cambell, *Personal Reminiscences*, 93.

975 Ibid., 93-94.

in the Battle of Cold Harbor, the siege of Petersburg. and the siege of Richmond. The regiment had suffered significant casualties in these engagements. Two members of the regiment had been awarded the Medal of Honor for their actions at Cold Harbor.[976]

Nevertheless, the Twenty-Fifth Massachusetts had much in common with the provost guard unit. The Minnesota troops quickly discovered that the Massachusetts officers were the classic "paper collar" soldiers who seemed far too concerned about appearance and regulations. "They were all for style and held us, who paid little attention to such things, in contempt" recalled George Cambell.[977]

The Eighth Minnesota had plenty of combat experience and little patience for being told what to do by some other regiment's stuffy officer. As a result, they had plenty of fun when the officer of the day for the brigade was assigned to an officer from the Massachusetts regiment.

The officer of the day was usually drawn from the field officers of the brigade, a major or above, although senior captains might serve in this capacity. The position rotated between the field officers of each regiment within the brigade.

An officer of the day served for a twenty-four-hour period during which he was responsible for a variety of matters. He was expected to visit all areas of the camp once or twice during each shift and make sure the camp was properly policed (cleaned and sanitary). In addition, the officer of the day would see that the drill and instruction schedule was followed by the troops, that the guards were at their posts and knew the signs and countersigns, and just about all other aspects of maintaining order and discipline within the camp.[978]

In camp at Charlotte, the men in Company E were appalled at how the officers of the day treated the troops from the younger regiments, or "yearlings" as the soldiers called them.[979] "As the war was over, we thought we were almost citizens again and were dead against this 'regular army business' as we called it, so we put the boys up to a thing or two."[980]

George Cambell described the games the men played with the officers of the day:

> One night the officer of the guard was around, trying to catch a victim. He came upon one of the guards who had been posted. The latter pretended not to know the officer, took him for a suspi-

---

976   James L. Bowen, *Massachusetts in the War: 1861-1865*, Springfield, Mass., Clark W. Bryan & Co., 1889, 382-392.

977   Cambell, *Personal Reminiscences*, 96.

978   Butterfield, *Camp and Outpost Duty for Infantry*, 58-64.

979   Cambell, *Personal Reminiscences*, 97.

980   Ibid.

cious character, halted him, made him mark time, wouldn't take
the counter-sign, pretending it was not the right one, and sent for
the Sergeant of the Guard...[981]

The sergeant of the guard in this case was from the Eighth Minnesota. Of course, he could not be found so the increasingly perturbed officer of the day was left to cool his heels for a good hour, much to the guard's amusement.

The men also targeted the regiment's sutler. The sutler was a civilian under license with the military to sell goods to the soldiers of a particular unit. The soldiers could buy a variety of items from writing materials to foodstuffs. Sutlers had to be mobile to follow the unit as it moved so they often sold goods out of a tent or wagon.

It is important to remember that the Eighth Minnesota generally had a very low opinion of vendors who sold goods to the army. The men believed that vendors were out to cheat the army and the soldiers any chance they could get. Company E's experience with hay suppliers at Paynesville and the arrest of Major Camp for standing up to the dishonest coffee vendors at Martinsburg, West Virginia reinforced this conception.

The Eighth Minnesota's sutler set up his large tent in the camp at Charlotte. He did brisk business with those freed slaves who had money—not Confederate currency, which was all but worthless, but those that had actual gold coin.

In addition to his other wares, the sutler got his hands on some barrels of whiskey and began selling it to the Eighth Minnesota soldiers out of his tent. This was strictly against orders. He was also probably selling the whiskey at inflated prices. According to George Cambell, some of the soldiers decided to take the initiative and punish the sutler for this offense.[982]

One of the soldiers set up his tent next to the sutler's large tent near the barrel of liquor. When the sutler was otherwise distracted, the soldier tapped the opposite end of the barrels and began doing business out of his own tent.[983] George Cambell noted that "Before the sutler found it out, he had lost money."[984]

Some sutlers were outright dishonest, which could be dangerous if the soldiers found out. George Cambell described one incident where soldiers of another regiment took revenge on their dishonest sutler: "One day, a couple hundred formed a kind of mob, charged on his tent, ran through it, and in two minutes had a fire and were getting their supper on the site of that tent."[985]

---

981 Ibid., 97-98.

982 Ibid., 94.

983 Ibid., 95.

984 Ibid.,

985 Ibid.

A Growing Resentment

Perhaps it was not surprising that the common soldiers would take out their frustrations on officers and vendors. The initial exhilaration the men experienced at the end of the war soon gave way to growing resentment as they waited to be mustered out. Days turned to weeks and weeks to months without any orders regarding their disposition and long anticipated trip home.

When there was a lack of news, as was the case regarding the Eighth Minnesota's fate in the early spring of 1865, rumor tended to fill the void. Every day that passed without being sent home bred more anger within the Eighth Minnesota. There was a general sentiment that they should have been sent home in early May. Now, they were just sitting around awaiting their time to muster out. Thomas Hodgson recalled that "It had become tedious to do military duty, we were anxious to get home and to continue the routine of military life became exceedingly irksome."[986]

Watching other "yearling" troops being sent home further inflamed the tempers of the troops in the Eighth Minnesota. The two Ohio regiments in the Third Brigade, the 174th and 178th were due to be mustered out at the end of June 1865, even though they had been in the service less than eight months. Meanwhile, the Eighth Minnesota, which had been formed in 1862, traveled thousands of miles in the past year, and had served nobly in a variety of extreme conditions, was forced to sit in North Carolina.

To add insult to injury, regiments mustered in on or before October 1, 1862, were all being sent home promptly. The Eighth Minnesota was mustered in on October 2, 1862, one day too late. As a result, they were told they had to stay in the army for the time being.

These perceived injustices further bred resentment towards the army among the men of the Eighth Minnesota. Discipline quickly began to suffer. "It was hard for the officers to maintain order and there was constant danger of insurrection."[987]

By the end of June, even William Houlton was getting irate. He wrote a letter to his father stating: "We feel it a great injustice and the boys are getting very indignant, but a private solder has no protection or redress."[988]

Charlie Gibbs wrote home on the same day as Houlton. "We had all made up our minds to go home soon and now to be disappointed makes most of the men

---

986 Hodgson, "Recollections of the Sioux War No. 32," *Dakota County Tribune*, May 7, 1891.

987 Ibid.

988 William Houlton to his father, Charlotte, North Carolina, June 26, 1865, Houlton Papers.

ready to do most anything."[989] He thought that if the soldiers in Company E got paid as they were supposed to, they would immediately start out for home on their own.

Some soldiers placed the blame on their officers. Thomas Hodgson of Company F later wrote:

> It was believed in the ranks that the officials were enjoying their pay and their rank and were loathe to give them up. Hence, they were not trying to have us returned to Minnesota.[990]

Other soldiers directed their anger higher up, at the War Department in Washington. Charlie Gibbs expressed his feelings on the matter:

> I wish we could have Old Stanton [Edwin Stanton, the secretary of war] here and every soldier that wanted to could kick his posterior once as hard as he wanted to. I would bet that I would either lift him or break a leg.[991]

Further adding to the misery were letters from home with news of all the other soldiers returning from the war. William Houlton, for example, received a letter from Albert Barker, who had been discharged on account of the wounds he received in the fight at Murfreesboro. Several members of unit had been discharged early due to wounds or other disability. Barker reported on all the Company E men who had already returned to Monticello. "We can raise quite a squad of Co 'E' here in town."[992]

Despite the resentment and anger over the injustice of being stationed in Charlotte when it seemed everyone else was going home, Company E and the rest of the Eighth Minnesota did their duty—not without grumbling and complaint, but they did it, at least to a point.

> "I will not do duty after the 14th of Aug. next. I will be put in irons first. I enlisted to serve the United States for 3 years and on Aug 14th about 9 a.m. that time is up and I will not do any more for him as a soldier after that date."[993]

---

989 Charlie Gibbs to his sister, Charlotte, North Carolina, June 26, 1865, Gibbs Family Papers, Wright County Historical Society.

990 Hodgson, "Recollections of the Sioux War No. 32," *Dakota County Tribune*, May 7, 1891.

991 Charlie Gibbs to his sister, Charlotte, North Carolina, June 26, 1865, Gibbs Family Papers.

992 Albert Barker to William Houlton, Monticello, July 2, 1865, Houlton Papers.

993 Charlie Gibbs to his sister, Charlotte, North Carolina, June 26, 1865, Gibbs Family Papers.

Homeward Bound

On July 6, 1865, the Eighth Minnesota finally received the news they had long awaited. A major arrived with the paperwork and instructions to muster out the regiment.[994] For the next few days the men went through the discharge process, finishing the paperwork and packing their equipment.

The Eighth Minnesota soon was ready to ship out for home. The final part of the mustering out process was scheduled to take place at Fort Snelling, where they would turn in their equipment and settle with the paymaster.

Traveling from Charlotte back to Fort Snelling was to be long and circuitous. From Charlotte, the Eighth Minnesota would take a train north through Virginia to City Point, which was located at the confluence of the Appomattox and James Rivers outside Richmond. From there, the regiment would travel by steamer to Baltimore and then by rail until it reached LaCrosse, Wisconsin. The last leg of the journey would be by riverboat up the Mississippi River to St. Paul.

On July 10, 1865, the men packed up and set out for the nearby Charlotte train depot. Before they did so however, the men rounded up all their comrades who were in hospital so the entire Eighth Minnesota could go home together. "We were bound to take them home dead or alive." recalled George Cambell.[995]

As they left, the men gave everything they didn't need or couldn't carry to the freed blacks who were camped around them.[996] At the depot, the men sat around waiting for the train. And they waited. No train appeared.

At the end of the day, the troops were forced to march back to their campground. Having given away much of their gear, apparently including the tents, lodging that night was not comfortable. George Cambell recalled "We stuck up some kind of shelter on the ground which we hoped we had seen the last of."[997]

The following morning, the Eighth Minnesota marched back down to the train depot with the band playing a popular rallying song of the Civil War, "The Battle Cry of Freedom."[998]

---

994 Paxson, *Diary*, July 6, 1865. Folsom took over for Major Camp, who resigned his commission in May and returned to Minneapolis.

995 Cambell, *Personal Reminiscences*, 101.

996 Ibid., 100.

997 Ibid.

998 Paxson, *Diary*, July 11, 1865. Paxson recorded in his diary that the band played "Union Forever" but there does not appear to be a song by that name from the era. It appears he was mistaken in the title and meant a different song, "The Battle Cry of Freedom." This song was extremely popular with the soldiers and played by most regimental bands throughout the war. The chorus begins with the lyrics "The Union Forever!"

We'll rally once again,
Shouting the battle cry of Freedom,
We will rally from the hillside,
We'll gather from the plain,
Shouting the battle cry of Freedom.
CHORUS:

The Union forever,
Hurrah! boys, hurrah!
Down with the traitors,
Up with the stars;
While we rally round the flag, boys,
Rally once again,
Shouting the battle cry of Freedom.[999]

When the regiment arrived at the depot there was great relief, for at long last, the train that would take them home for good was waiting. The only problem was that there were not enough rail cars. The train consisted of only freight cars, both boxes and flats.[1000] As a result, the soldiers had to take every available space, both inside and out.

George Cambell, along with many other soldiers, had to ride on the roof of one of the box cars. This was a rather precarious way to travel as the southern railroads were in very rough shape and it was a rocky ride. There was a very real risk of falling off the roof as the train was moving. To keep from falling, the men on the roof took precautions. "The way we did it was to lock arms across the center of the car with our baggage piled up on the ridge, then if we liked we could go to sleep and not fall off" recalled Cambell.[1001]

As the train moved along, the roof of the car on which Cambell was traveling began to sag under the weight of the soldiers. Those traveling inside the car saw the roof was in danger of collapsing upon them, so they fixed bayonets on their rifles and used them much like jacks to keep the roof stable.

Holding up the roof with a Springfield rifle and bayonet proved too fatiguing so the men in the car shouted up to the roof that they were not going to do it any

999   Lyrics retrieved from https://www.battlefields.org/learn/primary-sources/civil-war-music-battle-cry-freedom, accessed Jan. 1, 2020.

1000 Cambell, *Personal Reminiscences*, 101.

1001 Ibid.

longer. Those on the roof responded to go ahead, after all "we would still be on top if we fell in."[1002]

To lessen the weight on the roof of the box car, some of the men disbursed to the roof of a passenger car that had been added to the end of the train for the officers. Soon it became apparent that the roof of the passenger car was also weak, much to the apprehension of the officers, "who had no wish to come home in a disabled condition."[1003]

The train carrying the Eighth Minnesota slowly moved north from Charlotte, reaching Danbury on the night of July 11, where it paused until morning. The following day, the train set out again along the ill-maintained tracks.

Suddenly, and for the third time since the regiment had left Fort Snelling the previous October, the train derailed. One of the freight cars had jumped the tracks. This time, the men were in a hurry to go home and would not tolerate any delay. The solders jumped off the train, disconnected the car and rolled it down an embankment so it would be out of the way. Then they coupled up the remaining cars and off they went.

Shortly before reaching City Point, the Eighth Minnesota's train passed Petersburg, the scene of heaving fighting during the last year of the war. The soldiers on the train had read accounts of the Siege of Petersburg, as that battle would come to be called, and were curious to see the scene of the fighting. Some of the soldiers had chosen to travel on the roof of the cars just so they could view the sight, including George Cambell.

Nothing in the Eighth Minnesota's service so far had prepared them for the scene that awaited them at Petersburg. The regiment had participated in hard fighting, but not in any large-scale battles. Nor had it passed through any of those battlefields. They had seen the old Stone's River battlefield outside Murfreesboro, but that was fought in the country, not so much in the city.

Petersburg was different from anything the men had seen to date. As the train passed through the town late on the afternoon of July 12, the soldiers were shocked by the devastation that lay before them. "On every side was the wreck caused by war; fences burned, houses destroyed, etc."[1004]

As dusk approached, the train arrived at City Point, which had been Grant's headquarters during the Siege of Petersburg. There, the Eighth Minnesota left the train and boarded a steamship for the trip down the James River.

1002 Ibid., 102.

1003 Ibid.

1004 Ibid., 103.

As the troops were being fed their supper aboard the ship, they were startled by a small explosion and burst of steam.[1005] Something had gone wrong with the ship's propulsion system. Irked by another delay in their trip home, the troops were marched ashore while another ship was found to take the regiment to Baltimore.[1006]

Fortunately for the Eighth Minnesota, the wait was a short one. A new steamship was quickly arranged for the regiment, which boarded after only a short delay, and they traveled through the night. Shortly after dawn, it reached Hampton, Virginia, where it would exit the James and then travel north up Chesapeake Bay to Baltimore.

As the ship neared Fort Monroe at mouth of the James River shortly after daylight, the men were greeting with an amazing and chaotic sight. George Cambell described what he saw in the waters near the fort:

> *There were a great many boats on their way to Baltimore or other northern points lying there, loaded with soldiers and they were continually cheering or being cheered. It was, "Home boys;" "The war is over;" "Hard tack no more;" "No more drill;" "Shoulder straps to the -----;" and all such cries, and we were as happy as big sunflowers you might say. I don't suppose any of us will ever see so active a scene.[1007]*

Fort Monroe sat at the southern tip of the Virginia Peninsula, where it guarded the entrance to Chesapeake Bay and the mouth of the James River. It had been heavily fortified after the fall of Fort Sumter and remained in Union hands throughout the war. The Eighth Minnesota's ship paused at the fort for part of the day.

Some of the soldiers had time to go ashore and take a tour of the fort. They were astonished at the size of the artillery defenses. The twelve-inch guns were so large that George Cambell observed that he could almost have crawled inside them.[1008]

As they wandered around Fort Monroe, the Eighth Minnesota visitors were probably unaware that they were within yards of perhaps the man they most blamed for the war, none other than former Confederate President Jefferson Davis. Davis was at the time imprisoned within Fort Monroe. He had been brought there a couple of months earlier, shortly after he was captured by Union troops in Georgia on May 10.

1005 Ibid., 105.

1006 Ibid.

1007 Ibid., 105-106

1008 Ibid., 106.

After the short break at Fort Monroe, the steamship sailed on to Baltimore, arriving late at night on July 13. The troops spent the following day in camp, where they were fed hot meals and had a chance to rest. At 11 p.m. that night, the Eighth Minnesota boarded a train of the Baltimore and Ohio Railroad for the trip west.[1009]

For the next two days the regiment traveled slowing along the railroad until they reached Pittsburg, Pennsylvania. There, on an otherwise rainy miserable day, the regiment disembarked and were treated to a memorable dinner given by the citizens of the town. When they were done, the soldiers gave three cheers for the people of Pittsburg, re-boarded the train, and continued their journey west through Ohio.[1010]

On July 17, the regiment reached Chicago, where they disembarked and enjoyed supper at the Soldier's Rest Camp near the station. The meal included one exciting delicacy for the men on a hot July day: ice cream.

After spending a comfortable night in Chicago, the Eighth Minnesota again loaded up for the next leg of their journey to LaCrosse, Wisconsin. The regiment reached LaCrosse early in the morning of July 19. The steamboat *Keokuk* was waiting there to take them on the final leg of their journey back to Fort Snelling. It was at this point the soldiers really considered themselves to be almost home.[1011]

Keokuk steamed slowly up the Mississippi River until it reached St. Paul at about 2:00 in the afternoon on July 20. When the boat arrived at the landing, the troops were joyously received by the local citizens with cheering and cannonading.[1012]

The people of St. Paul turned out in great numbers to greet the returning troops. They had prepared a joyous welcome home event for the Eighth Minnesota. After disembarking from the boat, the regiment marched about a mile from the riverboat landing up to the capitol, where the ladies of the city furnished them with a sumptuous dinner, which the soldiers devoured with relish. In addition to this luxury, the mayor and governor were also on hand to deliver speeches to welcome the troops home.[1013]

While the men thoroughly enjoyed the reception, they were anxious to keep moving so they could finish the mustering out process and say their goodbyes at Fort Snelling. Parting would not be easy, as each unit had formed strong bonds amongst themselves. They were accustomed to the companionship within their close-knit units and could rely on each other. As one soldier from Company E of the Eighth

1009 Ibid., 108. The Baltimore and Ohio Railroad is well-known to players of the board game Monopoly as the "B&O" is one of the four railroad squares listed on the playing field.

1010 Paxson, *Diary*, July 16, 1865.

1011 Cambell, *Personal Reminiscences*, 108.

1012 Paxson, *Diary*, July 20, 1865.

1013 *Saint Cloud Democrat*, July 27, 1865.

Minnesota later wrote, "Army life is a crucial test of character and the friendships formed there were very very strong among manly men."[1014]

Finally, the regiment's commander, Brevet General Minor Thomas, gave a short speech to the assembly and expressed on behalf of the men their heartfelt gratitude for the greeting and refreshments offered by the people of St. Paul. Then, the men formed up and marched back to the levee to board the boat for the short trip to Fort Snelling.

When the troops arrived back at that steamboat levee, they were met by the mustering officer. He told the men that there was no room for them at Fort Snelling and that they were all granted furlough. They could go home and stay there until summoned by the army to return at a later date. Then they could settle their accounts and finally muster out.

And just like that, with no fanfare, pomp or ceremony, the Eighth Minnesota disbursed. The soldiers were left to go their separate ways. They said their quick goodbyes and set off for home. It was an anti-climactic end to the defining time of their lives.

Edson Washburn later wrote that the speeches at the capitol that day expressed Minnesota's thanks for "our little part in that great war that resulted in the freedom of 4,000,000 slaves, saving the Union undivided and the Flag unsullied."[1015] While the outcome of the war may not have depended on the Eighth Minnesota, Washburn's humble statement does not give enough credit to the service of his unit. It may not have been as famous as other Minnesota regiments, nor did it participate in the most historic battles of the Civil War. Nevertheless, the Eighth Minnesota had a remarkable story to tell about its time in the service of its country.

Return to Civilian Life

By the time the Eighth Minnesota went into camp at Charlotte many of the men were ill. Weakened by harsh conditions, poor nutrition, and lack of sleep, the soldiers were more susceptible to disease. Dysentery and other debilitating bacterial infections were common. Many of the soldiers could no longer function and went into the camp hospital.

Some had been so sick that the army released them early. Clay Helm, for example, came down with typhoid fever while Company E was camped at Wheat Swamp. When he was well enough, the army shipped him home. Helm made it back to Mon-

---

1014 William Houlton, *Autobiography*, 46.

1015 Washburn, *Autobiography*, 7.

ticello on June 30. By then, however, he had fully recovered and was described by Albert Barker, who had also been discharged early, as "looking first rate."[1016]

While the regiment was stationed in Charlotte the rest and improved food rations gradually led to improved health for the men. By the end of June 1865, all of Company E was out of the hospital with one exception: Private Elisha Sabin of Company E, who had been suffering various illnesses for months, contracted typhoid fever while in camp at Charlotte.

In a letter to his father on June 27, 1865, William Houlton wrote that Sabin was getting better and to "Tell Mrs. Sabin not to worry as he has good care..."[1017] Tragically, Elisha Sabin took a turn for the worse and died of typhoid at Charlotte only a week before the Eighth Minnesota left for home.

Despite the improving health of the regiment, some of the soldiers returned from the army in rough shape physically. Edson Washburn was one of those so afflicted. He had been suffering from dysentery off and on throughout his time in the army. The dysentery had recurred while the regiment was camped at Charlotte. By the time Washburn stepped off the *Keokuk* in St. Paul he weighed only ninety-two pounds and was very weak. He had trouble walking even a short distance.

With the excitement of being furloughed at the riverboat landing, Washburn somehow found the strength to travel from St. Paul to Minneapolis, probably by rail, and then walk the ten or so blocks from the depot to his sister's house on Hennepin Avenue in what is now Downtown Minneapolis. There, his legs gave out entirely and he was taken to bed with a high fever.

Washburn spent the next four weeks in bed at his sister's home, where she gradually nursed him back to health. Despite the toll the army took on his health, Washburn had no regrets for his nearly three years of soldiering.[1018]

One other member of Company E returned very sick from North Carolina. Private William Bazley had been seriously ill while in Charlotte, perhaps either with severe dysentery or some other infection. Bazley received an early discharge on June 12, 1865. He returned to Monticello but never recovered his health. He died from the illness on October 14, 1865 and was buried in Monticello.

The rest of Company E was reasonably healthy after their return from the south. None seemed to waste time getting on with their lives.

The Rest of Their Lives: 1866-1931

1016 Albert Barker to William Houlton, Monticello, July 2, 1865, Houlton Papers.

1017 William Houlton to his father, June 27, 1865, Houlton Papers.

1018 Washburn, *Autobiography*, 7.

When the Civil War ended, most of the soldiers from Company E returned to their families and resumed their pre-war professions. They tried to pick up where they left off when the war intervened in August 1862. Despite the return to normalcy, they were all changed men. There seemed to be a wanderlust among the men that didn't manifest itself immediately after their return. Within a few years, however, a significant number of the Company E veterans worked their way west. Some were seeking cheaper farmland or new business opportunities. Others, in their older years, perhaps were only looking for a comfortable place to retire.

California, Washington, and Oregon were popular destinations. At least eighteen veterans of Company E were living on the West Coast at the time of their death. Others were scattered about the western states, including Colorado, Wyoming, Montana, and Nebraska. Even though some veterans of Company E vowed never to return to Dakota Territory after surviving the brutal conditions during Sully's Expedition during the summer of 1864, several did. The rich farmland of North Dakota was simply too enticing for them to resist. Other Company E veterans had second thoughts about settling in Minnesota after the war. Several, including Captain Brookins, returned to their roots in New England or elsewhere in the east.

A surprising number of Company E veterans went on to play active roles in civic affairs wherever they ended up. Many served in various local government capacities, from village council to county sheriff or recorder of deeds. A few even served in their state legislatures.

The veterans also enthusiastically joined fraternal organizations. Many of the men were already Freemasons before the war or joined during their time in the service. Several more joined the fraternity after they returned. In all, nearly one in three Company E veterans became a Mason at some point in their lives.

Other fraternal organizations were also popular. During the post-war years there were many from which the veterans could choose. The former soldiers often joined organizations such as the Oddfellows or the Grange. Some joined multiple fraternal orders.

The most popular organization for the Civil War veterans all over the country was the Grand Army of the Republic or "G.A.R." The G.A.R. was formed initially as a fraternal organization where veterans could associate with others who had endured the same experiences. It later became a powerful political organization that advocated on behalf of Civil War veterans.

A substantial number of the Company E veterans joined their local G.A.R. Post. Numerous G.A.R. Posts formed throughout Minnesota, including the areas from which Company E drew its volunteers. In Clearwater, for example, A.C. Collins Post No. 112 was formed in 1868 with Charlie Gibbs as its first commander. Seven other members of Company E joined the Clearwater G.A.R. Post besides Gibbs: George Cambell, Dexter Collins, James Lyons, Homer Markham, Matthew Murphy, William Ponsford, and Charles Vorse.

The G.A.R. was an important organization for many veterans. There was a problem, however, in that an organization consisting solely of veterans from one conflict will eventually die out with its members. That's what happened with the G.A.R. The last G.A.R. member and last Union Veteran, Albert Woolson of Duluth, Minnesota, died in 1956.

In a sense, the G.A.R. did not entirely disappear. The work of the G.A.R. was handed off to a successor organization, the Sons of Union Veterans of the Civil War or SUVCW.[1019] The SUVCW continues its work to preserve the memories of those who served in the Civil War.

After seeing the leadership of Freemasons in the officers' ranks during the war and the closeness of those Masons in the ranks, several more veterans of Company E joined Lodges in Minnesota and elsewhere. Masonic Lodges in Anoka, Buffalo, Clearwater, Elk River, and Monticello all had members that were veterans of Company E.

There was so much overlap between the Freemasons and G.A.R. in Clearwater that the local chapters of both organizations built a dual-purpose building in 1888. The west side of the second story was occupied by A.C. Collins Post No. 112 of the G.A.R., while Clearwater Masonic Lodge No. 28 met on the east side.[1020]

Company E was never again all together at the same time in the same place after they left the steamboat levee in St. Paul on that warm July day in 1865. That does not mean they suddenly became strangers. Quite the opposite. Wherever they went and whatever they did with their lives, most veterans of Company E stayed in touch with their comrades. The Company held annual reunions in Monticello on December 7 each year, the anniversary of the battle at Murfreesboro.

The Monticello reunions were relatively small considering the size of the company. Too many had moved away and could not be physically present. Yet even those located half a country away stayed in touch. The veterans who remained in Minnesota sometimes made weeks-long trips to the West Coast visiting their comrades.

The last large gathering of Company E veterans took place on June 25, 1889. That day, Major George Camp and his wife hosted a reunion for the entire Eighth Minnesota. It was a grand all-day affair. Three hundred and fifty veterans of the regiment attended, along with wives and children.

1019 The last True Son of a Civil War veteran died in the late 2010s.

1020 The building still stands. It is on the National Register of Historic Places and is still used by Clearwater Lodge #28. In fact, nearly all of the Masonic Lodges mentioned in this text are still in existence, although none meet in the same buildings used during the Civil War.

At the reunion banquet that night, A.H. Bertram sat to Camp's left. The two had stayed close through their Masonic and G.A.R. activities. Also attending that night were thirty other veterans of Company E, including George Cambell, Edson Washburn, William Houlton, Charlie Gibbs, and Thomas Tollington.

Within a few short years after the 1889 reunion, the ranks of Company E veterans began to thin rapidly. Of the 105 men who served in Company E, only forty were still alive in 1910. The veterans knew that the inevitable march of time would take its toll. William Houlton perhaps best captured the sentiments of the veterans during a speech at one reunion in Monticello:

> Company E was exceptionally fortunate while in service in losing
> so few of its members. So since the war we have been remarkably
> exempt from disease and death, but two or three having died in
> the past 15 years. But it is not in the nature of things for it to con-
> tinue thus. The future will inevitably make wider and wider gaps
> in our ranks. As the years go by we shall meet, but we shall miss
> many who will fail to respond to roll call. But friends, if we each
> yield implicit obedience to the reasonable and loving orders of our
> Great Commander and put our trust in the good God who has so
> kindly guarded and cared for us all these years, we may hereafter
> have a grand reunion which will never end and where not one of
> our number will be missing.[1021]

The last survivor of Company E appears to have been Joseph Reed, who was only seventeen years of age when he joined Company E at Paynesville in 1864. Reed passed away in North Dakota on April 21, 1931. Perhaps then Company E held that long-awaited and celestial grand reunion of which Houlton so elegantly spoke.

1021 Houlton *Speech*.

Post-War Biographies

After being immersed in the tales of those who served in Company E of the Eighth Minnesota Volunteer Infantry Regiment, the reader may be curious as to what happened to these men after the war. Finding information on the soldiers' post-war activities is no easy task. While most of the Company E veterans could be tracked down through newspaper articles, public records, and other sources, a few seemed to simply disappear after the war. Joseph Fisher, for example, left little record of his activities following his discharge. In addition to Fisher, there is almost no record of what became of the following members of Company E:

Samuel Morgan	*John Morgan*	*John Moore*
Samuel Morris	*Thomas Phillips*	*Hugh Reedy*
John Russell	*Samuel Wilder*	

Nevertheless, some information was available about most of the men in Company E, as well as others who played prominent roles in the story. What follows are short post-war biographies of many soldiers mentioned in this book, beginning with the regimental officers, followed by the Company E officers, the Company E enlisted men, and ending with some of the other people mentioned or cited in this book.

Regimental Officers

Colonel Minor T. Thomas

After the war, Brevet Brigadier General Minor T. Thomas returned to his home in Minnesota with the rest of the Eighth Minnesota. He quickly re-engaged in his former profession—civil engineering—which was much in demand as the railroads quickly expanded following the Civil War. He was involved in the construction of the St. Paul and Pacific Railroad, which later became part of the Great Northern Railroad. For the next three decades, Thomas continued to work in civil engineering and moved wherever his work required. He resided at various times in New Orleans, Texas, California, and elsewhere.

Thomas finally returned to Minnesota and settled in the town of Worthington. His malaria, which he was never able to shake entirely, eventually caught up with him. General Minor T. Thomas died from complications of malaria while visiting Minneapolis on October 2, 1897 at the age of sixty-seven. His remains were sent to his birthplace in Indiana, where he was buried in the family plot.

Lieutenant Colonel Henry Rogers

Henry Rogers never fully recovered from the bullet wound that shattered his arm during the battle along Wilkinson Pike on December 7, 1864. He was discharged from the service because of his wounds on May 15, 1865. Rogers, however, chose not to retire from public life. That same year he ran for and was elected as the Minnesota Secretary of State. He won reelection in 1867 and continued to serve in that position until 1870, when he was appointed U.S. Pension agent for the state of Minnesota. Rogers lived in constant pain from the wound he suffered in the service of his country. He died of complications from his war wound on May 18, 1871. He was only thirty-seven years old.

Major George Camp.

Major George Camp resigned his commission on May 2, 1865 and returned to Minnesota. He resumed work in the lumbering business and also served as state surveyor-general for almost ten years. In 1871, he entered a partnership with Thomas B. Walker, a fellow Mason and lumberman. The partners purchased pine lands in the north and later entered the manufacturing business. The business, known as "Camp and Walker," proved successful and made both men quite wealthy. George Camp retired from the business in the 1880s, after which he spent his summers at his home on Lake Minnetonka in Minnesota and the winters in California.

George Camp stayed active in various Masonic organizations and served as Junior Warden in the Grand Lodge of Minnesota. He also used his wealth for philanthropy. In 1888, he donated land on Lake Minnetonka for the construction of a church. He then engaged the noted architect Cass Gilbert to design the building. Cass Gilbert's works still stand out and include the Minnesota State Capitol Building in St. Paul, the U.S. Supreme Court building in Washington D.C., and the George Washington Bridge in New York. The church donated by George A. Camp remains in use today and is known as St. Martin's by-the-Lake.

George A. Camp passed away from heart failure on May 4, 1892, several months after the death of his beloved wife. However, George was not alone in his last days. Alfred Brackett, commander of Brackett's Battalion during the 1864 Indian Campaign was at his bedside, as well as former regimental surgeon and Brother Mason Dr. John H. Murphy, his old business partner Thomas B. Walker, and many other old friends. So many people wanted to pay their respects at his funeral that a special train had to be run from St. Paul through Minneapolis to the service at Minnetonka Beach. James J. Hill, builder of the Great Northern Railroad headed up the pall bearers, among whom were Thomas B. Walker and Dr. John H. Murphy. Many soldiers who had served under Major Camp in the Eighth Minnesota attended, including Andrew Bertram, David Kingsbury, and William Eberman from Company E.

On a side note, while George A. Camp left behind the legacy of St. Martin's By-the-Lake, his business partner left a more widely known legacy. Thomas B. Walker and his wife began using their vast wealth to acquire a wide range of artworks for their house. The Walkers eventually began to open their house to members of the public so they too could enjoy the art as well. Eventually, the Walkers built a gallery to house their considerable art collection and made it available to the public. Today, that institution is still operating as the world-famous Walker Art Center in Minneapolis.

Dr. John H. Murphy

The popular regimental surgeon, Dr. John H. Murphy, was unable to accompany the Eighth Minnesota when it left Fort Snelling for the south, due to the wounds he suffered in the encounter with the mightily perturbed bull buffalo on the Dakota plains. He resigned from the army on January 12, 1865, but did eventually make a full recovery. Dr. Murphy continued to practice medicine and was heavily involved in a variety of Masonic, medical, and civic organizations, including the G.A.R.

DR. JOHN H. MURPHY

Dr. Murphy died in St. Paul on January 31, 1894. He touched so many lives and was so well-respected that every seat in the church was full for his funeral and more than 1,000 mourners were unable to gain admission. The funeral attendees included delegations of Masons from across the state, current and former governors, and various other state dignitaries.[1022]

Company E Officers

Captain Edward Hartley

Company E's first captain, Edward Hartley, resigned his commission shortly after the rest of the company voted him out. Although Edward Hartley did not make a good company combat officer, he was a skilled attorney and took an interest in civic affairs. It appears that he left Minnesota and went to Washington D.C., where he served as a special aid to President Abraham Lincoln.

After the war, he returned to his hometown of Portland, Maine, and practiced law until the mid-1880s, when he moved with his family to Mount Vernon, New York, only a few miles north of Manhattan. There, he continued to practice law and entered various business ventures.

Hartley became one of the wealthiest men in Mount Vernon and gave some of it back to the community. He donated five acres of land so the city could build a park. In 1915, he spent $1,500, a considerable amount at the time, to build a fountain in the park near the corner of Crary and Oakland avenues. Edward Hartley died in Mount Vernon on May 18, 1918, at the age of eighty-two.

Hartley's legacy can still be found in Mount Vernon, New York. The appropriately named Hartley Park was recently renovated and the fountain he built is still there. There is also a street in Mount Vernon that bears his name, Hartley Avenue. Despite the respect he earned in his adopted home of Mount Vernon, the humiliation of being voted out of his captain position by his men at Fort Ripley must have remained a bad memory. He may have wanted to forget his ties to Minnesota and Company E altogether. His obituary, for example, makes no mention of his life in

---

1022 *St. Paul Globe*, Feb. 4, 1894.

Minnesota or the prominent role he played in the early days of Monticello. The obituary merely states that he served with the Minnesota volunteers.

Captain Harvey S. Brookins

After being severely wounded at Murfreesboro, Captain Harvey S. Brookins was transferred to a hospital in Washington D.C. There, he made a slow but steady recovery. He was discharged from the Army on account of his wounds in mid-May of 1865. Brookins initially planned to head north to his hometown in Vermont for further recovery but was unexpectedly offered an appointment as a clerk in the Treasury Department.[1023] It proved to be a timely and convenient job. It required only light duty and relatively short hours, which helped in his recovery.

In 1866, Brookins resigned his position at the Treasury Department and returned to Shoreham, Vermont, his hometown. There, he married and took up farming. He also remained engaged in civic affairs, serving as town constable and other local offices. In 1876, Brookins was elected to the legislature on the Republican ticket. He remained active in the local Masonic Lodge and G.A.R. for the rest of his life.[1024] He continued to stay in touch with the men he commanded in Company E. Harvey S. Brookins passed away at his home in Shoreham, Vermont on September 1, 1907, at the age of seventy-three.[1025]

First Lieutenant Micah Croswell

Micah Croswell resigned from Company E shortly after Edward Hartley. He was then promoted on March 27, 1863 to Captain, Commissary of Subsistence (COS). He served in in that capacity during the 1863 expedition against the Indians led by General Sibley. Croswell was later assigned Chief of COS in Milwaukee until May 1864. After that, he spent the remainder of the war in Arkansas as Chief of COS until mustered out in 1866. He rose to the rank of Brevet Lieutenant Colonel. After being discharged, Croswell moved to California and lived there until his death on April 10, 1913.

First Lieutenant Thomas Tollington

1023 It should be noted that Edward Hartley's father was chief clerk in the Treasury Department at the time, having been appointed by Samuel Chase in 1863. It is possible that Edward Hartley, who had been serving Lincoln in Washington, arranged for Brookins' appointment.

1024 Jacob G. Ullery, *Men of Vermont: An Illustrated Biographical Story of Vermonters and Sons of Vermont*, Battleboro, VT, Transcript Publishing Company, 1894, 44.

1025 *Middlebury Register* (Vermont), Sept. 6, 1907, 10.

Late in the war, Thomas Tollington was rewarded for his leadership of the company after Brookins was wounded with a promotion to brevet captain. When the war ended, Tollington returned to his family in Clearwater. In 1866 he became a partner in a sawmill started in 1860 by Seth Gibbs, father of Company E member Charlie Gibbs. The partnership of "Gibbs & Tollington" operated the sawmill and furniture factory until Seth Gibbs was killed in a gruesome mill accident in 1874. After Gibbs' death, Tollington carried on the business in his own name.

Tollington expanded his business operations in Clearwater over the years to include retail furniture and even sold caskets and undertakers' equipment. He and his wife Sarah raised two children and spent the rest of their lives in Clearwater.

Thomas Tollington was an active member of both the Clearwater Masonic Lodge and the G.A.R. post. He also served in the Minnesota Veterans Association as president of the Eighth Minnesota reunion committee in 1904. Thomas Tollington died in Clearwater on December 8, 1910 at the age of seventy-seven and was buried in Acacia Cemetery just outside of the village.

Company E Enlisted Men

Albright, John

John Albright moved to Missouri after the war and lived there for several years. Later, he relocated farther west to Washington, where he spent the rest of his life. Albright died in Washington on August 4, 1907, at the age of sixty-seven.

Ambler, James

James Ambler, like so many of his comrades, returned to work as a farmer after his discharge. He farmed just outside of Buffalo with his wife and two daughters. Ambler passed away on April 27, 1900, at the age of seventy-three.

Anderson, Thomas

Private Thomas Anderson was left behind at the hospital in Murfreesboro after being seriously wounded during the action on December 7, 1864. He never was able to return to the Eighth Minnesota and army records are unclear regarding when he was discharged. In all likelihood, he was discharged early on account of his wounds and returned home in May or June of 1865. There he reunited with his wife and nine-year-old son at their farm outside of Monticello. Anderson farmed there until his death on July 14, 1889 at the age of sixty-nine. He was buried in Riverside Cemetery at Monticello.

Barker, Albert

Albert Barker was wounded during the regiment's engagement at Murfreesboro and discharged in the spring of 1865. He returned to Monticello, where he married and entered the furniture business. In September 1865, he was appointed Monticello Postmaster. The following year, he was elected clerk of the district court, a position which he filled for the next four years. He and his wife raised five children at their home in Monticello. Albert Barker died there on October 25, 1893 at the age of fifty-seven.

Batterberry, Michael (Batterbury)

While he was stationed at Paynesville in 1863 to 1864, Private Michael Batterberry put in a homestead claim for an acreage just about five miles to the west, in Burbank Township, Kandiyohi County. When he returned from the war, he moved his family onto this claim and commenced farming. He and his wife Hannah raised several children on that farm. Batterberry remained on the same farm for the rest of his long life. He died on March 18, 1913, at the age of eighty-two.

Bazley, William

Private William Bazley had been seriously ill while in Charlotte. As a result, Bazley received an early discharge on June 12, 1865. He returned to his home in St. Anthony, which was across the Mississippi River from Minneapolis.[1026] Unfortunately, his health never recovered. He died from the illness on October 14, 1865 and was buried in the Minneapolis Pioneers and Soldiers Memorial Cemetery. He was thirty-five years old at the time of his death.

Bertram, Andrew Hamilton

When Andrew "A.H." Bertram returned to Monticello he immediately took up farming. If the accidental killing of his friend Christopher Bailey weighed on his conscience after the war, he never let it show. His comrades did not blame him for Bailey's death and no written materials after the war mention that it was Bertram who shot Bailey.

In 1866, Bertram married Clara Bryant and together they raised four children on their farm by Monticello. Known by his initials, "A.H.," after the war, he was not only a successful farmer but also was deeply involved in a number of civic and philanthropic organizations. He remained an active Freemason in Monticello Lodge No. 16

1026 St. Anthony became part of the City of Minneapolis in 1872.

WILLIAM LANE AND ANDREW H. BERTRAM CA. 1900.

and served in a leadership role with the G.A.R. in Minnesota.

Bertram filled various positions with state agricultural organizations. He served as secretary of the Minnesota State Dairy Commission and was an officer in the Minnesota State Agricultural Society. He was also active in politics. For a time, he was the engrossing clerk of the Minnesota State Senate and briefly served as sergeant at arms during an impeachment proceeding in the same body. In 1884, Bertram was a delegate to the Republican National Convention in Chicago, which was the last Republican convention that refused to nominate a sitting president, Chester Arthur.

Unfortunately for Bertram, he contracted tuberculosis, which at the time was an incurable and usually fatal disease. He was sick for several years until it finally took his life on Christmas Eve in 1904. He was buried at Riverside Cemetery in Monticello.

Bloomer, Coleman

Private Coleman Bloomer was one of the last to enlist in Company E of the Eighth Minnesota. He joined the company in February 1864, only months before the regiment set out on Sully's Expedition. Bloomer was one of the very few members of Company E who were not from the Wright County area. He enlisted at St. Paul but lived in Morristown, which was about sixty miles south of the Twin Cities.

When the regiment was discharged, Bloomer returned to his wife and children at Morristown and got back to the work of farming. Sadly, Bloomer's young wife died the next year leaving him a widower with two small children. In 1867, Coleman Bloomer remarried. He and his new wife had five more children. Bloomer stayed on his farm near Morristown for the rest of his life. He passed away on February 9, 1914, at the age of eighty.

Bradbury, Edward

Private Edward Bradbury left Minnesota shortly after the war. He worked as fruit farmer in Illinois, where he married Amanda Gay in 1872. Later, the Bradbury's moved to California. There, he worked as a fruit farmer and orchardist at Santa Clara in what is now the heart of Silicon Valley. He died after a long illness on March 13, 1923, at the age of seventy-nine.

Bradley, James F.

James F. Bradley left Company E on November 16, 1863, for promotion to captain of Company F, 102nd Infantry, U.S. Colored Troops. He served with the 102nd in South Carolina until his discharge on September 30, 1865. In recognition of his service in that regiment, he was honored with promotion to Brevet Major in 1866.

After the war, Bradley moved his family from Minneapolis to Chicago, where he engaged in the insurance business until the 1871 Great Chicago Fire burned his establishment to the ground. He then moved the family west to Salt Lake City, Utah. There he took land claims and started in the mining business. He also published a newspaper, which he used to express his strong political views. Like most of those men who enlisted in Company E of the Eighth Minnesota, Bradley was an ardent Republican. In addition to his publication and mining endeavors, he served as a justice of the peace in Salt Lake City. He died in Salt Lake City, Utah on June 16, 1895, at the age of seventy-five.

Braughton, Henry

Henry Braughton was another Company E veteran who decided to travel west after the war. He left Minnesota and migrated to Salem, Oregon. He died there on July 22, 1915, at the age of eighty-five.

Brown, Milton

Milton "Milt" Brown quickly recovered after accidentally shooting himself in the head during the fall of 1863 while stationed at Paynesville. He stayed with Company E until the end of the war. After leaving the army he bought a farm near Anoka and married Sarah Kelly. Together they raised three children. Brown suffered from digestive trouble for much of his life. In 1892, his gut troubles took a turn for the worse. For twenty-eight days Milton subsisted on nothing but morphine and water until he died on September 8, 1892, at only fifty years of age.

Bryant, Alonzo

Alonzo Bryant recovered from the wounds he sustained during the battle at Murfreesboro. He returned home and began farming. He married in 1869. He and his wife had eight children. Bryant was active in the G.A.R. and attended the organization's national encampment that was held in Minnesota. Bryant farmed near Monticello for the rest of his life. He died on November 29, 1908. He was sixty-four years old.

Cambell, George Thompson

GEORGE AND MARTHA CAMBELL AT ABOUT THE TIME OF THEIR MARRIAGE IN 1866.

Upon his return to Clearwater, George Cambell went back to work as a carpenter and mechanic in the local mills. Several months later, George married his sweetheart, Martha Whittemore. Together they raised two daughters.

George joined A.C. Collins Post No. 112 in Clearwater but didn't seem otherwise interested in civic or benevolent organizations. In the 1880s he took a job with the Great Northern Railroad as a tie inspector. With the new job, Cambell moved the family twelve miles north to St. Cloud near the banks of the Mississippi River.

Cambell rarely spoke to his children of his service in the Civil and Indian Wars. It was about the time that his brother-in-law and fellow Company E veteran Charlie Gibbs died in 1890 that Cambell was motivated to sit down to write a reminiscence for his daughters. The result is a detailed and often humorous account of Company E's exploits.

George Cambell passed away in 1903 at the age of sixty-eight after suffering for weeks from "an anemic condition of the blood."[1027] Cambell was laid to rest in Acacia Cemetery near Clearwater, just a few feet from his close friend and brother-in-law Charlie Gibbs.

Carpenter, George Washington

Corporal George Carpenter returned to his wife and children at their farm near Silver Creek shortly after his discharge. He farmed there for many years. In the 1880s, George and his wife moved to Fargo, North Dakota to live with his son, who was a doctor. George Carpenter stayed in Fargo for more than thirty years until his death on April 19, 1922 at the age of eighty-nine.

Chaffin, Lewis

Private Lewis Chaffin returned to Monticello following his discharge and resumed his former trade as a blacksmith and laborer. In 1867, he married Francis Gaskill and started a family. He eventually saved enough money to buy a farm across the Mississippi River from Monticello in Big Lake township. Farming apparently didn't suit him for he soon returned to the blacksmith trade.

1027 *St. Cloud Daily Journal Press*, Friday, Dec. 11, 1903.

Chaffin was also an inventor. In 1895, the U.S. Patent and Trademark Office in Washington D.C. awarded Chaffin a patent for a heating stove he invented. Lewis Chaffin lived in Monticello until he passed away on April 15, 1898, at the age of sixty-one.

Clark, Henry P.

Henry P. Clark enlisted in Company E at the end of March 1864, not long before the Eighth Minnesota set out on Sully's Expedition. He was already forty-three years old at the time of his enlistment. Nevertheless, he served with Company E for the rest of the war. He received a minor wound at Murfreesboro, but otherwise made it through the last year of the war unscathed. When the war ended, he returned to his farm in Sherburne County. He farmed there with his son until 1892, when he moved to Princeton. There, he lived with his sister until his death on May 15, 1906, at the age of eighty-five.

Clifford, Franklin

Franklin Clifford returned to Clearwater after the war. He farmed near town with his wife until his death on May 15, 1895, at the age of fifty-four.

Colby, Frank H.

After his court martial, Frank Colby was transferred out of Company E. He remained with the Eighth Minnesota, spending the rest of the war with Company F. Colby accompanied the regiment on Sully's Expedition and was wounded at Murfreesboro. He was discharged after Murfreesboro and returned to his home in Hastings, where he was married in late 1865.

In the spring of 1867, Colby and his wife moved to Alexandria, Minnesota and began farming. In 1891, he moved to North Dakota seeking a better climate for his health (he may have suffered tuberculosis). Shortly after arriving at the new home, he caught the flu, which led to pneumonia and ultimately his death on February 15, 1892. He was only forty-seven years old.

Collins, Dexter

Dexter Collins rejoined his wife in Clearwater after the war. There, he opened a blacksmith shop and the couple raised two children. Collins was deeply involved in local affairs. He was a member of the Clearwater G.A.R. chapter and served four years on the village council. He passed away on November 23, 1920, at the age of seventy-six and was buried in Acacia Cemetery outside of Clearwater.

Crawford, Henry

Henry Crawford migrated west after the war and settled in Washington. He died in Retsil, Washington on July 30, 1929, at the age of eighty-six.

Dallas, William

William Dallas survived the wound to his wrist that he sustained at Murfreesboro. After the war, he returned to his Lynden Township farm just outside Clearwater. He farmed there until his death in in 1891 at the age of sixty-three. He was buried in Acacia Cemetery.

NANCY AND TIMOTHY DESMOND

Desmond, Timothy

Sergeant Timothy "Tim" Desmond returned to Wright County after the war. He married Nancy Blakely, who he had courted while Company E was stationed in Paynesville. Desmond became a successful farmer and later went into banking as part owner of the First State Bank of Maple Plain. He was also active in the G.A.R. Post at Buffalo. Timothy and Nancy raised six children. He retired in 1903 and spent the rest of his life in Wright County, where he passed away on May 5, 1915.[1028]

Dill, Thomas Jefferson

While in the service, Thomas Dill, sent his wife and children back to his native Maine so they could be safe with family. After the war, he apparently had no desire to return to frontier life and joined his family in Maine. There, Dill took up farming. He remained in Maine the rest of his life. Dill died there on April 21, 1917, of "acute indigestion" at the age of eight-two.

Duprey, Joseph

Private Joseph Duprey returned from the war and became a successful farmer in Wright County. In 1866, he married Mary Berthiaume and together raised five children. About 1890, Duprey moved to Minneapolis. It appears that all was not well with the marriage between Joseph and Mary. In 1903, Mary filed for a legal separation on grounds of desertion. Joseph Duprey remained in Minneapolis until his death on May 29, 1918. He is buried in Lakewood Cemetery in Minneapolis.

1028 Franklyn Curtiss-Wedge, *History of Wright County Minnesota*, Vol. I., Chicago, H.C. Cooper, Jr. & Co., 1915, 520.

Eberman, William

William Eberman, one of the most noted pranksters in Company E, worked as a druggist or pharmacist after the war, but he didn't stay put for long. He moved from Minnesota to North Dakota, back to Minnesota, and then to Wyoming. After the death of his wife in 1910, Eberman moved to Freeport, Illinois to live with his nephew. There, he worked as a chemist for a local company. He spent the rest of his life in Freeport. Eberman died there on January 20, 1921, at the age of seventy-four.

Ells, Charles

Private Charles Ells returned from the war to work as a mechanic in Monticello. Within a few years, he and his wife adopted a daughter and moved to Minneapolis, where he worked as a carpenter. Sometime before 1888, Ells relocated with his wife and daughter to Los Angeles, California. There, he served as a real estate agent and joined the local G.A.R. post. Charles Ells died in Los Angeles sometime after 1900. His dates of death and burial are unknown. He lies in Evergreen Cemetery in Los Angeles under a simple headstone marking him as a soldier in Company E of the Eighth Minnesota.

Erath, Albert

Albert Erath continued to serve in Company E after admitting his guilt to avoid court martial for the schoolhouse incident at Paynesville. After the war he returned to his family at Buffalo, where he resumed his trade as a stone mason. He later opened a saloon in Middleville, a few miles south of Buffalo. In 1886, Albert and one of his brothers moved to northern Minnesota to join a type of commune called the Pioneer Cooperative Association, which was also known as the "Bay Lake Colony." Albert Erath died on February 12, 1911, when he fell through thin ice while crossing Bay Lake on his way home.[1029] He was eighty-three years old.

Erath, Herman

Herman Erath was a bit of a world traveler before the war. He was born in Germany and lived in France and Africa before emigrating to the United States. He returned to his family at their home near Buffalo in Wright County at the end of the Civil War. There he settled down and farmed for the rest of his life. He passed away on June 9, 1915, at the age of eighty-six.

1029 Bay Lake is in Crow Wing County about midway between Garrison and Deerwood.

Fairbrother, Albert C.

Albert C. Fairbrother returned to farming at Monticello after the war and stayed there until the end of his life. He never married. It appears he may have spent time at the Minneapolis Soldiers Home before he died on January 5, 1897. He was buried at Lakewood Cemetery in Minneapolis.

Felch, John Henry

Private John Felch returned home to continue farming after the war. He was only home for two weeks when he married Jane Porter, who was eighteen years his junior. They lived and farmed outside of Elk River, where the couple raised four children. John and Jane lived in or around Elk River until after 1910. Late in life, the couple moved to Medford, Oregon, where John's brother was living. John Felch died there on July 28, 1917, at the age of ninety-one.

Flynn, Nicholas

After the war, Nicholas "Nick" Flynn initially returned to his farm near Buffalo in Wright County, where he and his wife raised five children. He later moved to St. Paul and worked as a river pilot on the Mississippi. In 1890, Nick Flynn took a job with the state as the door keeper at the state capitol building. He remained at that post for the next thirty years until his death on May 30, 1920, at the age of eighty-three.

Fuller, Henry

Corporal Henry Fuller had been a carpenter and cabinet maker before the war. When he returned home to Monticello following his discharge, Fuller decided to change careers and became a fire insurance agent. After a few years, Fuller moved his family to Wadena, about 100 miles to the northwest of Monticello and took up farming. He farmed there for more than twenty years until his death on December 17, 1901, at the age of sixty.

Gallow, Joseph

Private Joseph Gallow from Monticello was another of those who enlisted in Company E shortly before the Eighth Minnesota joined Sully's Expedition in 1864. He had been too young during the initial recruiting drive in 1862 and was still only seventeen when he enlisted. After the war, he returned to his family's home in Monticello. There he worked in a livery stable for more than twenty years. He married but never had children.

In the 1890s, Gallow moved to California. By 1910, he was living in the veterans' home in Napa. He was a resident there for the next twenty years. He died in the veteran's home on August 24, 1930, at the age of eighty-three. Gallow was buried in the Veterans Memorial Grove Cemetery near the veterans' home at Yountville in Napa County, California.

Gibbs, Charles H.

Charles "Charlie" Gibbs took up farming after the war as well as working with his father and Thomas Tollington at their factory in Clearwater. In 1873, he married Emily Whittemore, thereby becoming George Cambell's brother-in-law.

Charlie and Emily raised two daughters. He had been a popular member of Company E during the war and remained active in the community for the rest of his life. He was selected as the first Commander of the Grand Army of the Republic post in Clearwater even though he was the youngest member. He also belonged to the local Masonic Lodge, where he served as Master in 1873.

Gibbs suffered from kidney disease and died young in 1890. He was only forty-five years old. The large attendance at his funeral reflected how well-respected he was in the community. Among the mourners were at least fifteen veterans of Company E. His comrades William Houlton and Joseph Perkins both spoke at the funeral. Charles Hobart Gibbs is buried in his family plot at Acacia Cemetery outside of Clearwater next to his wife and children.

Goyette, Louis

Louis Goyette had been promoted to corporal shorty before he took a bullet in the chest during the battle at Murfreesboro. He survived the wound. After a long recovery, he was discharged in June 1865 and returned to his home at Buffalo, where he had a farm before the war. Farm work may have been too hard afterwards due to the lingering effects of his wound. In 1868, he married Harriet Brown, Milton Brown's sister. Louis and Milton thereby became brothers-in-law in addition to brothers in arms.

The next year, Louis and Harriet moved to St. Cloud, where he became a fruit dealer. They also started a family. Over the next few years, the couple had four children. Tragically, it appears all the children died at a young age. In 1876, Harriet also died. After that, Louis Goyette dabbled in other business ventures and eventually returned to farming.

Goyette left Minnesota in the mid-1890s and, like several other Company E veterans, moved to the warmer climate in California. He eventually settled in Oakland, where lived for almost thirty years. He died there on May 18, 1927. He was eighty-nine years old.

Hartley, John

JOHN HARTLEY, PROMOTED FROM COMPANY E TO REGIMENTAL FIRST SERGEANT.

John Hartley was promoted to sergeant major of the Eighth Minnesota shortly after enlisting in Company E. He remained with the regiment throughout the war. He was slightly wounded in the leg while the regiment was engaged in the battle at Murfreesboro but quickly recovered. He also suffered a wound to his right eye, which would plague him for the rest of his life.

In January of 1865, he was promoted to captain of the commissary (supply) corps. By the end of the war, Hartley had been breveted as major. After the war, Hartley accepted a commission in the regular army as captain and assumed command of Company B in the Twenty-second Infantry.

After putting in just over twenty years in the army, Hartley resigned. Sources indicate that the pain and suffering from his eye wound created mental health issues. He died on May 10, 1883, at the age of forty-five, and was buried in Oakland Cemetery in St. Paul, Minnesota. Although he loved his wife dearly, he left her penniless and destitute. In 1885, the U.S. Congress passed House Resolution 7952, which determined that Hartley's service-related eye wound was the cause of his death and granted a pension to his widow Julia.

Helm, Henry C.

Henry "Clay" Helm nearly died from the wounds he suffered at Murfreesboro but managed to pull through. He was discharged from the hospital and rejoined Company E in North Carolina. After the war he returned to farming at Monticello, but within a few years he moved to Duluth, Minnesota and then, like several other Company E soldiers, he migrated west. He lived for a time in Washington and then finally settled in Oregon. He died at Forest Grove, Oregon on February 1, 1920, at the age of seventy-six after suffering a stroke.

Holding, Randolph

After he mustered out of the army, that experienced forager, Randolph Holding, went into the shipping business. He ran freight from St. Cloud up to the Red River, which forms the border between Minnesota and what was then Dakota Territory. In 1868, Holding took a land claim about twenty miles northwest of St. Cloud, where he established the small town of Holdingford. There he ran a general store and served as postmaster. He was also involved in politics, serving two terms in the Minnesota State Legislature.

In 1895, at the age of fifty-one, Holding moved his family to Ransom, North Dakota. There, in addition to running a large farm, he again operated a general store and served as postmaster. He joined the local Masonic Lodge in 1903 and also the Scottish Rite of Freemasonry.[1030] In 1914, Holding was suspended from the Lodge for unmasonic conduct. The reasons are lost to history. He passed away the following year at his home in North Dakota at the age of seventy-one.

RANDOLPH HOLDING

An interesting footnote to the Randolph Holding story is that the town he founded would later become infamous during the Prohibition era. Holdingford and the surrounding area became known as the center for production of an illegal premium moonshine that came to be known as "Minnesota 13." This moonshine, named after the strain of corn from which it was made, was in demand all over the country until Prohibition ended in 1933.

Holgate, Levering

Private Levering Holgate never made it to North Carolina with the rest of Company E. He was left in hospital in Cincinnati with an illness. Holgate was discharged in May of 1865 and returned to Wright County. There, he resumed farming on land he acquired just months before he enlisted in 1862.

The following year, he returned to Cincinnati for a short time to marry Kate Murphy, who he must have met during his time in hospital. The couple returned to the farm and began a family. Holgate later moved the family to Elk River, where went into business as a woodworker and opened a meat market.

1030 The picture of Randolph Holding on the City of Holdingford web site shows him in the black cap worn by 32° Degree Scottish Rite Masons. The picture is available at https://holdingfordmn.govoffice3.com/index.asp?SEC=5DD7971B-84CC-4B7F-ABD4-6672ED128384&Type=B_BASIC, accessed Aug. 31, 2020.

Holgate was one of the founding members of Sherburne Masonic Lodge in Elk River, along with his Company E comrade William Houlton. About 1880, the Holgates moved to Minneapolis. There, Levering continued in woodworking as a railroad employee. Levering Holgate died in Minneapolis on July 27, 1892, at the age of sixty-four and was buried in Lakewood Cemetery.

Houlton, William

Corporal William "Willy" Houlton made it through the war unscathed and avoided any serious illness. He hadn't missed a day of duty in almost three years of service. When the company disbanded, he was held in such high esteem by his comrades that the men in Company E, by a unanimous vote, awarded him the company flag made by the ladies of Monticello.

Almost immediately after he returned home, Houlton was elected the Wright County Register of Deeds. He only stayed in that position for a short time before his brother in Elk River asked William to join him in business. The brothers ran a small store in Elk River and later entered the lumber business. In 1870, Houlton married Fredrietta Lewis in Elk River. He eventually went into business on his own and developed several blocks in the growing town. In 1900, he opened Houlton Bank in Elk River, which eventually became the First National Bank of Elk River and continues in business to this day.

Houlton participated in civic affairs and various organizations. He was an active Freemason, chair of the local temperance committee and a member of the G.A.R. In the 1870s he served as county treasurer and was later elected to serve two terms in the Minnesota state senate. Toward the end of his life he also served as superintendent of the State Reformatory at St. Cloud.

William Houlton made significant contributions to preserving the memory of the Eighth Minnesota Volunteer Infantry Regiment. His reminiscence speech delivered at the Company E reunion about 1880 served as the basis for the history of the Eighth Minnesota published in *Minnesota in the Civil and Indian Wars*, a work commissioned by the state legislature to memorialize the state's contribution to the Union cause. He left behind many letters with his fellow soldiers and their families, as well as other materials, which are now in the archives of the Minnesota Historical Society.

Of all the members of Company E, William Houlton perhaps rose the highest from his humble beginnings. Growing up in extreme poverty, he gained an education, served his country, became a model citizen and an astute businessman. He contributed to his community in many ways. William Houlton, to whom the author is greatly indebted for much of the material in this book, passed away on August 23, 1915, at the age of seventy-five. He remained so esteemed throughout his life that all the stores in Elk River closed on the day of his funeral.

Hulett, Asahel E.

Sergeant Asahel Hulett was discharged with Company E and returned to his home in Silver Creek. "Asel," as he was known, farmed outside of Clearwater for several years. In the late 1870s, the family moved to Minneapolis, where Asel worked as a teamster. On December 14, 1901, Asel Hulett suffered a cerebral hemorrhage and died at the age of sixty-five. He was buried in what is now known as the Minneapolis Pioneers and Soldiers Memorial Cemetery.

Keator, Charles H.

Charles Keator joined Company E in March of 1864 after having previously served in the First Minnesota Mounted Rangers. After the war, he settled in Minneapolis. There, he married Martha McCleod in 1868. He worked at a variety of jobs in Minneapolis, including as a bill poster and a baker. Keator died in 1895 at the age of sixty-six.

Kingsbury, David Lansing

David Kingsbury was promoted to lieutenant in the last days of the war and proudly used that rank for the rest of his life. He returned from the war and settled in Saint Paul, where he went into business as a hardware merchant. In 1869, he married Anna Braman. In his later years, Kingsbury became assistant librarian for the Minnesota Historical Society.

In 1898, Kingsbury published a detailed account of Sully's Expedition Against the Sioux. He was also active in documenting the experiences of other Civil War soldiers. He served as Recorder of the Commandery of the State of Minnesota Military Order of the Loyal Legion of the United States. One mission of the "Loyal Legion" was to "perpetuate the memory of those who fought to preserve the unity and indivisibility of the Republic and to honor the memory and promote the ideals of Abraham Lincoln."[1031] Kingsbury died in Saint Paul on January 24, 1912, at the age of seventy.

Kriedler, Daniel

Daniel Kriedler returned to Wright County and took up farming. He was married to Cordelia Beardsley, a widow with two children, on the same day in 1866 that his brother George married (which coincidentally was also the same day that Levering Holgate married in Cincinnati). Daniel continued to farm in Wright County for

---

1031 Military Order of the Loyal Legion of the United States web site at http://suvcw.org/mollus/org.htm, accessed Jan. 12, 2020. The Loyal Legion still exists as a hereditary association for descendants of officers who served in the Civil War.

many years. He and Cordelia had 5 more children. In the early 1890s, the family moved to Graceville, Minnesota, which was along the border with North Dakota. Daniel Kriedler died in Kenmare, North Dakota on March 27, 1903, and was buried in Graceville, Minnesota.

Kriedler, George

George Kriedler purchased eighty acres of wild land when he returned from the war. He set about the hard work of clearing it for farming and erected a log cabin. George had little education and had to have other soldiers, such as Edson Washburn, read and write his letters for him during his time in the service. He was nevertheless intelligent and, after learning to read, began consuming a wide variety of books.

In 1866, George married Margaretha Stoltz, an immigrant from Bavaria. The couple did well at farming and, before too long, added almost 100 more acres to the farm. They did well enough that the couple were able to replace the log cabin with a fine brick home, where they raised five children. George was active in the community, where he served on the school board and was a member of both the G.A.R and International Organization of Odd Fellows, a fraternal organization similar to the Masons. George Kriedler died on October 19, 1926, at the age of eighty-three. He is buried in Kriedler Cemetery near Buffalo.

Kriedler, Samuel

Samuel Kriedler, the oldest Kriedler brother to serve in Company E, returned to his wife and children in Wright County after his discharge. Like his brothers, he continued to farm in Wright County. In 1879, he relocated to Grant County, about 100 miles to the northwest of the old family farm. At the Grant County farm, Samuel raised livestock, farmed and cut timber. Together, Samuel and his wife Barbara raised eight children.

Samuel Kriedler was active in his church and well-known in the community. In 1909, Samuel and Barbara Kriedler retired to the nearby town of Herman, Minnesota. Later, when they were in their eighties, the couple moved to Minneapolis, perhaps to be near one of their children. Samuel Kriedler died in Minneapolis on March 19, 1928. He was ninety-three years old. He was buried in Lakewood Cemetery at Minneapolis.

Lane, William

William Lane, the Little Drummer Boy and occasional Company E barber, left Minnesota with his wife and children immediately after receiving his discharge. He moved the family back to his home state of Illinois and went to work as a clerk at his brother's pharmacy in the town of Momence.

In 1867, Lane opened his own grocery store at Momence. Three years later, he was appointed postmaster by President Grant and was later reappointed to the position by presidents Hayes and Garfield. After sixteen years as postmaster, Lane went into the insurance business. He served as an agent for Aetna Insurance Company for the next forty years.

Lane was an active Freemason for nearly his entire adult life, beginning while he lived in Minneapolis before the war and later transferring his membership to the Masonic Lodge in Momence. Lane stayed in touch with his comrades from Company E throughout the rest of his life. William Lane, "Uncle Billy" as he was affectionately known in Momence, passed away at his home after suffering a heart attack on March 12, 1905, at the age of seventy-two.

Locke, Joseph

Joseph Locke traveled west after the war and spent the rest of his life in Washington. There he was occasionally visited by members of Company E, including William Houlton. He died in Washington on May 6, 1900. His remains were returned to Silver Creek in Wright County for burial. His funeral was attended by several of his former comrades and other veterans from the G.A.R. post in Clearwater.

Lord, Martin

Martin Lord rejoined his wife and children at their Wright County farm when the war ended. He farmed there until his death on July 9, 1899, at the age of seventy-nine.

MARTIN LORD

Lord, William

William Lord returned to Wright County and took up residence in Buffalo after the war. There he opened a drug store in 1868. He was appointed the Wright County Sheriff in 1869 and served in that position until 1872. After he left the drug store business in 1874, he spent three years as a traveling salesman. In 1889, Lord moved to King County, Washington, where he lived for the rest of his life. He died in Washington on July 4, 1908.

Louisiana, John

John Louisiana returned to Wright County after the war and began farming. He was a member of the Montrose G.A.R. Post. He and his wife raised a large family. John Louisiana passed away on February 8, 1900, at the age of fifty-six and was buried in Kriedler Cemetery in Wright County.[1032]

Lyons, James

James Lyons returned to the Clearwater area after his discharge and pursued various ventures, including logging and rafting before he saved enough to buy a farm. He purchased 160 acres in Lynden Township, just across the Clearwater River from Wright County, and farmed there for many years. He married Mary Ridley from Silver Creek in about 1878. In 1900, he and Mary moved from the farm into the village of Clearwater, where he served as town marshal.

In 1913, at the age of sixty-six, James and Mary purchased a general store in Clearwater. There they sold ice cream, confectionery, canned goods, cigars, and tobacco. They also opened a restaurant and lunchroom. James was very active in the community and served as vice commander of A. C. Collins Post, No. 112, G. A. R., of Clearwater. James Lyons died on November 6, 1925, at the age of seventy-nine. He is buried in Acacia Cemetery outside of Clearwater.

Lyons, John W.

After the war, John Lyons bought a farm in Lynden Township, just outside of Clearwater in southern Stearns County. He married Harriett Dunklee in 1867 and had two daughters. John Lyons died of peritonitis on April 12, 1887. He was only forty-six years old.

McPherson, William

William McPherson, the young man who cracked up the company after he had a bullet pull his long hair through his cap in the cotton field at Murfreesboro, returned to Clearwater and began a stagecoach business. At first it ran from St. Cloud to the border with what would become North Dakota. Later, McPherson moved to North Dakota and expanded his stage line to the west into Montana. When the railroad came through, McPherson moved to Montana, where he lived until 1895. After the death of his first wife in 1897, he moved to Virginia City,

---

1032 It appears that Kriedler Cemetery was named after the same family that furnished 3 members of Company E by that name.

Washington where he remained for the rest of his life. He remarried in 1905. William McPherson died at his brother's home in Brewster, Washington on April 20, 1921 at the age of seventy-six.

Markham, Homer

Homer Markham from Clearwater came home after the war and worked at various jobs, including perhaps his cousin Randolph Holding's cartage business. In 1874, he moved across the Mississippi River to nearby Clear Lake, where he purchased a farm. He married in 1876 and had two daughters. Homer retired in 1900 and moved into the village of Clear Lake with his wife, where he lived for the remainder of his life. Homer Markham lived to the age of eighty-nine, passing away on March 6, 1927. He was buried at Clear Lake.

Merrill, Charles

Charlie Merrill, the young musician who enlisted in Company E at the age of only sixteen, finished his education after the war, married and then entered the ministry. He served as a minister at Pilgrim Congregational Church in Minneapolis for many years and then moved to Saratoga, California. He passed away in California on December 2, 1920.

Mitchell, Henry

Private Henry A. Mitchell moved to Minneapolis after the war, where he worked as a teamster. Mitchell operated a saloon for a time but went back to being a hack driver (one who drives a taxi or livery wagon) at some point. He was married but was widowed and it did not appear the couple had any children. In 1906, Mitchell entered the Old Soldier's Home in Minneapolis, which was on the grounds of the current Veterans Administration Hospital near Fort Snelling. He died there on May 11, 1906, and is buried in an unmarked grave in Lakewood Cemetery in Minneapolis.

Murphy, Matthew

Private Matthew Murphy, one of the Irishmen in Company E, returned from the war to his wife and young son, who were living at Clearwater. Soon after his return, Murphy began farming near the village. He remained a farmer for the rest of his life. Murphy and his wife Martha raised ten children. Matthew Murphy passed away on September 13, 1915, at the age of eighty-six.

Murray, Samuel

Samuel Murray, one of the veteran volunteers who joined Company E in 1864, returned to Monticello after the war, but later moved to Arapahoe County in Colorado. There he became a policeman. Later he settled in the city of Denver. He died there on April 30, 1905, at the age of sixty-six.

Nickerson, Alphonso

Alphonso Nickerson returned to farming near Monticello after the war. He was known in the community as a total abstainer from alcohol and became an advocate for Prohibition. On February 14, 1902, Nickerson was trying to drive his horse and cutter or mower across the tracks behind a freight train, when the train suddenly backed up and hit his rig. Seventy-eight-year-old Nickerson died as a result of injuries he received in the accident.

Parcher, Ellett

Ellett Parcher died in the cotton field on the Wilkinson Pike. He was initially buried with the rest of the dead from the Eighth Minnesota in a common grave. Later, the remains of those men were exhumed and reburied in separate graves at the Stones River National Cemetery.

Parcher, Frank

Frank Parcher returned to Clearwater after suffering a serious shoulder wound at Murfreesboro. The bullet had shattered the bones and rendered his left arm useless. Unable to do physical labor, Parcher decided to become a lawyer. He boarded with the prominent local attorney Hanford Gordon, the same man that had written Colonel Thomas in the summer of 1863 to complain about the Company E scouts. While living with Gordon, Parcher used the time to study law.

Parcher eventually became a lawyer and married. When Gordon moved with his family to California, Parcher decided to follow. He practiced law in the Los Angeles area and remained there for the rest of his life. He died on February 2, 1924, at the age of eighty-two. He was buried in Hollywood Cemetery, which has since been renamed as Hollywood Forever Cemetery, and is a well-known tourist stop because it is also the final resting place of many famous members of the entertainment industry.

Parks, Isaac

Private Isaac Parks had enlisted in Company E while the Eighth Minnesota was headquartered in St. Cloud. He had previously served for a short time with the First Minnesota Mounted Rangers following the Indian uprising in 1862. After the war he moved his wife and family to Sauk Centre, where the Eighth Minnesota had consolidated prior to setting out on Sully's Expedition. He worked there as a bricklayer until his death. He was seventy-four years old when he died on October 14, 1894. Parks is buried in Greenwood Cemetery at Sauk Centre.

Parvin, John

John Parvin was already forty-three years old when the war ended. He returned to farming at Monticello but was able to retire before the age of fifty. In 1871, he married Sarah Howe. Sergeant John Parvin died on April 13, 1901, at the age of seventy-nine.

Perkins, Joseph

Joseph Perkins made it through the war and returned to his wife Roxanne and children at their farm near Monticello. He continued to farm there for many years. Roxanne died in 1893. Two years later, at the age of seventy-four, Perkins moved to Iowa and remarried. He lived with his second wife in Iowa until his death on September 7, 1906, at the age of eighty-four. His body was returned to his longtime home of Monticello and buried in Riverside Cemetery next to his first wife.

Persons, Edwin

Edwin Persons, one of the latecomers to Company E, having joined in 1864, was also one of the last to be discharged. He was in a convalescent camp recovering from illness when he was discharged in September of 1865. Persons went straight back to his hometown in New York where his wife and children were living while he was away in the army. He decided to stay there and worked as a farm laborer for many years. In the late 1800s he moved to Albion, Nebraska. He died there on June 27, 1915, at the age of seventy-nine.

Philbrook, Amiel (Amide)

Private Amiel Philbrook returned to his wife Mary and their children at Monticello after the war. He resumed farming and worked the land in Wright County for several years before relocating the family to Superior, Wisconsin. There, Amiel and Mary lived out the rest of their lives. He died in Superior on October 18, 1917, at the age of eighty-two.

Ponsford, John

John Ponsford traveled with Company E from Fort Snelling bound for Murfreesboro but never made it. He died of disease in Louisville, Kentucky on November 22, 1864. He was only nineteen years old. He was buried at Louisville in Cave Hill Cemetery. Even though his life was short, he left behind a diary covering most of 1863, which provides helpful insights into the experiences of Company E during that year.

Ponsford, William

William Ponsford survived the bullet wound to his head that knocked him out cold in the cotton field at Murfreesboro. However, it took several months in the hospital before he was healthy enough for the return trip to Minnesota. He arrived at home in Clearwater after his discharge in May 1865. Later that year, Ponsford purchased a farm near Annandale in Wright County. He married Mary Anne Townsend in 1868. On their farm they raised their children and continued to reside there until Mary Ann died in 1906.

William Ponsford spent the last years of his life living with his daughter. When he died on March 5, 1930, at the age of eighty-nine, the newspapers reported that he was the last *local* survivor of the Civil War. That may have been correct but other members of Company E and the Eighth Minnesota outlived him.

Reed, Joseph

Private Joseph Reed was barely seventeen when he joined Company E at Paynesville before the Eighth Minnesota set out on Sully's Expedition. He returned to Paynesville after the war, where he lived with his parents and farmed. He married in 1880 at the age of thirty-three to nineteen-year-old Anne Mitchell. Reed and his wife lived with his parents on the farm until after 1885, when the growing family moved to a farm in north central North Dakota. Joseph and Anne had seven children.

Joseph Reed remained in North Dakota for the rest of his long life. He died on April 21, 1931, at Wolford, North Dakota at the age of eighty-four. He may have been the last surviving member of Company E. Joseph Reed may also have fathered the last surviving child of a Company E veteran. His youngest daughter, born in 1900, lived until 1994.

Sabin, Elisha

Private Elisha Sabin died of disease on July 4, 1865, shortly before Company E left for home with the rest of the Eighth Minnesota. He was buried in a Charlotte churchyard. After the war, his body was exhumed and reinterred at the Salisbury National Cemetery at Salisbury, North Carolina.

Stinchfield, William

One of the veteran volunteers who later joined Company E, William Stinchfield, took up farming after the war in Maine Prairie, a township in southern Stearns County just west of Clearwater. There he married Melissa Green in 1867 and together they raised three children. Stinchfield was a Freemason and active in the community. In the 1890s he moved the family west to Santa Ana, California, where he spent the rest of his life. He died there on November 1, 1905, at the age of fifty-nine.

Swain, John

Already forty-seven years old at the time of his discharge, John Swain returned to his wife Mary and their children at their farm near Monticello. By 1870, the children were grown and had left home. John and Mary moved into the Village of Monticello, where he worked as a carpenter. After Mary died in 1885, Swain moved to Minneapolis. He later entered the Old Soldiers' Home in Minneapolis, where he died on August 15, 1905, at the age of eighty-seven. His body was returned to Monticello and buried next to his wife in Riverside Cemetery.

Swartout, Cramer

Cramer Swartout was over forty years of age at the time of his discharge from the service. He returned to his wife and children at their Wright County farm. Despite his age, he made it all the way through the Indian campaign and the company's battles in the south. His only injury was a slight wound from a bullet. He returned to farming after the war and was active in his church and the G.A.R. Swartout died on August 30, 1909, at the age of eighty-six and was buried in Kriedler Cemetery near Buffalo.

Thompson, John

John Thompson, a resident of St. Cloud, enlisted in Company E of the Eighth Minnesota in March 1864. He had previously served as a private in Company I of the Third Minnesota Volunteer Infantry, having enlisted at the age of nineteen during October 1861. However, he was discharged for disability the following year. He apparently recovered sufficiently from whatever affliction led to his discharge and was determined to re-enlist. The Eighth Minnesota was headquartered in St. Cloud at the time, so he joined there and was assigned to Company E. He served with the company throughout Sully's Expedition and the campaign in the south. At the end of the war, he was discharged with the rest of the Eighth Minnesota and returned to his family's home in St. Cloud.

Tragically, John Thompson didn't live long after the war. In an incident eerily reminiscent of the accidental shooting of Christopher Bailey at Silver Creek, Thompson also was killed by mistake. In early November 1867, Thompson, his brother and some others, including a young German boy, set out on a hunting expedition near St. Cloud. The German boy was rather timid and deathly afraid of Indians. Late in the day, the party decided to shelter for the night at an abandoned house.

As the day grew dark, Thompson and the rest of the party thought they would have some fun with the boy and give him a good fright. They convinced the terrified youth that Indians were coming and even hung out a blanket not far from the house as a decoy. The boy was so scared that he fired at the blanket a few times from his position in the house. Meanwhile, Thompson and his brother made a commotion in a different part of the house to make it sound as if the Indians had gained entrance. Thompson then ran through the house to where the boy was sitting. In a panic, the boy fired his rifle, striking John Thompson in the abdomen. He uttered "I am killed," and then died. After having survived Killdeer Mountain, the Battle of the Badlands and the fight at Murfreesboro, Thompson died accidentally on that cold November afternoon in 1867. He was only twenty-five years old.[1033]

Tourtellotte, George

After the first winter at Fort Ripley, Private George Tourtellotte sought a transfer from Company E to the Third Minnesota Light Battery. The transfer came through on May 1, 1863. He served with the Third Battery on Sully's Expedition and again was deployed to Dakota Territory the following year.

After his discharge, Tourtellotte returned to Monticello. He married and had children while working as a brick mason. At some point he and his wife divorced and Tourtellotte moved to Elk River in nearby Sherburne County. In the mid-1910s, his health began to deteriorate. He spent time in Minneapolis seeking hospital treatment but eventually returned to Elk River. He died at the home of a neighbor in Elk River on November 2, 1918, at the age of seventy-four and was buried in nearby Orono Cemetery.

Vadner, Joseph

Joseph Vadner had some problems with authority during his time in the army, but he served with Company E all the way through the war and was discharged with the rest of the regiment. He appears to have struggled with mental health issues in the years after the war. By 1880 he was institutionalized in the Minnesota Hospital for the Insane at St. Peter. He was later sent to a similar state hospital at Fergus Falls. He remained institutionalized there until his death on August 9, 1910, when he was sixty-five years old.

1033 *St. Cloud Journal*, Nov. 7, 1867.

Vorse, Charles

Charles Vorse returned to Clearwater after the war and learned the wagon-making trade. He eventually opened his own wagon shop. He married in 1869 and with his wife raised two children while living in Clearwater. Vorse later got out of the wagon business and took over management of the Morrison House, a prominent hotel in Clearwater. He also joined the Clearwater Masonic Lodge.

In 1884, Vorse and his wife moved to Delano and continued in the hotel business. Four years later, he moved to Buffalo, and became the Wright County Clerk of Court, a post he held until 1903. He died on December 8, 1919, at the age of seventy-five and was buried in Acacia Cemetery outside his hometown of Clearwater.

Washburn, Edson

When Edson Washburn finally reached home after spending weeks recovering from his illness at his sister's house in Minneapolis, he had a nice nest egg waiting for him. Throughout his service he regularly sent a substantial portion of his army pay home for safekeeping. As a result, he had enough money stashed away to buy a small farm not far from Monticello.

On May 13, 1866, Edson married Amelia Wells, the "dark-eyed girl" with whom he corresponded almost daily throughout the war. Together, they raised several children. Their first born they named Orson after Edson's older brother who died of disease early in the war while serving with the Fourth Minnesota Volunteer Infantry Regiment in Mississippi.

Edson Washburn was respected throughout his life as a man of strong moral character. He was always proud that he kept his vow never to use intoxicating liquors, play cards, or be late for roll call while in the service. It was his first vote as a young man, however, of which he was most proud "… casting my first ballot for that good and great man, Abraham Lincoln…"[1034]

Washburn was active in civic affairs. He served two years on the Otsego town board and twenty years as a justice of the peace. In addition, he joined the G.A.R. in Monticello and was an active Freemason at Monticello Lodge No. 16. Edson Washburn passed away on November 18, 1918, at the age of seventy-six and was buried in Riverside Cemetery in Monticello.

Edson Washburn left behind diaries that covered the period from 1863 through mid-1865. Many of the entries provide excellent insights into the daily life of a soldier in Company E. Some of the entries were deeply and painfully personal, such as when he recorded the death of his brother Elbridge at Murfreesboro. The author is indebted to Edson Washburn for leaving behind this incredibly valuable resource.

1034 Washburn, *Autobiography*, 7. It was this statement that he chose to end his autobiography.

Washburn, Elbridge

Elbridge Washburn was killed in the cotton field outside Murfreesboro on December 7, 1864. He was initially buried in a common grave with the rest of the Eighth Minnesota dead. Later, the remains of those men were exhumed and reburied in separate graves at the Stones River National Cemetery.

Wedgewood, George R.L.

George R.L. Wedgewood, also known as "Russell," recovered from the wounds he sustained at Murfreesboro. He was discharged from the hospital in June 1865 and resumed farming near Monticello. In 1868, he married Sarah Smithson at Stillwater, Minnesota. They returned to the Monticello farm and raised a family.

When he wasn't farming, Wedgewood was active in Republican politics and the G.A.R. Farming worked out well for Wedgewood and he was able to save enough money to invest and provide an income for his later years. Sarah died in 1903. He remarried in 1910 to Mary Hager in Monticello. Wedgewood lived a long life. He passed away on January 7, 1930, at the age of ninety-one.

Wheeler, Stephen V.R.

Not much is known about what became of Stephen V.R. Wheeler after the war. He moved to California sometime after his discharge and worked as a laborer. In 1914, he was hospitalized in the California State Hospital due to alcoholism and dementia. He died in California sometime after July of that year.

Woodward, Emerson

After leaving Company E of the Eighth Minnesota in late 1863, Emerson Woodward was commissioned as captain of Company E in the 62nd Infantry, U.S. Colored Troops. His regiment spent most of the war guarding a boat landing in Louisiana and later was assigned to guard the mouth of the Rio Grande River on Brazos Santiago Island[1035] near Matamoros, Texas. By the end of the war, he had been promoted to brevet major. Woodward stayed in touch with his former comrades throughout the war and followed their service with Sully and in Murfreesboro in the Minnesota newspapers.

Woodward returned to Minnesota in 1865, married and settled on a farm in Richfield, Minnesota. There, Woodward and his wife raised four children.

1035 Now known as Brazos Island, this is now the launch site for SpaceX.

Although he saw little fighting, the war was physically hard on Woodward. He suffered from chronic diarrhea while his unit was stationed in Louisiana. At one point his weight dropped to 126 pounds on his 5'9" frame. His health was so bad that he resigned from the service on April 23, 1865. The illnesses he suffered in the south may have contributed to his early demise. Emerson Woodward died relatively young on August 25, 1892, at the age of fifty-six and was buried in Oak Hill Cemetery in Richfield.

One historical footnote on Woodward's Civil War unit. Shortly after Woodward resigned from the service, his former regiment, the 62nd Infantry U.S.C.T. participated in the Battle of Palmito Ranch near Brazos. It was during that battle on May 13, 1865, when John Williams of the Thirty-fourth Indiana Infantry Regiment was killed. Williams is believed by many historians to be the last Union soldier killed in action during the Civil War.

Woodworth, Edward

Sergeant Edward Woodworth left Clearwater not long after the war. He settled in Minneapolis for a time and then moved to Duluth. Later in life Woodworth moved to San Francisco, California, where he lived until his death on August 24, 1911. He was seventy years old.

Young, David

After his discharge, David Young returned to his wife and children and took up farming in rural Hennepin County. In 1871, he moved his family into the nearby town of Delano and opened a small hotel. The business quickly grew and expanded.

In 1879, Young opened a much larger establishment, described as "one of the finest in this section of the country," and added a livery stable. Young remained in Delano for the rest of his life. He died there on November 1, 1906, at the age of seventy-three.

Other Minnesota Volunteers

Atkinson, James B.

James B. Atkinson, who served in Company D of the Second Minnesota Cavalry, maintained a diary during Sully's Expedition in 1864 that provided helpful information for this book. Originally from Canada, he had lived in Philadelphia during the 1840s, where he became a lawyer and a Freemason.

Atkinson migrated to Minnesota Territory in 1857, where he started work as an innkeeper at Forest City. He quickly advanced in stature within the community.

368 | Sherman's Woodticks

By 1858, he was serving as chief justice of Meeker County and represented the area in the territorial legislature.

When word reached Forest City of the killings at nearby Acton on August 17, 1862, at the start of the Sioux Uprising, Atkinson was part of the group that traveled to the Jones and Baker farms to verify what had happened. He saw firsthand the results of the massacre.

After his return from Acton, Atkinson was elected lieutenant of the militia unit hastily formed to protect the residents and refugees at Forest City. When the threat abated after the Sioux were defeated in the fall of 1862, he enlisted in the Second Minnesota Cavalry.

Atkinson participated in Sully's Expedition, including the battles of Killdeer Mountain and the Badlands. After returning from Dakota Territory, Atkins transferred to the First Minnesota Battery of Heavy Artillery and was commissioned as captain of Company H.

He returned from the war in September 1865 and resumed his life in Forest City. Atkinson continued to practice law and regained his role as chief justice. In the 1870s, he moved the family to nearby Litchfield, which was growing rapidly due to the arrival of the railroad. He remained active in civic affairs in Litchfield until his death on July 12, 1894, at the age of seventy-one.

Brunson, Benjamin W.

Benjamin Witherell Brunson of Company K left behind valuable reminiscences of his time with the Eighth Minnesota, especially regarding Sully's Expedition. Brunson was a lawyer, engineer, and surveyor who arrived in Minnesota Territory during 1847. He helped survey sections of the town plot for what would become the City of St. Paul and served two terms in the territorial legislature. In 1856, he built a brick house in St. Paul, which still stands at 485 Kenney Street.

Already forty years old at the time of his enlistment, Brunson rose to sergeant and, just before the Eighth Minnesota set out for Tennessee, to lieutenant. After the war, Brunson continued to work as a surveyor for many years. Over the next decades, he variously managed the St. Paul Post Office, served as a justice of the peace, and became a manager of the St. Paul Union Depot railroad station.

Brunson was an active Freemason and member of the Odd Fellows, another fraternal and benevolent association. Brunson left a significant imprint on the city and a lasting legacy. Benjamin Brunson died at his home in St. Paul on May 14, 1898, at the age of seventy-five.

Brunson's legacy in St. Paul lives on. The Brunson House is believed to be the oldest brick house still standing in St. Paul. It was added to the National Register of Historic Places in 1975. The house is located in a neighborhood known as "Brunson's Addition" on the plat of St. Paul. In 2003, a bar and restaurant opened on nearby Payne Avenue and was named "Brunson's Pub" in honor of Benjamin Brunson's contribution to the neighborhood.

Cady, John S.

After his death at the hands of an Indian raiding party on June 11, 1863, the body of Captain John S. Cady was sent back to his family in Upstate New York. He was buried in the family plot at Dry Creek Cemetery outside his hometown of Moravia. Cady was not forgotten by his comrades back in Minnesota. When a G.A.R. chapter was organized at Anoka on October 28, 1880, it was named J.S. Cady Post No. 2 in his honor.[1036]

Doud, George W.

Private George Washington Doud of Company F maintained a detailed diary from the first days of his service in September 1862 until the Eighth Minnesota returned to Fort Snelling in October, 1864 after Sully's Expedition. He remained with the regiment until the war ended. Then, he returned to Cannon Falls in Goodhue County, Minnesota and began farming.

In 1867, Doud married Rebecca Ann Thomas Payton, the widow of James Payton, a member of Company F who was killed in action at Murfreesboro on December 7, 1864. Payton was advancing when a cannonball struck a nearby soldier and shattered the man's rifle. Fragments of the rifle struck Payton with the force of an exploding shell and killed him.[1037]

Together with Rebecca, Doud raised the children of his fallen comrade in addition to four more of their own. The Douds moved to Princeton, not far from where Company F had been posted in the summer of 1863 and farmed there for a time. Then the family moved on.

The Douds lived in Wichita, Kansas during the mid-1870s and then moved to Laramie, Wyoming. A few years later, the family moved to Pennington County, South Dakota in 1881, where Doud continued farming.

In 1909, Doud, by then a widower, checked in to the Battle Mountain Sanitarium in the far southwestern corner of South Dakota. The sanitarium opened just

---

1036 Winchell, et al., *History of the Upper Mississippi Valley*, 229.

1037 Hodgson, "Recollections of the Sioux War No. 29," *Dakota County Tribune*, Feb. 5, 1891.

two years earlier. It was the only short-term care facility for veterans suffering from lung or respiratory problems that was ever opened by the National Home for Disabled Volunteer Soldiers, which was later consolidated into the Veterans Administration.[1038] The sanitarium took advantage of nearby hot springs to treat the veterans both with mineral baths and the dry mountain air.

Doud entered the sanitarium with a variety of maladies, including respiratory ailments, rheumatism, and hemorrhoids. He remained there for almost two years. George Doud unexpectedly passed away on January 15, 1911, at the age of seventy-seven while on furlough from the sanitarium to visit his daughter in Rapid City, South Dakota. He was buried at Mountain View Cemetery in Rapid City.

Sometime around 1920, Doud's son Benjamin, a rancher near Gillette, Wyoming, allowed two copies of Doud's diary to be made. He donated one to the Minnesota Historical Society and one to the State Historical Society of North Dakota.[1039]

Hodgson, Thomas C.

Private Thomas C. Hodgson, also from Company F, mustered out and returned to his farm near Northfield in southern Dakota County. He married soon after the war. He and his wife raised several children.

In 1876, Hodgson moved the family from Dakota County to a farm in Grant County, which is in western Minnesota. There he became involved in several community activities. For a time, Hodgson served as superintendent of the Grant County schools. Though not an ordained minister, he preached frequently in local churches.

In 1887, he was appointed chief deputy inspector for grain by Governor Andrew McGill. That same year, Hodgson began writing a series of reminiscences of his time in Company F of the Eighth Minnesota Volunteer Infantry Regiment. The reminiscences were published in the *Dakota County Tribune* between 1887 and 1891 and provided great insights into the history of the Eighth Minnesota.

Thomas Hodgson was also well known as a political progressive and reformer. He was active in the Democratic Peoples' Party, a populist movement of the late nineteenth century, and served as an elector for Minnesota on behalf of the party in the 1900 presidential election. Hodgson died at the age of seventy on September 7, 1913, and was buried at Fergus Falls, Minnesota.

1038   https://www.nps.gov/places/battle-mountain-sanitarium-hot-springs-south-dakota.htm, accessed Feb. 19, 2020.

1039 Doud's diaries provided valuable detail of the Eighth Minnesota's experience during Sully's Expedition.

Paxson, Lewis C.

Lewis C. Paxson of Company G maintained a diary of his time in the Eighth Minnesota. It began on the day he enlisted and ran through the day he arrived home after the war.

After he was mustered out, Paxson remained in Minnesota only long enough to pack up and move back east to Philadelphia. There, he married and worked in the mercantile business for several years. In 1872, Paxson purchased a small dairy farm near Stockton, New Jersey. He remained on the farm for the rest of his life. He also served for many years as principal of the Stockton Public Schools. Lewis Paxson died at his home in New Jersey on May 28, 1915 at the age of seventy-eight.

Seelye, William E.

Private William E. Seelye of Company A maintained a journal and wrote about his experience in the Eighth Minnesota during Sully's Expedition. He apparently lied about his age when he enlisted at the age of fifteen in August 1862.

Still only eighteen years old when he returned to Anoka after the war, Seelye found work on the river as a lumberman. Several veterans of Company A worked together in this dangerous work. There was plenty of it as the rivers were the only effective method of transporting logs to the sawmills.

Seelye married in 1873. Shortly thereafter, he and his wife moved farther north to Brainerd, Minnesota, not far from the old town of Crow Wing, where the lumber industry was booming at the time. There he helped build a dam to power the lumber mills.

In 1890, Seelye and his family moved to Spokane, Washington, where he went into the mining business. He soon prospered as a stockholder and executive of a silver mining corporation. He enjoyed good health throughout his life and remained active in his mining ventures until the end. Seelye died at the age of seventy-seven in Spokane, Washington on October 5, 1924, after a brief illness.

Historical Figures Encountered by the Eighth Minnesota

Sibley, Henry Hastings

Henry Hastings Sibley was promoted to major general for his service during the war. He remained in the army until 1866. After his discharge, he was appointed to participate in the negotiation of new treaties with the Sioux.

Sibley later served in the legislature and held various government positions, including president of the state normal board, which oversaw the state university system. He became a regent of the University of Minnesota and served on the board of Indian commissioners. He was also active in the G.A.R. and Minnesota State Historical Society.

Over the years, he took on several business interests. Sibley was president of the St. Paul Gas Company, a director of the First National Bank and involved in the railroad business.

Sibley passed away in St. Paul on February 18, 1891, only two days before his eightieth birthday. The last fifty years of Sibley's life were deeply intertwined with the first fifty years of Minnesota history.[1040] Hastings, Minnesota and Sibley County were both named for him during his lifetime. In the twentieth century, Henry Hastings Sibley High School in Mendota Heights was named in his honor.

In recent years Sibley has become a controversial figure due to his actions during and after the Sioux Uprising. In 2021, the school district removed Sibley's name from the high school and renamed it "Two Rivers High School."

Wowinapa

Little Crow's son, Wowinapa, was tried for the murders of soldiers and settlers in Minnesota during the summer of 1863. He was convicted, sentenced to hang, and then sent to await his fate in a prison camp at Davenport, Iowa.

While awaiting execution, Wowinapa converted to Christianity and took the name Thomas Wakeman. Wakeman eventually escaped the noose. He was pardoned in 1865. He then relocated to a reservation in Dakota Territory near what is now Flandreau, South Dakota. There, he married and had six children. In 1876, he, along with some friends started the first Sioux Indian YMCA at Flandreau.

Unfortunately, Wakeman contracted tuberculosis, perhaps during his confinement at Davenport. As his condition deteriorated, he returned to Redwood Falls, Minnesota, the area where he spent his youth. He died there of his affliction on January 13, 1886, at the age of forty.

Sully, Alfred H.

Brevet General Alfred Sully stayed in the army after the 1864 expedition with the rank of lieutenant colonel. In 1866, he remarried to Sophie Henrietta Webster and the couple had two children. It is not clear if his Yankton Sioux wife was deceased at the time.

Sully continued to serve in the wars against the plains Indians for most of the 1860s. After a dispute with another former brevet general, Lieutenant Colonel

---

1040 *Minneapolis Tribune*, Morning Edition, Feb. 19, 1891.

George Armstrong Custer, over plans for an upcoming winter campaign, Sully was removed from frontline combat service.

In 1869, Sully was appointed superintendent of Indian affairs for Montana. Later, he was promoted to full colonel and assigned to command an infantry regiment posted in Washington Territory.[1041]

General Sully died at Vancouver Barracks, Washington Territory on April 27, 1879, while still in active service with the U.S. Army. His body was returned to Philadelphia, where he was buried in Laurel Hill Cemetery.

Ironically, Sully's descendants through his daughter Mary, also known as "Soldier Woman," became Indian rights activists. In 1969, Sully's great-grandson, Vine DeLoria, Jr., published his book *Custer Died for Your Sins: An Indian Manifesto*, which continues to have an influence on Native American policy to this day.

Forrest, Nathan Bedford

After the Confederate surrender, Nathan Bedford Forrest returned to his plantation near Memphis, Tennessee. It took him about three years to restore his property to production. Then, Forrest went into the railroad business. He undertook to build a railroad from Selma, Alabama to the Mississippi. This undertaking occupied his time for three more years.

Forrest is widely reported to have been an early member of infamous Ku Klux Klan in the 1860s and perhaps even served as the organization's first grand wizard. The Ku Klux Klan had used violence and intimidation to terrorize freed Blacks, Reconstructionists, and republicans in the years after the war.

In testimony before Congress in 1871, Forrest claimed that he had advised against all manner of violence and even urged that the organization disband, which it did in 1869.

Forrest's railroad venture didn't work out. The company went bankrupt, and Forrest lost most of his wealth. He returned to his plantation where he and his wife remained for the rest of his life.[1042]

It appears that Forrest contracted malaria, diabetes, or another type of chronic disease sometime after the war. His health slowly deteriorated over several years. By the autumn of 1877 it was reported that this once strong 6' 2" man had wasted away

---

1041 National Park Service, https://www.nps.gov/waba/learn/historyculture/lt-col-alfred-h-sully-1821-1879.htm, accessed May 31, 2020.

1042 Wyeth, M.D., *Life of General Nathan Bedford Forrest*, 615-623.

374 | Sherman's Woodticks

to no more than 100 pounds. He died at the home of his brother in Memphis on
October 29, 1877. He was only fifty-six years old.[1043]

During his later years, Forrest used what money he had left to support the
wounded and destitute soldiers who served under him, as well as their widows and
orphans. His wife continued this practice even after he died.

Milroy, Robert H.

The military career of General Robert H. Milroy only lasted another six months
after the fight at Murfreesboro. He resigned his commission shortly after the war
ended and returned to his native Indiana.

There, Milroy resumed to the practice of law and engaged in various business
ventures. He was appointed as a trustee of the Wabash and Erie Canal, and also
became involved in other railroad ventures. In 1872, he was appointed as superintendent of Indian affairs in Washington Territory.

In Washington, he served ten years as Indian Agent for various tribes in the
area, including the Puyallop, and Yakima. General Milroy died in Olympia, Washington on March 29, 1890, at the age of seventy-three. He was buried at Masonic
Memorial Park in Tumwater, Washington.

In 1902, a small town was incorporated in southwestern Minnesota and named
"Milroy" in honor of the general. Today, the City of Milroy has approximately 250
residents. It is about twelve miles east of Marshall, the nearest large town.

1043 The Daily Memphis Avalanche, Oct. 23, 1877.

Afterword

Company E
Historical Sites
1865 to Today

It has been nearly 160 years since Company E was formed and the Eighth Minnesota began its long march through Dakota Territory and later to the South. Nearly all the original locations significant to the story have since been obliterated by development, scavenging, or simply the ravages of time.

The town of Crow Wing provides one such example. It was once a thriving commercial center of more than 500 people and frequented by soldiers from nearby Fort Ripley. When the railroad came through in 1870, it bypassed Crow Wing in favor of nearby Brainerd. Thereafter the population quickly dwindled. The town site was finally abandoned by 1900. All the buildings were either torn down or moved to other locations.

Today only one of the original buildings from the town of Crow Wing still exists. Clement H. Beaulieu, who was an agent of the American Fur Company, built the largest house in Crow Wing during the late 1840s. After the town was abandoned, the house was moved to a nearby farm. The building survived there through the years.

In 1959, the State of Minnesota established Crow Wing State Park, which includes the original town site. Later, the state acquired Beaulieu's house and moved it back to its original location. Today, the town site and the Beaulieu house are accessible to the public.

The Forts

Company E spent time at several different forts during the Civil War. Nearly all traces of the original structures on these sites have been obliterated by scavenging. Wood and other building materials were simply too valuable to be left to rot. When a fort was abandoned. local residents often stripped the site of all the usable materials, especially in Western Minnesota and Dakota Territory, where wood was scarce.

Fort Snelling remained in use after the Civil War. However, the size of the military reservation was scaled back, and the surplus land sold to farmers. Most of the original buildings were torn down in the years after the Civil War. Nevertheless, portions of the fort were used until shortly after World War II. The fort was decommissioned for good in 1946.

The Minnesota Historical Society acquired what remained of Fort Snelling in the early 1960s. Unlike most of the other forts of the Civil War era, there were still four original structures at Fort Snelling, including the distinctive Round Tower, which dates from 1820. Today, portions of the fort have been restored so it appears much as it did at the time of the Civil War.

A small army garrison remained at old Fort Ripley until 1877, when the fort was decommissioned. Residents quickly dismantled the buildings to reuse the lumber and stone. By the early twentieth century almost nothing remained.

Today, the site of old Fort Ripley is within the Camp Ripley military reservation and not easily accessible by the public. The only remnant still standing from the Civil War era is a stone powder magazine.

The sod fort at Paynesville was abandoned for good the day Company E departed for Sully's Expedition in 1864. The sod walls and other remnants of the fort have long since been obliterated as the land was put to other uses. At one time it served as a school and later a national guard armory was built on the site. Today, almost nothing remains to note the existence of a fort in Paynesville.

In fact, almost no trace remains of the other sod forts built along the Minnesota frontier during the Uprising. Erosion, development, and agriculture have long since removed any sign of the forts at Green Lake, Mannanah, and elsewhere. The remnants of only one sod fort from the Sioux Uprising era remain in Minnesota, although it was not a post used by the Eighth Minnesota. It is located on private land and is not accessible to the public.

Despite its remoteness, Fort Rice on the Missouri River was not spared the ravages of time. Constructed by the Thirtieth Wisconsin Volunteer Infantry on the orders of General Sully, the fort was initially an important post in the area. However, it quickly became obsolete.

In 1872 the Army constructed Fort Abraham Lincoln approximately twenty miles north of Fort Rice and on the same side of the river. The new fort was in a better strategic location. There was little need for two forts in such proximity. Nevertheless, Fort Rice remained in operation for a while longer.

In 1873, Colonel George Armstrong Custer passed through Fort Rice with elements of the Seventh Cavalry on his Yellowstone River Expedition. Later, Custer would command the Seventh Cavalry at Fort Abraham Lincoln. Cavalry units from both Fort Rice and Fort Abraham Lincoln accompanied Custer on his 1876 expedition, which ended famously and tragically at the Battle of Little Big Horn.

Fort Rice was finally abandoned in 1878. Its buildings were quickly cannibalized of lumber and stone for use in construction at Fort Abraham Lincoln. Any materials left behind were taken by the local population.

The State of North Dakota took ownership of the old Fort Rice site in 1913. During the Great Depression of the 1930s, the state sponsored a W.P.A. project to mark out the corners of the old buildings. After that, the Fort Rice historic site became a park.

The park, however, was neglected over the years. Today, there are historic markers at the site and the building foundations are still marked, but what was probably a beautiful park clearly hasn't been maintained for a long time. The entire site has been left to decay and is now covered with a large prairie dog town.

Fort Berthold was abandoned as a military post shortly after the Civil War although it was used for other purposes for many years. In 1953, the Army Corps of Engineers built the Garrison Dam on the Missouri River about fifty miles northwest of Bismarck. The two-mile-long earthen dam formed a reservoir named Lake Sakakawea, which now extends over 100 miles to the west. The rising waters soon engulfed the site of the old fort. Today, the site of Fort Berthold lies far below the surface of Lake Sakakawea.

While nearly all of the forts disappeared in the years after the Civil War, some have been partially reconstructed as historic sites. In addition to Fort Snelling, Fort Ridgely, Fort Abercrombie and Fort Union have all been restored to some degree. The sites are now all either state parks or otherwise open to the public. However, few original structures from the forts remain.

Dakota Territory

The prairie seen by George Cambell, Edson Washburn, William Houlton, and the rest of the Eighth Minnesota was forever changed when Dakota Territory opened up for settlement. Trees and brush now grow where they were previously kept in check by prairie fires and the ravenous appetites of long-vanished buffalo.

Many soldiers who participated in Sully's Expedition thought that the territory was a wasteland that would not be settled for fifty or 100 years, if ever. They underestimated the pace of settlement in the west.

Less than ten years after Sully's Expedition, settlers began pouring into the eastern part of the state in pursuit of the rich farmland. The settlements spread west as the Great Northern Railroad progressed towards Montana. A few of those settlers had first visited Dakota Territory as part of the Eighth Minnesota during Sully's Expedition.[1044]

The settlers built roads and established settlements that grew into towns and cities. They marked out fields and began plowing the prairie. By 1889, only twenty-five years after Sully's Expedition, both North and South Dakota had gained statehood. Dakota Territory was no more.

Despite the changes to the landscape, visitors to western North Dakota can still get a good idea of what the area looked like in 1864. Buffalo still roam in Theodore Roosevelt National Park, and the Badlands look much the same today as they did in the mid-nineteenth century. The Little Missouri National Grasslands adjoin the park and, aside from the oil wells visible in all directions, gives the visitor a taste of what the Sioux and soldiers were up against.

The Battlefields

The Killdeer Mountain battlefield still looks much as it must have appeared in 1864, except that there are more trees and brush than existed at the time. Nearly the entire battlefield sits on private land. For many years, visitors could walk over much of the area. However, the landowners shut down access to the battlefield in 2014 after a dispute with the National Park Service, scenic preservationists, and state authorities.[1045] Sadly, as of this writing, only a one-acre portion of the vast battlefield is open to the public.

The site of the Heart River Corral is also on private land and appears much as it did in 1864. A marker erected in 1930 commemorates the site. Remnants of the fortifications dug by Edson Washburn and others are still partially visible during certain times of the year. Carvings in the rocks on nearby hills made by lookouts posted there during those long July days in 1864 are still faintly visible.

1044 After their experience with Sully's Expedition, most of Company E would have probably been happy never to return to the Dakotas.

1045 Lauren Donovan, "No More Hiking to the Scenic Medicine Hole," *Bismarck Tribune*, online edition, June 24, 2014, https://bismarcktribune.com/news/state-and-regional/no-more-hiking-to-the-scenic-medicine-hole/article_648762c6-fb1e-11e3-b9c0-001a4bcf887a.html, accessed November 20, 2018.

Much of the Battle of the Badlands took place in what is now the Little Missouri National Grasslands and is accessible by the public. North Dakota has placed some historical markers to commemorate the battle. With the exception of numerous oil wells visible in all directions, the battle sites and terrain are largely undisturbed. In fact, ruts cut by the wheels of the numerous wagon teams belonging to Sully's Expedition and the emigrant train are still faintly visible at the site known as "Sully's Waterhole," where the Expedition camped on the last night of the battle.

In Tennessee, the site of the battle along Wilkinson's Pike at Murfreesboro, where the Eighth Minnesota suffered so many casualties during its short pause in the cotton field, has been obliterated by development. The battlefield lies to the northwest of the intersection of Interstate 24 and Fortress Boulevard, a short distance northwest of Murfreesboro. Today, the site is a mixture of commercial buildings, housing developments and retail establishments.

Portions of Fortress Rosecrans have been preserved and are part of the Stones River National Battlefield. The site is maintained by the National Park Service. The nearby Stones River National Cemetery holds the remains of several Eighth Minnesota soldiers killed along Wilkinson's Pike on December 7, 1864.

APPENDIX

Roster of Company E

Eighth Minnesota Volunteer Infantry Regiment[1046]

Last Name	First Name	Initial	Rank	Hometown	Age	Birth	Death
Hartley	Edward		Captain	Monticello	26	1836	1918
Brookins	Harvey	S	Captain	Silver Creek	28	1834	1907
Croswell	Micah	S	1st Lieut.	Elk River	29	1833	1913
Tollington	Thomas		1st Lieut.	Clearwater	29	1833	1910
Post	Charles	E	2nd Lieut.	Monticello	32	1830	Unknown
Albright	John		Private	Monticello	22	1840	1907
Ambler	James		Private	Richfield?	35	1827	1900
Anderson	Thomas		Private	Monticello	42	1820	1889
Barker	Albert	F	Sergeant	Monticello	26	1836	1893
Bailey	Christopher	J	Private	Monticello	20	1842	1863
Bazley	William	F	Private	St. Anthony	32	1830	1865
Batterbury	Michael		Private	Maple Lake	32	1830	1913
Bertram	Andrew	H	Private	Monticello	20	1842	1904
Bloomer	Coleman		Private	St. Paul	29	1834	1914

1046 *Minnesota in the Civil and Indian Wars: 1861-1865*, vol. 1, 407-408. This list omits some soldiers that other sources identified has having briefly served with the company. The Hometown column provides the soldier's residence at the time of enlistment. Date of death has been added to the roster by the author.

Last Name	First Name	Init.	Rank	Hometown	Age	Birth	Death
Boyd	John	J	Private	Monticello	28	1834	Unknown
Bradley	James	F	Capt. USCT	Minneapolis	40	1822	1895
Bradbury	Edward	P	Private	Clearwater	21	1841	1923
Braughton	Henry	S	Private	Clearwater	32	1830	1915
Brown	Milton	B	Private	Monticello	20	1842	1892
Bryant	Alonzo		Private	Monticello	18	1844	1908
Carpenter	George	W	Private	Silver Creek	30	1832	1922
Cambell	George	T	Private	Lynden	27	1835	1902
Chaffin	Lewis	L	Private	Monticello	25	1837	1898
Clark	Henry	P	Private	St. Paul	43	1819	1906
Clifford	Franklin	W	Private	Clearwater	21	1841	1895
Collins	Dexter	E	Private	Silver Creek	27	1835	1920
Crawford	Henry	R	Private	Monticello	19	1843	1929
Dallas	William		Private	Lynden	34	1828	1891
Day	John	W	Private	Orono	33	1829	Unknown
Desmond	Daniel		Private	Monticello	21	1841	1908
Desmond	Timothy		Sergeant	Monticello	27	1835	1915
Dill	Thomas		Private	Big Lake	28	1834	1917
Dupray	Joseph		Private	Albion	24	1838	1918
Erath	Albert		Private	Buffalo	35	1827	1912
Erath	Herman		Private	Buffalo	33	1829	1915
Eberman	William		Private	Clearwater	18	1844	1921
Ells	Charles	G	Private	Clearwater	37	1825	1900s
Fairbrother	Albert	C	Private	Monticello	31	1831	1897
Felch	John	H	Private	Elk River	32	1830	Unknown
Fisher	Joseph	I	Private	Monticello	32	1830	Unknown
Flynn	Nicholas		Private	Buffalo	21	1841	1920
Fuller	Henry	W	Private	Orono	31	1831	1901
Gallow	Joseph		Private	St. Paul	21	1841	1930
Gates	James	M	Private	St. Paul	38	1824	1903
Gibbs	Charles	H	Private	Clearwater	18	1844	1890
Goyette	Lewis		Private	Buffalo	26	1836	1927
Hartley	John		Reg. Sgt. Major	Monticello	24	1838	1883
Helm	Henry	C	Sergeant	Monticello	18	1844	1920
Holding	Randolph		Private	Clearwater	18	1844	1915
Holgate	Levering		Private	Elk River	32	1830	1892
Houlton	William	H	Corporal	Monticello	23	1839	1915

Last Name	First Name	Init.	Rank	Hometown	Age	Birth	Death
Hulett	Asahel	E	Private	Silver Creek	27	1835	1901
Keator	Charles	H	Private	St. Paul	34	1828	1895
Kriedler	George	W	Private	Woodland	19	1843	1926
Kingsbury	David	L	Private	Monticello	20	1842	1912
Kriedler	Daniel	W	Private	Woodland	20	1842	1902
Kriedler	Samuel	G	Private	Woodland	26	1836	1928
Lane	William	D	Musician	Minneapolis	28	1834	1905
Lord	William	H	Private	Monticello	27	1835	1908
Lord	Martin		Private	Monticello	41	1821	1899
Locke	Joseph	N	Private	Silver Creek	18	1844	1891
Louisiana	John		Private	Woodland	18	1844	1900
Lyons	John	W	Private	Clearwater	21	1841	1887
Lyons	James	M	Private	Clearwater	17	1845	1925
Markham	Homer		Private	Clearwater	22	1840	1927
McPherson	William		Private	Buffalo	18	1844	1921
Merrill	Charles	W	Musician	Monticello	16	1846	1920
Mitchell	Henry	A	Private	Monticello	18	1844	1906
Morgan	Samuel	H	Private	St. Paul	34	1828	Unknown
Morgan	John	H	Private	St. Paul	24	1838	Unknown
Moore	John	W	Private	St. Paul	19	1843	Unknown
Morris	Samuel		Private	Faribault	34	1828	Unknown
Murray	Samuel		Private	Unknown	23	1839	1905
Murphy	Matthew		Private	Clearwater	25	1837	1915
Nickerson	Alphonso		Private	Monticello	38	1824	1902
Parcher	Ellett	P	Private	Clearwater	22	1840	1864
Parcher	Frank	M	Private	Clearwater	20	1842	1924
Parvin	John	B	Sergeant	Monticello	40	1822	1901
Parks	Isaac		Private	St. Cloud	43	1819	1894
Persons	Edwin	W	Private	St. Paul	28	1834	1915
Perkins	Joseph		Private	Monticello	40	1822	1906
Philbook	Amiel		Private	Monticello	26	1836	1917
Phillips	Thomas		Private	St. Paul	33	1829	Unknown
Ponsford	William		Private	Clearwater	23	1839	1930
Ponsford	John	B	Private	Clearwater	18	1844	1864
Reed	Joseph	J	Private	St. Paul	18	1844	1931
Reedy	Hugh		Private	St. Paul	21	1841	Unknown
Russell	John		Private	St. Paul	35	1827	Unknown

Last Name	First Name	Init.	Rank	Hometown	Age	Birth	Death
Sabin	Elisha	C	Private	Silver Creek	27	1835	1865
Smith	Charles	L	Private	Monticello	28	1834	1863
Stinchfield	William	Hanson	Private	St. Paul	18	1844	1905
Swain	John		Private	Monticello	43	1819	1905
Swartout	Cramer		Private	Woodland	30	1832	1909
Thompson	John	L	Private	St. Paul	21	1841	1867
Tourtellotte	George		Private	Orono	18	1844	1918
Vadner	Joseph	Jr.	Private	Maple Lake	18	1844	1910
Vorse	Charles	H	Private	Clearwater	18	1844	1919
Washburn	Edson	D	Corporal	Otsego	20	1842	1918
Washburn	Elbridge	F	Private	Otsego	24	1838	1864
Wedgewood	George	R. L.	Private	Monticello	22	1840	1930
Wheeler	Stephen	W.R.	Private	St. Paul	27	1835	1915
Wilder	Samuel		Private	Monticello	44	1818	Unknown
Woodward	Emerson	J	Capt. USCT	Richfield	26	1836	1892
Woodworth	Edward		Sergeant	Clearwater	21	1841	1911
Young	James	A	Private	Unknown	29	1833	1906

Sources

Manuscript Collections, Diaries and Journals

Washburn, Edson Dean, *Edson D. Washburn Diaries*, 1863-1865, Minnesota Historical Society.

Brookins, George W., George W. Brookins and family letters, 1861-1865, Minnesota Historical Society.

Gibbs Family Papers, Wright County Historical Society, Buffalo, Minnesota.

Brunson, Benjamin Witherell, Benjamin Wetherill Brunson and Family Papers, undated and 1850 - 1898, Minnesota Historical Society.

Colwell, Gardner B., Gardner B. Colwell diary and certificate, 1864 May 8-1865 July 20; 1898, Minnesota Historical Society.

Cumings, Bradley Newcomb, *Bradley Newcomb Cumings journal* (volume 1 of a journal kept in two volumes, 1828-1847). Massachusetts Historical Society at http://www.masshist.org/database/viewer.php?item_id=2445&img_step=1&pid=3&mode=dual#page1 accessed July 19, 2019.

Davison, Charles Edward, Charles E. Davison and family papers, 1852-1864, Minnesota Historical Society.

Doud, George W., *George W. Doud Diaries, Eighth Minnesota Volunteers, Company F, September 14, 1862-October 15, 1864*, bound transcript of three diaries, Minnesota Historical Society.

Ponsford, John Delano, *John D. Ponsford's Diary, May 31, 1863 to December 31, 1863*, typewritten transcript, Wright County Historical Society.

Strong, John Henry, *A journal of the northwestern Indian expedition under General Sully, 18641865*. Dakota Conflict of 1862 Manuscripts Collections, Minnesota Historical Society.

Atkinson, James B, *James Benton Atkinson diary, 1864*, Dakota Conflict of 1862 Manuscripts Collections. Minnesota Historical Society,

Silvis, William L, *Diary of Captain W. L. Silvis, Co. I, Eighth Minnesota Volunteers, January 1 to November 4, 1864*. Dakota Conflict of 1862 manuscripts collections, Minnesota Historical Society.

Reminiscences

Bertram, A.H., *Reminiscences & Incidents of Co. "E" 8th Minn. Vol. Inf.*, *being A Sketch of The Droll Side of Army Camp Life In Field and Garrison from actual facts, by one who was present,* December 7, 1878, Dakota Conflict of 1862 Manuscripts Collections. Minnesota Historical Society.

Brunson, Benjamin Witherell, "Reminiscences of Service with the Eighth Minnesota Infantry," *Glimpses of the Nation's Struggle,* Fifth Series, Military Order of the Loyal Legion of the United States, Minnesota (MOLLUS-Minn.), Saint Paul, 1908.

Brunson, Benjamin Witherell, *Ben W. Brunson reminiscence, undated,* Dakota Conflict of 1862 Manuscripts Collections. Minnesota Historical Society.

Cambell, George T, *Personal Reminiscences of the Civil War,* George T. Cambell family papers, 1857-circa 1890, Minnesota Historical Society.

Daniels, Jared Waldo, Jared Daniels reminiscences, Minnesota Historical Society.

Daniels, Arthur M., *A Journal of Sibley's Indian Expedition During the Summer of 1863 and Record of the Troops Employed: By a Soldier in Company "H," 6th Regiment,* Sherman & McNie Booksellers, Winona, Minn. 1864.

Davison, Charles Edward, Charles E. Davison, and family papers, 1852-1864, Minnesota Historical Society.

Hilger, Judge Nicholas, Campaign of General Alfred Sully Against the Hostile Sioux in 1864, as transcribed in 1883 from the Diary of Judge Nicholas Hilger, *Contributions to the Historical Society of Montana,* vol. II, 314, State Publishing Company, Helena Montana, 1896.

Hodgson, Thomas C, *Personal Recollections of the Sioux War with the Eighth Minnesota, Company F,* Transcribed by Robert Olson, Park Genealogical Books, Roseville, MN 1999.

Houlton, William, Company E, Eighth Minnesota Volunteer Infantry Regiment, Reunion Address, circa 1879, William H. Houlton and Family Papers, Minnesota Historical Society.

Kingsbury, David Lansing, "General Alfred Sully's Indian Campaign of 1864," *Glimpses of the Nation's Struggle, Fourth Series,* Military Order of the Loyal Legion of the United States, Minnesota, (MOLLUS-Minn.), St. Paul, 1898.

Kingsbury, David Lansing, "Sully's Expedition Against the Sioux In 1864," *Minnesota Historical Society Collections,* Volume Eight, St. Paul, 1898.

Lass, William E. "Inkpaduta (Scarlet Point)" *The Biographical Dictionary of Iowa*. University of Iowa Press, 2009, http://uipress.lib.uiowa.edu/bdi/DetailsPage.aspx?id=193, accessed Sept. 8, 2019.

Seelye, William E., "Early Military Experiences in Dakota," *Collections of the State Historical Society of North Dakota*, vol. III, Bismarck, 1910. State Historical Society of North Dakota.

Seelye, William E., *Narrative of the past and experiences and adventures of which the writer, W. E. Seelye, took part*, October 22, 1937, Dakota Conflict of 1862 Manuscripts Collections. Minnesota Historical Society.

Stillwell, Leander, Company D, 61st Illinois Volunteer Infantry Regiment, *The Story of a Common Soldier of Army Life in the Civil War*, Press of Erie Record, Erie, Kansas, 1917.

Babcock, Willoughby M., "Sioux versus Chippewa," *Minnesota History Magazine*, 41-45, March, 1925.

Letters

Robinson, James E, *John E. Robinson biographical memorabilia, 18591865*, Dakota Conflict of 1862 Manuscripts Collections. Minnesota Historical Society, Letter to his wife Libbie from Fort Wadsworth, Dakota Territory, Oct. 11, 1864.

Shotwell, James A, *James A. Shotwell letter*, January 15, 1898. Dakota Conflict of 1862 Manuscripts Collections. Minnesota Historical Society.

Ward, Chester C, Company D, Second Minnesota Cavalry Regiment, Letter to his son, January 15, 1898. Dakota Conflict of 1862 Manuscripts Collections. Minnesota Historical Society.

Bibliography

Album of History and Biography of Meeker County, Minnesota,

Anderson, Gary Clayton, *Through Dakota Eyes: Narrative Accounts of the Minnesota Indian War of 1862*, Minnesota Historical Society Press, 1988.

Atwood, E.H., Early History of Maine Prairie, Fair Haven, Lynden, Eden Lake and Paynesville, St. Cloud, MN, No Year Provided.

Baker, Robert Orr, *The Muster Roll: a biography of Fort Ripley Minnesota*, H.M Smyth Co. Inc., St. Paul, MN. No Year Provided.

Beath, Robert B., *History of the Grand Army of the Republic*, New York, Bryan, Taylor & Company, 1889.

Beck, Paul N., *Columns of Vengeance: Soldiers, Sioux, and the Punitive Expeditions, 1863-1864*, Norman, OK, University of Oklahoma Press, 2013.

Billings, John D., *Hardtack and Coffee: or The Unwritten Story of Army Life*, George M. Smith & Co., Boston, 1887. Retrieved from https://ia802305. us.archive.org/11/items/hardtackcoffee00bill/hardtackcoffee00bill.pdf

The Board of Commissioners, *Minnesota in the Civil and Indian Wars: 1861-1865*, vol. 1,, St. Paul, MN, Pioneer Press Company, 1891.

The Board of Commissioners, *Minnesota in the Civil and Indian Wars: 1861-1865*, vol. 2, St. Paul, MN, Pioneer Press Company, 1893.

Bowen, James L., *Massachusetts in the War: 1861-1865*, Springfield, Mass., Clark W. Bryan & Co., 1889.

Bryant, Charles S. and Murch, Abel B., *A History of the Great Massacre by the Sioux Indians in Minnesota: Including the Personal Narratives of Many Who Escaped*, Cincinnati, OH, Rickey & Carroll, 1864.

Butterfield, Daniel, *Camp and Outpost Duty for Infantry*, New York, Harper & Brothers, 1863.

Cabaniss, Jim R., *Civil War Journals and Letters of Sergeant Washington Ives 4*[th] *Florida C.S.A.*, 3rd Ed., 2008.

Cambell, David, *The Graham Journal of Health and Longevity*, Vol. 1, no. 1 (Apr. 4, 1837)-v. 3, no. 25 (Dec. 14, 1839). Boston, Mass., 1839.

Casey, Silas, *Infantry Tactics for the Instruction, Exercise, and Manoeure of The Soldier, A Company, Line of Skirmish, Battalion, Brigade or Corps D'Armée*, Vol. I., New York, D. Van Nostrand, 1862.

Curtiss-Wedge, Franklyn, *History of Renville County Minnesota*, Vol. I., Chicago, H.C. Cooper, Jr. & Co., 1916.

Curtiss-Wedge, Franklyn, *History of Wright County Minnesota*, Vol. I., Chicago, H.C. Cooper, Jr. & Co., 1915.

Davis, Elaine, *Minnesota 13: Stearns County's "Wet" Wild Prohibition Days*, St. Cloud, MN, Sentinal Publishing Co., 2007.

English, A.M., *Dakota's First Soldiers*, South Dakota Historical Collections, Vol. IX, Hipple Printing Company, Pierre, South Dakota, 1918. p. 241.

Fletcher, R. S. (1943). *A History of Oberlin College: From its Foundation Through the Civil War*. Chicago, IL: R.R. Donnelley& Sons Co. Retrieved from http://ia700802.us.archive.org/12/items/historyofoberlin01flet/historyofoberlin01flet.pdf

Folwell, William Watts, *A History of Minnesota*, Vol. II, Saint Paul, MN, Minnesota Historical Society, 1924.

Fritsche, L.A., M.D., Editor, *A History of Brown County Minnesota: Its People, Industries and Institutions*, Vol. 1, Indianapolis, B.F. Bowen & Company, Inc., 1916.

Garrison, Wendell Phillips and Garrison, Francis Jackson, *William Lloyd Garrison: The Story of His Life Told by His Children*, New York, The Century Co. 1885.

Halleran, Michael A., *The Better Angels of Our Nature: Freemasonry in the American Civil War*, Tuscaloosa, AL, The University of Alabama Press, 2010.

Holder, Naomi Dail, *History of the Wheat Swamp Christian Church Including the Conditions in Europe and the Colonies*, New Bern, NC, 1977.

Hubbard, Lucius F. and Holcombe, Return I., *Minnesota in Three Centuries*, Vol. Three, Mankato, MN, Free Press Printing Company for the Publishing Society of Minnesota, 1908.

Kelly, Fanny, *Narrative of My Captivity Among the Sioux Indians*, Hartford, CT, Mutual Publishing Company, 1872.

Larson, Constant, *History of Douglas and Grant Counties Minnesota; Their People, Industries and Institutions*, Vol. 1, Indianapolis, B.F. Bowen & Company, Inc., 1916.

Lass, William E., "Inkpaduta (Scarlet Point)" *The Biographical Dictionary of Iowa*. University of Iowa Press Digital Editions, 2009, http://uipress.lib.uiowa.edu/bdi/DetailsPage.aspx?id=193, accessed Sept. 8, 2019.

Libby, O.D., Editor, *Collections of the Historical Society of North Dakota*, Vol. III, Bismarck, N.D., Tribune, State Printers and Binders, 1910.

Merrick, George Byron, *Old Times on the Upper Mississippi: The Recollections of a Steamboat Pilot from 1854 to 1863*, Cleveland, OH, Arthur H. Clark Company, 1909.

Michno, Gregory F., *Dakota Dawn: The Decisive First Week of the Sioux Uprising, August 17-24, 1862*, Savas Beatie, LLC, New York, 2011.

Mitchell, William Bell, *History of Stearns County, Minnesota*, Vol. I and II, Chicago, IL, H.C. Cooper, Jr., & Co., 1915.

Myers, Frank, *Soldiering in Dakota Among the Indians in 1863-4-5*, Huron, Dakota Territory, 1888 (Reprinted by State Historical Society, Pierre, S. Dak., 1936).

Pattee, John, "Dakota Campaigns", *South Dakota Historical Collections*, vol. 5, State Publishing Company, Sioux Falls, South Dakota, 1910.

Paxson, Lewis C., *Diary of Lewis C. Paxson: Stockton, N.J. 1862-1865*, Bismarck, ND, (Reprinted from Vol. 2, Collections State Historical Society of North Dakota, Bismarck, N.D.) 1908.

Pfaller, Rev. Louis, Sully's Expedition of 1864 featuring the Killdeer Mountain and Badlands Battles, *North Dakota History*, vol. 31, no. 1 (January 1964).

Roberts, Allen E, *House Divided: The Story of Freemasonry and the Civil War*, Richmond, Virginia, Macoy Publishing & Masonic Supply Co., Inc., 1961, 1990.

Smith, A.C., *A Random Historical Sketch of Meeker County, Minnesota: From its First Settlement to July 4th, 1876*, Litchfield, Minn, Belfoy & Joubert, 1877.

Spence, John C., *A Diary of the Civil War*, Murfreesboro, Tenn., Rutherford County Historical Society, 1993.

Stillwell, Leander, *The Story of a Common Soldier of Army Life in the Civil War*, Erie, KS, Press of the Erie Record, 1917.

Stone, Ebenezer W., *Compend of Instructions in Military Tactics and the Manual of Percussion Arms with Extracts from the U.S. Army Regulations*, Boston, William White, 1857.

Skelton, Constance Oliver and Bulloch, John Malcolm, *Gordons under Arms: A Biographical Muster Roll of Officers named Gordon in the Navies, and Armies of Britain, Europe, America and the Jacobite Uprisings*, Aberdeen, Aberdeen University, 1912.

Sully, Langdon, *No Tears for the General: The Life of Alfred Sully, 1821-1879*, Palo Alto, California, American West Publishing Company, 1974.

Ullery, Jacob G., *Men of Vermont: An Illustrated Biographical Story of Vermonters and Sons of Vermont*, Battleboro, VT, Transcript Publishing Company, 1894.

U.S. War Department, *The War of the Rebellion: A Compilation of the Official Records of the Union and Confederate Armies*, Washington D.C., Government Printing Office, 1880-1901.

Utley, Robert M., *Sitting Bull: The Life and Times of an American Patriot*, New York, Holt Paperback Edition, 1998

Watkins, Sam. R., *"CO. AYTCH," Maury Grays, First Tennessee Regiment: or, A Side Show of the Big Show*, Chattanooga, Tenn., Times Printing Company, 1900.

Winchell, N.H., et al, *History of the Upper Mississippi Valley*, Minneapolis, MN, Minnesota Historical Company, 1881.

Wright, Henry H. *A History of the Sixth Iowa Infantry*, Iowa City, IA, State Historical Society of Iowa, 1923.

Wyeth, John Allan, M.D., *Life of General Nathan Bedford Forrest*, New York & London, Harper & Brothers, 1899.

Water Cure in America: Two Hundred and Twenty Cases of Various Diseases Treated with Water, Edited by a Water Patient (David Cambell), New York & London, Wiley and Putnam, 1848.

Newspapers

The Weekly Minnesotan (St. Paul), 1856.

St. Cloud Journal, 1860-1865.

Dakota County Tribune (Farmington), 1889-1891.

The North-Western Weekly Union (Monticello, Minnesota), 1862-1863.

The Daily Memphis Avalanche, 1877.

Saint Paul Pioneer Press

The St. Paul Daily Press

Weekly Pioneer and Democrat (St. Paul).

Mankato Weekly Union

Los Angeles Times

New York Herald, 1864.

Websites

Ancestry, ancestry.com

Find A Grave, findagrave.com

Library of Congress, Chronicling America: Historic American Newspapers, chroniclingamerica.loc.gov.

Newspapers.com

Soldiers and Sailors Database, National Park Service, nps.gov/civilwar/soldiers-and-sailors-database.htm

Table of Illustrations

Index

Y